KENYON COX
1856–1919

KENYON COX

Courtesy of the Oberlin College Archives.

KENYON COX

1856–1919

A LIFE IN AMERICAN ART

H. WAYNE MORGAN

THE KENT STATE UNIVERSITY PRESS

KENT, OHIO, AND LONDON, ENGLAND

Library of Congress Cataloging-in-Publication Data

Morgan, H. Wayne (Howard Wayne)

Kenyon Cox : 1856–1919 : a life in American art / H. Wayne Morgan.

p.   cm.

Includes bibliographical references and index.

ISBN 0-87338-485-7 ∞

1. Cox, Kenyon, 1856–1919.   2. Painters—United States—Biography.

3. Art critics—United States—Biography.   I. Title.

ND237.C8M67   1994

759.13—dc20

[B]   93–33967

CIP

British Library Cataloging-in-Publication data are available.

To the memory of

KATHARINE SMITH

1904–1992

CONTENTS

PREFACE

I N THE FIRST TWO DECADES OF THIS
century Kenyon Cox was among the best known cultural figures in the
United States. This reputation rested on his activities as a painter and critic.
After five years of rigorous training in Paris between 1877 and 1882, he returned to his native Ohio, and then settled in New York City. Like many
other aspiring young painters, he earned a living drawing illustrations for
magazines, teaching, and from the occasional sale of an easel work. He
painted in a realistic manner and attained considerable reputation for landscapes, portraits, and genre studies. Cox took all his art seriously and was
always a conscientious craftsman and careful interpreter of his subjects. He
enjoyed working in a variety of styles and subjects, but his natural bent was
toward intellectual and emotional idealism, which he expressed in art
through figure painting, especially of the idealized nude, and in murals with
classical appearances and themes. This interest in ideals reflected both his
high regard for the grand European art tradition and his belief that modern
cultures could extend it without losing their own special qualities. He was
ultimately able to paint murals that expressed these ideals about the roles of
art in society and in expanding individual emotions.

Cox's murals and easel pictures brought him reputation in the art world
and a modest living, but his public stature rested chiefly on his criticism.
Beginning in the 1880s, he became a well-known contributor of book and
exhibition reviews and regular essays for such magazines as the *Nation, Century,* and *Scribner's,* which carried his views to influential tastemakers. He
dealt with a wide range of both historical and contemporary art. He saw
both art production and appreciation as expressions of personal ideals and
emotional needs that had civic consequences. In due course, he became
well known for holding that art could and must temper materialism in
modern life, be a force for cohesive social ideals, and expand the individual

imagination. He called this general attitude *classicism,* and expressed it best in a major book entitled *The Classic Point of View* (1911).

Cox and his peers had returned from Paris in the 1870s with a sense that their generation would produce art that was technically better, intellectually broader, and less parochial than that of their predecessors. They were interested in depicting current life in an intimate and vigorous manner that employed skilled drawing and rich coloration. They were certain that a revitalized American art could both become a major national school and enrich the world tradition. Cox retained a lifelong belief in the future of American art, provided that it was thoughtful, expertly painted, and projected overtones of idealism, whatever its subject or style. He wanted art to become a major and accepted part of life, and for the artist to become a protagonist in the development of American culture.

He was thus a logical opponent of the modernism that began to reshape contemporary art in the years before the Armory Show of 1913. He saw this modernism in all of current life, and especially in the arts, as a potentially anarchic romanticism that exalted the individual over the polity. He also disliked its apparent disregard for technical skill in painting and drawing. In the largest sense, he feared that the new approaches would undermine the role of art in American society and would separate artist and public, thus placing cultural matters on the margin of life and in the care of a self-serving elite. These general views doubtless expressed those of most art patrons. In his later years, Cox both reflected and enhanced that mainstream opinion. Modernism in its various forms finally triumphed among those who dominated the debate over art, but Cox's views never entirely disappeared. His art and life thus deserve a reexamination.

A word about my approach is in order. This is a biography, not art criticism. Art was central to Cox's life. His work and the works he criticized represented large ideas and ideals to him. I have made this clear at appropriate points, but the focus is on Cox's developing and varied life and his roles in the art world rather than on the formal qualities of pictures. Analysis of his easel work is also hard to do because so much of it has been lost. A biographer's task is always difficult because the subject does so many different things at the same time. I can only hope that my coverage is logical. The notes are full and indicate my sources for both his life and times. To avoid a large number of citations, I have clustered them logically and they are keyed to the text. All italicized passages in quotations are in the original. A final note: historical monetary values are always hard to judge, but the dollar of Cox's youth and middle age was worth at least ten of today's.

Every book is a cooperative enterprise, and it is a pleasure to thank some of the people who helped me most. Richard Murray of the National Museum of American Art, Smithsonian Institution, Washington, D.C., shared his knowledge of Cox's art. I benefited from Patricia Ronan's knowledge of the

Cox family, derived from her biography of Louise King Cox. Virginia Colby, president of the Cornish Historical Society and a wonderful friend, furnished information about the Cox family in that locale and was a delightful hostess on two occasions. Janet Parks of the Avery Architectural and Fine Arts Library, Columbia University, answered numerous questions about the Cox papers in her custody. Gerald Ackerman of Pomona College, Claremont, California, gave me information about Jean-Léon Gérôme, Cox's mentor. Karen O'Brien of the Commonwealth Fund took a morning to help me examine Cox's glass windows at the Harkness House in New York City. Richard Lothrop of Christ Episcopal Church in Oberlin, Ohio, photographed Cox's stained-glass window there and found additional archival material. Geoffrey Blodgett of Oberlin College, an old friend and generous helper, photographed Cox's two murals in the college administration building. Elaine Evans Dee and Gail S. Davidson patiently helped me through the enormous collection of Cox's drawings at the Cooper Hewitt Museum, New York City. Abigail Booth Gerdts and Betsy Arvidson of the National Academy of Design, New York City, answered more questions than I had a right to ask. Leonard E. Opdycke of Poughkeepsie, New York, and Henry Peltz of New York City kindly furnished photographs of Cox works in their possession.

I owe a great debt to the staffs of each depository mentioned in the text, but especially to: Roland M. Baumann, Oberlin College Archives; Mary Beth Betts, print room, New-York Historical Society, New York City; Timothy Q. Cleavenger, Cliff Dwellers Club, Chicago; Catherine L. Corcoran, Albright Knox Museum, Buffalo, New York; Philip N. Cronenwett, Dartmouth College Archives; Lydia Dufour, Frick Art Reference Library, New York City; Charles E. Greene, Rare Books Collection, Princeton University Library; Peggy Hammerle, Art Commission of the City of New York; John F. Nelson, district director of the U.S. Customs, Janet M. Opaskar, General Services Administration, and Helen M. Lybarger, all of Cleveland, Ohio, who described or photographed Cox's murals in that city; Nancy Johnson, librarian at the American Academy and Institute of Arts and Letters, New York City; Cheryl Liebold, Pennsylvania Academy of Fine Arts, Philadelphia; Peter McDonald, General Research Division, New York Public Library; Harold L. Miller, State Historical Society of Wisconsin, Madison; Cynthia Ott, Archives of American Art, Smithsonian Institution, Washington, D.C.; Cynthia Sanford, Jersey City, New Jersey Museum; Barbara Sevey, Philadelphia Museum of Art; Norma Sindelar, St. Louis Museum of Art; John W. Smith and Catherine Stover, Art Institute of Chicago; Cynthia Wall, Newberry Library, Chicago; Melanie Wisner, Houghton Library, Harvard University; and Deborah Wythe, Brooklyn Museum.

Others were important for different reasons. Dean Kenneth Hoving of the University of Oklahoma Graduate College supported my research with funds and leave time. Harriet Peterson of Norman, Oklahoma, as usual was a wise and careful editor. My wife Anne lived much longer with Kenyon Cox than either of us planned, but never faltered. I dedicate this book to the memory of Katharine Smith of Wooster, Ohio, the granddaughter of Cox's sister Helen. Mrs. Smith generously allowed me to see and use paintings, family letters, and inscribed books in her possession. She answered questions about the extended family that I otherwise could not have solved. And most important, she became a kind friend as well as a link to the past.

I wish to thank the following institutions and persons for permission to use unpublished materials from the holdings noted: the McKinney Library, Albany Institute of History and Art (Will H. Low); Albright Knox Art Gallery Archives (Kenyon Cox); Avery Architectural and Fine Arts Library, Columbia University in the City of New York (Kenyon Cox); Archives of the American Academy and Institute of Arts and Letters (Kenyon Cox); Archives of American Art (Kenyon Cox and Louise King Cox, Allyn Cox, Miscellaneous Manuscripts, August Jaccaci, and James Henry Moser, with the consent of his heirs Margaret Longwell, Samuel Fetherolf, Ralph Fetherolf, David G. Griggs, and Robert M. Griggs); Beinecke Rare Book and Manuscript Library, Yale University (James B. Carrington, Royal Cortissoz); Bowdoin College Museum of Art (Kenyon Cox); Dartmouth College Library (Augustus Saint Gaudens, Winston Churchill); Rutherford B. Hayes Presidential Center (Rutherford B. Hayes); Houghton Library, Harvard University (Miscellaneous Manuscripts); Isabella Stewart Gardner Museum (Kenyon Cox); Library of Congress (John Sherman, Cass Gilbert, Central Services Division Files); Massachusetts Historical Society (Grenville Norcross Autograph Collection); Metropolitan Museum of Art Archives (Kenyon Cox); New-York Historical Society, Manuscript Department (Edwin Howland Blashfield) and Architectural Collections (Cass Gilbert, Minnesota State Capitol and Essex County Courthouse files); Rare Books and Manuscripts Division, New York Public Library, Astor, Lenox and Tilden Foundations (Richard Watson Gilder, and Century Company Records); Oberlin College Archives (James Monroe, Jacob Dolson Cox, Henry Churchill King, and Kenyon Cox alumni file); Pennsylvania Academy of Fine Arts Archives (Kenyon Cox); Princeton University Library (Scribner Archive and Frank Jewett Mather, Jr.); State Historical Society of Wisconsin (Capitol Commission Records); Yale University Library, Manuscripts and Archives (John Ferguson Weir).

I

AN UNUSUAL
YOUNG MAN

I N 1786, CONNECTICUT RETAINED
possession of a large tract of land when it ceded its western territories to
Congress. This finally encompassed the northeastern corner of Ohio and became known as the Western Reserve, set aside chiefly for citizens of the
Nutmeg State. The area boasted rich and varied natural resources. It was
heavily wooded and well watered, with good soil for farming, once the land
was cleared. It also had numerous navigable streams and a large front on
Lake Erie, which promised an efficient transportation system to sustain long-
term settlement and economic growth. In the ensuing decades many kinds of
people came to the Reserve, but the educated middle-class element drew on
a sense of mission derived from New England. They saw themselves as the
bearers of settled civilized values on this promising frontier. Theirs was an
errand into a wilderness, in which sobriety, belief in education, and culture
accompanied the desire for economic success. They did not see such concerns
as mutually exclusive. They believed in the American success ethic, tempered
with care for the less fortunate, and were generally antislavery.[1]

Education figured largely in the settlers' ambitions, both to provide a
learned clergy and to reinforce the personal and civic values they thought
necessary for sound social development. The Reserve soon boasted colleges
and seminaries dedicated to this task, but none figured more in the area's
intellectual history than Oberlin College. It was literally hewn out of the
flat, scrubby wilderness some forty miles southwest of the growing city of
Cleveland. It opened in the mid-1830s and rapidly gained considerable no-
toriety for its policy of coeducation, a concern for temperance and abolition,
and attention to community service. Though it seemed radical to many ob-
servers, the Oberlin tradition really rested on ideals of individualism, self-
help, and civic probity. Its religious emphasis was somewhat freethinking in

stressing evangelism and the individual's role in salvation. But except for its antislavery ideals, Oberlin emphasized sobriety, duty, and reason to temper American materialism.[2]

The Reverend Charles Grandison Finney was a major figure in the Reserve. Born in Connecticut in 1792, he became a lawyer but underwent a religious conversion that took him into the turbulent scene of American evangelism. He modified traditional Calvinism to emphasize the individual's role in personal salvation, which required a strong emotional response and commitment to living out personal ideals. He finally embraced the loose structure of the Congregational church and became a founding father of Oberlin. Finney taught theology at the college after 1835, served as president from 1851 to 1866, and was pastor of its principal Congregational church. Tours and writings made him a major religious figure in the nation and in Europe before his death in 1875.[3]

Finney's home was naturally a center for intellectual and social affairs in Oberlin. In the fall of 1847, he began to notice a tall, attractive student named Jacob Dolson Cox, who was already noted for dignity and a precise analytical mind in debate and classroom exercises. Cox had encountered Finney at a revival meeting in 1843 at Niblo's Gardens in New York City, was converted, and decided to train for the ministry at Oberlin.

The young Cox, born in Montreal in 1828, was one of eleven children, seven of whom lived to adulthood, not an unusual number at the time. His father gained modest success as a carpenter and builder in New York and Canada. His mother instilled in her offspring a strong regard for learning and ideas, and for an independent cast of mind, which had mixed effects on Dolson's life. He believed in free discussion and was an idealist about people's motives and the power of reason to affect life. This gained him respect but cost him advancement in a world in which such niceties did not prevail.

Dolson's visits to the Finney home and elsewhere in Oberlin brought him into contact with Finney's daughter Helen. Born in 1828, she was dignified, with a cultured demeanor beyond her years. Gracious but aloof, endowed with a dry wit and common sense, she attracted many young men. In 1847 she married Professor William Cochran of the theology department. The couple moved to New York City, where he was to edit the *New York Evangelist,* but Cochran died suddenly of cholera in August 1847, leaving Helen pregnant. The child was born in 1848 and given Cochran's name. Helen returned to Oberlin to help her ailing mother, who died soon afterward. By the time she met Dolson, she had suffered misfortune and unexpected loss, which seemed to intensify her disciplined reserve.

Dolson's suit was successful, and the couple married on November 29, 1849. They first kept house with her father while Dolson finished his degree. Religion, of course, was ever present in the home and family, and Dolson expected to follow that calling. But relatives and others had noted Helen's apparent lack of deep piety, despite her genuine religious beliefs. Dolson's commitment weakened as he found even Finney's theology too constricting for an independent mind. By 1851, when Dolson received a bachelor's degree, he and Finney had parted company. He became a member of the Episcopal church but did not pass on to his own children any strict dogma. Like so many people of his class and circumstance, he seemed to see religion more as a restraining and civilizing force than as a body of revealed doctrine.[4]

As he verged on making a career and raising a family, Dolson's personality and values were well formed. He was reserved, though not pompous or self-important. He had a strong sense of self-worth and of high ideals, which he believed in even if they were unattainable. He could be amusing and playful within the family, but his seriousness about life and the world naturally affected the children, who inevitably held him in awe as well as in regard. He was an authoritative but not a frowning presence to friends and family. His son Kenyon was "extremely fond and proud of his father, and loved to pass on information" about him later to his own daughter. After his father's death in 1900, Kenyon wrote a sound epitaph: "If he had been less modest, less honest, and more self-seeking, he would have occupied a larger place in the eyes of the world, but we could hardly have been so proud of him."[5]

In their sense of their own worth, and of obligation to society, Dolson and Helen were well matched. She raised the children to live with rules suitable to their heritage and station, and to succeed in the world while emphasizing values beyond self. Though always concerned and caring, she was a trifle aloof even with them, conscious of their destinies as an extension of her idealized view of her own family. The family believed in earnest and intense discussion of individual positions, and in ideals that were not to be surrendered lightly, or at all. They must also give to society more than they took from it. Helen's children would surely do well, become leaders of their communities, break no moral codes. But material success was not enough. As she told her son Kenyon late in life: "My ambition has always, from childhood, been for *fame,* and although my own life has been in the quiet domestic lines, the fame of my father, my husband, my son, has been dearer than life to me."[6]

Helen kept this sense of family destiny and importance alive with a steady flow of visits and correspondence with her children and other relatives. She passed around the family's letters, insisted on responses, and noted each member's progress or troubles. And for families like hers, terms such as *Honor, Duty,* and *Ideals* were not words but concepts and goals to be spelled with capital letters. Small wonder that she and Dolson adopted as a motto LABORE ac VIRTUTE: With Labor and Courage. This family would win life's race and honors through self-help and application, but also because it deserved victory.[7]

Dolson received his bachelor's degree in the late summer of 1851, and obviously could not continue to live with his father-in-law. More to the point, he already had a family and needed a viable profession. Will Cochran was an active three year old, and the couple's own first child, a daughter named Helen, was born in July 1850. The best opportunity seemed to be the school superintendency in Warren, a small community east of Oberlin near the Pennsylvania border.

Warren was home for more than two thousand people, engaged in various commercial and agricultural enterprises. It was ragged around the edges and, like any frontier community, offered few civic amenities. But its citizens thought that these would come as the region's economy developed. By the 1840s, plank roads and canals tied the area to its natural markets, and the railroads came in the late 1850s. In due course, it would be part of the great manufacturing triangle of the Reserve, producing metal goods, containers, food, and fiber products. Warren had prospects, as the natives said, and was not the worst place to start a family and career.[8]

Dolson focused on the school district's business but quickly became a community leader. He was active in various church affairs and often spoke to the literary societies whose members were determined to remain linked to civilization. He was hard working and serious and more than earned his inadequate salary of six hundred dollars a year. Education, like the ministry, had its rewards, but Dolson soon saw that he could not support a family on any likely income from education and turned to studying law, which had been his first choice of profession. He was admitted to the Ohio bar in April 1852 and joined a local firm in June 1853. He was bright, attractive, and intellectually impressive. Many people marked him for success in politics, if that was where the law led.[9]

Life as a budding lawyer was a struggle, especially because the family continued to grow. On May 15, 1852, Helen gave birth to the couple's first son, named after his father and known as "Dol" to the family. Then on October 27, 1856, a second son was born to their modest home on Bazetta Road, near the county fairgrounds. He was named Kenyon, in honor of his father's younger brother, and added "Junior" to his name until he was a mature man.[10]

Kenyon was an unusual child. He was thin and "poorly," as frontier folk wisdom said, but bright and curious. The parents worried about his health but tried to let him behave as normally as possible. Dolson entered politics as a state senator for the term 1860–61 and began the pattern of being away from home much of the time. Helen spent a great deal of time with the children and thus became their role model as well as teacher and nurse. She expected them to excel and, true to family ideals, made each one seem special, of whom great things were in order.

Kenyon attended public school, though he did not reminisce about the experience. Winters were hard and most students remembered the freezing rooms, numb hands, and snow-covered playgrounds rather than substantive learning. Kenyon worked through the standard curriculum, which emphasized English, history, geography, and mathematics. He was not an enthusiastic student and spent considerable time drawing crude pictures for classmates. He apparently knew the dunce cap, usually applied for inattention to duties.[11]

Kenyon's real education was private and self-motivated. He cared little for sports but was studious and enjoyed reading on his own. The fare ranged from the predictable primers to material he did not fully understand but enjoyed, such as the novels of Sir Walter Scott or current periodicals that discussed public questions and cultural issues. Throughout youth, he read widely and developed a retentive memory. All the while, he decorated books and papers with drawings, often simple but always reflecting a growing interest in the arts.[12]

From youth, life seemed to be a serious business to Kenyon. His appreciation for facts led to an insistence on accuracy in the smallest comment. He thought nothing of correcting other people's grammar or of defining an unusual word. He had a firm opinion on most things. Partisan attacks on his father, reported in the press, often upset him, because he knew they were untrue. Exaggerated advertising especially irked him. This insistence on accuracy became a major character trait, adding to his serious demeanor, though sometimes it amused those who saw its naïveté. In later years, his younger brother Charles delighted in going around the house making obviously absurd and untrue statements "just to see Ken squirm."[13]

The family's fortunes seemed to parallel those of the country. Dolson was in the Ohio senate when the Civil War began and took a strong unionist stand. He then served in many of the conflict's campaigns in West Virginia, Tennessee, and Georgia, emerging as a major general. He was governor of Ohio from 1866 to 1868. He was an unlikely figure in the hurly-burly of politics, never a backslapper, always serious, unwilling to compromise ideals for any partisan advantage, concerned with his conception of the public good, however poorly this sat with other politicians. But these very qualities made him attractive to those who wished to purify politics, and he became an important figure in the liberal wing of the Republican party. By the war's end, he seemed poised for a national career and the fulfillment of the family's sense of destiny.

At the same time, the parents worried over Kenyon's health. He spent a good deal of time in bed after age nine and did not attend school after age fourteen. In the spring of 1868 in Cincinnati, where Dolson practiced law after his governorship, Kenyon developed serious nosebleeds, and a tumor appeared in his left cheek. His brother Dolson recalled running fearfully for his mother after Kenyon fainted and bled profusely from the mouth while playing. The doctors offered little explanation and not much more therapy and treated the tumor, apparently some kind of hemangioma, with ice and iodine. They cautiously suggested an operation, warning that it might be fatal. The family hesitated. Throughout the anxiety-laden ordeal, Kenyon remained cheerful. "It used to break my heart as a boy to see him suffering with that awful tumor," Dol later recalled, "and never a complaint, always loveable, always cheerful, always patient. If he had a book to read nothing else mattered."[14]

The tumor continued to grow, involving the neck and mouth, even threatening the blood vessels leading to the brain. The operation was risky and painful, with the added dangers of shock, blood loss, and possible infection. But the family finally had to accept the risk and entrusted Kenyon to the famous Cincinnati surgeon Dr. William H. Mussey, who operated on February 20, 1869. The following days were critical, but Kenyon's youth was in his favor. "Kenny continues to improve slowly and we trust that with ordinary good fortune now we may regard him out of danger," the elder Cox wrote his brother Charles on March 3, 1869. Though no one described the operation clinically, even for the family, it was clearly major. Kenyon was bedridden for some time, unable to do anything for himself. "You will not wonder at this when you learn that the surgeons say that the operation itself in severity is equivalent to amputating both legs."[15] A few days later, Helen wrote Will Cochran that the patient could sit up and eat a little. She read to him, and he soon called for drawing paper and pencils, and even a watercolor set to make pictures for various friends and relatives. By May he could go to the cool Tennessee mountains with his mother and siblings, exercise moderately, and eat well, on the road to recovery.[16]

During this crisis, Dolson's political fortunes appeared to advance another step, when he became secretary of the interior for President U. S. Grant, in March 1869. This move took the family to Washington, where Dolson rented a pleasant house on New Jersey Avenue near C Street, southeast of the Capitol. The house was built on a slope, with a large back yard. Its rooms were spacious and even included an area for billiards and dumbbells. The family joined Dolson that fall. Kenyon approved of the house, despite the mess of remodeling, and was well enough to take in the city's sights. "The Capitol is a splendid white marble building with a white dome," he wrote Dol. He also found the Interior and Post Office departmental buildings impressive.[17]

Unhappily for everyone, Kenyon's tumor recurred. By early September 1869, his father was almost distraught over the case. The surgeons advised another operation, this time with even greater risks. Dolson first planned to have it done in Cincinnati, then arranged for Dr. Mussey to come to Washington. "The result is doubtful," he wrote Governor Rutherford B. Hayes in Ohio, "though we do not abandon hope. If he survives, weeks of the most incessant watching and of continuing danger must follow before we can feel that he is safe."[18] The day before the operation, the reserved and dignified Dolson broke down and cried with his wife at the prospect of their son's suffering.[19]

The second operation took place on September 23, 1869, probably at home, under ether or chloroform. Kenyon reported on his condition just three days later with the detachment of a twelve year old. He noted matter-of-factly to Dol that the doctor removed a tumor from his nose and throat. He could not write but was dictating to his mother. Breakfast was a bowl of oyster soup and a bunch of grapes, which did not seem odd to him. Neighbors stayed with him so that Helen could rest or do errands, and everyone had been very kind. There were many visitors, including President Grant, "although I was too sick to see him." His nose was sore but he could breathe through it, and the incision in the cheek seemed to be healing rapidly. "I can smell and hear first rate." He was looking forward to a special fowl dish with sweet potatoes, and complained of the mosquitoes. The brightest spot was the presence of his father, who was obviously relieved at the patient's condition. "Pa is at home today and he teases me almost to death. He wanted to know if I thought I could eat two or three turkeys for dinner!" Dol was working hard in the ore trade in Cleveland, trying to establish his own business. Kenyon was sympathetic, with reservations. "I am sorry for the trials you have, but would be willing to go through them and be as well as you are, if you could take my place."[20]

Helen was a solicitous nurse but kept the patient on a careful regimen of study. He was soon moving about and eating well. She had five children now, Will Cochran, Helen, and Dolson, more on less or their own, and Kenyon and young Charles, born in 1858. There would be a final child, Charlotte Hope, born in 1871. Two others, William born in 1861, and Dennison, born in 1867, had not survived infancy. Some of the family thought that she babied Kenyon and kept him immature, worrying over his health and habits, attending to his demands and complaints. He, of course, thought otherwise, but was always grateful for her special concern and care. In 1886 he inscribed a copy of his first artistic success, the illustrations for Rosetti's "The Blessed Damozel," with unusual emotion: "To my beloved mother, to whose care and nursing I owe it that I have ever lived to produce anything, this volume, as containing the best work I have yet done, is presented with tender love by her affectionate son."[21]

Kenyon became careful about his health but did not refer much to these traumas. He was prone to catch colds, which always revived fears of recurrence of the tumor. In 1870 he had a significant relapse, and the family did not expect him to live, but he recovered, and the tumor did not recur. The operations did have lasting effects, which became obvious with time. The surgeons had cut the facial nerves and the left side of his face remained immobile. It did not age much, which made his face asymmetrical, especially when he smiled. In time, he covered this with a beard and was almost always photographed from the right side.[22]

For the moment the youthful Kenyon continued to enjoy Washington. Not attending school left him with time to visit the city and see various effects of Washington and Franklin, as well as models at the patent office and other curiosities. He liked receiving mail, especially from his oldest friend, Leonard Opdycke. "Leo" was the child of Emerson Opdycke, a wartime friend of General Cox's. Two years younger than Kenyon, he was slow in writing, which provoked the senior adolescent's officious wrath. He sent Leo a postcard decorated with a grinning ogre that would eat him if he did not obey. If he could not write well, he could at least print a card or letter. "I want you to understand that I will not write you another letter until you print me an answer to this and my former one," he wrote in September 1870. "I think I have performed my part of our bargain. Your friend, Kenyon Cox." The threat apparently worked, for a few weeks later he wrote Leo again, this time on a card with a grinning jester. Through it all, and much to come, Leo remained docile and was a lifelong friend. Like others, he found Kenyon's personality fascinating even when irritating.[23]

Dolson's probity and idealism did not suit Washington in general or the Grant administration in particular. Though a loyal cabinet member, he was bound to disagree with Grant and ultimately to see these divergences as matters of principle. He was more interested in a merit civil service and honest campaign contributions than were the president and powerful congressmen. He also chafed under Grant's increasing tendency to interfere with departmental rules for political reasons. Their break came in the fall of 1870, and Dolson resigned November 1. There were few public animosities; Dolson was probably right in his view of the public good and wrong in supposing that he could change policies. He returned to Cincinnati to practice law.

Kenyon was approaching the time of deciding on a profession. He would go to college, of course, and was perhaps more prepared than young men who had completed public schooling. His parents probably thought him suited to some scholarly pursuit, given his health and tastes, but did not press him. This was just as well, for he had decided to be a painter, however unlikely this choice seemed in a family of theologians, lawyers, and politicians. Kenyon was remarkable in choosing this path in early youth, a time when most peers were unaware of the world or alternated among inappropriate career choices before settling down to do the expected. He thus displayed from the first a determination, even obstinacy, to succeed that marked his coming artistic career.

The family was probably not surprised. Even as a small boy he drew with pencil and charcoal. While Dolson was at the front, Kenyon wrote him in a childish but legible scrawl or in block printing, including drawings of scenery, objects, or people. The ever-practical Dolson doubtless found this curious, especially in one so young, but was proud of the boy's talent. "Dear little Ken's progress delights me," he wrote Helen after receiving a note. "His letter I will try to answer soon. Let him write current hand. He does it quite as well as his *print*." Kenyon continued to sketch for his father, who always responded with praise. "Little Ken's drawing of a horse's head does great credit to so small a youngster," he wrote home in 1863. "Tell him papa thinks it very nice."[24]

At some point, Kenyon's interest in art crystallized. Years later he recalled his youth of invalidism and reclusive study. "I saw little art but chanced to be taken to the studio of a bad painter called Crawford, and from that time determined, in my own mind, to be a painter." This unremembered artist was John Crawford of Warren, who apparently had some eye for color and the patience to explain his work. He was doubtless grateful to find anyone in town, however young, who liked his painting. "He took a great fancy to Ken," Dolson remembered, "and I think Ken's taste for art was acquired through the friendship of Crawford."[25]

The acquaintance with Crawford at least focused, if it did not cause, Kenyon's art interests. Anyone's choice of a profession, and the needs it represents, is psychological as well as practical. Kenyon no doubt found art, as he first perceived it, an escape from poor health and a cloistered existence. It was a doorway to a wider world of colorful and creative experience beyond his sober household. It was also eminently respectable, however uncertain its rewards. A career in art could satisfy his expectations of himself and please the family if he worked with the proper subjects. For Kenyon, art could present truth and facts in ordered and meaningful ways, but with the controlled and elevating emotion that seemed normal in the family. He was too young to analyze such feelings, but certainly had them. His lifelong tendency to balance ideals and verities found a sound outlet in the forms of art he finally chose to study and create.

The family accepted Kenyon's decision calmly, perhaps thinking that he would change his mind. The poor prospects of making a living in art gave any parent second thoughts, and General Cox may have been more skeptical than he appeared. Kenyon's parents realized that he found art a great comfort during his illnesses and obviously needed to create. Dolson was proud of his son's efforts, which he often circulated among friends and family. By 1872, when Kenyon seemed recovered, Dolson told a friend that he was "a natural student, and his bent seems to be artistic."[26]

Kenyon apparently attended some classes at the McMicken School of Design in Cincinnati as early as 1869 and copied from book reproductions and

FIG. 1. Kenyon Cox, *Spring House* (1873). Pencil on paper, 5 × 9 ins.
Allyn Cox Papers, Archives of American Art, Smithsonian Institution.

prints. The family bought many periodicals and illustrated books, and he
had access to a fair cross-section of both contemporary and historical art. He
roamed the countryside during visits to relatives, armed with sketchbooks
and pencils. He drew in a stilted, amateurish way, employing heavy outlines
and literal detailing, but sometimes used hatching and shading to create
mood and light effects. The subjects included rocks, leaves, trees, and some
small figures. His approach was not facile, but revealed careful observation
and an earnest effort to depict reality.

In one example from 1873, he sketched a spring house in Gambier, Ohio.
He set the image firmly midpage, delineated the appearance of the logs and
bricks in the house in careful detail, and bisected it with a tree trunk for
added interest. And he cropped the scene, leaving rather large unfinished
edges to give a sense of ongoing space. Though studied and literal, the small
work had its charms (fig. 1). He also sketched people, trying to create mood
and character with hatching and shading, detailing costume and equipage
for interest.[27]

The mid-seventies brought significant changes to the maturing Kenyon. His father became receiver for the bankrupt Wabash Railroad, and between 1873 and 1877 his parents spent a good deal of time in Toledo, the company's headquarters. Kenyon was thus free from constant supervision for the first time. He stayed with relatives in Cincinnati, where Will Cochran was starting a law practice, and wrote his parents a steady stream of letters about his situation and thoughts. His cheek sometimes hurt and he visited Dr. Mussey, but the tumor did not recur. Helen worried about his regimen and wanted regular reports. "Tell mama that I have four eggs a day usually," he wrote Dolson early in 1876. Sometimes he had oysters, and he ate a good deal of nourishing meat. He loved classical music and went to many concerts and recitals. He read widely, both for the content and the illustrations, in books such as *Don Quixote,* Thackeray's social novels, and Motley's histories. He also attended many meetings of the U.C.D., a literary society whose initials derived from the phrase *Utile cum Dulce,* or Useful with Pleasure. These groups of educated, affluent people, many of whom resembled the Coxes in taste and prospects, met often in each other's homes and staged larger events for the public.[28]

The great question, of course, was how to become an artist. Cincinnati did not seem the most propitious place to begin such a career. It was a significant western city, but cultural offerings were uneven amid the great drive for economic development. The city wanted to become more than "Porkopolis," and its leaders supported music and literature but were less certain of their tastes when it came to the plastic arts. Some affluent citizens collected paintings, but they tended to be minor examples of old masters, safe recent French works, and the historical and anecdotal works of the Düsseldorf school. Through reading, and to some extent from having lived briefly in Washington, Kenyon was more aware than most of the world beyond the Queen City.

The logical place to begin his studies was near at hand, the McMicken School of Design, which opened in 1868 and was affiliated with the University of Cincinnati. On paper its program resembled those of European academies. Beginning students emphasized shading and perspective, drawing from prints. Second-year students advanced to drawing from plaster casts of famous works. Third-year pupils could use color, draw from nature, and employ dressed models. Day students tended to be young women interested in adding art to their social talents. Night classes were full of young men trying to learn skills for the job market. For a person of Kenyon's tastes and growing ambitions, eager to enter the world of high art for its own sake, the school offered few attractions. He enrolled, probably at his parents' request, but was an indifferent scholar. As always, he resisted authority from people he did not respect. The routine was boring, and he "passed more of his time sketching the animals in Robinson's menagerie than he did in the classroom."[29]

He did meet some interesting peers, and it was comforting to know that he was not alone in his ambitions and tastes. One of these peers was the engaging Robert Blum, already noted for his facility in drawing. He liked exotic subjects and employed a flowing line that, later combined with rich coloring, gained him considerable reputation before an untimely death in 1903. Kenyon also became close to Alfred Brennan, talented draftsman and an energetic personality with a cutting wit. A native of Louisville, he had studied in Canada and knew at least something of the world beyond Cincinnati. These and others became close friends. They fancied themselves rebels and inevitably resisted authority and criticized established taste. They were hardly bohemian or radical, but saw the art life as something more exciting and important than farming, practicing law, or speculating in commodities.[30]

Impatient youth found the McMicken School and the Cincinnati cultural scene stodgy and dull, but there was an occasional breath of fresh air. The art shops offered prints of modern European works. The readily available eastern newspapers and magazines reported on the art world abroad. And for Kenyon's group there was the special excitement of having the artist Frank Duveneck in the city from late 1873 until the summer of 1875. Duveneck was just developing what became a large reputation as a member of the Munich school. These younger painters emphasized free handling of paint in rich, old-masterish tones. They seemed vital and modern in trying to create a sense of motion and vitality. They also depicted daily life, exotic human types, and any subject they thought colorful and intriguing for its own sake. This approach inevitably emphasized the painter's act as much as the subject, an attitude that had profound consequences on modern art. Duveneck and his friends seemed facile, slipshod, and devoid of ideas to critics who had matured on older works and ideals which involved morality or stories. But both their techniques and subject matter attracted younger people trying to break with convention and precedent.

Duveneck kept a studio and tried to spread his gospel. He taught a special night class at the Ohio Mechanics' Institute. His sixteen pupils included Cox, Brennan, and Blum, who knew of his reputation and were eager to see what he had learned from European study. Duveneck emphasized naturalistic studies of heads, which combined the free use of paint with a search for character and vitality. The class also treated subjects from daily life and drew from the nude male model.[31]

Duveneck returned to Munich in August 1875, but left behind at least an example of some of the things missing in the McMicken approach. Kenyon did not reflect on this experience, but like his friends was ready to challenge the system. That fall Brennan got permission to conduct a night class along more modern lines, and Kenyon joined the rebels. The group met in the basement of the classroom building, was very enthusiastic, and discussed art in all its ramifications. They wanted to be modern and used strong color and realistic drawing, trying to infuse their work with motion and richness.[32]

Kenyon sometimes instructed in Brennan's place. The students appreciated his seriousness and talent, and he was usually patient, though blunt in criticizing work. Any such group was bound to have its tensions. Kenyon often delighted in Brennan's wit, at least when it was directed at others. Brennan liked Cox, but sometimes found his opinions and learning pretentious. Kenyon once used the word "madrigal," only to have Brennan suggest loudly that people employ normal English. Kenyon explained that the word said exactly what he meant, but sulked over his friend's wounding remark. Early in 1876, he finished a picture that Brennan offered to buy, then changed his mind. Now he would not have it as a gift; Kenyon promptly gave it to him.[33]

Thomas Noble, the staid director of the school, did not quite know what to make of such people. He sometimes came down to see their work and tiptoed about like a mouse, though he was lionlike elsewhere. He would then return to the cast room where the mood was hushed and solemn, things were in order, and he was in charge. Kenyon had mixed feelings about it all. They had changed some things and made some progress, but where was it leading? The program seemed marginal, and there was never enough of anything— models, materials, or enthusiasm. He thought a lot about how to enter the world of high art somewhere else.[34]

Kenyon's situation was frustrating, but his knowledge of art was in fact expanding. He was more aware than ever of the European modernists who were moving away from the allegorical and historical painting that had dominated art for so long. The French painter Henri Regnault captured his attention. This brilliant young man, clearly marked for fame, and perhaps greatness, died in the Franco-Prussian war in 1871, but not before producing several canvases that shocked or gratified critics and patrons. His *Moorish Headsman* (1870) showed a gruesome beheading and fairly rang with drama. A Moorish executioner calmly wiped blood from his blade while looming over a decapitated corpse, the entire scene set dramatically on rising steps with a background of rich decoration. It was both an unusual and disturbing subject and an exciting technique. Regnault's 1869 portrait of the Spanish General Juan Prim depicted the victorious soldier on a horse that fairly reared at the observer, with a background of soldiers and tattered flags fresh from action. The brushwork was rapid and nervous, the coloring dramatic, and the drama palpable in these works.

This sense of life and action in Regnault's work was most dramatic for Kenyon in *Salome* (1870). The legend of Salome in both literature and art shocked many people in the nineteenth century. But Regnault seemed to capture her essence in a painting of a dark gypsylike woman, resting after a dance. Her costume was loose, revealing bare legs and arms. On her lap was a dagger in a large brass bowl. She sat with her right hand on hip, curly hair tousled from exertion, decolleté at the right breast, with a look of frank sensuality.

On January 8, 1876, Kenyon went to the public library and looked up the engraving of *Salome* in the *Gazette des Beaux-Arts*. "It must be a wonderful picture," he noted rather drily. The next day between attending church and eating dinner he and his friends saw the etching again. A week later he wrote his father the usual letter and decorated the upper left corner of the page with a small sketch of the work. Of course, it lacked the vitality of the original. "She is like a panther, an agile, springy, beautiful beast, that one could play most charmingly with, only keep away from the claws," he noted with some boldness. He was beginning to see the work's sexual resonances. "It is a wonderful imagination, and if so much [so] in this etching, what must the painting be?"[35]

Kenyon and his friends reserved their greatest enthusiasm for another modernist with a worldwide reputation, the Spaniard Mariano Fortuny. His amazing talent had burst upon the scene a dozen years earlier when he was a young man, and his life quickly became a model for the new generation of young artists committed to change. *Exotic, sumptuous, exciting* were words that came easily in describing his work. He loved color and light, whether in painting Moorish or North African scenes and types or in dealing with his native Spain. His work seemed to be an open door, beckoning to new subject matter, color, and self-expression in style. His portraits tended to be informal, catching character while displaying movement and life. He did outdoor scenes with overlaid colors, broad strokes, and thick surfaces, and was not afraid of sunlight and unusual tones. His studio works combined rich finery and decor with a nervous line that made the canvases seem jewel-like to a generation reared on sober works. In *The Choice of a Model* (1874), he showed a group of eighteenth-century academicians examining a nude female in a large salon with fancy decorations, which with the costumes, were jewels for his brush. The painting combined artistic dexterity and expression with an interesting scene and an acceptable female nude.[36] In a larger sense, Fortuny's career also showed that the artist's life could be exotic, imaginative, and unusual, touching on themes and experiences that the sober professional world could not offer. This was certainly one of the appeals of art-life for Kenyon.

Kenyon may have seen his first Fortunys in the fall of 1875 at the Sixth Cincinnati Industrial Exposition. This fair also showed some works that Fortuny's followers, such as Giovanni Boldini, had done. In January 1876, Kenyon saw a local collector's photograph of *The Choice of a Model*. He noted engravings of other works, and an oil copy of Fortuny's *Arquebusier* (1869) at a local auction house. "It is composed in a remarkable manner," he wrote in his diary. "The color is not good nor is the painting as full of snap as the original must be, but the drawing and the character is [*sic*] good. The original must be immense." He wrote Dolson that Fortuny was "the prince of all the etchers I know anything of." Kenyon's circle became frankly "Fortuny-mad" and spent hours talking about and trying to copy the master's techniques. The craze went so far that when someone substituted a copy for a Fortuny work in a Cincinnati show, Kenyon and his friends were suspects in the case. Fortunately for them, the perpetrator, an itinerant artist, was apprehended.[37]

Kenyon's fascination with Fortuny continued unabated and began to have subtle results. Like most beginners, he first saw nature as something to be copied with suitable expression, and he focused on acquiring technical skills. But he was beginning to see art as a means of capturing feeling and of extending the imagination and emotions. In short, he was thinking pictorially. Early in 1876, he noted an attractive young lady in church. She was pretty, to be sure, but her curves, drapery, and jewelry created a new effect on him. She was a picture.[38]

This approach affected him in daily life. He knew examples of the popular Barbizon school and was beginning to see what painters such as Corot were trying to do. He could equate their pictures with nature and, more to the point, with broad emotional responses that enriched his sense of self and the world. Early one January morning in 1876, he noted the effects of sunrise in artistic terms. The combination of delicate sky and gray landscape "kept reminding [me] all the time of Corot, and showed me his wonderful delicacy and accuracy of painting tones of nature." A few weeks later he and Brennan went to see a local collector's Corots. "I think Brennan's comparison of Corot's works to music is just right. Such a picture as that I could *love* and keep around by myself in a corner somewhere." He could not resist adding: "It's a pity it should be in a house among such a lot of German stuff." By the spring of 1876 he still often felt depressed about his progress, but sensed that he was expanding his perception of art's functions. When things went well at the easel or sketch pad, the feeling was wonderful. "I have passed a day gloriously and have felt like an artist," he recorded after a successful morning in class. In the afternoon he worked at a new canvas "and had as wholesome, broad artistic feeling [as] I have had for some time." After a long walk with Brennan, he noted: "I am glad to put down here that I am growing broad, and more of a universal *artist* all the time."[39] He was changing from a painter to an artist, a broader, more intellectual role in his own imagination.

Of course, the proof of any progress was in the work. He continued to fill sketchbooks with studies of leaves, animals, and ornaments of various kinds. He copied famous persons from prints and photographs. He depicted himself in varied poses, now dejected, now elated, as a jester or as a costumed figure. He used his Fortuny techniques in sketches of cavaliers, pirates, and historical figures in fancy dress. He practiced shading and light effects, often with consciously dramatic poses, in dealing with heads and figures. His surviving oils showed the influence of both Fortuny and Duveneck. A little oil of 1875, called *The Whistler,* was amateurish and hesitant, but charming. It showed a satyrlike head of a boy whistling through pursed lips, a favorite Duveneck subject, broadly painted in flesh tones, with swirls of white around the edges for effect.[40] He did a small self-portrait in pencil, depicting a rather pensive adolescent, facing the viewer in a romantic attitude. The detailing was realistic, and he used a rather fluid line in depicting the clothing (fig. 2). He doubtless saw himself this way, at least while in confident moods, a pensive young man with aspirations.

Kenyon was working and changing, but progress seemed very slow. He could not shake the belief that he was better than the situation in Cincinnati. He had no illusions about his present stage of development. "I *must* learn to draw," he instructed himself early in 1876. And he tried to be patient, remembering Dolson's advice: "Don't theorize, but *paint!*"[41] Still, he felt strongly that somehow he must move on. And just recognizing his limitations while aspiring to do more was surely an ironic kind of progress.

He understood better what he wanted than how to attain it. His irritation and frustration with the McMicken program grew daily. He always seemed to be copying someone else's art, at the mercy of mediated ideas and subjects in prints and photographs. The school routine did not lead anywhere, or even prepare a good student to go someplace better. "We have learned what little we know away from the McMicken and we have had to unlearn almost everything we learned there," he confided to his diary in February 1876.[42] His reading and survey of what art was available locally told him that there was much more to both training and art-life than he could get in Cincinnati.

Later that February he began to campaign as only a determined youngster could, in a frank letter to his father. He reported that Brennan was pacing their room like a caged lion, frustrated at not having been out of Cincinnati for years. All of their circle were weary of studying from casts and prints. They wanted to see the world. "And, indeed an artist must see the world. His business is to paint what he loves most, and how can he find it without seeing what there is to paint?" His horizon had certainly grown. "But when spring comes can't you manage it that I may travel and see something? I want to see Europe, *not* to attend an academy, not even to see pictures, although pictures are much, but to see nature and art, men and countries." His ambitions grew as he wrote. "I want to see Spain and Morocco, and find out what there *is* to paint, and *see* it and *study* it." This kind of experience made artists good. "What made Fortuny great, more than anything else, was his chance to travel through Morocco with unlimited sketchbooks and portfolios at hand and sketch *everything*. Corot learned his wonderful art of tones through seeing nature at all hours and times." He assured Dolson that he was

FIG. 2. Kenyon Cox, *Self-Portrait* (1876).
Pencil on sketchbook paper, ca. 6 × 9 ins.
Kenyon Cox Papers, Archives of American Art, Smithsonian Institution.

well and old enough to strike out on his own. "I feel that the time *is* come, or, by spring, *will be,* when I must find out and learn, and when more time spent in digging by myself were lost." Could he not at least go to the Centennial Exposition in Philadelphia and see the collections of art from all the world's countries, "and then not stop till I cross the ocean?" This plan, or fantasy, had a happy ending. "Then after a year of travel I feel that I would know enough at twenty-one to settle down in some place where art is taught and models are plenty [*sic*] and keep myself, travelling in summer and painting in winter for a year or two, and then come back, perhaps, an artist and a recognized one." He wanted to experience life as well as paint it. Doubtless somewhat surprised at his own boldness, Kenyon noted in his diary that night: "Wrote a letter to father today speaking of how much necessity there is that one should see something in the world to paint."[43] Dolson's response did not survive, but the talking and planning continued. By late April, Kenyon had discussed with Will Cochran plans to visit the Centennial Exposition. After that he might settle for studying at the Art Students League in New York, established in 1875 and made up of pupils who were dissatisfied with the traditional teaching methods of the National Academy of Design (NAD).[44]

Visiting the Centennial Exposition made some sense to Dolson, and he might have suggested it without prompting, simply as part of Kenyon's education. He was as interested in the scientific and technological displays as Kenyon was in the art. They could meet there. In late August, Kenyon made the rounds at the exposition and reported back to Blum in a long letter. Most important, there was the prestigious Pennsylvania Academy of Fine Arts, which seemed his likely destination for the fall term, which opened on October 1. Applicants were judged and placed on the basis of anonymous drawings. He and Blum could probably escape the beginners' class in drawing from antique casts. If they got into the life drawing section, they would work from good models three days a week and have the rest of the time for independent study. They could also model in clay at night. "There is a tremendously large park left wild to wander in, and there will be, when [the] exposition is over, a permanent museum containing many rich things brought from said exposition." It was not Europe, but might be second best. "I have written these things to my father and rather expect he will have me stay here." The point was that Blum could come too. "We two could hire a couple of rooms, sleep in one and paint in the other, strike out against the old fogy's [*sic*] and paint as we liked and be happy as two ducks in a mudpuddle." They could live cheaply with hand-me-down furniture and old clothes, and might even earn something from their art.

That suggested, he reported on the art at the fair. Alexander Wagner's much discussed *Roman Chariot Race* (1876) was poorly executed and overwrought. Gonzalo Alvarez Espino's equally noted *Annual Fair Attended Only*

by Men (1874) was awful. The celebrated Austrian Hans Makart had sent
Venice Paying Homage to Caterina Cornaro (1873), done in his sumptuous, expansive historical style, but it left Kenyon cold and disappointed. He disliked the grandiose works that attracted so much press attention, preferring
more intimate subjects and treatments. The Japanese arts and crafts were
best of all. He went through the Japanese house erected for the exhibition
and was much impressed with the simplicity and grace of oriental life. Although the art work was elegant and refined, it was richly colored with a
controlled sumptuousness. "The Japanese art is magnificent—far beyond
anything I ever saw, *too* magnificent for me to copy," but he included two
small drawings of a Japanese girl on the letter.[45]

Helen and Dolson probably did not quite know what to do with their ambitious son, who was now expressing the family's idealism quite forthrightly.
At some point in the discourse they agreed, and Kenyon duly reported to the
Pennsylvania Academy for the fall term in 1876. Blum and Brennan joined
him shortly thereafter, and the three lived together.

Cheap and appropriate housing was hard to find. They advertised in the
paper but got no suitable replies. In due course, after almost giving up, they
tried the last location on their list, Shingle's Commercial Building at 247
Elbow Lane. They took modest rooms on the top floor, where the air and
light were good whatever the demerits of the decor, which was all second-
hand and make-do. Suitably parsimonious, they first thought of eating
breakfast in to reduce restaurant costs and bought a huge supply of oatmeal.
They tried to vary this with a custard, which almost exploded. They finally
settled for eating out at cheap restaurants. Classwork was demanding, and
they walked around the city a good deal. They visited galleries and auction
houses to see available art and tried to sell their own work, with no luck.
Their comings and goings seemed strange enough to provoke momentary
police surveillance. But for all their apparent bohemianism, they were very
proper; the limit of their daring was a game of whist or checkers. Kenyon
concluded one letter with a fair description of their allegedly glamorous existence. "In a room furnished with two easels, a chair, a trunk, a box, and a
broken-legged saw-horse, with the wind whistling through the partitions and
under the door, with some thirty-odd canvases and panels painted and un-
painted lying and hanging wherever there is a hook, and sketchbooks in the
interstices, and pieces of paper countless as the sea sands," he catalogued,
"with torn clothes, no shirt-buttons and a frightful cold, resting under the
dark suspicion of being a counterfeiter or something equally dreadful, and
seeing no escape from spending the remainder of my existence so, writing by
a lamp with a sheet of paper for a shade . . . in our atmosphere of poetry and
art—I wish you a merry evening and a good night."[46]

Helen doubtless had decided not to worry. Kenyon was rambunctious but
not foolish, and at least was not alone. She had also reared enough children

simply to hope for the best. From Toledo, where Dolson had just been elected to Congress, she wrote Will Cochran in Cincinnati about Kenyon's progress. Dolson "seems to think that Ken must have all the money that he wants," she noted somewhat drily. "I do hope the boy's [illegible] will be commensurate with the labor and expense that have been put upon him all his life. I sometimes fear that he never will amount to anything."[47] This was realism rather than criticism, and she remained supportive, sending food, advice, and concern to the trio regularly, as Brennan later recalled.[48]

The Academy's program looked impressive and was prestigious. The antique drawing class met on Tuesday, Thursday, and Saturday mornings. The life drawing class met the other days of the week. Dr. W. W. Keen, a famous Philadelphia surgeon, lectured on anatomy on Saturday. There was a good library, and costumes and accessories for the classes.

Kenyon entered life drawing and at first worked very hard, but was blasé. "You say that all my Cincinnati friends express a great deal of satisfaction at my whereabouts," he wrote home. "For myself I must say [that] one place is much like another. The only advantages here are a life class and a *very* good painting room." The instructor was not impressive. "The professor is an old man who, judging from his paintings, never did know much and who is now far behind the times, and has palsy to boot." This was Christian Schussele, a noted historical painter whose tastes were not likely to please young turks like Kenyon or Blum. "Robert and I are working on entirely different principles from all the rest and rely simply on ourselves for all improvement." Cox did not mention a young man named Thomas Eakins who assisted Schussele.[49]

Kenyon's sketchbooks revealed some progress, whatever his complaints. In one large drawing he depicted a woman in an elaborate hooded costume walking along a wall that had an impressive Spanish gate. It was loosely drawn, with swirled lines and open edges to create a sense of motion. Fortuny's influence was obvious. Other drawings showed male nudes in various poses. The informal ones often lacked specific features, with the pencil's emphasis on costumes and accoutrements as much as on the person. In more elaborate figures, some sitting, reclining, or standing, he was more careful to opt for firm drawing with some shading to create a sense of solidity and presence (fig. 3). He was more enamored of informal genre scenes and loose drawings of people than of the elaborate figure studies so common in academic instruction.[50] He still decorated letters home with doodles and sketches, including costumed figures (fig. 4).

He continued to find great pleasure in things Japanese. He went back several times to the exhibitions at the Centennial grounds. He also wrote home for books and prints dealing with Japan and read the country's history. His letters home often had drawings of Japanese subjects. Some of his classwork had Japanese themes, such as an 1877 sketch of a woman in traditional

FIG. 3. Kenyon Cox. Untitled Study of Standing Male Nude (1874–1876).
Charcoal on paper, 24⅞ × 19 1/16 ins. Courtesy of the National Museum of
American Art, Smithsonian Institution, bequest of Allyn Cox.

FIG. 4. Kenyon Cox, *Sketch of a Cavalier*, from a letter to his parents,
February 7, 1877. Pencil on paper, ca. 7½ × 3½ ins.
Kenyon Cox Papers, Archives of American Art, Smithsonian Institution.

kimono, holding a parasol. He wrote a lengthy poem, "A Dream of Japan," or "To a Picture," which detailed the emotional appeal of a mythical Japanese woman and what she represented about her exotic culture. His most ambitious effort was a small oil showing a Japanese woman herding a line of cranes across the picture plane. It had a heavy, scumbled finish without modelling or drawing, that emphasized the paint's texture. The colors were strong and, for a student, well handled, another reminder of Fortuny. He was equally interested in the ancient Peruvians and read a good deal about their customs and artifacts. He started on a small oil that depicted Incas feeding alligators, an interesting pictorial idea, however unlikely it was. He also painted some Peruvian jugs at the Academy and attracted unwanted attention from passersby. In the end, he did not like the finished pictures but retained an imaginative streak that paralleled his formal training.[51]

He kept his sights on European training and clearly saw the Academy experience as a way station on a trip abroad. Old habits reasserted themselves, and he was soon cutting classes, disdainful of the academic routine. His complaints and actions produced fatherly discipline. "Sometime since, Mr. Bartlett remonstrated with me for my very irregular attendance at the Academy," he admitted to the Academy director in December 1876. "As I thought I could employ my time more profitably outside, I could not promise any better, so gave up my ticket of membership. I reported this to my father, and he has requested me to ask that my ticket be given me again, and in such case, to attend more regularly in future."[52] This was probably a mild summation of instructions from home. By the spring of 1877, he was explaining to Dolson: "I do not think anyone at the Academy would accuse me of ill manners toward him. I have tried to bear myself politely, and indeed the curator once expressly said that I had acted like a gentleman. But the Academy authorities did not like my independence of them in study."[53]

More than youthful dissatisfaction lay behind Kenyon's persistent desire for European study. He had begun to see art and the art life in a broader context than did most of his confreres. He understood that large changes were at work in cultural life, just as in economics and politics. The mere fact that he could be aware of the art world while in Cincinnati or Philadelphia showed how much communication, knowledge, and ambition had changed in his generation. He certainly wanted to perfect his technical skills, but hoped to be part of what he saw as a renaissance in cultural tastes and production. "Indeed, I believe as I have so often said, that modern times are coming to a second renaissance," he wrote in his diary early in 1876. He respected the inherited art tradition, but saw no reason why moderns could not add to it. This required careful training, wide experience, and much thought.[54]

He also knew that he would not likely succeed in the competitive art world without European training. There was a growing migration of bright young Americans to the art academies and ateliers of Munich, London, and, especially, Paris, the artist's lodestar. Part of this was probably mere snobbery; insecure Americans naturally found European tastes and credentials impressive. But in a larger sense, art was developing a cosmopolitan context, which the United States could and should enter. This did not imply merely copying European art for the American scene. It meant integrating the United States and her new generation of artists into a world cultural order. And Kenyon saw his personal ambitions and hopes as part of that large process.

He had done some homework on the problems involved in studying abroad. First and foremost, of course, was money. While at the McMicken School, he thought of a European tour, simply to see art and broaden his horizon. At the least, this would require about a hundred dollars a month, fifty when he settled in a city. He talked this over with Brennan and Will Cochran. His sources were reports from people who had been or were hoping to go abroad, and there was a good deal of comment in the art journals and press. One could live cheaply in Paris and learn a great deal about art. He alternated between enthusiasm and depression. Would his parents let him go? Could he live alone in such circumstances? Was he mature enough after all? For every moment of enthusiasm, there were times of doubt. "Had a long talk with Brennan," he noted in March 1876, "who thinks neither of us is ready to go to Europe yet."[55]

By early 1877 he returned to the assault upon his parents. He shrewdly approached his mother first. Now he was ready to attend a European school, he said, not just to take a tour. He complained ceaselessly of the Academy's instruction and intellectual tone. "The Academy is an abomination," he noted, with the usual exaggeration. He remained irritated and depressed at not seeing more real art work; copying was not preparation for success. Fortuny remained his example of an artist who was grounded in quality technical education, and profited from seeing the world, especially exotic and unusual places. He quoted prices in Paris as he had heard them, and mentioned attending the state-sponsored Ecole des Beaux-Arts. This was the most prestigious art school in Paris, or in the world for that matter. He could probably live there for little more than it cost to stay in Philadelphia. And if he could not go to Paris, perhaps he should go to the Art Students League in New York City. He did not dwell on New York City's high cost of living, but his parents knew about it.[56]

Dolson visited Philadelphia early in March 1877, and Kenyon met him at the train. The two talked, and the subject of further training inevitably arose. Dolson was cautious, obviously thinking that Kenyon would need supervision if he went to Paris. After all, it took at least ten days to send or receive a letter across the Atlantic. What if he became sick again? Would it not be best for him to study with a well-known artist? Perhaps George Peter

Alexander Healy, an expatriate American with a large reputation for portraits of leaders in politics and business? And this example of success might sober and benefit Kenyon.

Kenyon did not likely argue, but as usual he wrote a reasoned reply after Dolson left. He did not dismiss Healy but obviously was not interested in his old-fashioned way of painting. If he studied with an artist, it would be someone like Boldini. But truth to tell, he wanted independence. "My idea is that to get the proper good from study, one should *apply* everything constantly to pictorial purposes," he wrote with a seriousness that was bound to appeal to his father. "I do not want so much to learn the shape of a leg or color of a shade as 'What about this thing is artistic?' I do not think the knowledge can be attained without the constant presence of nature. And one would learn much more if the nature is of just the kind you then want." This meant choosing models and approaches on his own. "Now, do you not think that this sort of study would be impossible in another man's studio?" he asked rather gently. "I should have either to paint with no models, or if he was especially good natured, work from his already posed model." He needed his own studio, with the freedom to choose his own pace of development. "Again, if I am to work to the very best advantage, I should have the chance to make pen drawings, water colors, etc., whenever I feel like it, and it would be better on every account that my studio should be next door to my bedroom."[57]

A few days later he followed this letter with one to his mother, whom he clearly expected to speak for him in family councils. He reiterated the desire for privacy and independence. He would work hard and confidently expected to send "a picture to the Salon at the second year." He hoped to live on a hundred dollars a month, but less was probably impossible. He would profit from the environment as much as from any schooling. "Of course, I should expect to learn much from the constant viewing of the best in modern art, which always comes to Paris." He was obviously in an agony of suspense, which heightened all of his irritable immaturity. "I wrote you several letters that I did not send," he admitted. "They were written from time [to time?] and when the sheets were full I found that they consisted of so much complaining at my situation and were so vacillating, weak and boyish that I was ashamed and did not send them."[58]

Life went on in the midst of all this anxiety and discussion. He continued to copy works, and for a moment thought he could sell a copy of Fortuny's *Arquebusier.* He offered it to a dealer for a mere thirteen dollars, only to hear that times were hard, everybody was "Fortuny-mad," and there was no market. In the end, he took it on consignment for an auction. Kenyon might get five dollars for it, more likely nothing. "Poor I had flattered myself that a copy after Fortuny was far more likely to sell than anything original I could do." The dealer showed him some water colors no better than his own, but they were from Paris. "Nice prospect for a young man in this enlightened country," he said in a moment of pique. "I want no more of America, where there is no chance to do good work and where people prefer that you should paint badly rather than try to do as well as circumstances permit." But his moods were improving, as he understood from a letter his parents had written to Brennan that they were serious about study abroad. "I can never be enough thankful to you and father for providing the way, as I gather from your letter to Brennan, you intend to do, for my exit from this stage of artist life."[59]

A week later he reported home the usual litany of troubles—not enough clothes, shoes worn out, too little coal, and very cold weather. He even had bought the poverty-stricken Brennan a meal. "But for myself, knowing that it won't last long, and that 'there's a good time coming' next year, it is rather a matter of rough enjoyment, especially when I am walking about to keep warm and being blown about by the wind."[60] School ended and he joined his parents in Toledo, able to report to Leonard Opdycke: "I expect to go to Europe some time this fall and spend a year or two in Paris studying painting. I am not hopeless of meeting Boldini himself there."[61] Just how long he would stay was an open question. The family had many financial obligations, but Helen apparently spent some of her own money, probably inherited from her father, to help finance the trip. Kenyon understood that this was his inheritance, and was properly grateful.[62]

Going to Paris was a great challenge, but for all his immaturity, Kenyon was probably as well prepared as most of his peers. He did not leave many examples of work at the Pennsylvania Academy and clearly did not like the institution. But if the training and experience were not critical, they did not harm him. The Academy was one of the best art institutions in America and had quality students, even if he thought the instruction sometimes seemed old-fashioned. Given his impatient desire to go abroad, Kenyon got from the Academy about as much as it could give him.

He went back to Cincinnati, eager to practice drawing and study French. His friends were pleased at his prospects, but inevitably some were jealous. Brennan was hostile, seeing foreign training as a rejection of the ideals and modernism he and Kenyon had championed. But this was partly a cover for disappointment at losing a friend, and was simply Brennan's way. By late September, Kenyon was packed and ready, sorry to leave friends, but eager for the great adventure.[63]

I I

PARIS

THE FALL WEATHER OF OCTOBER
1877 sharpened Kenyon's anticipation. He went by train to New York City
and visited Dolson's brothers, Theodore and Charles, who were in business
there. They were helpful and doubtless reported fully to the anxious parents.
On October 12, Kenyon wrote home that he had forty-five dollars in French
coins. This would suffice until he had to draw on a letter of credit for a hundred pounds, about five hundred dollars, at an English bank in Paris. In the
rush he managed to visit the major galleries and was much taken with several
of Boldini's works, though he did not care for those of Jean-Léon Gérôme,
one of the most fashionable French modernists in America. Late in the afternoon of October 13, his uncles helped him to the dock, checked his bag-
gage, waved goodbye, and the steamer *Mosel* of the North German line
pulled away for Southhampton. He would go from there to Le Havre, then by
rail to Paris.[1]

He dreaded the prospect of seasickness, but the voyage was reasonably
calm, and he actually ate well. The passengers were an interesting and varied
lot of tourists, businessmen, and several young ladies he watched carefully.
He made friends, played deck games, and observed the majestic ocean. At
Southhampton on October 24, he dined with friends from the boat, then
took a packet to Le Havre, a journey that did make him sick. He spent the
day at a hotel, then went to Rouen, stayed overnight, then tried to see at
least the major sights in this ancient city where Joan of Arc had died. He
liked the Gothic architecture of churches such as St. Ouen. Like most newcomers, he had preconceived notions of France, and his first impressions were
exhilarating. There was "so much artistic material here that one might almost be content to stay here and paint for years," he wrote home. "One can't
dive down a crooked street or turn a sharp corner without finding more to
paint than he could by hunting months for a subject in America. If Paris is
at all like this it must indeed be a paradise for artists."[2] Between Rouen and

Paris he noted the pervasive sense of settled existence. The villages were compact and solid; houses had thatched or tiled roofs, with sturdy walled gardens. He found this sense of order and of layered civilization very appealing in contrast to the slapdash, temporary look of American life.

His excitement grew as the train approached the City of Light. Once it stopped, he retrieved the luggage and showed a cabman where to go from a map in the guidebook. The choice probably came from friends on the boat, as he knew nothing specific about lodgings in Paris. At the Hôtel Corneille he found no one who could understand his French or speak English. After some gesticulating, the proprietor took him to another guest, Dr. Karl Magnus Thordén of the University of Uppsala in Sweden, who was in Paris studying higher education. Thordén settled matters genially, and Kenyon took a fourth-floor room that was small but clean, at two francs a day. He immediately rushed out to see the Luxembourg Gardens. The lodgings were temporary, and he naïvely thought he might find a nice inexpensive house.

The following week was busy. He moved to the Hôtel du Mont Blanc at 63 rue du Seine, for a small suite of a bedroom and sitting room. With maid service it cost forty francs a month. He was in the art quarter near the Ecole des Beaux-Arts, close to restaurants and cafés. Dr. Thordén joined him. "I am very glad that the Doctor is with me," Kenyon wrote home. "To say nothing of the considerable lessening of expense, I find it in every way pleasanter, enabling me to spend many evenings pleasantly at home, when, otherwise, I should either be moping in the blues or going to a cafe." Thordén was blond, about thirty, and in some ways reminded Kenyon of Brennan. He had traveled on the Continent and was thoroughly upright and moral. Thordén had little aesthetic sense and was not much interested in the arts or music, but that might be a welcome relief with Kenyon settled into the grind of study.[3] Kenyon adopted a reasonable routine, visiting the public baths, treating himself to a shave at the barber's, dining with new friends at a bistro.

The France to which he came held an ambivalent place in American thinking. Ties between the two countries went back to the American Revolution. France represented ideals of political liberty and social equality that appealed to Americans. It was now a republic in a sea of European monarchies. Educated Americans accepted the country's cultural leadership. It stood for the perceived best in aesthetic expression, as revealed in both great collections and famous contemporary artists. But Americans disapproved of the other side of French life, at least as it was detailed in the press and novels. There were, after all, the scandalous cancan, the smoky and bibulous music hall, and alleged lapses in Victorian morality. Contemporary novelists such as Emile Zola rode a wave of naturalism with sexual innuendoes that made the term "French novel" suggest license. Kenyon's parents must have thought of all of this when consenting to send him.

The French naturally had stereotypical ideas about Americans. All were rich and uncultured. Why else would they come to Paris? Kenyon's contemporary, Julian Alden Weir, who studied with Gérôme at the Ecole between 1873 and 1877, encountered such attitudes. He attended a fashionable dance where a charming French girl asked if he were an American. "Cousin Jules told me he was a savage, with feathers in his nose, a red tint and rings in his ears," she said. Weir had developed a sense of humor, or weariness, about such preconceptions. "I assured her I had gone to a good doctor and had all these signs removed."[4] But all cultures were tolerated in Paris, and Americans and French coexisted easily.

Paris was an ancient city but a new capital. In the preceding twenty years, Napoleon III had brought it into modern times. The city had a relatively uniform building height, which gave it both a cohesive appearance and a human scale. The planners had developed numerous parks and squares to alleviate urban density. Old monuments were repaired, new ones built. Gaslight and then electricity, pure water and good sewerage, and other technical systems made it a very modern place. Above all, planners emphasized its role as an art mecca. The monuments, refurbished buildings, and grand new structures such as the Opéra all testified to the Second Empire's determination to combine elegant style with the appearance of authority. Its successor, the Third Republic, agreed on the importance of culture to France's greatness. This interest was also developed in countless smaller ways, as in the moldings of a shop window, a corner flower stall, or a decorated department store, which added to the cultural air.

The city had its drawbacks, as Kenyon and countless others discovered. The weather was often vile, and the cost of living high. Life was not easy or exciting for the typical working citizen. Beneath the glitter, as Zola and others showed, ran currents of despair and poverty. Art students partook of the glories of French and world culture, but most were at the bottom of the economic pyramid, likely as not shabby in appearance, undernourished, living in drab rooms. Nor had the city recovered completely from the effects of the war with Prussia in 1870 or the frightful Commune uprising of the poor in 1871. There was ample evidence of strife. When Kenyon arrived, for instance, the Tuileries Palace, which had joined the west wings of the Louvre complex and housed the imperial family, was a heap of rubble and foundations, testifying to the mob's action.

All of this did not detract from the city for the art students who came from nearly every other country. Most, like Kenyon, were apolitical, focused on their studies to the exclusion of local affairs. Art and Paris were what mattered and would change their lives. A friend noted of the American art student Henry Bacon, a contemporary of Kenyon's, that "he would rather live in this city on a crust than in any other on six courses and dessert."

Everything seemed pictorial and imaginative, especially to Americans armed with an ideal of the art life. "The streets, often as he has seen them, form an ever-new picture for him. A French crowd seems to be spontaneously composing all the time without giving the artist the trouble to set the model." Above all, Paris was exciting not merely as a museum of past glories but as a home of hopes and prospects. "In Italy [the student] will live among the treasures of bygone ages," another observer noted, "here, though surrounded by representative work of all time, he is at the center of the most active, earnest efforts of the present."[5] Kenyon understood these broad currents of thought. He was there to learn the best technical skills he could acquire. But he also wanted to live in an artistic context where his work and ideas were respected.

Kenyon dutifully fulfilled obligations to his parents. He took his father's letter of introduction to Edward F. Noyes, former governor of Ohio and now minister to France. He called on G. P. A. Healy, comfortably ensconced as a fashionable portrait painter, something of a latter-day Sir Joshua Reynolds. Kenyon met Healy several times later and never liked his unctuous and slightly condescending manner. Years of treating with the rich and powerful made him seem insincere in dealing with lesser mortals. Kenyon eagerly visited the home of the expatriate collector William Hood Stewart, who had a large number of Fortuny's works, and was impressed. "I think the work of Fortuny's which he has is even greater than I expected."[6]

He got other intellectual stimulation from visiting various monuments and collections, especially the Louvre. He immediately went several times, and did some copying. His first impressions were mixed. Inevitably, such a huge collection, gathered over so many centuries, had marginal works, even some dross. In some ways this was comforting to a beginner. "There are many intensely interesting things," he wrote home. "But there is *nothing* before which I could say, 'This is the height of art. There is no use hoping that anything will approach this again.' On the contrary, the more I see the more I feel that one or two modern men have advanced far beyond them in all the technical parts of art. As to mind, that is an entirely different question, and [one] which I am not prepared to discuss."

Of course, real works looked very different from photographs and engravings. He thought Leonardo da Vinci still impressive, but surprisingly cold and lacking in spontaneity. He liked Titian and Hals, but found Rubens disappointing. "I always knew that his drawing was coarse, but had expected to find tremendous vigor and beauty of color. I do not at all like his flesh, and his work shows no sign whatever of powerful and rapid painting." Fragonard and Watteau were charming but uneven. He disliked the moderns descended from Delacroix. The antique collections were superb, but not exciting to him just now. For the moment he preferred the moderns he knew. "I have been to Mr. Stewart's collection twice and find that Fortuny holds his own as a supremely great artist," he insisted two weeks after arriving. "He was, however, improving up to the last hours of his life and would, I think, have gone on to do much better things in color than he has. In drawing he could hardly go further." Many of Fortuny's early works seemed dark, but his late sketches pointed toward a great looseness and energy in drawing. "But I doubt if he ever could have produced such delightful color as Boldini sometimes does."[7]

In that first hectic week, Kenyon naturally focused on entering an art school. Unhappily, Boldini did not take pupils, and the Ecole des Beaux-Arts was full. He then turned to a famous and controversial painter, Carolus-Duran. This was somewhat surprising, because the name had not figured in his discussions before coming to Paris. He probably had read about Carolus-Duran, saw his works at the Centennial Exposition, and picked up information on him from the student grapevine. Kenyon was not ready for the Ecole and needed preparatory work in a congenial setting. He liked the atmosphere of Carolus-Duran's atelier, and the students. "They have very good models at Duran's and a good light room [in which] to work, and a very decent set of fellows, so I did not see my way to do better and decided to try them," he wrote home. He showed Carolus-Duran some drawings, doubtless with the hesitation of a newcomer with provincial training. The master was kind. "He said they had the 'sentiment of nature,' but lacked proportion, which last was true enough. The students also seemed much pleased with them." The fee was one hundred francs a year, with a fifty-franc admission charge and a few francs for a stool and easel.[8] The atelier was at 81 Boulevard du Montparnasse, squarely in the artist quarter where Kenyon could savor the atmosphere.

Born as Charles-Emile Auguste Durand, this painter had suffered poverty as an ambitious youth. When success came, he adopted the more striking, some said pretentious, name of Carolus-Duran. By the time Kenyon arrived, he was widely known as a painter of the rich and famous, working in a sumptuous and dramatic style. He had not planned to teach, but he opened an atelier in 1872 at the suggestion of an American student, Robert C. Hinckley of Boston. Carolus-Duran doubtless remembered his own days as a penurious student, but he also surely saw teaching as a way of creating disciples for his methods. He accepted nothing for instruction, beyond an occasional testimonial dinner. Student fees paid for the building and materials. An assistant, or *massier,* ran things, and Carolus-Duran appeared for criticism at regular intervals.

No one ever accused him of modesty. Now at the height of his powers, Carolus-Duran was a handsome man who radiated vigor and intensity. He was the subject of much comment and moved among the powerful. He strove to look the part of an unusual artist who was not averse to reminding others that he had won after hard struggle and meant to enjoy the role. "He wears tight pantaloons and little pointed boots," Kenyon wrote home, "has a head of hair and wears a beard and moustache, elaborately curly, and is very fond of waving and gesturing with a diamond-ringed hand." Will Hicock Low, an American who just preceded Kenyon in the atelier, recalled the master's careful attention to clothes, or at least to their shock value. It was not unusual to see him in something like a black velvet coat, with a ruffled orange silk shirt, green tie, and ample gold jewelry, all of which set off his dark hair and complexion. He carried himself regally, with appropriate hat, gloves, and cane. An occasional striking public display did not hurt his image either. Low remembered seeing Carolus-Duran clad in something resembling a bullfighter's outfit, driving an exotic vehicle behind a team of pure white horses. He nonchalantly explained that all of this was a gift from the king of Portugal, whose family he had painted. His studio, to which he invited the public and students, was filled with bric-a-brac and the exotic stage props of one who saw the art life as very special and exciting indeed.[9]

All the attention to his personality sometimes obscured Carolus-Duran's ideas about art and how to paint. He rejected the academic approach that laboriously trained the eye and hand with drawings from casts of famous works. He wanted modeling, truthful representation, and concern for form, but painting needed to emphasize surface texture, color, and motion. His own success testified to the rise of new classes of patrons and collectors who wanted rich effects and vigor in art. Only painting directly on the canvas, with little or no preparatory drawing, could produce spontaneity and a truthful sense of life. William-Adolphe Bouguereau, a brilliant academic technician, once asked a student: "Does M. Duran ever make you draw?" Carolus-Duran could have answered yes, but in basic forms, and with colors and surfaces that created character and vitality. "Draw? Of course," he once exclaimed. "But why not draw with the brush? Anathema to the conventional, delight to the students."

For all his panache and individualism, Carolus-Duran was a careful painter and serious teacher. He did not want painting to be sensational, or to reflect mere whim. He had studied the Spanish and Flemish masters, such as Velázquez and Rubens, with great care and wished to join that tradition. But the arts must now satisfy people's fascination with change and variety. "In the French school, since Ingres, the tradition comes from Raphael," he told students. "That was all very well for Ingres, who freely chose the master from whom he really descended; but we who have other needs, who desire reality—less beautiful, without doubt, but more passionate, more living, more intimate—we should search a guide among the masters who respond most fully to our temperament." He believed in the grand gesture but disliked the formality and artificiality, as he saw them, of current academic art. Many young people doubtless thought his method was a shortcut to mastery, and it was easier to enter his atelier than the Ecole. But Carolus-Duran did not offer them an easy approach as much as a sense of being part of the art process. "It is in seeking the human side, the intimate side, that you will solve the enigma," he told them. "Your joy, your conviction, your entire nature should contribute to your work. You must live that which you would paint."[10] Young students ready to defy convention and express their own ways responded eagerly. The Russian Marie Bashkirtseff adored Carolus-Duran's paintings. "After that everything else seemed to be mean, dry and daubed." Kenyon's American friend Eliot Gregory remembered that after a year with an old-fashioned instructor, "the vivid enthusiasm and dash of Carolus-Duran's studio was like stepping out of a dusty cloister into the warmth and movement of a market-place."[11]

Kenyon liked the students and the atmosphere at the atelier. He worked hard at drawing and tried his hand at painting with Carolus-Duran's methods. "Classwork goes on evenly. I find myself lacking a little in some qualities and ahead in others," he noted in late November 1877. "The professor is down on me a good deal, but I think I stand fairly among the first of the class." A hint of uncertainty began to creep into his reports home. "What I principally lack is a long study of the figure, which many of these fellows have had." And he appreciated the tolerance among the group. "Far from regretting it, I find that I like my choice better every day," he wrote in mid-December. "For though I do not entirely like Duran's methods or notions, yet I see that there is much to be learned here, and that his ideas are less distasteful to me than those of most other professors here, and also that he is less strict in forcing them down his pupils' throats than are most of the teachers."[12]

He kept a regular schedule of hard work, but there was also time for recreation and relaxation. He went to the cafés with friends, generally to nurse a drink of coffee or watered wine, relying on conversation to carry the evening. He also read magazines and newspapers at the American social clubs. After Christmas 1877, he went on a hiking trip to the Barbizon area with friends from the atelier. He began to see something of the Parisian environs that were so famous to artists. But the work was remorseless. "I am bending my efforts principally now to learning what the French call 'the values,' " he wrote home, meaning light and shading, or chiaroscuro. "For I find that my principle fault has been in exaggerating the details of light and shade and of color at the expense of the whole, not getting the true value of the various tones. I suppose the professor's 'pas mal' marked a partial success in this direction, as simplicity and true value are his great requisitions."[13]

Carolus-Duran thought enough of him to include Kenyon among the students who were laying in background, draperies, and figure outlines for an enormous ceiling he was doing for the Luxembourg Palace. Kenyon usually joined Carolus-Duran at his home, then they drove to the large studio where the group worked. The master was always courteous, careful to comment on his good progress. The thirty-by-thirty-foot work, *The Apotheosis of Marie de Medici,* was impressive but caused Kenyon some apprehension. "It is a gorgeous piece of color and very well composed," he wrote his mother. "The drawing is not so good, but its chief fault, and indeed the chief fault of all his work, I think, is a certain coarseness, a lack of refinement and delicacy in color, in drawing, in execution, and in feeling. He is strong but a little vulgar." These were large doubts, but "at the same time I like him much better than the dead coldness of Gérôme and some others."[14]

Through the cold winter months of 1877–78, Kenyon worked, but his doubts grew. He began to see that Carolus-Duran's technique was successful only in the hands of an outstanding talent. Ironically, only one like himself who had studied past masters and understood design and composition, with the touch of a great draftsman, could make it succeed. And Carolus-Duran's showmanship offended Kenyon. His was not a proper example for the high calling of art. These doubts came together at the annual banquet the students gave their master in February 1878. Carolus-Duran was at his haughty worst. "He was neither a dignified professor among students nor a man on friendly equality with others, but had a sort of condescending familiarity that I did not like." Carolus-Duran suggested in a toast that his pupils should establish a great school of art with his principles. Kenyon thought that someone else should have said this. Carolus-Duran then criticized a portrait that Jules Bastien-Lepage had on display, a marvel of realism and character depiction to Kenyon. Carolus-Duran quibbled about lights and shades, then suggested it owed a good deal to his own methods. He left, and the students, some tipsy, did the cancan and were foolish. They were only letting off steam, but it all seemed undignified. "Please don't think I see nothing but faults in Duran," Kenyon wrote his father. "I appreciate his strong color, breadth, etc., etc. But I thought you would like to know just how he impresses me, and I must say that a predominating vulgarity grates on me."[15] The "etc., etc." indicated a growing impatience and a certain contempt. He was preparing himself, and his parents, for a change of instructors.

In later years, Kenyon praised Carolus-Duran as a major figure in modernism, one who let in the light and color to painting. But he could not hide his dissatisfaction with the direction of his studies, or deny that he needed more rigorous work. "Duran is not a fine nor careful draftsman himself," he wrote shortly after leaving the atelier, "and the tendency in his atelier is too much to neglect drawing. To make a few hasty scratches for the form and then dash at the effect and color."[16]

Kenyon knew that he needed more careful training in draftsmanship, and in a setting that emphasized discipline and quality work. He logically turned to the Ecole des Beaux-Arts. This venerable institution, dating from the mid-seventeenth century, was the focus of the government's support of the arts. Since the late 1830s, the school had occupied a site on the rue Bonaparte, close to the Louvre, the Luxembourg Palace, and other artistic sites. The visitor entered from the street into a courtyard filled with copies of ancient and Renaissance statuary. A glassed-in area contained architectural models. The ground floor of the main building, "downstairs," as students called it, housed the collection of plaster casts from which beginners drew. The second floor, or "upstairs," contained the painting ateliers.

The Ecole offered instruction in painting, drawing, sculpture, architecture, and gem cutting. It was open and free to Frenchmen between the ages of fifteen and thirty. Foreigners could be admitted on the same basis, and the head of each atelier accepted students as he wished. The painting teachers were Alexandre Cabanel, Jean-Léon Gérôme, and Henri Lehmann. Adolphe Yvon taught special classes in drawing. These famous artists received a modest honorarium, but teaching at the Ecole was prestigious and offered each the chance to develop a school of followers.

The internal workings of the ateliers resembled Carolus-Duran's. A *massier* attended to routine operations and was usually a fountain of gossip and unwanted advice. Every *nouveau,* or newcomer, treated the students to a modest repast, usually bread and wine, or perhaps cheese, was at their beck and call for errands for awhile, and was expected to tolerate some hazing. This was sometimes violent among the French. Entering Americans usually faced what Frenchmen thought were Indian war whoops.

Advancement was slow. The typical *nouveau* drew from the casts of antique sculpture for some time before moving to the more prestigious drawing and painting from the live model. *Concours,* or examinations, determined the student's place in class. Work began early in the morning and continued until noon, or later. Students also maintained private studio space elsewhere.

There were about nine hundred pupils at the Ecole when Kenyon arrived. They represented a cross-section of French talent and a generous sampling of foreigners. Many other aspirants were enrolled in nearby private ateliers. Current and future prospects, the whims and merits of instructors, personal problems, all were grist for student gossip mills. The pupils worked long hours, huddled in cafés for warmth and companionship, and escaped to the country in summer. Competition was intense and anxiety suffused their lives. Outbreaks of raffishness or violence relieved the strain, to the irritation of neighbors and the police. Ecole authorities sometimes closed ateliers in punishment for such behavior. But Paris was accustomed to eccentric behavior from artists and usually took it all in stride.[17]

The Ecole's approach assumed that technical training focused natural talent, and that individualism could be expressed well only if disciplined. The most facile pupil, in this view, had no future outside the boundaries of traditional art and could express originality only when properly trained. The ability to draw was basic. In copying casts and other objects, students were not supposed to seek mere realism or exact detailing. They were to use shading and line with a sense of volume to express a subject's inherent qualities, symbolism, and power. This often tedious and lengthy training was also designed to make students feel part of an ongoing tradition. The experienced pupil copied paintings at the Louvre and other collections, and in due course painted from the live model. This involved careful preparatory sketches, thoughtful composition, and reworking. Figure painting was the most prestigious work for the academician, partly because of its ancient lineage. But portraiture and the decoration of public buildings with allegorical figures was also a mainstay of the successful painter in Europe. Figure study was inherently difficult. It required careful shading of light and tints and especially challenged the artist to capture the subtle sense of motion and power in the anatomy beneath appearances. The figure was an allegory of much in human existence, involving energy and rest, action and repose.

Although weary students often thought otherwise, Ecole instruction was not dedicated to mere repetition of the past. A steadily enlarging audience for art demanded both new technical approaches and fresh subject matter drawn from life. Of course, change must not be sudden or bewildering. The academic looked backward to precedent for contemporary work and opposed any sharp breaks with tradition. But the larger aim in art instruction in Kenyon's time was to incorporate the modern interest in light and color, reality and motion into that tradition. Only discipline, a sense of composition and order, could make any such changes endure in cultural history. Like most of his peers, especially the Americans, Kenyon wanted both modern training and its linkage to tradition.

Kenyon tried unsuccessfully to work in Yvon's special evening class in drawing. This and other developments convinced him that he had to have more rigorous training. By late March 1878, he was thinking of trying to enter Alexandre Cabanel's atelier at the Ecole, which offered what he thought was the best instruction in Paris. The added advantage was a serious milieu, "and the being among a set of strong men is even more important than having a fine master because you see them at work and understand their processes and get the spirit of them."[18]

On Sunday, March 31, 1878, Kenyon gathered up his best drawings, and in company with his friend Theodore Robinson, then studying with Gérôme at the Ecole, went to Cabanel's home in the exclusive Parc Monceau. Cabanel was courteous but adamant; the atelier was full and he simply could not admit anyone else. Robinson politely suggested looking at the drawings, noting shrewdly that Kenyon was unhappy with Carolus-Duran and wanted very much to study with Cabanel. For whatever reasons, the master looked through the drawings and suggested that they come back in a week. Kenyon did so twice, but Cabanel was out. He persisted, which may have impressed Cabanel, who finally received him at eight-thirty, Monday morning, April 8. He gave the anxious aspirant a letter to the Ecole director admitting him to the beginning class. "Everyone says I am lucky to get in, for Cabanel is very particular, has always more applicants than places, etc."[19]

Cabanel was a logical choice for Kenyon. He was a fine draftsman and figure painter, noted for portraits and for nudes that were often sensual. His approach was academic and his standards high, but he also tolerated diversity among students. He was a good taskmaster, but not a tyrant. He dressed and behaved like one willing to enjoy worldly success, with "the air of a very superior *bourgeois,*" according to one observer. Kenyon thought him somewhat dramatic but not condescending. "Cabanel is a large, pink-complexioned man with a vulgar mouth and a carefully trained white beard and moustache," he wrote home. "He dresses in the most gorgeously 'swell' style, with fur collars, rings, etc., and never exerts himself in the slightest, being always slow, mild, and pompous."[20] This was the kind of view students often had of professors; the point was Cabanel's talent and reputation.

Kenyon went to work determined to prove his worth both to Cabanel and himself. "This week I made drawings of the 'Torso Belvedere,' and of the 'Illisos,' " he wrote home. "Cabanel saw the first and seemed to think it not very bad." He was steadily improving in the ability to draw volume and to indicate light and shade. His studies were beginning to have presence. "I am extremely glad I entered Cabanel's," he reported in late May. "The severe training of drawing from the antique among the fellows here is extremely bracing." By mid-June, Cabanel looked over his work and said he could go upstairs to life drawing after making one more antique study. On Monday, June 17, after paying the necessary fees, he went upstairs with some trepidation. The atelier was to be closed the following week because the students had injured a French pupil in hazing. Perhaps because of this, or because of end-of-term exhaustion, or because they recognized Kenyon's rather staid dignity, they were all polite. After the usual courtesies and refreshments, they left him alone. "I was not even obliged to sing, and have only been out twice on errands." He even got some work done. "I made two drawings from the life, which was quite refreshing work after so much [drawing from the antique], and Cabanel did not criticize them too severely."[21]

Entry into Cabanel's atelier marked another stage in Kenyon's maturity as a person and as an artist. At the Ecole he was among the best people in the Paris art world. He worked hard as spring turned to summer, but had some leisure time. He visited more churches and monuments, attended the annual Salon, which opened on May 1, and eagerly toured the lavish Paris Universal Exposition of 1878. The great fair celebrated the new republic with a cross-section of the world's technology, culture, and art. The huge exhibition of French and foreign art works fascinated Kenyon, and he walked its halls and galleries when not working at the atelier. For the first time, he saw how much current art there was in all its variety.

He reported many of his feelings home, and his father suggested that he write an article for a Cincinnati paper. This was tempting, especially if the editor paid something. Kenyon had never written for the public, but tried it. He was not surprised that the words did not flow, for he realized that his tastes and attitudes were changing. He began to see the effects of experience and education, which broadened one but also reduced certitude. After a month of the exhibition he decided against writing anything. "My ideas, my likings, are constantly changing here. I think I am broader. I think I know much more than when I came, but what I write today seems false or weak or exaggerated tomorrow." Someone else who was less knowledgeable or intense could write a better article. He simply had not digested the effects of all the art.[22]

Given this mood and the tensions of the last few months, he could afford a vacation. In late June 1878, he decided on a painting trip to Rouen and surrounding cities. Kenyon showed considerable maturity and enterprise in organizing such forays. He packed bags, got painting supplies, bought tickets, and drew funds from the bank. His natural curiosity and desire to learn made such trips exciting. He paid close attention to the look of the land and towns, the people and their customs, architecture, and especially the artistic appearance and feel of a given place.

Early in the morning of June 27, he left his room without waking Dr. Thordén and took a train for Rouen. The trip was hot and dusty, but summer had raised a spectacle of flowers and trees northwest of Paris.

In Rouen he found cheap lodgings and began to explore the city, which he had barely seen en route to Paris the preceding fall. His parents and the family members who read his letters enjoyed descriptions of life and scenes. This time he kept a running journal filled with comments on architecture and markets, and on people and their activities. The varied styles of the numerous churches impressed him. "Churches are thicker than blackberries here. As Robinson says, 'The people must have been awfully pious in the old times.' " He carefully inspected major churches such as St. Ouen and St. Maclou but did not overlook smaller ones. His favorite was St. Eloi, "the most outrageous, cranky, and altogether charming specimen of flamboyant [Gothic style] I have yet seen." Of course, the trip was really about art, and he soon unpacked the painting kit. June 30 marked a great national celebration in honor of the foreign visitors to the exposition and on behalf of the republic. The town was decked in flags, flowers were everywhere, and some people wore traditional costumes. This was too much for any painter to resist. At nine o'clock that morning he sat down under the famous Gros-Horloge, or great clock, to sketch a tower of the Cathedral of Notre Dame. A crowd immediately surrounded him. "Of course I was obliged to work at lightning speed, but I was in high good humor with myself and the world, and in about an hour and a half made the best thing I have yet done," he wrote home. "Of course it is extremely unfinished, almost unintelligible in parts, but there is the cathedral, the tower standing up gray against the white windy sky, and the varied tones of the crowding gables (and a couple of tri-colored flags) set in broadly. I am really pleased with the sketch, much more than I have been with anything I have done in a long time" (fig. 5). His pride was justified. It was a sketch, of course, not a finished product. But the central focus that drew the viewer's eye toward the dramatic tower was good. The perspective was sound and the buildings bordering the angle of vision to the tower were done in deft strokes. The fluttering flags imparted both color and motion to the small scene, which was charming and spontaneous. Its composition and the care in rendering testified to his training at the Ecole, but there were hints of Carolus-Duran and Fortuny in the broad strokes and color.

He canvassed the sights in Rouen again, then went to Honfleur, across the Seine estuary from Le Havre. The town was not interesting, but he noted the changing colors of the water as the river met the sea in a line of purple clouds. Enroute to Amiens, he fell in with a voluble train passenger whose French he could understand, but to whom he could not reply in like measure. This was another reminder that his French needed attention, though he was fluent enough for daily living and reading. His goal was the famous Cathedral of Amiens, a masterpiece of mature Gothic architecture. He described it in detail for the family, with appropriate sketches. After a brief stop at Beauvais, he returned to Paris, tired but satisfied with the excursion.[23]

Kenyon resumed work on *concours* drawings, due in mid-August, which would determine his ranking in the atelier for the fall term. But too much concentration was counterproductive after awhile, and he saw sights in Paris and toured the exhibition at the fair. He focused much of his thinking on somehow arranging and paying for a trip to northern Italy with Robinson. He would have to save money for the fare and hotels, but living there was cheap from all reports. Now that he was settled in Cabanel's atelier, the time seemed ripe to sample Italy's art treasures. He would be the good tourist, seeing all the famous sights, but the trip had artistic goals. "I want to drink in color and to get thoroughly acquainted with the architecture," he wrote his mother. He first wanted to include a walking trip through Switzerland, but that was too expensive. The *concours* results were available late on the afternoon of August 13. He placed forty-second out of seventy, and second among the Americans.[24]

He left immediately for two weeks of sketching and relaxing in Grez-sur-Loing, the artist colony south of Paris near the Barbizon forest. The weather was poor, and Italy loomed larger than work in his mind. Late in the afternoon of August 28, he and Robinson made the train connection for Turin, the first significant stop after thirty hours of bad food, poor company, and a rattling third-class carriage. They arrived in Milan in high spirits about

FIG. 5. Kenyon Cox, *From the Grosse [Gros-] Horloge, Rouen* (1878). Oil on canvas, 13⅝ × 9½ ins. Courtesy of the National Academy of Design, New York.

noon, August 31, and immediately "did" the galleries. The celebrated cathedral seemed to Kenyon a mélange of conflicting styles without presence or beauty. The next day they saw their first great Italian work in place, Leonardo's *Last Supper*. Kenyon had seen Leonardo's works in the Louvre and thought the *Mona Lisa* unsurpassed. But the disintegrating *Last Supper* was disappointing. Perhaps he had been reared on a false view of it from etchings and photographs. "It is utterly ruined, past any recognition of what it may once have been," he wrote. There is not a head or hand that is perfect. It is a total wreck. It would be almost a charity to the great name of Leonardo to obliterate it altogether and cover the spot with white plaster." They climbed to the top of the cathedral, but could not see the Alps for haze. They were also aware of the artistic possibilities in the scenes and people. "The women here all wear the bewitching mantilla, which if it cannot quite make the ugly ones pretty, at least makes the pretty ones altogether charming." The next morning they left for Verona. "Just outside the town we got a glimpse of the Alps at last, standing up big and white and quiet." A few hours in Verona did not suffice even to sample that famed city's history or art. "Such a marvelous, beautiful old place I never had imagined. . . . If I did not know that Venice must be still finer I could hardly bear to leave."[25]

They approached the magic city of Venice as only artists filled with its mythology could, prepared to revel in its architecture, art, and natural setting. They were not disappointed. Arriving late, they took a gondola to the hotel, rose early the next morning, and plunged into sightseeing. St. Mark's Cathedral and its piazza lived up to their expectations. "The city is just a dream of color and beauty," and no photograph or picture did it justice.[26]

Kenyon came to Italy chiefly for color and was dazzled. As usual on trips, he sent home numerous photographs. "The photographs are black; Venice is white, or nearly so," he reminded them. "There is everywhere such a blinding glow of light as almost hides the color. It is like violet and pink and pale yellow fire." St. Mark's was impossible to depict because of the delicate tones in its decorations and architecture. "And then there are the centuries of association with the church, the delightful quaintness, and the splendid costliness of it, which add immensely to one's pleasure."[27]

They stayed at a reasonable but cheap hotel and ate in the restaurants that lined the streets and squares. Every meal offered fresh fruits and vegetables, with unusual entrées, at low prices. Their favorite place was a garden restaurant with a buffet. Two hungry young artists made short work of its bounty, and usually took something back to the room or to eat while walking the streets.

Kenyon was cautious in describing the great works they saw, because he lacked the scholarly background for measured judgments, and because they were outside his current tastes. But he had come to paint and sketch as well as to look and feel, and filled letters home with drawings and descriptions of works in progress. He liked colorful subject matter set amid historic associations. He wanted to depict color, pictorial values, and associations, as in a proposed painting of the Ca' d'Oro, a palace famous for its elaborate facade. "I intend to paint it as best I can in the glowing afternoon sunlight with deep blue sky beyond and its rich marbles tremblingly reflected in confused and glorious coloring way below." Such a work would thus be modern in effects, yet emphasize the place's historic connections. He also hoped to do a genre scene at Andrea del Verrocchio's fifteenth-century monument to the Venetian general Bartolommeo Colleoni. "Then another thing which I have just begun is of Colleoni's monument with its equestrian figure (viewed in perspective from the rear) with some interesting buildings in the background," he wrote. "On the left is one of the public cisterns so common in Venice, a very fine one this, with carvings of cupids and so on. Around this I mean to make some girls drawing water, and in the foreground a couple of figures with their filled buckets, coming right beneath the statue." The attached sketch probably did not reveal "how the composition of the buildings 'builds up,' in such a way as to make the monument dominant over everything, all lines leading to it, and the figures beneath it." This canvas was about two feet high, large enough, he hoped, to send to the Salon or perhaps to show in New York.[28]

He also worked in the open air, on a sketch of a girl's head, despite the model's refusal to sit still very long. But most of the projects remained unfinished. He abandoned the studies of the Ca' d'Oro and of the Colleoni monument, but did a good many sketches and small oil copies of famous works. He repainted the picture of the young girl one afternoon in a fit of impatience with her antics. *Jeune fille vénitienne* was his first Salon entry, the following year. There was always an excuse for not finishing a work—bad weather, the blues, too much or too little inspiration. Most such hesitation reflected Kenyon's uncertainties about his abilities and the undigested impact of Venice on his thinking. There was a lot of truth to a friend's observation later that "the only thing Cox finished in Venice was Macaulay's *History of England.*"[29]

He took in a great many impressions of high art. Many of these masters were not well understood, however famous. Others would become giants shortly, as art historians and critics began studies of Italian art. Kenyon knew the works of Leonardo, Titian, and Michelangelo in the Louvre. But he was less familiar with Bellini and Carpaccio. He liked Tintoretto. "He puzzles me greatly. I should think him a gigantic intellect, yet he is evidently the beginning of the fall. There is a terrible power about his work, which constantly reminds one of Michelangelo, yet it impresses you as in many ways false and bad and wrong. . . . The quiet sweet strength and carefulness of the early men is all gone." Paolo Veronese "seems to have been a quiet, happy, thoughtless sort of a man, fond of brilliant color and gay scenes. A very good fellow."[30]

For all his curiosity and desire to travel, Kenyon appreciated routine and by mid-October was ready to end the trip. He was overloaded with information and experiences. He also alternated between the desire for freedom of expression in informal works and for the rigors and discipline of careful study. "I shall be glad to get back to Paris and to serious work, but I shall stay here another week and then take a short trip to Florence, whose galleries I cannot miss when I am so close to them." On October 15 he and Robinson had a hearty farewell dinner of roast goose and potatoes, topped off with ice cream and coffee for dessert. Robinson planned to remain in Venice another month, then go to Munich, "so I shall have to bid him goodbye tomorrow for some time. I shall be sorry, as I have formed quite an attachment for him."[31]

The next day he left for Florence, with stops at Padua, Ferrara, and Bologna. He greatly admired Gothic architecture and had a corresponding dislike for the Renaissance and baroque styles. But in Padua and elsewhere he saw several churches done at the height of these styles and began to change his mind. They lacked the overdecoration and self-consciousness he associated with the baroque, and he saw that any style at its best was striking. Once in Florence, he secured a good room with an excellent kitchen. The northern Italian cuisine was new, but he ate copiously.

For the next few days he examined the great paintings, sculpture, and architecture in this center of the northern Italian Renaissance. Titian's *Bella* (1536), *Flora* (1516-20), and *Venus of Urbino* (1538) confirmed this master's stature. Naturally, his work varied in quality, but he was a superb colorist and figure painter, as well as seeker of character. The complex at the cathedral, including Giotto's famous campanile and the heavily decorated baptistery, were beautiful and impressive. "I have taken a very great fancy to an odd old painter called Sandro Botticelli. Have you ever heard of him?" he asked his mother. "To me his pictures are altogether delightful in their quaint sweet feeling. And in spite of the slight flatness of his backgrounds, and the thinness of his figures with their feet not properly foreshortened, it is astonishing the amount of solid, hard-earned knowledge of nature and power of draftsmanship that he has." And he studied the tomb figures that Michelangelo had done for the Medici family at the Church of San Lorenzo. These famous works, depicting Night and Day, and Dawn and Dusk, had influenced generations of sculptors and artists, both for their technical power and for their evocation of mortality and the mystery of life. They became major works in Kenyon's later canon, but for now he merely noted: "I have seen Michelangelo's great figures on the tombs of the Medici and wondered at them. I have seen nothing else by him that seems to express his strange nature as they do."[32] He passed his twenty-second birthday in Parma, ready to return to Paris and resume the familiar routine.

With the passage of a little time, the impact of the Italian trip on Kenyon's thinking was large. In Paris, he was the art student, focused on learning technical skills, in constant competition in a narrowly defined program. But this tour began to show him just how broad and deep was the art tradition that lay behind that training. He saw numerous masterworks, some familiar, others not. Each showed the painter's technical skills, rendered in a personal style. More to the point, such works evoked ideas applicable to life, rather than the clever anecdote or sensational story. Both painting and architecture also revealed a range of emotional associations and cultural values when seen in place that he could never get from seeing similar works in reproduction, or even in museums. The individual facts he learned and the sensations he felt were important, but the total effect of the trip mattered most in showing the importance of art to culture in general. He did not articulate these feelings in detail but realized they were there. "The trip, I think, did more to broaden and define my notions of art than anything that ever happened to me before," he wrote the following spring.[33]

Kenyon returned to Paris, which seemed strange after the quiet Italian towns. But this was the least of his concerns. On arriving he heard that dramatic changes were in the offing at the Ecole. The faculty was dissatisfied with the large numbers of students, and proposed to eliminate those not making real progress. Lehmann, whose atelier Kenyon thought weak, dropped about sixty pupils. Gérôme had announced a special *concours*. Cabanel had done nothing, but rumor said he had a list of survivors. "Whether I am in it or not is of course a great matter of anxiety to me," Kenyon wrote home. "If I should be sent downstairs to work from the antique again, it would seriously interfere with the work I wish to do this winter, and I have been so short a time in the atelier that I am afraid my chance is none too large."[34]

He learned shortly that his name was not on the list. Only two Americans were, one a reasonable success, the other without prospects. There did not seem to be any pattern for those who remained in the three ateliers, which somewhat softened the blow for Kenyon. He could now either return to the antique class or go elsewhere. He simply could not face the routine drawing from the antique. He was beyond that and needed to move on. He did not even think of what his parents shortly suggested, the discreet use of some special pressure. "Cabanel has the undoubted right to regulate his atelier and to send just such students as he sees fit to draw from the antique, and from his judgment there can be no appeal." To ask Minister Noyes or perhaps G. P. A. Healy to speak on his behalf would be "a sort of breach of student honor." If Cabanel had made a mistake, Kenyon would have to prove him wrong. There would be another *concours* soon, and he might be able to re-enter. Nor did he think of going to an academy elsewhere, as in Munich.[35] He would not return to Carolus-Duran's, which would be another backward step. In any event, his regard for his first teacher was low, and events proved him right. Carolus-Duran asked the *massier* for a list of those who had left his atelier for the Ecole, and decreed that they could not come back. "If they had been anxious to come back, even then, I think this would have been undignified and foolish, but when one knows that not one student has offered, or thought of going back, it becomes very absurd." The cafés were filled with anxious students debating what to do. Kenyon decided to enroll in the private atelier of Rodolphe Julian, where there were "some very clever fellows."[36]

Students invested Julian with a romantic and dramatic past, some of which was true. He was then thirty-nine years old, a native of Provence, with a muscular build that lent credence to stories that he had been a wrestler and strongman. He had studied art, but found art life more appealing. About 1868 he established a teaching atelier to meet a real need among students who could not enter the Ecole. This was a business proposition, and it prospered mightily over the next decades. But Julian was a sympathetic personality and realized that he could help apprehensive students prepare for the Ecole, or give others whatever their talents merited. Anyone could enter for a small fee, and got a clean, well-ordered studio with good models. As at the Ecole, noted painters regularly criticized the work and there were prizes for *concours* winners. The staff included Bouguereau, Jules-Joseph Lefebvre, and Tony Robert-Fleury. Julian emphasized sound training and personally was a classicist. But he tempered the regular classwork with informality and a genuine interest in his charges. The Ecole did not admit women, for whom he provided both integrated and segregated classes, as they wished. The atelier contained a cross-section of students and was a genial place, where pupils actually elected the *massier*. Work at Julian's was quite respectable, and many artists who later succeeded saw it as a sound entryway into the art world.[37]

Kenyon paid monthly at Julian's, hoping to return to Cabanel's, but he quickly grew to like the routine and the people. The informality was refreshing and the staff was encouraging. He somewhat apprehensively described his Italian tour and showed Lefebvre the painting of a young girl from Venice. "He told me that it was 'pas mal du tout,' and as my friends call it 'very pretty' and say that it has much the open-air effect, I gather that it is really very fair for a youngster of my limited time of study and experience." On another occasion the students auctioned off some *concours* works and Julian bought one of his sketches for ten francs. Kenyon appreciated the money but was doubly pleased to see it hanging in the impresario's office. By December he had settled into the routine, and was well liked among both students and staff. At the monthly *concours* the prize went to an oil, but his drawing was first. Lefebvre "was extremely complimentary. He said that I had made a 'dessin charmant.' That I had much the character of the model, great *finesse* in the details, and, above all, 'beaucoup d'ensemble.' " Of course, every day was not prize day and he did not like some things. Because Julian was attempting to prepare people for the Ecole, he naturally adopted some academic methods and subjects. Kenyon spent a full day working up a study of a formal problem, "Caesar turning away his eyes when presented with the head of Pompey." The subject was characteristic of the French approach, which did not make it any more palatable. "I have no sympathy with classical subjects—still less with ghastly ones." Given this, it was a compliment to his work that he won eleventh place in the *concours*.[38]

Julian's atelier was comfortable, but Kenyon soon realized that it lacked the rigor he needed. He did not know how long he could stay in Paris, but could not continue to change ateliers. Both he and the family required real progress, which meant the Ecole. He still hoped to reenter Cabanel's but had developed some hesitation about him for his alleged inattention to atelier work and criticism. No doubt after talking to friends and analyzing the situation, Kenyon approached Jean-Léon Gérôme, probably the best known Ecole instructor and an international figure. Kenyon knew that he was a strict taskmaster, who took teaching seriously, appeared regularly in the atelier, and had high standards.

On February 8, 1879, Gérôme admitted Cox to work in the antique section. After a few weeks, he took Gérôme a sketch of the reclining female figure of Michelangelo's *Night,* which he based on antique studies and his visit to the Medici tombs in Florence. This showed his advancement within the academic tradition. It revealed the exact appearance of the work, down to cracks and shadows in the marble. But it somehow bespoke more than realism. The shading was effective, and he produced a good sense of the figure's volume and emotional appeal (fig. 6). It was student work, but that of a promising young person. Gérôme must have seen that Kenyon had both talent in drawing and an ability to look beyond surface effects. Gérôme liked the work and advanced Kenyon to life drawing.[39]

This was a somewhat unexpected choice for Kenyon. On the day before he left for Paris in 1877, he visited the New York galleries and pronounced against Gérôme's works. He even spelled the name wrong. "Jerome is more distasteful to me every day." While studying with Carolus-Duran he heard a great deal about Gérôme and once looked into his atelier at the Ecole. He professed surprise. "I went in Jerome's atelier one day and was astonished to see no better work than I did. After all the talk about the 'severe drawing' of Jerome's school, the drawing was very little better than that at Duran's, although Duran's atelier has no such reputation." But as he worked under Cabanel, listened to students talk, and began to realize that there was a lot more to art than technique, his opinion of Gérôme's approach, if not his art, rose.[40]

Gérôme's reputation did often seem curious. He specialized in historical scenes drawn in meticulous detail, with carefully modulated color. He also was known for elegant genre scenes taken from life in northern Africa and other exotic locales. He was an outstanding figure painter and a master

FIG. 6. Kenyon Cox, sketch of Michelangelo's *Night* (1879).
Graphite and charcoal on paper, 18 × 24 ins. Gift of Allyn Cox, 1960-83-349.
Photo by Ken Pelka. Courtesy of Cooper-Hewitt, National Museum of Design,
Smithsonian Institution/Art Resource, New York.

draftsman. These works, which commanded high prices and respectful or adulatory criticism, somehow did not seem suited to the current era. Yet there were good reasons for Gérôme's appeal. He offered order and certitude in a period of great change and was exact without being literal. He depicted the exotic and historical, but in ways that most art lovers could comprehend as expanded experience. The thoughtful understood that he was symbolic without using elaborate symbolism. He preached attention to details at a time when too many people prized hasty success. His work clearly rested on a thorough understanding of past masters and was emotional without being flamboyant. The themes of his best canvases were timeless, whereas his careful technique seemed contemporary.[41]

Gérôme was a realist in demanding fidelity to nature but was equally concerned with character and meaning. He allowed no student a shortcut in draftsmanship or design but never stressed the importance of mere details. Every drawing or painting had to reflect reality to be understood, but in the end art was about expression. The artist could not paint a North African subject, for instance, without knowing about the culture. "He pleads constantly with his pupils to understand that although absolute fidelity to nature must ever be in mind," his American student George De Forest Brush recalled, "yet if they do not at last make imitation serve expression they will end up as they began—only children."[42]

Though a strict disciplinarian and hard worker, Gérôme did not require imitation from his students. He sought chiefly to make fine drawing second nature to them, and to introduce them to the art tradition. After that, they could make personal statements. "Do not try to imitate me," he said. "Seek out effects in nature which are sympathetic with your perceptions." Kenyon saw that Gérôme was more tolerant than his reputation implied, and in due course took his criticisms to be suggestions rather than commands.[43]

Gérôme could be informal, even genial, but radiated authority. There were about seventy students in the atelier, in varying stages of progress or dismay. He appeared promptly on Wednesday and Saturday mornings to mark their works for placement in the atelier contests, and to criticize. He never raised his voice, adopted airs like Carolus-Duran, or missed appointments like Cabanel. He offered suggestions, which "had the effect of making the student reconsider his own performance, a far harsher judgment than any he might make." Though never familiar, he obviously liked the students and watched their progress closely. His praise was worth a great deal to them. Like other successful painters, he kept a large home and exotic studio, where students could visit when he was not working. For a great many young people, especially the Americans who were intent on acquiring culture as well as skill, he was an ideal mentor, larger than life, always demanding their best, yet real.[44]

Kenyon was satisfied. "I like the atelier better than any other I have been in, and I like Gérôme's teaching very much," he wrote home in early April. "He has criticized me a good many times in the antique, and I find his opinions and ideas most valuable. As he has always had *concours,* and as I draw quite as well as the others, I have no fear of being turned out and feel that I am at last permanently placed for as long as I may remain in Paris." His entrance into Gérôme's atelier marked Kenyon's maturity both as a person and as an artist, even though "I may not love his work." As the weeks passed, Kenyon liked the order and purpose that Gérôme symbolized. "I do not now, any more than I ever did, admire either Gérôme's choice of subject nor his manner of painting, but I am sure that he is a fine draftsman and that his influence is so far good," he assured his father, "that he believes in and insists on thorough truth and simplicity and discourages all *chic* and cleverness."[45]

He had found a mentor, though not necessarily an example, someone he could admire and emulate, and who above all well represented the high calling of art. Kenyon had a quick eye for personality as well as appearance in analyzing Gérôme. "In person, Gérôme is tall and thin, erect and soldierly, with gray hair and large gray moustache, a small head, hook nose, and sharp eye," he noted. "He looks like a rigid disciplinarian and a brave soldier." But like the other students, he saw another side to Gérôme. "In spite of this he is in fact a singularly kindhearted man, and rigid as he is in his requirements of himself is easily moved by perseverance to anything." Unlike the theatrical Carolus-Duran or "swell" Cabanel, he was dignified. "I like him very much, as I know him better, and respect him as a man, more than as an artist."[46]

At this point, Kenyon preferred looser composition and less literal realism than Gérôme did. The influence of Fortuny, and even of Carolus-Duran, was evident. He had also learned a suave style at Cabanel's. Kenyon never liked exact realism and always sought a strong, if controlled, emotional response in art. Gérôme's art seemed formal, lacking in moving ideas or the mere love of gesture. But Kenyon took from Gérôme the teachings appropriate to him at the moment—careful observation of nature, concern for form and volume, and attention to useful detail.

For now, he quickly adapted to the atelier routine and progressed rapidly, which testified to Gérôme's regard for his potential. After his regular rounds on Wednesday, May 7, 1879, Gérôme looked over his work and told him "to go to painting."[47] Kenyon began to write home with a fresh sense of confidence and purpose, the feeling of arriving at last as an art student with prospects.

This sense of security helped Kenyon define himself amid the currents of art practice and thought. Like many Americans, he was ambivalent toward fashionable French art. He admired the dexterity and confidence of French painters but thought their work was often false. He realized that students had to learn the grand tradition, but disliked formal problems drawn from history and mythology. They did not speak to him, or by implication, to modern life, whatever their merits as copybook studies. French painting also often lacked refinement and an elevated mood. On the whole, "most of the French, though magnificent painters, are *not* artists. They are coarse, hard, vulgar, brutal."[48] The system of patronage and instruction intensified these tendencies. To make a mark, any painter had to be overly dramatic, and the Salons were thus crowded with complex but empty canvases. Every aspiring artist had to "do something striking, *éclatant,* which shall call attention to his work or gain him the coveted medal," he wrote in reviewing the Salon of 1879. "In this race beauty, simplicity, sentiment, even truth, are forgotten, and the salon is filled with gigantic canvases, exaggerated muscularity, and impossible effects. The subject either becomes a mere excuse for the display of skill and learning, or is chosen to draw the attention by its horror and ugliness, and the same well known model serves for Charon, Abraham, Lazarus, and St. Jerome. It is all one, so [sic] only the action be forcible and the anatomy correct." He equally disliked the suave, fashionable work that sanitized great themes into preciosity. "In the picture of the Italian mother that you speak of," he wrote his father of a Bouguereau canvas, "the baby is undoubtedly very angelic and pretty, but it seems to me that a real live vulgar kicking baby would be much better. And this same fear of any ruggedness, this same ultrapurism runs through his execution, giving it that 'licked' smoothness that I dislike."[49]

A growing need for subtlety and for inner meanings in art now led him to reevaluate Fortuny. For some time in Paris, he remained enamored of the Spaniard's brilliant and popular works. Fortuny lacked the power of an old master, "but before his *Choice of a Model* one is lost in a dream of perfect color," he wrote early in 1878. "The superbly subtle modulations of ever-varying and commingling units, the shimmering and glancing of the light, and the sinuous delicacy of line, wrap up the senses like the finest music, and there is no more question of morality or immorality than in listening to a symphony of Beethoven's." Such a frankly sensual reaction was not the only or highest aim of art, but Fortuny used it for striking and legitimate reasons. Kenyon saw a range of Fortuny's work at William Hood Stewart's private gallery. The Universal Exposition of 1878 offered a retrospective showing of forty Fortunys, and Kenyon remained entranced. "I believe more firmly than ever that Fortuny is the bright particular star of modern art."[50]

But the further Kenyon went in formal training, and the more he knew of great art, the more his doubts about Fortuny grew. These sumptuous works began to seem artificial, lacking in ideas. By the spring of 1879 he reassured his mother that "I do not think you need be afraid of Brennan's and Blum's outdistancing me," simply because they were gaining attention using Fortuny's methods. A more sober, substantive painting would outlast fashion. And "the best result so far of my stay here I take to be that I have ceased to be Spanish-struck. The attempt to be brilliant and clever grows daily more distasteful to me, and what work I exhibit will at least be sober and honest, if it is not good." In the fall of 1879, he wrote Blum a long letter suggesting that he too would see Fortuny's limitations in a larger context. "If I could go to the Salon with you, and get you candidly to study and examine the work I like best I think that even if you preferred Fortuny and Boldini . . . you would still see that there may be great merit in other kinds of painting." The steps in this evolution of taste were slow and hard to plot, but testified to

Kenyon's growing personal maturity and critical acumen. "Perhaps the most important factor in it was my Italian trip, which I think was of incalculable benefit to me," he wrote his father in September 1879. That trip had showed him that technical skill could join with elevating and timeless ideas. As Fortuny's attractions faded, he noted curious ironies. By midwinter 1879, he thought that "it seems odd now that the entree to that set should seem open to me if I care to take it, while when I would have given anything for it, it was not to be had."[51] His tastes changed, but as with Carolus-Duran, some of Fortuny's influence remained.

Kenyon found another kind of popular modernism appealing, the realism and *plein-air* painting that seemed a viable alternative to the Salon. This broad trend rested on an ideal of absolute fidelity to perceived nature, whether depicting people, scenes, or objects. It suited the modern temper, which was concerned with facts, exactitude, and the present. Its practitioners did not reject the classical tradition but emphasized their own times. The realist assumed that current life had a past, was important, and reflected enduring interests. The approach was new in emphasizing light and meticulous drawing. At its best it set major human themes in a personal rather than allegorical scale, with treatments that viewers could understand. At its weakest, it was merely photographic.[52]

Kenyon viewed this realism with a certain caution, but admired the work of its chief practitioner, Jules Bastien-Lepage. This painter developed a style that brought overnight fame, especially among young artists seeking to escape official formalism while remaining within the French art tradition. His facility with the brush was astonishing, and he could delineate the smallest aspect of a scene with absolute accuracy. He painted outdoors in an evenly modulated light that did not overwhelm the subject but that seemed modern. He employed subtle tones, especially of gray and blue. The mood was informal, inviting the viewer to participate, but the works were impressive and dignified.[53]

Kenyon was much taken with some of these works, and wrote home a great deal about the ones he saw on exhibition and in the Universal Exposition of 1878. He especially praised *Les foins,* or *The Haymakers,* in the Salon of 1878. This painting showed a dozing man and a seated woman, resting at midday after hard field labor. The picture tilted slightly toward the viewer, with a high horizon line that showed a village scene and trees. The atmosphere was grayish blue, and every detail was clear. The theme was an old one, the relation of people to nature, and the power of hard work. The subjects' character was clear. "They are ugly and coarse and common enough, but there is in the original [painting] a dazed stupid expression in the girl's face, an expression of one just awakened and almost wishing she had never waked, that is wonderfully poetic." The technique was equally potent. "There is an absolute truth in tone and value, a perfect representation of all-pervading daylight that is marvelous. The girl's figure swims out of a surrounding atmosphere in perfect relief, and yet things seem almost shadowless. The distant hayfield alone, with its haycocks and men working, and the sky and thin bit of trees against it would make a splendid landscape."[54]

Like most art students struggling for technical skills, Kenyon admired Bastien-Lepage's dexterity. But he thought the realists were naïve to suppose that they could capture nature exactly as they saw it, or that this would be art if they could. No artist lived in or for the moment. Memory and the urge to order and to intensify the art experience always ruled. This technical skill astonished him but left other emotions untouched because the painting had no real ideas. The greatest fault of realism was "the lack of intelligent and artistic selection of subject, and the feeling that it makes no difference what one paints so long as he paints it truly."[55] A hundred exact studies of peasant life, for instance, would not delineate man's relation to nature or the meanings in their history together. Bastien-Lepage could not equal Jean-François Millet, whose peasant studies moved millions precisely because they recalled epic themes in a distinctive personal manner. Kenyon continued to admire Bastien-Lepage's skill, but this kind of realism did not suit his changing needs.

Nor did Kenyon like the new impressionists, who were making some impact after their initial showing of 1874. Few people expected the style to triumph, and Kenyon did not mention it in letters home. He did not object to painting outdoors, as he and fellow students did regularly in the summer. The impressionists' interest in the momentary was not especially striking either. Even Gérôme used a snapshot technique in depicting the death of Caesar or moments from history. And the realism of Bastien-Lepage glorified the present and the recording eye. A much more basic belief in the importance of palpable form separated Kenyon from the impressionists. He admired more the earlier Barbizon school's efforts to combine volume, light, and color into a poetic mood without sacrificing nature. He also saw the impressionist emphasis on light as false, because the mind did not in fact allow light to dominate but used it to interpret nature. "I do not like the effect of sunlight much anyhow," he wrote while painting outdoors in the summer of 1879, "preferring much [more] gray days when there is full color and everything is not eaten up with light."[56] Like most early critics, he disliked the impressionists' apparent lack of ideas and the haphazard appearance of their canvases. He suggested that Manet's *Boating* in the Salon of 1879 was contrived and unfinished. Manet "seems carefully to have avoided all appearances of drawing, of modeling, or of detail, and laying in two or three broad tones, more or less true, and a number of apparently aimless daubs with the brush—behold an impressionist picture!"[57] The approaches of both Carolus-Duran and Bastien-Lepage seemed more durable than impressionism. Carolus-Duran's painting satisfied the desire for color and motion, involved modern life, and was linked to the grand tradition. Bastien-Lepage's works were striking, dealt with contemporary life, and were in the tradition of fine painting.

In descriptions of work in progress and in a few early pictures that survived, Kenyon revealed a spectrum of tastes. In the studio, he worked from the model in approved manner and became a masterful draftsman. During the summer he was more informal in both style and subject matter. He did several landscapes in subtly worked masses of paint that captured the effects of foliage, light, and water within a formal design. Other outdoor studies were informal yet carefully organized.

Kenyon also began to develop an intellectual basis for his art. However much he admired technical skill, he believed that enduring art involved some kind of ideas. Above all, art communicated between a special creator and an audience of like-minded people. The artist selected from his experience and intensified with his skill and special personality those attributes of life that would enhance the experience of others. The artist was "not to invent something not in nature, but to choose from nature those truths which come home to the individual mind, so making you see, not nature, but the artist's view of nature," he wrote early in 1878.

> Then, as I conceive it, his business as an artist is not to reproduce the landscape just as it is, which if it were possible, would leave everyone free to be impressed or not, as nature would; but to choose from the scene those aspects and forms which should convey perforce to any beholder of his work the same impression which nature herself conveyed to him. And he is the noblest artist who succeeds in reproducing the greatest and truest feelings and conveying to the beholder the noblest emotions, and in this, I think, is [the] true morality of art, which has no business to instruct but only to move.[58]

Painting had to reflect substantial and intelligible form and represent unifying ideas that expanded the imagination. These ideas were hardly new or unique to Kenyon, but his thoughtfulness was unusual in one so young and revealed his steady commitment to art as a way of life, not just a profession.

Gérôme's injunction to start painting early in May 1879 was welcome news to Kenyon. He had worked hard and had some tangible evidence of progress. In 1878 he sent a small pen drawing to the Salon jury, though without much hope of acceptance. "I hardly expect it to get in, and if it does I shall be neither helped nor hurt by it, only that I shall have a free ticket," he cautioned his parents, and probably himself. Because about seven thousand works were rejected and four thousand accepted, he was not surprised when he did not appear in the list of winners. It was good enough, but hardly great, he told himself, and it did not hurt to show some ambition. On returning from Italy, he showed the students and professors at Julian's the study of a young girl's head he did in Venice. They liked its open-air effect and charm, and he sent it to the Salon jury. *Jeune fille vénitienne* gained entry, which was quite a compliment to a student at his stage. His parents were obviously proud, and suggested that he take visitors from home, and perhaps Mrs. Noyes, to see it. Kenyon thought the idea premature, to say the least. "It is a very insignificant thing indeed, among the 3040 pictures in the Salon, and to take Mrs. Noyes there to see it would be exquisitely absurd." Kenyon had gained self-confidence, but had no illusions about his status. He was among the better students, but had no rank as a real artist. "Only a few people know of my existence and I have yet made no mark of any kind. To take the trouble to say anything about my head at the Salon would be extremely foolish. If I do anything worthy of mention it will get mentioned. Until I do, do not mention what is unworthy."[59] Still, a Gérôme student with anything in the Salon had reason to feel successful.

As the term drew to a close in late May, Kenyon decided to spend the summer outside Paris. He was familiar with the area around the capital from excursions and walking tours with friends. He liked the medieval villages of Moret and Recloses, which he and Robinson had visited. Fontainebleau was the most popular area, and its forest was inviting to the hiker and the painter. There were, of course, noted colonies in Brittany and Normandy, farther away and more crowded. Kenyon chose to go to the small village of Grez-sur-Loing, about twenty miles south of Paris, which the writer Robert Louis Stevenson, a fair-haired figure among young people, had helped make popular. It was self-contained, not overrun, and charming.

The hamlet dated from the middle ages and was on the Loing River just below its junction with the Seine. A low bridge with several graceful arches crossed the stream, whose water fed large areas of floating lilies. Carpets of sedge, grass, and flowers and stands of trees ran down to the edge of the river and the canal that paralleled it. Cattle, sheep, and chickens roamed the single street. There was a good inn and a genial keeper, with a shaded garden for al fresco meals. The inhabitants were reserved but tolerant and took the artists in stride. The presence of foreign students added a dash of cosmopolitanism to the scene.[60]

These summer excursions were part of the grand mythology of artist life. A summer at Grez was a kind of heaven for art students. They were warm at last, could swim, boat, or exercise, and take in color and sun. The food was cheap and the companions interesting. But these were working vacations, and the students painted outdoors to vary their classroom experience and interpret nature. They differentiated between these informal studies and the "serious" art of school. Gérôme and other masters did not judge such works with the calm severity they applied to studio efforts, though they expected adherence to academic rules of composition, painting, and intention. The range of subject matter increased, and students could experiment with light and color. Most such summer work naturally emphasized personal expression and was a significant transition between being a student and a full-fledged artist.

Kenyon was in Grez by early June, ready for a change from atelier work, eager to relax, hoping to make new friends. He had visited the village in the summer of 1878 before going to Italy and it was still charming. The weather was rather chilly and he returned to Paris once to nurse a bad cold. But by midsummer the foliage and grasses were green, flowers profuse, and the water comfortable. In mid-June, he sent his mother a wordless letter, consisting of a self-portrait and drawings showing him boating, swimming, painting under an umbrella, and playing billiards. He soaked up the local color, which included a spectacular fête at nearby Nemours, complete with fireworks, clowns, and whirligigs. On another occasion he made some hasty sketches of gypsies and their animals passing through Grez. Late in the season, a group of cuirassiers on maneuvers settled down in the village. Kenyon was amused to see one officer inquire about a place where artists had scraped their palette knives: "What is this supposed to represent?"[61] Apparently not every Frenchman understood or appreciated art.

Kenyon sketched and painted in the open. He started half a dozen works and hoped to finish at least four before leaving. The most elaborate was a landscape with figure that allowed him to use an informal subject, rich colors, and sound composition. "The picture represents an oat field, ripe and yellow (perhaps you don't know what a charming color ripe oats are), on a sloping hillside which suddenly breaks away almost precipitously as it reaches the left of the picture," he wrote. "There are bushes and trees and a glimpse of a distant village, and the foreground is a mass of grasses and many colored wild flowers, growing with a richness and profusion hardly credible in America, I think, in the midst of which is seated a lady in black silk with a straw hat and pale blue ribbon, who has let her parasol and book fall neglected in the grass while she looks or thinks, just as you please." The picture was a fair statement of his views and methods, as there were few painters yet in Grez to influence him. As usual, uncertainty lurked under his confidence. The painting was good, but the family should not expect too much if they got a chance to see it.[62] As usual, from the description, he had tried to combine modern themes and methods with traditional aims. This was probably *Dans les herbes,* which won admission to the Salon of 1880, though it did not survive.

He made several new friends, including some young women who were visiting Paris and had an interest in art. He sketched them, all the while improving his social skills, which easily withered at the Ecole. In one study he placed a young girl in a straw hat against poppies and had to catch the scene quickly because she "doesn't like posing."[63] He made these small studies quickly and then retouched them. In sound academic manner, he posed the subjects, but created the figures with masses of paint rather than careful drawing. He relied on the effects of strong colors in broad, short strokes to create a sense of informality and immediacy. Many of these sketches had a rich, if unfinished, appearance, testifying again to the lingering influence of Fortuny and Carolus-Duran.

He completed a small landscape that revealed unusual progress. "At any rate it *is* a picture, not merely a sketch or study, and the first I have painted since I came abroad." This work depicted trees and foliage seen across the river, and he tried to capture several natural effects in an orderly composition. "The sky is [full] of light cirrus clouds, through which the blue sky shows itself in the darker parts, and across which float great white cumulus, the highest lights in the picture," he wrote his father. "One of them, however, [casting?] a purplish shadow comes dark against the background of cirrus. The effect is of late afternoon, the trees taking strong warm lights and dark shadows, and upon the reeds, of all the still deeper shadows cast by the trees on this side of the river, the water jumbling and reflecting all."[64] He used rather broad masses of color and rich brush strokes, and its craftsmanship and mood made the picture a mature work (fig. 7).

Kenyon passed many happy hours in Grez, and the summer of 1879 was both restful and productive. He sketched or completed several works of future importance. But once again, as in Italy, he missed a routine and by early September was ready to return to the Ecole. "It would be a treat to sit down to a little hard academy drawing again." And a respite from the summer's crowded sensations would give him a better perspective on just what he had accomplished.[65]

When the confusion of starting the new term subsided, he took the summer work to Gérôme for criticism. The master looked at the sheets and canvases and uttered a "bien," even a "très bien" on seeing several. Then he "finally wound up by saying what of all things he could possibly have said pleased me most, 'All these things show a man who will arrive at something.' " Kenyon thought this a real compliment and was flattered but also sobered. "From him I think such a remark means a great deal, and that I have a right to feel that my confidence in my own ability is not unwarranted," he wrote home. "As I have said, that confidence grows quieter, steadier, stronger all the time. I begin to feel my own individuality assert itself, to know what I wish to do and what I am fit for." He hoped in four or five years to be "among the best artists we have."[66]

One residual challenge from summer remained. Kenyon had met an attractive young woman he simply called "Miss Brown" in letters home. She was staying with his married friend Ben Gilman, an Ecole student, "and the ladies fancy themselves more or less artistic." They were generous hosts, "and their rooms have a family, home-like air that is refreshing to a Latin

Fig. 7. Kenyon Cox, Untitled Landscape (1879). Oil on canvas, 10¼ × 15½ ins. *Courtesy of the late Katharine Smith, Wooster, Ohio.*

Quarter student." He and his close friend Lowell Dyer were much in evidence there for tea, cookies, and conversation. "Miss Brown is exceedingly good natured and has a piquant face and pretty brown hair," he noted in mid-November. "She is going to sit for a portrait, which I hope to make something of a success." He worked rapidly, as Miss Brown was leaving for home soon, and finished by early December. He took the work to Gérôme, who criticized it "in a very tender and delicate way," saying that it was refreshingly naïve and sincere, but that the flesh tones were too warm. Then as he prepared to step through the atelier door, Gérôme turned and said clearly, as if speaking to the entire group, "C'est bien, le petit portrait. C'est d'un bon sentiment." Once again, Kenyon was flattered, almost overwhelmed. "His taking enough interest in it to do this I consider a good deal of a compliment."[67]

The portrait merited attention. Kenyon had posed Miss Brown in the canvas center, leaning her head to one side enough to seem both informal and interesting. She was smiling in a natural way, with a rich arrangement of hair, and a fine white scarf at her throat. The figure rose out of modulated shadows, which made the face all the more dramatic, yet the effect was simple and natural. The white lace offered good contrast to the dark color scheme, and the total effect was one of charm and technical skill. He had embodied both academic composition and modernistic interests in motion and character (fig. 8).

Of course, there was a nonartistic issue. Kenyon's mother naturally would conclude that he had a crush on Miss Brown, which might lead to all sorts of changed relationships. He hastened to reassure her in late December 1879, after cataloguing his activities with the young lady. "From all these things, though I was somewhat reticent, I doubt not that the watchful maternal mind conceived certain suspicions and alarms. Tranquilize yourself. It is Dyer, not I, that has fallen. I have played the role of disinterested mutual friend." A week later he somewhat stiffly assured her that all the proprieties were safely in place. "On the business of Miss B. I have nothing to add to what I said before, except that she never did pose for me *alone*, but was always accompanied by her married friend." In late January 1880, he responded to the family's praise of his good sense for not falling in love. He always thought this an odd phrase, "for it seems to me that one falls in love because he can't help it." He congratulated Dyer on winning Miss Brown, and they all remained good friends. But he did indeed seem smitten.[68]

Kenyon professed dissatisfaction with the portrait; more time and greater care would have produced a better result. He was probably wrong, for the picture's sense of spontaneity was its greatest merit. It won entry into the Salon of 1880 as *Dame en noir*, along with *Dans les herbes*, and was then shown at the Pennsylvania Academy in the fall of 1880 and at the annual exhibition of the Society of American Artists in May 1882. It received considerable

FIG. 8. Kenyon Cox, *Dame en noir* [Lady in Black] (1880). Oil on canvas,
20¾ × 12⅞ ins. Courtesy of the National Museum of American Art,
Smithsonian Institution, bequest of Allyn Cox.

notice for a beginner's work. Miss Brown's brother bought it, doubtless as a wedding present. Years later it somehow came back to Kenyon and hung in his Cornish, New Hampshire, studio as a reminder of the Paris years and of special friends.[69]

By now, Kenyon was well established among the art students. Though he remained somewhat defensive and dogmatic, he was actually quite gregarious. Life naturally centered on long days of hard work, which often extended into the evenings in studio space he rented or shared with others. But Paris life was a legitimate part of the art experience, and Kenyon enjoyed it. He ate reasonably well and occasionally treated himself to an unusual dinner, as when he visited an inn in the utopian community of Robinson south of Paris. He went part of the way on horseback, and then ate with friends in a summer house on the grounds, though one could actually eat at tables in trees, amid colorful lanterns. He also frequented restaurants that catered to Americans, and found such things as griddle cakes, turkey, and pumpkin pie welcome reminders of home.

His circle of friends was varied. He knew the principal star among the Americans, John S. Sargent, a pupil of Carolus-Duran and already noted for amazing dexterity in both drawing and painting. Kenyon posed for the hands of a guitar player in Sargent's famous work depicting a Spanish dancer, *El Jaleo,* which was a sensation in the Salon of 1882. But Sargent was self-contained and not especially close to Kenyon or anyone else. Kenyon's good friend Theodore Robinson accompanied him to Italy in 1878. He appreciated Robinson's dry wit and geniality, as well as his talent and intellect. Robinson returned to the United States in the spring of 1879, but they corresponded until his death in 1896. By then, Robinson was gaining a justified reputation for a rather subdued impressionism. Not everyone in the group was destined for success, of course, and Cox knew people such as Thomas Shields, James Johnson, and Ben Gilman who did not become well known. His closest companion after 1878 fell into that category, one Lowell Dyer, who married Miss Brown. Kenyon liked Dyer's easy conversation and rather sharp observations about life. They visited sights in Paris and passed evenings in conversation about art and their future prospects. Kenyon also liked William Stott, "a ruddy and somewhat vulgar Englishman, but a good fellow and a charming artist." He enjoyed visiting the Stotts as a reassurance that family life was possible after the routine of the Ecole. And although Stott liked Kenyon and admired his abilities, he gave as good as he got in any critical free-for-all. Kenyon also became known for rapidly executed caricatures of friends and critics, so effective that just beginning one drew a crowd.

The popular press imagined that art-student life was carefree and raucous, if penurious. There was a grain of truth in the stereotype. H. Siddons Mowbray, another American, recalled many lonely restaurant dinners after an exhausting day's work. "Occasionally a crowd of wild men from the Beaux Arts would surge in—Kenyon Cox, Stott, Dyer; and pandemonium would reign, scandalizing the sober clients and bringing a frown to Père Fuchs, notwithstanding the consumption of his villainous wine." Kenyon knew that such behavior was merely letting off steam and anxiety. Most such students would become sober citizens, however turbulent they now seemed. And he assured his parents that for all they heard about the disorder and alleged immorality of student life, the fellows were a respectable and sincere set underneath everything.[70]

Kenyon enjoyed these friendships, but often as not passed the time alone, especially reading. He read some English novels and liked Richard Blackmore's exciting *Lorna Doone* (1869), set in seventeenth-century Devonshire. He read historical and biographical works to practice his French and liked an old favorite, Charles Perrault's *Mother Goose* (1697), which contained all the great fairy tales. He was chiefly interested in the broad histories and moralistic essays so dear to his class and generation. He did not comment much on either French or American public affairs, though he received a gift subscription to the high-minded *Nation*.

He continued to love music and almost every weekend went to the free concerts at the Théâtre du Châtelet. His tastes were basically classical, but he also heard a range of contemporary music, including works by Bizet, Saint-Saëns, Gounoud, and Massenet. He admired the controversial Hector Berlioz, and one performance of the magnificent *Requiem* (1837) made his hair stand up. He was an avid fan of Félicien David, and went to many performances of his symphonic odes *Le Désert* (1844), which depicted a caravan in the desert, and *Christophe Colomb* (1847). He admired David's gift for melody and tonality. Much else he heard was destined for oblivion, such as works by Charles-Marie Widor, Nils Gade, and Charles-Edouard Lefebvre.

Kenyon also attended the theater. His mother was watchful of this form of entertainment, which carried overtones of questionable morality, especially in Paris. She rebuked him for trying to attend a performance of the glossy musical revue *Rothomago* (1838) on Christmas evening 1877, despite his protests that he did not actually get in; and anyway it was only an effort to do something unusual on a holiday. He insisted that the theater was educational and assured his mother several times that he received no unescorted women in his rooms. Although he might watch a game of billiards, or even wield the cue, no money changed hands. And he drank only watered wine, never to excess. He was candid about the loneliness and boredom. "What *can* we do with our evenings is the universal cry," he commented after a year in the city. "After a hard day's work at drawing or painting one is too tired in eyes and brain to work or study. Reading is not good for the eyes, even if one had more to read, and living on the small allowances that most of us do, we can hardly dress well enough to call, even if we knew people to call on," though he made the rounds among visiting Americans. "We manage to afford a gallery seat in a theater now and then, and the rest of the time we talk over our suppers as long as we can and then go to a cafe and talk more, coffee being generally cheaper than fire."[71]

His mother worried constantly about his health, and filled her letters with admonitions against exposure to cold, bad food, and brooding. Kenyon suffered from colds and dyspepsia, but the tumor did not recur and he reported no real poor health. He did have bouts of "the blues" or mild depression, usually from loneliness or troubling doubts about his abilities.

Kenyon followed family affairs as closely as possible and often nagged his parents for more information and frequent letters. "Please write once a week, will you not?" he asked late in 1878. "I think you hardly know how much a letter from home is to one of us exiles."[72] Will Cochran, Dolson, Helen, and Charles all married while he was in Paris. The antics of the younger sibling Hope provided him some long-distance amusement. He decorated letters home, which he knew would circulate among them all, with drawings. None of the family had any deep understanding of art. But they knew that Kenyon was not easily deflected from a course once adopted and supported him well.

The problem of money was always on Kenyon's mind. He apparently tried to live on a basic stipend of five hundred dollars a year at first, though the family supplemented this as they could. He ate cheaply, had few clothes, lived in a bare room, and sought out free or cheap amusements. He carefully reported expenses to his father, always emphasizing his penury and the high cost of everything in Paris. He also complained to his mother, obviously seeking her intercession. He cut costs to the bone, but at the same time could not imagine any way to earn money. He occasionally fantasized about receiving commissions, but none came his way.

Behind the money problem lay the more basic issue of how long he could stay. He was barely settled with Gérôme at the end of two years. Revealing again the persistence that had brought him to Paris, he talked of a four- or five-year stay. He reminded his parents that art education was tedious and complex; many French students took longer than five years to gain proficiency. In addition, what would he do if he returned? He could go to New York, perhaps study at the new Art Students League and illustrate for the magazines, as many artists did. But that would simply halt his progress toward real art and would be equally expensive. If not that, he would have to stay in Cincinnati. "A sufficiently dismal prospect for me, either as regards progress or moneymaking." The most obvious recourse was some kind of position at the McMicken School, which might allow him to save enough to return to Paris. "How I could learn anything to speak of there I can't see." He shrewdly noted that with four or five years of study he could surely be self-supporting.[73]

In late spring 1879, his parents apparently agreed to another year. He carefully reported on his work in Grez that summer, clearly hoping for still more study. He wrote Will Cochran of his condition and aspirations, knowing that he would circulate the letter in the family. Kenyon was resigned to coming home after the spring term 1880, the end of his third year. "The first was spent in finding out what I had to learn, the second in learning how to draw, and I hope the next will be spent in learning how to paint. So, though of course a longer term of study would do me no harm, if father can keep me over here until June next I shall feel in a sort ready to go home." In September he responded to hints that his father might be named president of the University of Cincinnati with a long letter about modernizing the McMicken School, concluding that he was suited for the job.[74] The elder Cox instead became president of the Cincinnati Law School, though he would be president of the university from 1885 to 1889.

By early 1880, Kenyon was resigned to returning that summer. He could not face the McMicken School and hoped instead to go to New York and somehow develop a clientele. "New York is, and must be, the only center in America." His father agreed. "He will come home next summer and probably set up for himself in New York," he wrote a relative. By mid-March Kenyon was bustling with plans to paint several pictures before leaving Paris, "so as to take my stand at once as an *homme arrivé*." Robinson wrote of speaking to editors at Scribner's, who knew of Kenyon, and thought he could make a modest living illustrating. Then an unexpected opportunity appeared. John S. Sargent recommended him for work on a large panorama of the Battle of Tetuán of 1860, to be displayed in Brussels. Success at this might lead to other jobs, and he could come home with a nest egg. He promptly packed and bought a train ticket, but was back in Paris a week later. The painters in charge had expected him to do Moors and Arabs from memory or imagination, and at a killing pace. This immediately reminded him of the early bad training he had escaped. "I cannot and will not, at least so long as my very bread does not depend upon it, give myself to work where it is impossible to study *anything*, drawing or color or value or action or anything else. It would be too like a return to those horrid times of three years ago when I painted imitation Fortunys without models. I cannot afford it." He had been naïve in taking the job "but was carried away by my desire to earn something."[75]

Kenyon returned home in early summer, abandoning a plan to see the galleries of London. He spent some time in Cincinnati, visited relatives in Oberlin, then stayed on a friend's farm in Franklin County, Pennsylvania. Through family contacts or luck he met several people who commissioned him to do portraits or other works. Perhaps as a result of this good fortune, and to satisfy his ever-present demand for further study, the family agreed to more time in Paris. Robinson wrote him at the farm, detailing his own lone-liness and dissatisfactions, but noting: "How I envy you going back next September!"[76]

Kenyon left for Europe early in October and by midmonth was reporting home on the London galleries, which he stopped to see this time. The hold-ings of old masters were good, though the Louvre's were better, but he came to see British painting. Much of it was popular in America for its story-telling, but the French held it in contempt because of sentimental subject matter and poor execution. Kenyon thought that the scenes of courtship, country life, and animals so dear to British collectors were awful. The Pre-Raphaelite painters offended him with their insistence on heavy modeling, bad drawing, and garish colors. He thought J. M. W. Turner a great failure. He obviously could paint and had grand ideals, but for Kenyon, the work lacked any substance or reality. Turner's efforts to capture transitory effects disappeared into meaningless blooms of color. He simply did not know the proper limitations of art in depicting interpreted reality. "The greatest mas-ters have known what they could do and have done that. The frantic scrabble after the unattainable of many moderns is wearisome."[77] Kenyon was soon back in Paris, settled in the routine of a mature art student. Securing some commissions and the prospect of further study gave him a fresh sense of maturity. His letters home declined in number and took on a brisk, busi-nesslike tone.

In 1881 he published a small sketch in the *Century Magazine,* one of the country's best journals, which was sure to attract some attention. It was one illustration in a long article on American students at the Ecole, done in 1879 but delayed because other artists did not meet deadlines. It depicted a corner of the "chapel," the large room in the Ecole that contained antique and re-naissance statuary. He included some modern objects, but the focus was on two cherubs on a pedestal to the right center of the formal composition. By 1881 he had moved beyond this approach, but the work was well drawn, with enough modulation and perspective to create interest.[78]

The paintings promised for 1882–83 posed some problems. He appar-ently took a commission for some works, including a portrait of a young son, from Henry Elliott Johnston, Baltimore banker and collector. Johnston was probably a friend of Kenyon's father, who warned him to finish the work and not become a "deadbeat." Johnston in fact did not seem worried, and gave Kenyon "carte blanche" to do anything he wished except landscape. Kenyon wanted to do a good job, but thought that like so many collectors, Johnston was interested in signatures rather than paintings. This prompted an uncon-sciously forceful statement of his new self-confidence. "He thinks I am a ris-ing painter and wants to buy cheap and sell dear and at the same time get the reputation of having patronized [me] when I was still unknown." Johnston, who visited France in 1881, was difficult to work with and Kenyon apparently did not do the portrait. He did finish at least one work for him, *Hay time,* which was shown at the Pennsylvania Academy exhibition in the fall of 1882.[79] Neither painting survived, and Johnston died in 1884.

Kenyon worked hard on a small canvas entitled *Blanc et rose,* which the Dyers and other friends liked. It was finished by March 1881, when he drew a small sketch of it on a letter to his mother. The jury accepted it for the Salon. It marked a small but interesting change in Kenyon's direction, as it was a nude study. "It represents a little girl with wavy brown-blond hair sitting on a white fur with white drapery behind her," he explained. "The only color in the picture is a delicate pink ribbon in the hair and some pale rose-colored peonies in a vase, at which she is looking." The point was to display his skill with these unusual colors. But he also wanted to go beyond mere realism for a decorative, abstract effect, the nude for its own sake. The sketch at least showed a good deal of informal charm. It illustrated an interest in the ideal, which paralleled his concern for informal subjects. One review criticized the picture's apparent lack of a subject or purpose, and thought it inferior to *Dame en noir.* Kenyon took the criticism in reasonable stride; the pictures were simply different, for different reasons.[80]

While working on pictures, Kenyon had at least one chance to make more money. For about the last half of 1881, he assisted Georges Becker, a painter of portraits, genre, and military scenes. He worked closely with Becker on a large canvas of undescribed historical subjects, laying in figures and draperies (fig. 9). Becker had to make a living, of course, and kept an assembly line of decorative pieces, such as girls in pulcinella costumes. A former assistant had started many of these, and Becker now expected Kenyon to repaint them, "and then he signs them and sells them or gives them away." Kenyon liked Becker, who became something of a confidant, but this was journeyman work and offended his sense of propriety. He did one, then balked.[81]

Fulfilling the other commissions was slow work. He started a bust portrait of an Italian girl for Dr. Groesbeck, who was apparently a family friend. Kenyon thought the model resembled those of Leonardo and Raphael, which again showed his growing interest in classical allusions. He did not note finishing this but sent Groesbeck a painting titled *Autumn sunshine* for his hundred dollar advance. It was shown, but not described in the Pennsylvania Academy exhibition in the fall of 1882. J. M. Brown, Mrs. Dyer's brother, also bought *Afternoon.* This was apparently a landscape showing a hillside, with an old woman, horses, and a farm laborer who was sitting in the grass.[82]

Kenyon was determined to take home as much reputation as he could, to help in starting a career. This meant steady showing in the prestigious Salon. He decided to submit two small portraits in 1882. One, *Portrait de M. E.G.,* was of his friend Eliot Gregory, with whom he had worked at Carolus-Duran's. Gregory was a good companion and later became a stage designer

FIG. 9. Kenyon Cox and Georges Becker in Paris, 1881–82.
Allyn Cox Papers, Archives of American Art, Smithsonian Institution.

in New York, but he apparently did not like the picture. Kenyon was miffed to receive "the magnificent sum of 200 francs [forty dollars], including the frame," for it. The other work, *Le Miroir;—portrait de mon ami U.*, was of his recent friend Walter Ullmann. This young English painter died under unnoted circumstances in Grez in June 1882. Ullmann wanted an informal portrait in profile, wearing the old jersey in which he worked. Kenyon and mutual friends thought the result a good likeness. Ullmann had drawn attention for a landscape with figures in the Salon of 1882, *Jour d'automne*. Kenyon gave the portrait to Ullmann's brother as a memento. The works were too small to attract much attention, whatever their merits. "If I exhibit again in the Salon I must try to have something in the way of a *picture* and of some size." The Ullmann portrait was shown in London at the Fine Arts Society exhibition late in the summer. Reviews did not mention it, but Kenyon was in good company.[83]

Kenyon's stay in Paris was to end with the fall term in 1882. He went to Grez that summer, determined to complete the commissions, to do some work to take home, and to start a Salon entry for 1883 that would attract some attention. By mid-September, he had begun an elaborate composition about four by six feet, entitled *Thistledown*. In its foreground, a young girl in a dark blue dress picked pinkish blossoms from a thistledown bush. Two companions sat in the grass beyond her. The scene rose up gently to a long wall, which ended in the house and tower of a country place, outlined against a high horizon for dramatic effect. The dominant tone was carefully brushed green. The buildings were in gray buff and the sky in subtle pink. The figures were loosely but solidly modeled, and the general tone was relaxed and charming (fig. 10). The placement of the figures, sense of distance, and high horizon recalled Bastien-Lepage, though the coloration was stronger than his.

Kenyon finished *Thistledown* by December 1882 and left it with friends to submit in the spring. The Salon jury did not accept it, perhaps because it was not especially distinguished among many similar works. It followed him home to appear in the Pennsylvania Academy exhibition that fall, priced at a thousand dollars. Kenyon wrote the academy secretary that he would take anything over five hundred. Will Cochran visited the show and reported that the picture was well placed and looked handsome. "I have, however, very little hope of selling it, as it is too big a picture to sell in this country unless it had a reputation behind it," Kenyon wrote his father. "It may sell some years hence." It did not, though it won some notice. He showed it again with the Society of American Artists (SAA) in 1884, and it remained in the family until going to a museum many years later. *Thistledown* did not win Salon honors or sale, but it did show Kenyon's growing self-confidence in tackling such a large and complex work.[84]

FIG. 10. Kenyon Cox, *Thistledown* (1882). Oil on canvas, 46 × 78 ins.
Courtesy of The Washington County Museum of Fine Arts, Hagerstown, Maryland.

By mid-September, Kenyon was preparing to leave Grez for Paris and a final stint at finishing the work in progress. He had ambivalent feelings. He would miss Grez but thought that a cycle had ended. "I daresay a change and the getting away from the impressions of this place will do me good. Since Ullmann died I have been nervous and almost hypochondriacal." Leonard Opdycke visited Paris, and they met briefly, though Kenyon was busy packing pictures. He stayed in Paris until early December, then left for home. In New York, he visited friends, looked over potential studio space, and tried unsuccessfully to see Robinson, who was working in Albany.[85] He then went on to Cincinnati.

Kenyon left Paris after five busy years in a somewhat curious situation. Most American artists trained abroad eagerly relived their student days and wore a symbolic badge that read "Elève de Gérôme," or whichever master had directed their studies. Kenyon did not reminisce much about these years, perhaps because for all he had learned and liked, they were filled with penury and very hard work. And while he was proud of his training, he did not identify with a single teacher. For all his criticism of Carolus-Duran, he retained a certain breadth of style gained in that atelier. He had learned some good drawing techniques from Cabanel, though he seldom mentioned him in later years. He agreed with Gérôme's demands for precision and drawing that produced volume and form, with expressive shading and intellectual fidelity to nature, but he did not follow his example in subject matter or painting style. Kenyon was a realist, devoted to sound composition and interpreted form, but had begun to see the appeals of idealism, especially in figure painting. Though he did not use the term, he was something of an academic modern, dealing with contemporary life, but with the restraint and sobriety of the grand tradition. He was an acute and curious observer and began to see the symbolism in nature. His stay in Paris and travels to the countryside and to Italy reinforced his belief in combining technical skill with traditional unifying ideas. This broad tradition was his real teacher.

He came home with assets. As a person, he had clearly matured. As an artist, he had the credentials of a fine draftsman and promising painter. More to the point, perhaps, in developing a career he had shown at every Salon between 1879 and 1882. These and other works were then exhibited at the Pennsylvania Academy and the SAA in New York. A new generation of painters was at hand, determined to make American art the equal of Europe's, armed with fresh ideas and strong skills. Kenyon was part of that large movement. The art life was always hard, but he seemed poised for a successful career in the burgeoning art world.

III

⚜

AN ARTIST
IN NEW YORK

Cincinnati seemed somewhat larger, but otherwise not much different, to the returning Kenyon. The family, however, had gone through many changes during his absence. His father was elected to Congress from the Toledo district in 1876 and served the single term of 1877–79. As usual, he found politics distasteful, disliked the district, and often disagreed with the Republican party. After leaving Washington, he practiced law in Cincinnati with Will Cochran and other partners. In late 1879 there were rumors that he would become president of the University of Cincinnati, but he declined. He became dean of the Cincinnati Law School instead, a post he held until retiring in 1897. He was also president of the university from 1885 to 1889. The elder Cox was a good lawyer but found the legal life unchallenging and spent a good deal of time studying science and practicing microscopy, a new and popular subject on which he often lectured. He was "General" to those who remembered his wartime service, and "Governor" to those who liked his politics. Helen, of course, was always the daughter of Charles Grandison Finney, with a powerful Oberlin heritage and a large family to supervise. She and her husband were leaders in civic affairs and maintained an attractive home in the affluent Mount Auburn section of Cincinnati.

Will Cochran had married Rosa Dale Allen, of whom Kenyon heartily approved, in 1878. He had once toyed with an artistic career, but his stepfather urged practicality. Perhaps he thought that one artist in the family was enough; maybe he did not see talent in Cochran. Now thirty-five, the sober, industrious Cochran was settling into a successful law practice. He too was a community leader, in the mold the elder Coxes expected.

Kenyon's older sister Helen also married in 1878 while Kenyon was abroad. Her husband, John G. Black, was an Ohioan, born in 1847, destined for the ministry. He graduated from Kenyon College in 1874, studied a year at Princeton Theological Seminary, then took a term at New Kirk Divinity School in Edinburgh, Scotland. After a brief stint as a missionary in Nova Scotia, he became superintendent of schools in St. Clairsville, Ohio. By 1880 he was pastor of the Rock Hill and Wegee Presbyterian churches in Bellaire, on the Ohio River east of Columbus, nearly at the Pennsylvania border. In 1887 he would be president of the struggling Franklin College, then join the faculty of the College of Wooster, where he taught science and mathematics until the early 1920s.

The younger children had different stories. The lanky Dolson, with a prominent jaw and strong gaze, was beginning his climb to success in business. He was clearly not meant for the law or ministry. He wanted to enter business and settled on making machine tools, now in great demand. His father sympathized but in the best tradition of the watchful paterfamilias, expected him to succeed on his own. This was fine with Dol. In 1876 he borrowed two thousand dollars at 7 percent interest from his father and bought a small firm in Dunkirk, New York, that made twist drills. He moved it to Cleveland, and after much struggle became the wealthiest member of the family. He was outspoken in the best Cox tradition, prosaic and utterly practical. He too married in 1878, to Ellen Atwood Prentiss, daughter of a prominent Cleveland family. Kenyon spent a good deal of time with the couple, and they figured largely in his later life.

The youngest brother Charles tried his hand at cattle ranching, then fruit raising, and finally real estate in Colorado, but failed, and steadily drifted to the edge of family affairs and out of Kenyon's life. The youngest child, Hope, was only twelve in 1883, the subject of much brotherly affection and amusement. She was pretty, charming, and spoiled, clearly the family's darling, with an impish streak that seemed wholly out of place in her sober family. She married John Pope, an engineer whose work building railroads and port facilities took them around the world as "Swiss Family Pope."[1]

Kenyon was glad to see the family, but focused on what to do next. The prospect of immediately entering the highly competitive and risky art world in New York City was daunting. His training marked him for success, and he had a small network of friends in the East who could help him get started. He could not risk stagnating in Cincinnati and yet shrank from independence. Much of this, of course, was normal in a young person. But he was in a position common to favored children, alternating between intellectual certitude and emotional uncertainty. He sought praise, but resented any control that followed. He was intellectually precocious, but emotionally immature and inexperienced. He was sure of his talents, or at least of his potential, yet dreaded the world's judgments. He understood and accepted the family's expectations, but feared failing them, as revealed in constant warnings against expecting too much of his work. These feelings and reactions kept him tied to his parents longer than usual and were intensified because of a favored upbringing and unusual intellectual interests.

Kenyon renewed some old friendships in Cincinnati but did not join the McMicken School staff, as he had once suggested to his father. He visited relatives, including Dol and Nellie in Cleveland, where some interesting things were happening. In 1882 local artists secured space in the upper floors of the new city hall on Superior Street. The Cleveland Art Club, dating from 1876, organized a school, or academy, and set about trying to make the city conscious of the arts. The members worked in the assigned rooms during winter and went outside in warm weather, and staged lectures, receptions, and exhibitions of local work. An increasing number of Ohio students, such as Otto Bacher and Joseph R. De Camp, returned from studying abroad and like Kenyon were not quite ready to strike out on their own. Kenyon became popular in this group, who admired his obvious talent and the European art world he represented. "I remember that we thought he had made a lucky start," one recalled years later. "We didn't do much criticizing of each other's work. I guess we were pretty bad. He made a good impression on us socially—which was the best kind of professional introduction in those days." Kenyon understood their need for companionship and for a sense that their work and ambitions were important.

The club had the appearance of a going concern, including a board of directors, but no funding. This did not prevent their publishing the *Sketchbook*, which "was hurried into existence with but a modicum of premeditation, and entirely innocent of organization." It appeared monthly from January 1883 to March 1884, at $2.50 a year. It was something of a grab bag, with art news, a few advertisements, and reproductions of the group's work. The editors were proud of a new lithography process, but in truth the reproductions were often muddy. Kenyon contributed eleven items, and De Camp did a portrait head of him. His works included sketches of other members, a scene of people on a pier, a French girl in a big hat with ostrich feathers, and a *Diana* that touched on allegory. All were competent, well composed, drawn with ease.[2]

It was all very well to be among these painters who were of like mind, however amateurish, but Kenyon must have had some sinking feelings. It was too much like the McMicken days. He was drifting, waiting for something to happen. He wrote Georges Becker of his dissatisfaction, who answered with fatherly advice to persist. "I wish to repeat to you, my dear friend, that I have the most absolute confidence in your future," he replied from Paris. Will Stott also wrote from there to commiserate on the failure of *Thistledown* to get into the Salon. He comforted Kenyon with a sharp review of the bad pictures that did make it. Like Becker, he tried to reassure Kenyon that "some day Cox will find his own peculiar subjects which he will paint in his own peculiar way, and which will be greater and better than this [*This-tledown*], and which I am sure we shall like and be astounded at."[3]

Robinson also continued to urge Kenyon to face facts and come to New York, even if it meant making a marginal living at illustrating for the magazines and newspapers. He would at least be in congenial surroundings, where important things were happening. Kenyon should not live in the uncultured West. The country as a whole could not match the artistic resources of Europe, but "the eastern and middle states almost anywhere are not so hopeless. One is in a country two hundred years old instead of fifty," as he knew from personal experience after a year in his home state. "I don't believe Millet himself would have continued painting in Wisconsin, had he found himself there. At least come east before the end of the summer." He reported that Kenyon's *Afternoon* showed well in the SAA exhibition that May, perhaps a harbinger of things to come. And he remained sure that Kenyon could work for his own employer decorating hotels and the new Metropolitan Opera House, which paid five or six dollars a day. One could live and do real art at night and on the weekends.[4]

As spring arrived, his father nudged Kenyon toward moving on, at least in stages. It would do him good to visit John and Helen in Bellaire. He could improve his landscape technique, "so as to have a stock in trade to go to New York with in the fall." The ever-practical father believed that Americans were most likely to buy landscapes and that his son did them well when he tried. Kenyon went, and predictably complained about the cold weather. He had few friends, and no one to discuss art with, although Robinson did write.[5]

Kenyon always professed to dislike landscape painting and believed he had no talent for it, but his father's confidence was well placed. He did at least two fine landscapes while at Bellaire that spring and summer. *Flying Shadows* was especially successful. In it, Kenyon adopted a high vantage point, which enabled the viewer to look down on a sumptuous open scene that rose up smoothly and dramatically to a high horizon line marked with trees and greenery. Softly rounded hill forms dominated the almost square picture, and a rail fence snaked through its center. The hillsides were green and yellow, and there was a touch of purplish blue in the upper left corner. Kenyon painted in soft brush strokes, with a feathery touch in the high colors, that combined with the sense of great height to create a dual feeling of drama and poetry (fig. 11). The second landscape, which Leonard Opdycke ultimately bought, was more conventional but equally striking. It was rectangular and emphasized a horizontal view set at a lower height than *Flying Shadows,* done in modulated russet, green, and buff tones. Hill forms cut across it in dramatic diagonal lines. Kenyon again painted in soft strokes that blended the colors into a poetic mood. As usual, he emphasized form and tone rather

FIG. 11. Kenyon Cox, *Flying Shadows* (1883). Oil on canvas, 30 × 36¼ ins.
Courtesy of The Corcoran Gallery of Art, Museum Purchase, Gallery Fund,
Washington, D.C.

than light effects. Both pictures were well composed and richly painted, and created strong moods.

Some time that year he did an equally impressive portrait. Henry L. Fry was well known in the arts and crafts movement in Cincinnati, and Kenyon may have worked with him at the McMicken School. Frank Duveneck painted a head of Fry in 1874, which showed a realistically depicted face rising out of a dark background in the best manner of the Munich style. Kenyon now did a full-length study, which he carefully lettered with the legend HENRY FRY WOODCARVER AGED 76. Fry was rather short, with a full set of gray whiskers, gray hair, and a rugged face. He wore a brownish black work coat and stood squarely in midcanvas against a thinly painted curtain, near which hung a brightly colored lamp, and beyond which several objects were shrouded in gloom. The face stood out in the composition, which gained drama from the arrangement behind the figure and the floor that seemed to tilt slightly toward the viewer. Kenyon painted in soft blended strokes and gave the face a feeling of the character that came with age and achievement. A rather flattened sense of space added drama. It was an attractive and effective work, which Fry was proud to have in the Cincinnati Industrial Exposition that fall[6] (fig. 12). This portrait and the two landscapes showed that Kenyon was capable of quality work and that he could appeal to imagination as well as to realism.

Kenyon's dissatisfaction and drift were obvious, but he still hesitated about going to New York. In later years, he seldom referred to these unhappy months in Ohio and often implied in biographical sketches and correspondence that he stayed there only a brief time before establishing a studio in New York. His parents knew that he needed to become independent for both emotional and financial reasons and urged him to move. They could continue a small allowance and give him introductions to important people. He clearly would not starve. His friend Will H. Low, settled into the routine of magazine and book illustrating in New York, offered to help him get started. By late September 1883, Kenyon proposed to go and wrote Low that he "may be called upon to fulfill rash promises." Low had studied briefly with Gérôme and then with Carolus-Duran between 1873 and 1877. He painted and sketched French country scenes and peasants and was enamored of Jean-François Millet. Kenyon apparently had not met him in France, but the genial and helpful Low knew almost everyone in the art world and doubtless learned of Kenyon through mutual friends such as Robinson. He would be an important friend the rest of Kenyon's life. The group in Cleveland wished Kenyon well. "The sterling worth of the man, his eminent ability as an artist, and his scholarly attainments must win for him high rank among the strongest and best of our American students." By early October, the *Studio,* a clearing house of art information and criticism in New York, reported: "Kenyon Cox is in town."[7]

He did not stay with the Lows but took a small room at 35 West Eighteenth Street. With considerable enterprise, he immediately went to the offices of the Century Company, which published books and the prestigious *Century Magazine.* Doubtless after looking over his portfolio, the editors commissioned him to illustrate an article on the French sculptor Antoine-Louis Barye. He brought one of the sculptures to his room to sketch and reported proudly that he received twenty-five dollars for each of the drawings. By the last week in November, it was clear that he could not live and work in such cramped quarters. Probably on the advice of friends and the

FIG. 12. Kenyon Cox, *Portrait of Henry L. Fry* (1883).
Oil on canvas, 39³⁄₁₆ × 17¹⁵⁄₁₆ ins. Courtesy of
the Cincinnati Art Museum, gift of William H. Fry.

[76]

Century people he took studio space in the Holbein Building for artists on West Fifty-fifth Street. A shrewd developer built these small studio apartments over a row of stables in the late 1870s, chiefly to accommodate artists returning from foreign training, and in the correct hope that the city's art world would expand. Kenyon's was number 145 West Fifty-fifth Street. He sometimes stayed late in the studio but apparently lived in a nearby boarding house and ate in local restaurants.[8]

New York lived up to its billing as the center of national art activity. A beginner like Kenyon could hardly expect to succeed at once in showing and selling works. Like many others, he entered a highly competitive but exciting system that employed artists in new capacities. The burgeoning industrial order demanded designs for home furnishings, equipment, and accessories. The book publishing industry absorbed a good deal of art in both designs and promotional material. Makers of greeting cards, posters, advertising, and games and toys also employed artists. But the steadiest demand for art work was in magazine illustrating. A new literate middle class was eager for information on current issues, and also had expanding cultural horizons. They wanted to know more about the various art forms and the world, which required illustrated texts. Photography was expensive and difficult to use, so artists sketched or painted illustrations that engravers prepared for the press. The ability to transfer art to plates in photogravure processes was just opening further prospects for artists.[9]

Kenyon did not perceive these large implications in the rush to make a living. He was sure he would succeed if only he became known in art circles. The Century editors liked his first work and there was so much demand for illustrations that any new person with talent looked good. "I feel certain that I can do the work they want," he wrote home shortly after getting the first commission. He sought out potential employers and used family connections for introductions to important people, such as George William Curtis of Harper Brothers. "I am *determined* to make a living this winter." Little by little he managed to pay the bills, but as always, alternated between gloom and hope. He wrote home dejected in early November 1883, out of money and with no immediate prospects. His father sent fifty dollars, which helped, and Kenyon apologized for his gloominess, which suddenly lifted with a fresh job. He simply had to accept the normal ups and downs of earning a living at art.[10]

Kenyon's illustrative work naturally conformed to publishers' needs rather than to his own tastes or abilities. He drew the actors in a production of Aristophanes's *The Birds,* and did the same for an article on the Chinese theater. He could be whimsical or amusing, as in decorations for a poem dealing with the seasons, in which he depicted allegorical nude females and other figures representing the seasons, all amusingly posed. Illustrations had to catch the reader's fancy and be logical for the text. Kenyon liked best those that let him use expert draftsmanship or probe for character. On January 11, 1886, he spent several freezing hours sketching Houdon's famous bust of Benjamin Franklin at the Metropolitan Museum, for an article in *Century Magazine*. Working with frozen fingers in poor light, he fancied that he saw beneath the marble. "He impresses me as having been all his life laughing at the foolishness of everybody else," he wrote his mother. "A shrewd old boy who used everyone to gain his own ends and let them take the credit. As his ends were good ones, it was all right, but if he had been a rascal, what a tremendous one he would have been!"[11]

Kenyon also did colophons and headpieces. He became part of a cooperative effort to illustrate a special edition of Thomas Moore's *Lalla Rookh: an Oriental Romance* (1817) for the Boston firm of Estes and Lariat. It was to have about 150 illustrations, assigned to Low, Blum, Cox and other younger people. He welcomed the money but also was gratified that the reproduction would be done with photogravure, so that there would be no "hacking of it to pieces by bad wood engravers." The rising artist Thomas Wilmer Dewing had recommended Kenyon for the work, which spoke well of his growing stature in art circles. The project dragged on through 1884, with payments late and a receding publication date. The book appeared in 1885 but was not successful either commercially or artistically. Reviewers inevitably noted a lack of unity in the illustrations, though they lauded the effort to employ younger people. More to the point, the reproductions were indistinct and lifeless. Cox's were not his best work, but he did reveal a growing tendency toward allegory.[12]

Cox had no illusions about the qualities of the large volume of illustrative work he turned out in the 1880s. Publishers tended to approach artists with immediate deadlines, which did not permit much reflection or the use of models. Helen Cox praised one set of illustrations. "They are as good as I could make them for the money, but if the Century Co. paid for more time it would get better work," he replied realistically. "After all, it would hardly be worthwhile to do them better, as they were far too good for the engraver as it is." About all an artist could do was to make his best sketch or painting and surrender it to the engraving department. Its fate after that, no matter how many proofs he saw, was problematical. And given the medium's limitations, it was no wonder that most engravings lost the subtleties in the originals. By the late 1880s, armed with considerable experience and a weary realism, he thought it well to remind critics and readers that most engravings did not resemble originals. "My own experience is that even the best engravers habitually destroy the most individual qualities of their originals," he wrote in 1887.[13]

Accepting the medium's limitations, Kenyon never knowingly lowered his standards, and his illustrational work bore comparison with anyone else's.

Especially in treating objects, he often let subtle shading create mood. In dealing with people he relied on strong lines and hatching to produce volume and to depict the subject's character. These studies were well composed and often striking, since this technique was well suited to engraving (fig. 13). He was always careful to note "after photograph," if he had used one, "not to 'acknowledge the source of my inspiration' as someone once put it," he wrote years later, "but to avoid responsibility—for I always believed I could do much better work from nature." He could also use oil and soft mediums to create smooth, full surfaces. Given enough time, he could develop an elaborate composition that resembled painting. In one of these, a whimsical illustration for one of his own poems, he literally copied from an old photograph of himself playing the pipes while in a jester's costume. The rest of the scene showed a couple strolling in meadows, with a castle near a high horizon. The result was informal and amusing, but also showed strong composition, good perspective and the ability to balance details in what was really a rather complex picture, not just a routine illustration.[14]

Cox did a great deal of illustrative work and it provided welcome income into his middle age, but it was always second to painting for him. "I must illustrate to pay my bills, but hope to find time for work of a more serious nature between whiles," he told Leonard Opdycke in 1885. It was inferior to painting, and also represented a lower taste. "Much as I should like to do so, I find it impossible to avoid a certain amount of rather commonplace illustrative work, and I find such drawings the most popular with publishers, models, etc., whom I take to be fair indexes of popular opinion," he wrote Opdycke in 1886. By then he was well established as an illustrator, but as he told Low, "I've an itch for painting upon me, and fairly loathe the sight of black and white."[15]

The expanding art world that needed illustrations also required a new range of critical comment. Art was now varied and complex, and the United States was part of a world cultural order. Public interest was high, and the number of exhibitions and the variety of art shown steadily increased. The critic needed to be familiar with new techniques and philosophies, and be able to communicate with an intelligent amateur audience, many of whom were patrons and collectors. Gone were the days when a reporter could simply summarize an exhibition. These needs made an articulate, dependable and well-trained artist like Cox a natural candidate for writing criticism. The role was not altogether new or unexpected. He had done a three-part review of the Salon of 1879 for a Cincinnati newspaper while in Paris. He had at least tried to discuss the intentions and philosophies of painters as well as techniques. And though a callow youth, he realized that criticism invited response, which was not always measured. His parents signed only his initials to the reviews for the newspaper, but even this gave Cox pause. "Particularly

Kenyon Cox
after photograph
1891

FIG. 13. This illustration from W. F. Apthorp, "Paris Theaters and Concerts, I,"
Scribner's Magazine 11 (January 1892), is of Jean Mounet-Sully (1841–1916),
a famous French actor. It shows Cox's attention to realistic detail,
and to character.

if I have to criticize American artists, I should want to remain incognito and not draw down envy and malice and all uncharitableness on my own head when it comes my turn to exhibit."[16]

The editors who sought illustrations from Cox apparently recognized his literacy and candor. He wrote some short articles for the art press soon after arriving in New York. By late 1885, he accepted an offer to do unsigned criticism for the *New York Evening Post,* noted for controversial reporting, and the *Nation.* Writing took time and energy from painting, but he frankly needed the money. And for all the dread of personal animosities, "I like well enough to write and it is of course pleasant to have a pulpit from which one can deliver his opinions to the world." In written work to date he had tried to adopt Matthew Arnold's advice that the critic try to gain authority through disinterest and a large view. Like Arnold, he used the best culture, which meant the ancient and Renaissance tradition, as a standard for modern work. This was all very well, but a popular audience lacked the knowledge for any fine discussions. Perhaps he knew he had to deal in blunt language and vivid judgments.[17]

By early November 1885, Cox was making the rounds of exhibitions at the height of the season. An elaborate review of a typical eclectic show at the American Art Galleries was among his first. One section featured recent works of American painters trained abroad. The paintings of people such as Edward Simmons and Arthur Hoeber were competent enough but uninspired. "There is no air and no light in them—the light is *on* the figures but it is not *around* them; there is no 'envelopment'; and the eye cannot penetrate beyond the canvas, or see between and around the figures. The pictures are dry and all on the surface." Upstairs he found a lot of "shop," pictures he thought reflected time-worn themes, such as those of Sanford Gifford, or that were mere flashy decorations. He was especially harsh with Frederic A. Bridgman, a student of Gérôme's who worked in the master's style, but without his dignity. The artist's technical skill in rendering effects and exotic subject-matter, especially from the Near East and Orient, sacrificed "every sober truth of form and color." The third section of the exhibition contained watercolors, which Cox thought competent.

This tartness became familiar in art circles in the following weeks. Cox praised fashionable French work only when it contained some large idea. He disliked anecdote and was caustic with John Everett Millais, whose *Little Nell and Her Grandfather* was "calculated by its childish sentimentality to 'touch the great popular heart.' " Nor did the autumn exhibition of the prestigious NAD escape. He noted that the best young people did not exhibit, and that some older academicians would do well not to. He thought most of the work "so frankly amateurish that it is hard to take the exhibition seriously." Some artists were stung to reply. Cox had called Francis A. Silva's work *Clearing After a Southeaster,* "utterly worthless." Silva protested to the *Post* editor that the jury had thought otherwise. And he adopted Cox's pedantic tone and said the picture was worth at least a dollar, making the statement factually incorrect. The editor laconically supported Cox.[18]

Cox naturally reported all of this home, and provoked some sage advice from his father. " 'Slashing criticism' is very tempting, but it does not teach the public, nor does it impress the knowing, as more temperate and kindly criticism will do." Kenyon could easily moderate his language without surrendering principles, and must not become known as a troublemaker. Cox must have pondered this as his secret came out. It was utopian to think that the closely knit art world would not discover his authorship, and he was shortly the object of unwanted comment. One offended artist confronted him in a public shouting match. Another refused to speak to him. Still others wrote him angry letters. If duelling had been in fashion, he would have spent time finding seconds. His own critics made the common rejoinder that he wrote because he could not paint. This produced a defensive sanctimoniousness in Cox. "I think he was perhaps a little in a hurry to proclaim the failure of one who in so short a time has attained the position I have among the best artists here." By late January 1886, he wrote Leonard Opdycke that he wanted to stop writing but hated to "back out under fire" and frankly needed the money. He realistically agreed to modify his tone and to criticize in generalities. But even so, artists would object. "Artists are certainly the *irritable genus,* and can't bear anything less than unlimited soft soap apparently."[19]

He reviewed into the new year of 1886 and included collections of oriental painting and porcelain, contemporary etchings, as well as current paintings. By February he had received a major illustration commission and decided to end his critical career with a review of the Mary J. Morgan collection, chiefly of Barbizon paintings, at the American Art Galleries. He had apparently hit his stride, for the resulting essay was measured and thoughtful about work he liked. He praised Jean-François Millet for the simplicity, grandeur, and evocative moods in his work. He enthused over the ability of Troyon, Diaz, Corot, and Daubigny to harmonize the essentials of nature into a poetic mood rather than deal with mere facts. The work created reflective analytical moods, expanded and harmonized the imagination, and pleased the eye. Here was work that anyone interested in ideas in art could study with profit. He had some reason to write his mother: "I am rather proud of it and think it a good article to wind up on."[20]

Cox bade criticism farewell without regret, little knowing that he would become a widely read art critic in later years. For now, he wanted to paint rather than write. "Besides, there is more hard work for less pay in writing art criticisms for the papers than in almost anything I know of," he wrote his father, "and nothing is so exasperating as being forced out at all times to trot around to see collections of bad stuff and get into rows by saying that the stuff is bad." He also thought that other critics as well as artists now disliked him, a double penalty. And he was defensive about their main charge: " 'The critics are the failures,' etc., sticks in my throat," he wrote Will Low that fall.[21] Cox doubtless regretted this brief foray into newspaper criticism, fearing that the animosities involved would affect his career. He did gain a reputation for bluntness and intemperate language, but in fact these irritations passed. Many people disliked him; others granted him a grudging respect as his art developed. One reviewer in 1886 noted, after praising Cox's works in the SAA show: "Mr. Cox, by reason of his strictures on his fellow artists, is one of the most cordially disliked men in New York, but his works show some ground for his conceit."[22]

People who knew him doubtless dismissed his tone and manner as aspects of a rather prickly, defensive personality who did not know when he was offending people. And the content of his reviews was often impressive. He praised what he knew best and believed in and criticized work that fell short of sound standards. He lauded quality workmanship, fidelity to significant details in nature, and seriousness of purpose. Perhaps most important, time proved him right in many judgments. The people most wounded did not develop. And he praised artists who would dominate the coming generation, like William Merritt Chase, J. Alden Weir, Abbott H. Thayer, and Thomas Wilmer Dewing. At a time when few critics praised Winslow Homer, Cox appreciated his economy of means, eye for the symbolic detail, and love of truth, no matter how roughly executed.[23] All in all, writing art criticism was beneficial in forcing Cox to see a spectrum of current work, to organize his thoughts, and to establish canons of taste.

Teaching was an equally unexpected career for Cox. In the summer of 1883, before Cox came to New York, Theodore Robinson complained of earning a meager living decorating houses and public buildings, but the only alternative he could think of was teaching, "that great resource of the impecunious painter in America."[24] The growing art world needed teachers as well as critics and illustrators, though it did seem ironic that a painter who could not live from selling work could teach others to do the same.

New York City rivaled Paris in the number of students seeking instruction in several art schools. The oldest was at the NAD with a basic curriculum much like that of the Ecole des Beaux-Arts. A group of students hostile to this approach formed the Art Students League in 1875 on more democratic principles. Students there could enter any class with the instructor's consent. The regimen was difficult, but ability seemed more important than persistence in advancement. Students also advised about the curriculum, regulations, and even the staff. The student body of several hundred came from all over the country and contained a large number of women. The school had a library, and examples of good work, in quarters at 38 West Fourteenth Street. There were other programs, as at the Cooper Union and the Metropolitan Museum of Art, but the League seemed the most modern and freest of them. Relations with the NAD were good, and many League teachers were academicians. In time, some of the best people taught at the League.[25]

By the spring of 1884, the League was considering Cox for an instructorship in drawing, which spoke well of his standing in the art community. People liked his illustrations and realized that his excellent training and studiousness suited him for teaching. He thought the idea intriguing, and as always welcomed the small but steady income. By summer he had joined the staff for the term beginning in October, teaching two half-days a week for six hundred dollars. He still did illustrations and hoped to sell some paintings, but the salary at least covered base living expenses. He liked the work and was popular with the students. They found him young, still a little glamorous for foreign training, and a hard but interesting taskmaster. "My teaching has been very successful this winter and my pupils say they have learned more than they ever did before in their lives," he wrote his mother in May 1885, "and were unanimous in asking the League to engage me for next winter." Within four years he was earning more than a thousand dollars a year for two full days of teaching, and had eighty or ninety students[26] (fig. 14).

Cox also joined the staff of the Gotham Club of Art Students. It was designed for working people, and he taught drawing on Tuesday and Thursday evenings. The original students founded the club in 1879 after meeting in a beer hall on Broome Street, then settled into quarters at 17 Bond Street for an array of classes. They also entertained visiting artists who displayed their skills in free sessions. The staff was good, and the students clearly appreciated Cox.[27]

Cox was naturally the subject of students' comments and gossip as he settled into teaching. They knew of his recent past in Paris, and of his reputation as an illustrator and draftsman. He also quickly became noted for sharp criticism and a rather subdued manner. Louise Howland King enrolled at the League in 1883 and recalled the anticipation among her friends who heard that the noted Mr. Cox was coming to teach the women's life class. They awaited his first appearance, quietly composed in a semicircle, and were surprised to see a rather tall, slender, bearded young man enter the room. It "did not seem possible he could be the severe, caustic individual we feared." She soon decided that he was simply shy, but his bluntness in criticizing work became legendary. His comments reduced some students to tears, much to his own surprise, and he was always apologetic and distressed at being misunderstood. King, of course, got to know him better later as his wife.[28] During his long tenure to come, students respected him, even though some finally thought his teaching was too formal. He represented discipline and tradition, which many other people thought salutary as the art world changed.

His classes drew chiefly from the life. He gave the students the same meticulous instruction he had received from Gérôme. He designed a new seal

FIG. 14. Photograph of Kenyon Cox with Art Students League Class, ca. 1900.
Courtesy of the Peter A. Juley & Son Collection, National Museum of American Art,
Smithsonian Institution.

for the League in 1889 that symbolized his commitment to drawing as the basis of all art. It depicted a seated woman with nude bust seen from the right, poised to paint on a canvas. The motto was *Nulle Dies Sine Linea* (No Day Without Drawing), which was a fair statement of what he thought artists should do. Cox did this small work in one of the styles he taught. He drew the figure in thin, flowing lines that tempered its realism with a sense of idealism. The lady was a person but clearly represented Art. He delineated the drapery on her lap with subtle shading rather than details. The arms and hands possessed the strength to paint, and he enclosed the work in a continuous circle.[29]

He insisted that students master realistic details, but that they never merely copy. His own first efforts were often rough and heavy, but he refined the drawing to an elegant, stylish statement, especially in the figure. Like Gérôme, he emphasized volume, tonality, and suave yet energetic line. Cox's teaching was not innovative, but his demands for controlled expression were sound enough and did not prohibit individualism within the academic tradition.

Cox sympathized with the students' struggles but expected them to be as dedicated as he was to the quest for meaningful, well-presented art. He could be impatient and cutting in erasing or redoing drawings and often left a trail of charcoal dust or erased pencil, as well as of acerbic comments. Many students inevitably disliked or rebelled against discipline, emphasizing their feelings over studied reflection. But Cox was adamant that their finished product evoke the solidity, function, and structure of the figure. He hit upon one especially challenging, or irritating, way to force students to develop their memories and to analyze, compose, and delineate feeling and function as well as appearance in the figure. He often held class on one floor and posed the model on another, forcing students to go back and forth until they could reproduce from memory something more than transitory appearances.

Cox always believed that drawing was the basis of all sound art because it focused and extended the artist's ability to perceive and interpret nature. It permitted composition, mood, and the proper use of complementary color. He did not think that everyone could learn to draw, but training created a kind of reflex that transferred the mind's interpretations of nature to paper or canvas. "Drawing as a training of eye and hand is a kind of physical culture," he told students at the Metropolitan Museum of Art late in life. "It shapes the senses, broadens the powers and stimulates the observation and the intelligence, making of the student a finer and in every way more efficient being than he could become without it." Students may have dreaded Cox's demands for excellence, but the good ones benefitted. And he did not let age or continuous teaching erode his standards. Toward the end of his teaching career, he was still sending marginal students back to drawing from casts.[30]

Cox was very knowledgeable about the technical aspects of painting but apparently did not teach it much. He had some special students, with whom he took an academic approach that emphasized orderly composition, careful modeling, and complementary coloring. He also became famous for demonstrating anatomy, for men only. Like any good faculty member, he tried to raise funds, judged exhibitions of student work, contributed some of his own works, and in general helped make the League experience important to students who were often far from home and with few anchors, as he was once. And although he did not teach art history or theory, he tried to make students understand that the technical skills they so eagerly sought were only the beginning of an art career. The great tradition mattered most.[31]

Writing criticism, teaching, and illustrating kept Cox busy through 1885. Then at the beginning of the new year he suddenly received a major commission that might establish him as an artist if done successfully. The publishers Dodd, Mead asked him to do an elaborate set of illustrations for a special edition of Dante Gabriel Rossetti's famous poem "The Blessed Damozel" (1850). They first approached Will Low and then Thomas W. Dewing, both of whom were busy. The firm then asked Cox, whom the two older artists recommended as a rising person, with the training and talent necessary to do the figure work involved. The book would appear in a small trade edition, bound in fine cloth with plates on heavy paper. A special collector's edition would have calf binding and plates on handmade paper, suitable for framing. The fifteen hundred dollar fee was substantial, though Cox would have to pay for numerous models. He had to do twenty paintings, to be photographed for printing plates, due at summer's end.

This was indeed a coup, and Cox understood that the other artists' recommendations carried the day, but he took some credit for having reached this point. "This is a proof of what I have always believed, that the way to real success in art or anything else is to do the highest one knows and wait for those who can recognize its merit to inform the rest of the world," he wrote his mother. He might have made a little more money with popular art, but it would not have brought the recognition they both wanted. In practical terms, he hoped to pay off debts to his father and others, and perhaps save enough for a short trip to Europe.

His mother answered at once: "All things come to him who waits." He should spend this "golden egg" on a nice home, and she even mentioned matrimony. Now he seemed on the verge of the fame she had not expected "would ever come to you in your lifetime." Cox's father cancelled the modest debts, and Kenyon thanked him for past help, especially the years in Paris. "I hope I may achieve success enough to make you feel that it was not money spent in vain." He naturally wanted their approval, but was mature enough to remind them that his stubborn adherence to ideals had gained recognition among artists. Perhaps *The Blessed Damozel* would do the same in a larger public.[32]

The set of illustrations was elaborate and the deadline remorseless. Cox was not sure that he could handle the pressure and had to deal with temperamental models in a cramped studio. Much of the work would go on during the broiling summer. He also had sieges of colds and other ailments. But he was determined, and set to work on February 22, 1886. He started with drawings in black ink, then painted the final works in *grisaille*, a gray monotone that would become sepia in photogravure. He did twelve paintings of 24- by -18 inches for stanzas from the text; one each for title, half-title, and illustrations pages; a dedication and signature; and three head and tailpieces, plus initials. By the beginning of fall he had done sixteen of the paintings and a third of the letters. The days were long and he even worked some nights. The end was in sight and none too soon. The studio was a "kind of private hell in hot weather such as you can have no idea of," he wrote Will Low, to whom he dedicated the work. He finished on October 16, 1886, and the book was ready in time for the Christmas season.[33]

Cox did not especially like Rossetti's poetry. "The Blessed Damozel" dealt with the loss of loved ones and was written in a cryptic, refined style. The tone was one of brooding regret and exalted melancholy, but the language and metaphors were cosmic, dealing with the meanings of life, death, and love. The poem's message was that exaltation could relieve sorrow. And literate readers recognized the work's purified eroticism. Cox attempted to parallel this tone as much as possible, but really saw the commission as a chance to make a special statement in figure painting. He wanted realistic figures to look modern but embody large ideas, and to be decorative in the best sense. He knew the result would be controversial. The American public generally did not care either for nude figures or for rarefied ideas, much less a combination of the two. "I can't imagine how my book is likely to succeed," he wrote Leonard Opdycke. "I imagine the best things in it will be of too severe a taste for the general [public]." But he could reasonably expect attention and success where it mattered most, among peers. Determined to get the maximum coverage for his effort, he arranged to display the completed paintings at Reichard's Gallery on Fifth Avenue. One critic noted that "neatly framed in plain, dull-gilded oak, they form a frieze the possession of which one might well envy the publishers."[34]

These pictures were Cox's best work to date, and showed great technical skill. He painted thinly and evenly in a suave manner. Shadows were subtle and tones well modulated. The best figures, whether single or grouped, had volume and energy. Draperies were light, but covered real bodies. The nudes were idealized yet genuine people. Some of the scenes were cropped for effect, and though all were academically composed, the best had a sense of action. The landscapes in several pictures were striking. The figures were at the front of the plane, with an illusion of great distance in the backgrounds. These small scenes were detailed, yet had an ethereal quality that matched the text. There were subtle references to past masters throughout (figs. 15 and 16).

Cox immediately dispatched copies of the book to friends and family in late November 1886. He proudly wrote in one: "A Mon Cher Maître, J.-L. Gérôme, Son Elève Reconaissant," and sent it to Paris. Gérôme's reply, if any, did not survive. Will Cochran was pleased, but had to be frank. He did not like Rossetti and had heard others say that "your illustrations overweight the poem, and are too good for it." His mother disliked nudes, and apparently did not say much, though she was proud. From Florence, Will Low thanked Cox for the dedication. He thought that some pictures inevitably were better than others, and especially liked the initials. The drawing was fine.[35]

Cox was now on the receiving end of criticism, and awaited the results with the prickly dread common to writers and exhibitors. Friends were congratulatory, but some people clearly envied his success. Others did not like his style, or simply did not care for figure work. He heard criticism that his figures were not ethereal enough for the "Damozel." If Michelangelo's frescoes appeared in 1886, he wrote his mother, these same critics doubtless would find them "singularly 'realistic' and 'unspiritual.' How shocking to put real bones and muscles to heavenly and ethereal beings! And how 'gross' and 'overmature' are his ideals of feminine beauty!"[36]

The book received considerable attention, though the reviews inevitably were mixed. The complaint that the elegant and substantial illustrations did not match the limpid and ethereal text was most common. But even so, critics praised Cox's technical skill and high ideals. The most thoughtful and interesting review appeared unsigned in the *Nation*. In general, the critic did not find the illustrations moving, but he thought that several were among the best ever done in America. He also shrewdly concluded that the pictures were decorative rather than illustrative, derived from sculpture and relief, and resembled wall paintings. Cox agreed. "The only piece of real criticism I have seen is that in the *Nation*, the writer of which has seen clearly what the drawings are and what they are not, and his praise of them as decorative compositions in the style of the Renaissance wall-paintings is very welcome, as it is praise of what they were meant for." He had always thought they were "a splendid bit of training in composition and drawing that I shall be better for all my life." And in later years, he thought that "I showed my decorative bent for the first time" in these works.[37]

The criticism was actually quite mild, rather normal for any such work. Dodd, Mead quickly offered another commission, this time of Cox's choosing, for the Christmas market in 1887. After some thought, he declined. "I cannot do again what I have done on the *Damozel* in so short a time without too great a strain, and to do anything less good now, or even not better, would be fatal." He also wanted to paint independently. And just as he did not wish to be trapped illustrating magazines, so he did not want to become dependent on book illustration at the expense of painting.[38]

The Blessed Damozel was critical to Cox's development. He had completed a major commission on time and in good order. He had tested his skill and done something more than the bits and pieces of work that earned a living. He had glimpsed the satisfactions of decorative art, and had raised his stature in the art community. And he earned a significant fee, was the subject of considerable public discussion, and thus bolstered his self-confidence as a person as well as an artist.

Working on *The Blessed Damozel* allowed Cox to refine his views about the nude and allegorical painting. He incorporated both of these in illustrations where possible, as in the work for *Lalla Rookh,* and in some smaller magazine

FIG. 15. Kenyon Cox, *Surely She Leaned O'er Me* (1886).
Grisaille on canvas, 24⅛ × 18⅛ ins.
Courtesy of the Brooklyn Museum, 25.840.I, gift of Mrs. Daniel Chauncey.

commissions, but was careful to avoid figures that might be controversial.
But in his steady production of mundane drawing there were always hints of
a need to express classical ideals through the figure. The intense work on
pictures for Rossetti's poem made him want to use his training as a figure
painter. "But oh! how I long for a chance to try what I can do at painting on
a large scale subjects with nude figures!" he wrote Will Low as *The Blessed*

FIG. 16. Kenyon Cox, *The Stars Sang in Their Spheres* (1886).
Grisaille on canvas, 24 × 18¼ ins.
Courtesy of the Brooklyn Museum, 25.840.K, gift of Mrs. Daniel Chauncey.

Damozel work came to an end. "I shall do it yet if I live ten or twenty
years."[39] These illustrations showed him both the limitations of the usual approach, and the possibilities for a large statement of the idealism he felt.

Cox, of course, had received the very best training in figure work from
his Parisian masters, especially Gérôme. In that setting, the nude figure
caused no controversy and was at the top of the artistic hierarchy. The greatest

painters in history had done nudes, and artists understood that the figure appealed on several complex levels. The technical difficulty of depicting the qualities of flesh challenged any painter. Only the best could combine realistic appearance with a sense of the underlying structure and actions of the body, which symbolized the complexities and order in nature. The energy and motion in the body were parables of the subtle workings of life. As allegory or symbol, the figure idealized emotions and grand conceptions, promoted harmony over discord, and offered safe expression of basic feelings to artists.

By the nineteenth century, the nude was also an outlet for the controlled sensuality that permeated a great deal of formal art. Many modern painters, such as Cabanel and Bouguereau, tried to express classical ideas with nudes that often hinted strongly of sexuality. The Salons were filled with allegorical pictures drawn from mythology or history in which nudes seemed both symbolic and erotic. A sumptuous female figure might be a Venus or Virtue but could also appeal to other than ideal emotions.

American painters faced the added complication of working in a society that was uncomfortable with sex, however controlled or refined. The same culture that tried to regulate drinking, or to promote religion, also regularly crusaded against pornography in literature and the arts. In the largest sense this represented efforts to retain a set of dominant core values in a period of rapid change. And the painter or sculptor might see a nude as pure, chaste, ideal, all terms that neutralized eroticism, but the public simply saw nudity. There was the added irony that many tolerated European nudes as expressions of high art, especially if labeled as old masters, but would not accept or purchase similar works from Americans. The traditionalist art critic and historian Frank Jewett Mather, Jr., later suggested that this attitude represented a belief that such decadence was good enough for Europeans but should not threaten purer American values. Or perhaps it was all just cultural snobbery. As Mather said, these people "may have felt that a conscientious nude, like a cask of sherry, needs a sea voyage to make it desirable."[40]

Cox had done many nude studies as an art student and his interest in the figure and in allegorical compositions grew as he matured. He usually emphasized architecture, power, and authority in depicting the male figure. In 1878 he explained to his father that good artists hoped to capture the figure's surface and actions, which put them in the line of the old masters. But they also sought something more profound. "But I think the greatest is he who goes deepest and seizes the essential characteristic, the construction, the anatomy and building of the man, his great barrel of ribs for holding his lungs and heart, his soft and fleshy abdomen, the great jointed column of his back, and the sinewy supple limbs." He held the same ideals fifteen years later in 1893, and especially remembered the power of the *Illisus,* a fragment of a male torso from the Parthenon which was a staple in student cast drawing exercises. "The 'Illisus' is, in my opinion . . . the finest male figure in all art," he wrote a correspondent who asked his advice on drawing. "It is reclining on one side and is marked by the splendid definition of the thorax and the falling away of the softer parts of the body, and by the magnificent sense of weight in the fleshy parts of the thigh." In all such considerations of the technicalities of observing and depicting the figure, he understood what the male form symbolized.[41]

The female form was a different matter. Cox followed the precepts of his teaching and study, and his own inclinations to let it personify high ideals of personal purity and civic virtue. Like most spokesmen of his class and circumstance, he saw women as guiding forces of civilization, personifications of ideals that tempered materialism and disorder in masculine life. His era prized realism and the mundane yet had a parallel need for exalted expression and for the pursuit of ideals, which female forms symbolized in the arts. Cox was in good company. Idealized women figured in the works of leading artists, such as Augustus Saint Gaudens, Thomas W. Dewing, Abbott H. Thayer, and many muralists. Once again, in the largest sense, idealization of women in this way reflected a desire to establish unifying purposes and tastes in a period of rapid and bewildering change. The female nude also expressed and symbolized an unconsciously controlled eroticism.[42]

Cox's advocacy of the nude encountered strong opposition, not least in his own family. His mother feared that this controversial interest would ruin his career. For women like herself, standing as she thought for the best in personal taste and civic values, there was no room for such nudity, however idealized. She thanked him for a sketch of a nude woman in 1885. "Yet I don't fancy nude female figures, and wish there would never be another one painted. . . . It is wholly unnecessary to portray them in that manner, and not pleasing to any but the [illegible] few." This response brought out all of Cox's brusqueness. "I am sorry you feel as you do about the nude," he replied. "It is just such feeling that makes great art almost impossible in this country." Controversy over the nude was old-fashioned, especially in circles such as theirs with artistic interests. "I insist that there is nothing immodest whatever about the nude when treated from a high artistic point of view, and that it is impossible for it to be as suggestive and lascivious as a figure partially draped and knowingly uncovered. The nude is pure. It is the *undressed* that is impure. If any person not corrupt sees anything immodest in my picture it is because I have failed." A few weeks later he insisted that "the *intention* is everything, and that the striving after beauty is *never* immoral or immodest."[43]

This fear of the nude was also part of the hoary view that art life was dissolute, and that artists and models were prey to sexual temptation. Once again, Cox found this view astonishing and read his mother a stern lecture. "It seems as if no one would ever understand that an artist's models are tools, like his palette and easel, equally indispensable to his work and of as little importance to his life." Models were certainly not glamorous temptresses. Some were really plain, in fact, and all earned their meager two or three dollars a day. They had "no more to do with the feeling of the artist than so many paintbrushes." He certainly had no desire for romance in their presence. "Do you suppose painting and drawing such easy things and so little absorbing that one can think of anything else while carrying them on?" he demanded. "When I am working on anything serious and difficult, I haven't a word to throw at a dog and would absolutely forget that the model was human were it not that her fatigue and inability to hold still any longer reminds me that she is not a plaster cast." His mother also need not worry about his personal life. "I had thought you knew me well enough to know that if I ever marry it will be a woman not inferior to my own friends in all that constitutes lady-hood." But this all had little to do with his art. "I believe in art and in its nobility and I believe that the nude human figure is the highest vehicle for the expression of high artistic thoughts. If the world does not know enough of art to understand this, I must suffer its misconstructions."[44]

Cox stubbornly went his way on this question. His friend William A. Coffin wrote an important biographical article about him in 1891, and noted that "no painter among us has a purer sense of beauty in the ideal, and no one has a keener perception of grace in form and distinction of color in nature. He is impelled to paint the nude simply because he considers it beautiful." Cox spent a good deal of energy attempting to educate the art public to accept idealized nudes. He and Will Low wrote a carefully reasoned explanation of the appeals of figure work in 1892. They noted the usual challenges in depicting form and function, but in the end great figure work was conceptual. "Ideas, if they are to be expressed in graphic or plastic art, must be incarnated, and the human figure is the one great medium of expression for abstract ideas in the arts. That the figure should be nude if it is to express great and simple ideas, seems also natural." And Cox freely adopted the advice he gave students, saying in 1910: "I enjoy drawing from the nude for its own sake, and find it a continuing and valuable discipline."[45]

Cox's best known female nudes were those in *The Blessed Damozel,* but he painted many other such works. They were often technically skillful, in smooth brush strokes that created an even but not enameled surface of carefully blended and delicate flesh tones. He used fine shading to highlight the body's contours, and modeling to create presence in the figure. Many of these nudes were reclining, in good academic manner and to attain complex pose and structure. The models were sometimes languid and relaxed, but also faced the viewer. In some such works he introduced classical symbols, such as a cupid stealing up on a drowsy nude female in *The Approach of Love* (1890), which also tempered any eroticism involved. Other works, such as the elegant *Brune* (1888), were tangible in appearance but also abstract celebrations of the female form and of the artist's skill (fig. 17). Most bore titles that symbolized a season, a time of day, a mythological character, or were simply abstract studies, which also distanced the viewer from mere nudity. Like any good traditionalist, Cox tried to update the inherited tradition in this figure painting. He thought that the modern nude came from classical and Renaissance models, but should have "some element of realism" to avoid being derivative and to appeal to modern tastes. The painter could deal in gods and goddesses, but they had to have "real flesh and bodily presence," or he had failed to link past and present sensibilities. The results of this theory were mixed, and the more elaborate such easel works, the more staged they often seemed. He was most successful in abstract figures such as *Brune,* and least successful in combining formal classical settings with modern realism.

Cox liked these works, and exhibited many in the late 1880s and 1890s, but he simply could not sell them. A fellow artist or collector occasionally bought one, but most returned from shows unsold and stayed in the family until they were lost, destroyed, or given to a museum. Some critics praised them, however mildly, as efforts to ennoble current painting or to revive figure painting in the grand mode. The praise was often faint. Those critics who did not like the nude, or who disliked Cox's efforts to combine classical values with modern techniques, were outspoken about the works, and used them to denigrate his talents and purposes. In the end, he was fortunate to subsume this interest in the figure into the mural painting that occupied his late years.

Year after year, Cox paid a price for this idealism. In 1891 a group of women protested over several nude studies, including some of his, in the annual show at the Pennsylvania Academy. He publicly suggested wryly that Philadelphia must be more philistine than New York, and let it go at that. Privately he told Louise King that he had laughed over the tempest, but could not resist adding: "It tickled me greatly to find others getting the same sort of thing I have been used to taking alone." He did not think the controversy would affect much. Still, the animus against the nude persisted. In 1895 he objected to the removal of photographs of nudes from an article he wrote for the staid *Century Magazine.* Five years later, he privately protested to his friend Edwin H. Blashfield at being thought "an erotic maniac" in certain quarters.

The controversy even struck close to home. In 1906 the antivice crusader Anthony Comstock raided the Art Students League for distributing publications with nude studies. Cox was not involved, but it was a sobering lesson. About 1908 he gave the League a painting from the late 1880s titled *The Girl With the Red Hair.* "The canvas represented a nude figure, in an attitude of repose, seated on the floor of a studio. A mass of auburn hair fell loosely over the face, and the white sheet in the background, against which the

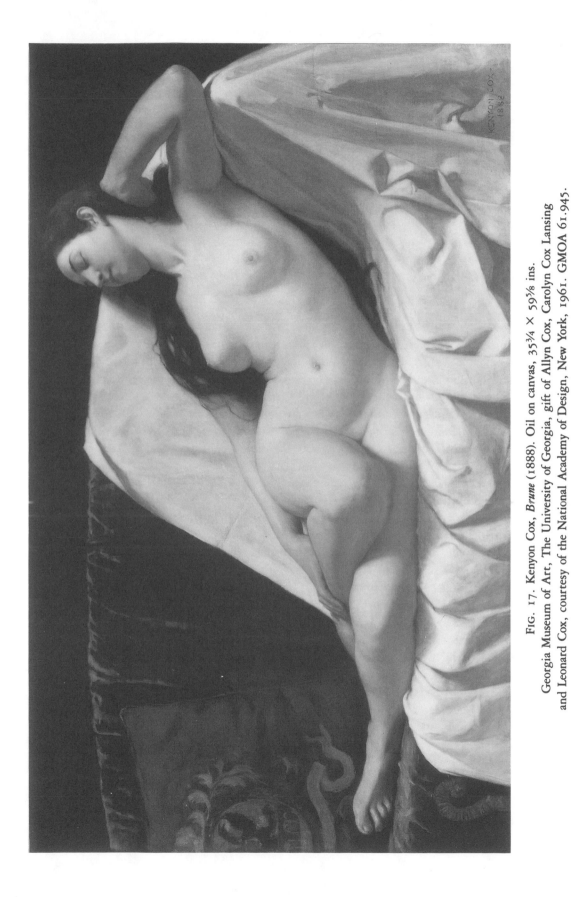

FIG. 17. Kenyon Cox, *Brune* (1888). Oil on canvas, 35¾ × 59⅝ ins. Georgia Museum of Art, The University of Georgia, gift of Allyn Cox, Carolyn Cox Lansing and Leonard Cox, courtesy of the National Academy of Design, New York, 1961. GMOA 61.945.

model posed, gave much color to the setting." In 1910 someone discovered it behind a radiator, slashed to pieces, apparently a protest. Dolson, who bought several of Cox's works, suggested drily that he might have to cover a leg in an allegorical painting. Another partial nude embarrassed a maid who told Nellie: "I will be ashamed to come into the room if Mr. Cox is in there." In 1909 Cox asked the Albright Art Gallery if they would accept a painting for an exhibition. "It is a half-nude figure, and it may be that this is an objection in Buffalo? I know it is in some places." Two years later, Henry Moser, an old friend from Ohio student days, reported finding an early sketch Cox did of a red-haired girl poised on a wave, "so shockingly nude, and *natural,* that cold chills ran up and down my back when I fancied what would happen if the police, or my friends, 'found it on me' at some unexpected moment!" This prompted Cox to insist that "I don't think I ever did anything with a smutty intention, but even the most harmless and classic nude is apt to be misunderstood," as he knew from anonymous letters protesting the showing of his works while he lectured at the Art Institute of Chicago. He offered to replace the drawing with a newer one, if Moser would destroy it. And as late as 1913, he stiffly assured one inquirer that he did not use nude models at his studio in Cornish, New Hampshire, but certainly would not reveal their names if he did.[46]

By the late 1890s, Cox employed some nude or partially nude figures in allegorical paintings and murals. He also developed a way of writing as a critic that allowed the wise to know when he was describing nudes without saying so. He did not abandon his commitment to the nude, but with time accepted the limitations of popular taste. In 1918 he warned his son Allyn, studying at the American Academy in Rome, to cover the male genitals to avoid criticism. "As art you are right, but you are likely to get into trouble with the prudish, and I know by experience how difficult it is to get it out of people's heads that you are indecent if you once get it in."[47]

Cox was a formal thinker, not a mystic, and logically adopted classical forms in the 1880s and 1890s to express idealism. This was not entirely new. While studying at the McMicken School, enamored of Fortuny and the reigning modernism, he retained a strong interest in Renaissance precedents. "I believe I have always had a classical-natural feeling in art, and that my natural bent is towards such pictures as the Venus and the centaur that I will paint someday," he wrote in his diary in 1876. He proposed an allegorical painting of Night and Day. "Day perfectly nude, with long hair, if in color, rich gold, flying back in long lines as she joyfully leaps into the air, a glorious life! Night, entirely wrapped in clinging gauzy drapery . . . covering probably even the hands and feet but not hiding them, and *floating gently upward* as the figure descends. In one, the morning star, day's harbinger, and in the other a thin thread of crescent moon." Such an allegory was serious yet sensuous, rich in color and active, satisfying a dual need for order and emotion. Theodore Robinson also wearied of treating the mundane, and hoped to do something large perhaps drawn from the Bible or mythology, in the style of Millet. And Cox had not been in New York a year when he sought decorative work, "which is the work above everything else I should like."[48]

Cox worked out these ideas in a series of complex canvases. He described the first of these, *Vision of Moonrise,* in a letter to his mother in late March 1885. It drew on Renaissance Italian precedents, depicting a "young man on a hillside in the evening, seeing a beautiful female figure, with rose-colored wings and a wealth of red hair, floating down to him from the air as the moon rises over the hills beyond." He had done some preparatory work, including the reclining male's red drapery, but the four-by-five-foot picture was complicated and would require a great deal of effort to finish. Later that same day he sent her another letter with a sketch of the work. This was well-drawn, suggestive yet solid, composed, with two strong figures, and a pastoral background of trees and shrubs, with a steep hillside whose top was a high horizon line for the moon. "I do not know of any other American artist who has attempted anything of the kind, and if I succeed at all with it, it ought to give me a reputation."

The picture soon fascinated Cox, and he worked at it steadily in the midst of regular obligations. By late May he had the female figure photographed and sent a proof home, "which does not do it complete justice." His mother disapproved of the nude figure, and the photo provoked a long-range quarrel with his father, who thought he was wasting time on projects that would not sell. He should tend to illustrations and above all paint landscapes. Cox answered hotly in the best family tradition, resentful of parental criticism and irritated that such educated and thoughtful people still did not understand his motives. He had not foregone any illustration work and insisted that "I have no ability whatever to paint [landscape] except directly from nature," which was hardly possible in New York City. Besides, landscapes gained him neither income nor stature. The people whose opinions he valued saw him as a figure painter and said in effect "that's all well enough, but why should an artist with your training and knowledge of the figure waste his time on landscapes? We expect figure pictures from you." Even if *Vision of Moonrise* failed, he would learn a great deal from such a large and complex project. "I believe that one can do best what one loves best, and even if I never make a success, I prefer a struggle for what seems to me the best, rather than an easy attainment of something lower." He intended to illustrate and teach, and do informal works that might sell, but his heart was in classical allegory that expressed his ideals. "I must be allowed, I think, to keep some such piece of work on hand as this picture, in which apart from all considerations of money or success I will strive for what I love most in art. Otherwise, I should as lief be a clerk or a cobbler." Succeed or fail, he would continue to do classical and ideal works. "Art is my religion, and it is the only thing worth living for, to struggle for the expression of what I like best in art."

There was no arguing with him, and by mid-June 1885, he had finished the picture. He certainly did not compare it to Giorgione or Tintoretto, but "I'm also certain that it is as good as I can make it, and that whatever its shortcomings, they don't come from carelessness or flippancy." He vacationed that summer in Pennsylvania, working on landscape and genre pictures, and returned to the studio to find that *Vision of Moonrise* needed some work, but "on the whole I like it better than I thought I did. I think I have no reason to be ashamed of it." The old ambivalence about whatever he finished compelled him to retouch the picture that winter.[49]

The picture was in the SAA annual exhibition in the spring of 1886. The critics did not quite know what to say. They praised its intent and understood its references to the masters. Cox was clearly talented and dealt with large themes. But the work seemed out of place in a modern exhibition dedicated to less portentous themes. And for all its meanings and the effort involved, at least one critic thought it static. It did not move the spectator. Yet it meant something special to Cox, for he continued to show it and repainted it for the National Academy fall exhibition in 1911 (fig. 18). He was undoubtedly proud of this first large-scale effort, and it symbolized youthful ambitions that he fulfilled in later years. But its emotional meanings for him were complex. He saw it as a variation of the Endymion theme in Greek mythology, a confrontation between a poet-shepherd in this case and a goddess from another plane. "My attempt, of course, is to embody the poetically voluptuous delight that one feels when the disc of the moon swings into one's sight," he wrote Leonard Opdycke. At another level, the picture surely represented his own demands for a higher level of consciousness than the world provided. And the female figure symbolized an idealized superiority in these realms, while neutralizing eroticism.[50]

Cox turned to another ambitious painting. An anonymous reviewer of *The Blessed Damozel* illustrations commented that "the dedication, with its two figures of Painting and Poetry, is one of the best things in the whole work." In this picture, a nude seated female held a paintbrush to symbolize the pictorial arts. She was turned toward another draped female, representing poetry, who strummed a lyre. At their feet, roses and a laurel wreath indicated fame and immortality. Above the heads in an elegant ribbon design ran the legend Ars Picturae, Ars Poetica. A canvas between them held Cox's dedication of the drawings to Will Low. The composition was balanced in the best classical manner. The figures were elegantly painted and almost monumental yet remained real. Their poses owed something to Titian's *Sacred and Profane Love* (ca. 1514), but the picture really drew on the general Renaissance tradition for its idealization of the arts, and on numerous masters such as

FIG. 18. Kenyon Cox, *Vision of Moonrise*. Frontispiece from NAD 1911 annual
exhibition catalogue. Original painting done 1885–86, repainted 1911.
Oil on canvas, 4 × 5 feet, location unknown.
Photo courtesy of the National Academy of Design, New York.

Veronese for its style. The *grisaille* coloring did not detract from the work's elegance or the tradition it echoed.

Various comments about the picture apparently intrigued Cox. The *Blessed Damozel* illustrations enhanced his self-confidence in figure painting, and he now wanted to express classical ideals in a large way. By early 1887 he was at work on a five-by-eight-foot canvas derived from this picture, entitled *Painting and Poetry*. "I have greatly improved it in drawing, and those in whose judgment I have the most confidence tell me that it is vastly better both in form and color than what I have done before," he wrote Low. "I find that my long course of black and white has helped me much in color, making me so much surer of my ability to draw a thing that my mind is free to think of it."

The expanded composition naturally had a new sense of monumentality, but the figures remained real persons. Cox replaced the dedication to Low with a terse Latin epigram, Sororibus Divinis, Picturae, Poesi. This raised the guardians of these arts to divine status, reflecting his belief in their idealizing power, showing that the arts could extend the imagination and emotions in harmonious ways. The picture did not survive, but its coloration was apparently rich. The flesh tones of the nude figure for painting were appealing, and she had flowing red hair. Poetry was draped in white, which Cox painted with easy lines and shading. The roses and laurel wreath added touches of bright color, and there was a flat blue sky behind the figures (fig. 19).

Cox was proud of this canvas and showed it in the spring 1887 exhibition of the SAA. Reviewers praised his intentions and skill and the work's breadth. The picture was impressive, dignified, and serious, but it was hard to see how such work could appeal to modern audiences. In Europe it might win Salon prizes then be purchased as a public decoration. But in America it seemed to be merely an elegant and praiseworthy *succès d'estime*. Cox probably did not expect public approval or appeal, but as usual, praise from peers pleased him. In the meantime, he would go his way in trying to depict ideals. *Painting and Poetry* well expressed his classicism and interest in the Italian Renaissance, whose ideals and aspirations he thought could be adapted for modern life. The work was an important step toward the mural painting to come.[51]

Cox expressed classical ideals in a formal and decorative manner in *Painting and Poetry*. He hoped to do so differently with landscape and figures. "There is a certain ground in art that I particularly love and most intensely desire to excel in," he wrote his skeptical father in 1885. "A mingling of landscape and the human figure."[52] Such a composition could express many traditional ideals and had distinguished antecedents, yet it might also seem modern and expressive.

FIG. 19. Kenyon Cox, *Painting and Poetry* (1887). Oil on canvas, 5 × 8 feet.
Location unknown. Photograph, gift of Allyn Cox, 1959-69-25.
Photo by Ken Pelka. Courtesy of Cooper-Hewitt, National Museum of Design,
Smithsonian Institution/Art Resource, New York.

In late 1889 and early 1890, Cox worked on a four-by-five-foot canvas he
titled *An Eclogue,* which referred to the pastoral ideals of ancient and Renaissance writers and painters. Four female figures dominated the foreground in
the right half of the picture. One, entirely nude, sat on a white sheet, back
to the viewer. Another, fully nude, reclined at her side, facing front, one leg
drawn up, an arm on a sheaf of wheat. Two others stood, loosely embracing
while facing forward, and gave the group a pyramidal composition. One of
the standing figures was nude to the hips, with brilliant red drapery around
her legs. The other wore a blue-and-white-striped robe. The placement of the
three nudes allowed Cox to depict the figure in simultaneous views. Three of
the women had bright red or reddish hair and the other's was black. They
stood against green foliage and a russet tree, with touches of red poppies in
the grass at their feet. The figures were well painted, with a strong sense of

volume, expressing Cox's effort to make the nude seem modern in appearance and traditional in intent. The left half of the picture drew the viewer's eye to a distant landscape. A bright yellow field dominated this small landscape, which contained a nude shepherd holding a staff across his shoulders with both arms, drapery covering his front. A black dog stood at his side. Cox painted the foliage and richly colored field with a feathery touch that recalled the Barbizon mood. The light was vivid but did not dominate the scene. The figures were well realized and the coloring sumptuous. The picture symbolized classical ideals of order, repose, and thoughtful harmony in a bucolic setting. The work was attractive rather than exciting, and it had the gravity and sense of importance that permeated the best of Cox's painting in this style (fig. 20).

Cox sent the picture to the monthly exhibition of the Union League Club in March 1890, and then to the annual spring show of the SAA. His friend William A. Coffin, who did not especially like symbolic works, praised it in measured phrases. As usual, he lauded Cox's breadth of vision and technical skills. The picture obviously did not move him, but he recognized its large intent. "It is an excellent canvas to cite as proof that the art of *picture-making* is not lost sight of by some of our figure painters, in these days when so much praise is given to the more dashing successes obtained by striving not for all, but only for one or two of the many things in the wide range of the painter's art."[53] The picture attracted similar comment elsewhere, but did not sell and remained in the family until given to the national collection.

Cox was busy earning a living and seeking a reputation in the hectic late 1880s. But he had the time and will to express his growing interest in classicism in these varied works for which there was only a small audience and no financial reward. He believed that American art needed complex statements of traditional ideals. Too much attention was focused on the realistic and the mundane, on transitory bits and pieces of nature and life. Someone should express life's wholeness, if only as an ideal, and draw from past masters in art. Such work also would elevate America's whole art into the world cultural order. And of course, there were personal reasons he did not always understand or analyze. For all his often brusque demeanor, Cox was emotional, but it was not his nature to be dramatic or highly responsive. He sought expanded imaginative power and psychic intensity in art, but chiefly in forms with classical overtones resting on harmony, order, and a thoughtful response, thus controlling any disturbing power in feeling.

Although Cox remained personally fascinated with the nude and allegory, he had to earn a living with other kinds of work. His illustrations naturally covered a spectrum of subject matter. Like many artists, he spent fall through spring in New York and some of the summer in the countryside or at the seashore. This schedule helped sustain his interest in landscape, genre, and informal work in general. He also painted some studio genre, most

FIG. 20. Kenyon Cox, *An Eclogue* (1890). Oil on canvas, 48 × 60½ ins.
Courtesy of the National Museum of American Art, Smithsonian Institution, gift of Allyn Cox.

successfully in *The Harp Player* (1888), which showed a woman in a bright red dress playing a large harp in a drawing room or studio. The clothing and instrument contrasted well with the shadowed background. The old-masterish tones made the work dignified. It was well reviewed and became the property of Cox's friend William Merritt Chase. The Metropolitan Museum of Art ultimately purchased it in 1912. Cox saw the work as "a genre in the Dutch vein," which he did "for discipline, and to prove to myself that I could."[54]

Cox also gained a reputation for portraits. He had painted some in Paris and had considerable skill in depicting both the character and appearance of sitters. In the summer of 1885 he took a vacation at the family farm of his friend William A. Coffin in western Pennsylvania. Cox welcomed the rustic atmosphere after a long winter in New York, as he had done in Grez after a siege of Paris. He loafed, ate, and started numerous genre pictures and landscapes. One hot day Coffin appeared in white clothes and a straw hat that captured Cox's fancy. "I have begun a picture of him sitting under an apple tree with spots of sunlight," he wrote his mother. "We think it will be pretty good." Coffin returned the favor with a study of Cox smoking a pipe at work in the farm's carpentry shop. These two informal studies won favorable comment among friends that fall and appeared in the SAA spring exhibition the following year.[55]

Cox also painted some portraits of family members and friends. The most supportive of these was Leonard Opdycke, who had graduated from Harvard Law School and was practicing in New York. Opdycke had been Cox's friend through good times and bad and had long since learned to ignore his occasional surliness and biting tongue. He probably understood Cox better than anyone else and believed in his greatness. Privately wealthy, he offered loans in hard times, which Cox did not take, and bought several paintings. Cox drew elegant designs for two books that Opdycke translated in special editions. In 1888 he did a small portrait of Opdycke's mother, which was well displayed at the NAD autumn show. "I received several compliments on it. People seem to like it better than I had expected them to." In 1897 he essayed a portrait of Opdycke's wife. He disliked the yellow background that the couple wanted to highlight her black dress. Cox explained at length how color produced and complemented character, and that yellow was too high for Mrs. Opdycke in this case. In the process, he showed attention to detail and understanding of the portraitist's art. In the end, after much repainting, the yellow remained, and he satisfied Opdycke.[56]

Cox also did an interesting portrait of his friend Will Low. In it, Low sat at a working table, facing the viewer to his right, one arm on the chairtop, the other on the desk holding a cigarette. He had an assured, purposeful air. Shelves on the wall held the usual bric-a-brac associated with painters, pots of color, brushes, props. A window admitted light and provided a truncated view of the world beyond the room. The strong angles of objects in the picture formed interesting designs, and a sense of flattened space made the work seem complex and somewhat mysterious without losing its authority. Cox dedicated this effective picture, *A Studio Corner*, to Low's wife.[57]

Cox was able to combine his interests in individual character and classicism in a magisterial portrait of the sculptor Augustus Saint Gaudens in 1887. Cox had met Saint Gaudens briefly in Paris when both were students, but knew him better as part of the circle of aspiring young artists he encountered in New York City after 1883. The sculptor helped Cox get illustration commissions, some of which involved his own works. By the spring of 1884, Cox was writing an article on Saint Gaudens for the prestigious *Century Magazine*. Saint Gaudens quickly gained fame for portrait statues of prominent people and for elegant relief work in medallions and plaques. He became an ideal as well as a friend for Cox, who saw him as a harbinger of the second Renaissance he so often discussed. He praised the sculptor's stylish combination of realism and classical values in work after work. In Cox's view, Saint Gaudens depicted individual character and yet linked sculpture and design to the grand tradition. The work was elegant but never chic, real but not merely realistic, heroic but not bombastic. He praised Saint Gaudens over emerging modern sculptors because he sought order, harmony, and the appropriate design for an idea or emotion rather than mere self-expression.[58]

Cox's portrait showed his respect for a master sculptor, affection for a friend, and homage to an ideal. The large picture, about three by four feet, depicted the sculptor in the studio in right profile, cropped at the waist, with right forearm bared, working on the clay model of a portrait medallion of their mutual friend William Merritt Chase. The strong angles of the stand holding the clay added to the figure's sense of authority. Pieces of Saint Gaudens's work in the background emphasized his ties to tradition. Behind the sculptor, in middle view, sat the enigmatic bust *Femme inconnue* from the Louvre, which had captivated Cox and many other artists with an elegant appearance and repose that seemed to mask hidden emotions. Cox painted the subject's white shirt with great skill, and there was a compelling sense of energy in the flexed wrist. Saint Gaudens's dark hair and beard contrasted well with the buff tones that gave the picture a sense of calm authority (fig. 21). Cox showed the work in the spring 1888 SAA exhibition, and it was an immediate success. Critics recognized it as a great academic portrait and understood its larger intellectual implications. In 1889 Saint Gaudens returned the favor with a likeness of Cox in an oblong bronze medallion. The picture was destroyed in a fire in Saint Gaudens's studio in 1904, and Cox created an almost exact replica in 1908 as a memorial after Saint Gaudens's death.[59]

In the relatively short time since coming to New York in 1883, Cox had become a significant figure in the art world. He earned a reasonable living

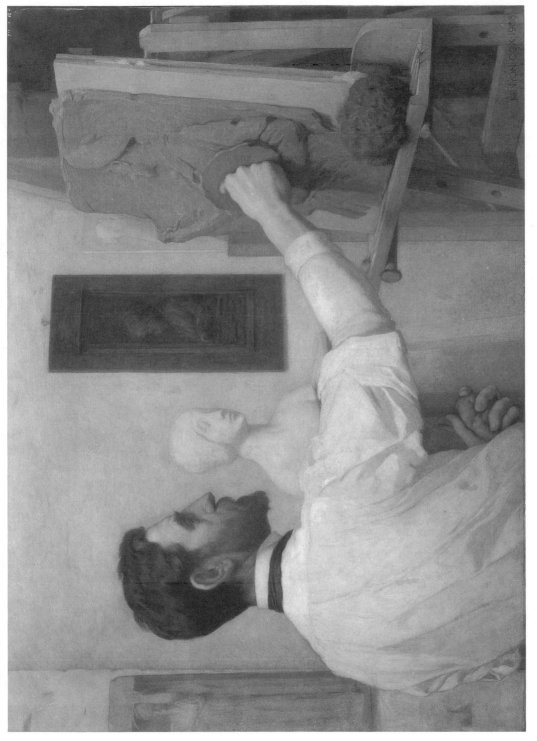

FIG. 21. Kenyon Cox, *Augustus Saint Gaudens* (1908). Oil on canvas, 33½ × 47⅛ ins. Courtesy of the Metropolitan Museum of Art, gift of friends of the sculptor, through August F. Jaccaci, 1908 (08.130).

from teaching, illustrating, occasional sales, and writing. He had met influential friends among the rising generation of moderns who could help his career and with whom he generally felt at home, despite his steadily growing interest in more traditional forms of art and expression. In spite of uncertainties, he liked the busy art life and had a strong sense of accomplishment and growth. He was already known as a rising spokesman of classical ideals, which fulfilled his ambitions for respectable attention and authority, if it did not always pay the bills. By 1891 an old friend from Warren was justified in writing Cox's mother of "Ken's rising fame as an artist."[60] And she could take pride that he was well on the way to achieving the status she thought his due.

IV

ART LIFE

&

NEW RELATIONSHIPS

THE 1880S WERE HECTIC FOR
Cox, absorbed as he was in making a living and in trying to extend his art
into personally satisfying realms. Art was the focus of his emotional and professional life, but his long-standing interests in other intellectual activities
continued. He remained a steady and somewhat eclectic reader, enjoying
both current literature and the heavier art history that helped refine his ideas
and support his formal criticism. Poetry was also a significant outlet for his
emotions. From childhood he kept notebooks of verse, often mere doggerel
but sometimes elaborate narratives. These works reflected a need to state and
clarify intimate thoughts and to express expansive romantic or sentimental
ideas within controlled emotions.

Cox published several poems that revealed the range of his thought and
ability in the medium. In the summer of 1884, he essayed a light emotional kind of verse in a full-page illustrated poem for the *Century Magazine*. In the small but elaborate picture accompanying the poem, he drew
himself from an old photograph done in student days, seated in tights
and a jester's cap, playing the flute. On the right edge of the picture
he placed a kissing couple, and on the left another duo strolling arm
in arm. These figures made a balanced composition. A romantic castle
and landscape filled the background, which he drew with finesse and a
strong sense of both poetic intimacy and good perspective. The entire
scene balanced whimsy, romance, and historic associations in a fine small
illustration that was under firm artistic control. But the poem attracted the
most attention:

Buss me, buss me,
Bauble mine!
Be my love and
I'll be thine.
All the court
has come a-maying
All the court at love
is playing.
Men are sighing, maids
are singing.
Through the woods their
laughter ringing,
Gathring flowers, giv-
ing kisses—
We poor fools have no
such blisses.
Be my love and I'll be
thine.
Buss me, Buss me, Bauble
mine.

The sentiments were sophomoric or romantic, as the reader wished. But many people thought both the scene and poem frankly sensuous, with the open invitation to kissing and the carefree atmosphere. Art students quickly adopted the illustration as a kind of coy talisman of at least modest rebellion against conventional mores.[1]

Cox's emotions were more subtle and complex in another poem he published that fall. The small bust in the later Saint Gaudens portrait, *Femme inconnue,* played a significant role in his emotional life. Shortly after arriving in Paris in 1877, he saw it at the Louvre and returned several times to study both its technical qualities and emotional meanings. It was attributed to an unknown fifteenth-century Florentine sculptor, who had used low relief and smooth flowing lines to create a unified mass that was realistic as a portrait yet highly charged with subdued general emotion. The expression of calm melancholy hinted at feelings that time and life had harmonized after struggle. Cox wrote his mother in 1878 that it was "the most delicately sweet and pure [sculpture] of anything I know." This partly resulted from the sculptor's willingness to speak through the subject rather than with technique. "The head set square on the long neck above the flattened breasts and inconspicuous modeling, the hair covered by a close-fitting cap down over the forehead, no fluttering of draperies and twisting of attitude, but everything almost puritanic in its quietness, yet a bewitching subtle smile round the fine-lined mouth and out of the slanting eyes under their flat brows." He made several drawings, including one only 5-by-2½ inches. He and others appreciated the work's calm understatement of large ideas. It was both realistic and symbolic, speaking to the classicist's need for intense but controlled emotion. Casts of it adorned the studios of many artists, and there was "a regular cult of the Unknown Lady" in the 1880s and 1890s.

In the summer of 1883, Cox wrote a poem on the themes that she symbolized and incorporated it in his first article on sculpture the following year. He was enamored of the work's "lowness and vagueness of relief, the floating, undefined modelling, the delicate finish of surfaces, the exquisite modulation and subtle curvature of line, the frank simplicity of aim, the individuality and vitality of the whole, all in their utmost perfection." The bust symbolized many emotional aspects of the ideal nude as well as of larger classical ideals. "What a work of art and what a pearl of woman!" The poem's emotions were surprisingly frank, told in a credible story with mystery and romance, but controlled with a classical mood and object:

> She lived in Florence centuries ago,
>   That lady smiling there.
> What was her name or rank I do not know—
>   I know that she was fair.
>
> For some great man—his name, like hers, forgot
>   And faded from Men's sight—
> Loved her—he must have loved her—and has wrought
>   This bust for our delight.
>
> Whether he gained her love or had her scorn
>   Full happy was his fate.
> He saw her, heard her speak; he was not born
>   Four hundred years too late.
>
> The palace throngs in every room but this—
>   Here I am left alone.
> Love, there is none to see—I press a kiss
>   Upon thy lips of stone.

The poem was an immediate success in art circles and gained Cox considerable attention. The poem and its Unknown Lady symbolized the need among artists, especially those with classical interests, for intense emotion expressed through acceptable forms, and for the idealization of women. Such outlets were safe expressions of desire. The bust had enduring significance for Cox, who used it in illustrations and always took care to reproduce it well.[2]

As time passed, the tone of his public poetry became more lofty, as befitted his growing reputation as a classicist. A decade later in 1895, he published another poem that summarized his idealism about the artist's role in
intensifying emotion through sacrifice, and on the function of art in culture:

> Work thou for pleasure; paint or sing or carve
> The thing thou lovest, though the body starve.
> Who works for glory misses oft the goal;
> Who works for money coins his very soul;
> Work for the work's sake, then, and it may be
> That these things shall be added unto thee.

This poem, titled "The Gospel of Art," was equally popular and was included
in the standard reference work *Bartlett's Quotations*.[3] Cox steadily gained a
reputation for having broad culture, which added to his stature as an artist of
ideals that others respected even if they did not follow his example.

These poetic sentiments, whether romantic or elevated, were important to
Cox and helped his reputation, and perhaps alleviated the daily grind. As
with many painters, life seemed to alternate between periods of calm and
intense labor against deadlines. This had emotional drawbacks, given his
fears of failure and tendencies to have the "blues" when under pressure. The
daily routine provided a sense of personal order, however. He rose early,
breakfasted at a local restaurant, then went to the League on class mornings.
At noon he had lunch and gratefully sat "a half hour or so over my coffee to
talk with other artists who dine there. Then back to work until it gets too
dark to see or I get too tired to work." He often dined with artists who
drifted in and out of a boarding house on Fifty-fourth Street. A French
woman, one Madame Harral, offered a room for socializing and good, inexpensive cuisine. For those who had studied in Paris, she seemed to echo the
boulevards and ateliers. For those who had not, she was exotic and unusual,
almost "bohemian." She was indulgent and allowed the men to visit the
kitchen to sample the contents of pots and skillets. During meals they sang,
composed doggerel, and reported artistic news. For a group of single men
who worked long and tiring days, the scene recalled more exotic times as
students in Paris, substituted for home life, and hinted at domesticity.

The art world was close knit and supportive, and most painters kept open
house in their studios at least one day a week, as Cox did on Friday after-
noons. He served modest refreshments, but most of the time passed in earnest conversation about work in progress, hoped-for commissions, or small
talk that relieved the hard work at the easel and drawing board. Time could
hang heavily. "Sometimes I drop in at a friend's studio and gabble," he wrote
his mother. If he had the money, he might attend the theater but was more
likely to play whist with equally lonely and penurious friends. Married art-

ists sometimes took pity on his single state and invited him for dinner and some non-art conversation. The family in Ohio probably thought art life was glamorous, but he assured them that his days were pretty much alike.

His mother naturally worried about his tendency toward self-absorption and nagged him to be more sociable. He appreciated her concern but resisted such efforts at control. "I'm sorry you don't approve of my conduct in not going out more," he responded testily in 1886, "but really I haven't time—what with teaching and writing and illustrating and painting how is one ever to get very many hours in the day-time to go down to Broadway in the hope of meeting some Vanderbilt or other? Some artists do what is called the 'society racket' counting on acquaintanceships and society connections for commissions and success, but that's not my line." The family also worried about his health, and he did suffer from colds, including a bad "quinsy," or tonsillitis, that interrupted his work on *The Blessed Damozel* illustrations in the summer of 1886. He finally spent late July at his physician's home at Sag Harbor, Long Island, and allowed the doctor's wife to mother him. "I read vast quantities of bad novels and one good one (*Kidnapped* [1886]—what a ripper it is!) and thoroughly enjoyed myself," he wrote Will Low. His health and emotional state were variable during these years, but for one allegedly so frail, he produced an extraordinary quantity of varied work.[4]

Cox developed a social life, but many people found him difficult. He spoke without considering the effect on others and was likely to snap at people who did not know their facts. To some degree, these were defenses against uncertainties, but he took art very seriously and assumed that everyone else did so. His friend William A. Coffin wrote the most perceptive analysis of his mind and demeanor in 1891. He noted that Cox simply did not realize that others could not follow his rigorous mind, or be as totally informed as he. "Self reliant and persistent, he reasons clearly and logically, and acts upon his conclusion." Criticism did not change his course, but he could be kind, and no one worked harder for causes that the art community valued. "High minded and absorbed in his own world, he takes little heed of the concern of others except when he is appealed to, and then he is always ready and willing to give his friends the same conscientious thought and the same energetic action that he brings to his own affairs." Coffin understood that his friend wanted art to be elevating, and to be central to a society that could afford to temper materialism with culture and ideals. He overlooked Cox's demeanor because "he has energy of intellect sufficient for a whole company." And Cox really did not perceive his effect on others. Once when an acquaintance left the room after speaking rudely, he asked innocently of fellow guest William Merritt Chase, "Why should a man speak like that?" Chase could not resist the opening and answered with good humor, "For God's sake, Cox, don't you know that *you* always speak like that?"[5]

Cox soon became a regular participant in the social activities focused on Washington Square and Gramercy Park. He circulated among painters and sculptors and knew writers such as William Dean Howells, and the visitors they hosted from home and abroad. He gained the attention of Richard Watson Gilder, the influential publisher of the *Century Magazine* and a noted author, who with his wife Rosamund was an arbiter of taste. He could see and hear such luminaries as Mark Twain, the Belgian violinist Eugène Ysaÿe, and the Polish pianist Ignace Jan Paderewski.[6]

He continued to love music and attended as many concerts and operas as he could afford. He saw a production of Verdi's *Rigoletto* (1851) with a family friend, "which I think we both thought rather stupid." He was more taken with Wagner's *Lohengrin* (1850), which he saw with the visiting Will Cochran. They had uncomfortable balcony seats in the new Metropolitan Opera House, "but I think I never enjoyed opera so much before," he wrote his father. "I came home with the swan song haunting me and could hardly get rid of it all night. I think it is a lovely thing altogether. One can't but wonder at the thick-headedness of the world that took twenty years to find it out."[7]

Cox especially enjoyed the social events organized around Saint Gaudens. He quickly idealized both the sculptor and his work. Saint Gaudens was a perfectionist who often took years to attain a desired effect, but whose finished work seemed effortless. His elegant compositions combined realism and personal gesture with a sense of harmony and classical perfection. He also had a potent personal charm and self-assurance, which impressed the insecure Cox. The sculptor's interest in good living, music, and literate conversation was also attractive. Saint Gaudens liked Cox well enough, and admired his idealism, but came to think that he wrote better than he painted. If Cox ever realized this, he did not say so, and the two often exchanged visits, criticism, and art news, both in New York and later in Cornish where they were neighbors.

Saint Gaudens enjoyed music and started hosting chamber concerts for friends in 1882 with musicians from a local beer garden. These affairs were so popular that he engaged professional musicians to play on Sundays between October and May, usually in the spacious studio building at 148 West Thirty-sixth Street, which he had renovated for his larger works. These events were opportunities to wear formal dress and mingle with famous and unusual people, as well as to hear good music. "That long white studio became a familiar meeting place for all who were interested in any form of art," Cox recalled later. "I meet clever people there," he wrote his father in 1884. "Everybody in the literary or artisic world that comes to New York seems to be brought there as a matter of course." At one gathering, the English critic Edmund Gosse suavely said that Cox's was "one of the names best known in

England." He was flattered but realistic. "Flummery mostly, I take it, though I suppose they know my *Century* work there."[8]

Cox enjoyed city life and studio work, but summer brought the desire for a change of scenery and routine. Artists tried to leave New York after the exhibition season ended in May, for the seashore, mountains, or backcountry in nearby states. As in Paris, summers in the country were a release from routine, times to challenge received wisdom and accepted methods. In the summer of 1884, Cox visited the small seaport of Magnolia, Massachusetts. The painter William Morris Hunt had become interested in this fishing village in the late 1870s. He persuaded the inhabitants that a few improvements would make it an attractive summer resort and artist colony. It looked like many places in Europe, with picturesque fishermen and reticent local types. Rocky coves, beaches, and cliffs were good subjects for painters. Cox shared rooms and dining facilities with several other painters. The locale brought out his romanticism. "It's lots of fun to climb around the rocks," he wrote Leonard Opdycke. "I always imagine myself a melodramatic smuggler with two brace of pistols in my belt." He meant to do some seascapes and genre studies but was more tired than he thought. "I have ground out such a quantity of stuff last winter that my brains don't seem to be equal just yet to the serious work I thought I wanted to do," he wrote Opdycke again at the end of his first week's stay. "Perhaps a spell of loafing is the best thing for them." As summer went on, he started several canvases but let nature take its course and relaxed. He read the works of Pepys, Trollope, and Thackeray. Dolson and his family arrived and they all went sailing on his boat. Dolson was "an enthusiastic sailor, and when I say I sail I mean only that I sit in the boat while he manages it," he wrote Will Low. In addition, he played tennis, swam a little, and read to a group of ladies doing needlework. "In short, I have discovered a number of little *talents de société* in myself of which I was unaware and am surprised to find myself so valuable a personage." At the summer's end he had not finished many pictures but had thoroughly enjoyed himself.[9]

A year later at the end of May 1885, Cox was eager to leave New York again. He wanted to do some informal work after doing a lot of illustrating and wrote his mother that "I've got the landscape fever pretty bad." By mid-June he had accepted an invitation to stay with Coffin on the family farm near Jennerstown, southeast of Pittsburgh. The German butcher, at whose establishment he and friends often ate, gave them a fine send-off with a buffet of spring chicken, lobster, champagne, "and *tout le tremblement*." He and Coffin took the train to Pittsburgh, then went over awful country roads to the farm, which was in wooded, rolling terrain. They earned their keep haying, feeding livestock, and repairing fencing and buildings. "I have been haying with the others and have got fairly skilful with the horse-rake," he proudly wrote home. He ate continuously and gained some needed weight and became bronze under the sun.

He also started several pictures, including landscape and genre studies, and one of evening. "The moon is breaking through the clouds at the top and the sky is pale with a few twinkling stars," he wrote his mother. "The distant hill is dark with a road dimly seen winding up it to a village whose yellow lights show against the sky. The foreground is in broad moonlight. A big black oak tree, massive and dark, fills the left side of the picture, and a row of little sapling maples in perspective cuts the sky on the right."

The preceding summer in Magnolia had reminded him of the wealth of subjects outside the studio and had sharpened his interest in natural contrast and drama. The farm now opened his eyes to a fresh sense of color in nature. He knew this, especially from the summers at Grez, but it was easy to forget in New York. "Color is my great study now," he wrote home. "Drawing one can learn in the school, and the ability to paint faithfully a bit from nature, but pictorial color one must get, if at all, afterward, and I think I am improving in that direction." And the American landscape was both more subtle and more dramatic than its painters had revealed, as the oncoming fall showed in late September. "The reds, yellows and greens are all of a singular metallic richness like the colors of some rare water fowl," he wrote his mother in a felicitous phrase. "I never saw, since I can remember, anything so fine, and am lost in wonder at the stupidity of the painters who have painted 'autumn scenes' in crude reds and yellows until they have made people believe that an American autumn is ugly." Back in New York, he thought the summer had been critical in his development as a colorist. In years to come, he took working vacations in such places as Put-in-Bay, Ballast Island, off Toledo in Lake Erie. He also revisited Magnolia, then settled in a permanent summer home in Cornish, New Hampshire, in the late 1890s.[10]

Cox's social life indicated growing stature and familiarity in the art community. Despite fears of failure, he was ambitious and tenacious once he set goals. The first months in New York in 1883 were filled with uncertainty, but his self-confidence grew as it became clear that he would succeed at least in making a living. He understood that knowing the right people would make that success certain. Even by the winter of 1883, he had made numerous contacts among rising artists. "I am getting into the best artistic crowd here, St. Gaudens, Dewing, and other of the best men we have," he wrote home, "and they all compliment me on my landscapes and other work." As illustration commissions, writing assignments, and occasional teaching jobs appeared, he savored some modest self-congratulation. "I think on the whole that I have every reason to congratulate myself on my good fortune in getting into work so soon," he wrote his mother, and could not help adding: "You see that an acquaintance among the artists does count for something after all." He attributed success in getting *The Blessed Damozel*

commission in 1886 to a reputation among artists, which he could only hope
would someday translate into popularity.[11]

Even Cox's brief stint as a critic did not cost many friends. Knowledgeable
artists recognized that however caustic his tone, his judgments were usually
right. His intensity and earnestness reflected idealism, and he obviously
wanted art to be important in American life. He also had considerable organizational ability and was willing to spend time and energy on art matters,
which marked him for roles in art organizations, including the SAA. The
influential writer and editor Richard Watson Gilder, his wife Rosamund,
Saint Gaudens, and other younger artists established this group in 1877 in
reaction against the exhibition policies of the NAD, which allegedly favored
older members. Cox was elected a member and began exhibiting with them
in 1882.

The SAA annual spring exhibition became a major focus for the work of
younger people. Even by May 1884, while still a relative newcomer to the
scene, Cox was involved in the society's affairs. Though busy making illustrations, he worked hard as a juror and on the hanging committee for the
spring exhibition. This reflected both regard for him among artists and their
understanding that he would do the work. Cox was gratified to be asked but
felt that the society work was "the hardest and the most thankless work I ever
undertook." And who could tell how long the wounds opened in the selection process would remain open? "I believe that all the members of the jury
did their work honestly and impartially, but we have raised a storm of exe-
cration not only among the refused, but among the newspapers. However, I
am not sorry to have gone through with the thing if it does not lose me half
my friends," he wrote his mother. He assured Leonard Opdycke that he had
tried to be impartial. But "the hardest thing has been to vote against the
pictures of personal friends from a feeling of duty, and to meet them afterwards." By 1890 he thought the society offered the public the best in current
art and was a viable alternative to the NAD. He was the organization's secretary for many years, handling routine matters and a flood of correspondence. He became a member of the governing board, and then vice president
in 1905. In the following year he was on the committee that negotiated the
society's merger with the Academy.[12]

Cox was less enamored of the Academy in the early 1880s. This venerable
body, dating from 1825, was the most publicly prestigious art institution.
The most famous American artists had been members, and it was the closest
thing to an official supporter of native art. Its autumn and spring exhibitions
were major cultural events. But Cox naturally first thought of himself as
something of an iconoclast, though hardly a radical, and was more comfortable with the younger people in the SAA. On arriving in New York in October 1883, he sent two unnamed pictures to the Academy jury for the fall
exhibition. Having exhibited at the Paris Salons between 1879 and 1882, he

had some reason to hope for acceptance, but the jury rejected both. He affected indifference, especially because a newcomer's work probably would not have been displayed well. He grew closer to the Academy each year and exhibited regularly after 1884. In 1889 he won the prestigious Second Hallgarten Prize for a figure study entitled *November*. This was gratifying, because the exhibitors chose the winners. Equally important, he received two hundred dollars. He was elected an associate in 1900 and a full academician in 1903. These dates were somewhat late for an artist of his ability, and may have reflected some hesitation among other painters about his candid personality, as well as the limited appeal of his chosen style. In any event, he devoted considerable time to the body's business as a juror and committeemember the rest of his life.[13]

Cox's increasing visibility in the art world took him into national politics as part of a movement to exempt imported art works from tariff duties. The protective system was a major issue between the two national parties and figured in every presidential campaign between 1880 and 1912. Republicans generally favored high duties that shielded American business from competition with cheaper foreign goods. This kept some prices high but protected American workers while allowing domestic business to develop and compete with foreigners whose wage rates and production costs were lower. This stance thus appealed to many in the labor movement as well as in business. In the late 1880s, the Democrats began to favor lower rates both to help their constituents buy cheap foreign goods and to reduce the role of government in the economy. The issue was also highly emotional, with Republicans defending the country against foreign economic power. The coalition behind the tariff was always insecure and militantly opposed reducing the rates for any import, including art, as this might start a process that would destroy the system. The Morrill Act of 1860 levied a 10 percent rate on imported art, which the so-called Mongrel Tariff of 1883 raised to 30 percent. The tax was not applied to art works imported for museums or educational institutions, or to those simply to be exhibited. To protectionists, art was a luxury, and the tax justifiably fell on rich collectors. Politicians would not very well reduce or repeal it and tax imported clothing, tools, or household goods. To them, dealers in art were like dealers in anything else and deserved no special treatment. And supporters of free art tended to be affluent, urban intellectuals, an ideal foil for politicians speaking for ordinary voters. Artists who embarked on this crusade talking of high cultural and esthetic values entered an arena fraught with animosity.

Richard Watson Gilder spoke early for free art. After returning from a European trip in 1880, he began to press friends in Congress to remove the duty but got nowhere. The idea nevertheless developed with the rising interest in tariff reform during the decade. In 1884 Cox's old mentor Jean-Léon Gérôme wrote a comprehensive letter to the New York art dealer William

Schaus that outlined how foreigners saw the tax. He thought that a rich country like the United States could easily do without the small revenue involved. The tariff did not foster any home industry, because art production and consumption defied the usual economic rules. The tax also prevented Americans from buying or seeing some great art. And, of course, France had educated many American artists at the Ecole des Beaux-Arts for nothing and did not tax imported art. He thought posterity would find it odd that "in one country alone were they [art works] saddled with an excessive tax, and that country was the youngest, the greatest, and the wealthiest of nations." In the same year the Union League Club of New York circulated a questionnaire among artists and found that only a small fraction favored any duty on imported art.

Artists soon began to organize like any other interest group. Several met in February 1889, as a new debate on the tariff loomed in Congress, and appointed a committee to plan a national campaign. In March they founded the National Free Art League, with J. Carroll Beckwith as president, William M. Chase as vice-president, and Cox as secretary. A year later they had more than twelve hundred members.[14] Cox worked hard for the cause, both as an officer of the league and as a true believer. The new administration of Benjamin Harrison favored protection, and a Republican Congress would meet to revise the tariff in December 1889. Cox and fellow reformers began their campaign with resolutions from art societies and bodies, articles in the press, and lobbying among sympathetic politicians. Cox, Coffin, and Beckwith testified before the House Ways and Means Committee in Washington on December 30, 1889. They cited the heavy support for repeal among artists and insisted that this would promote domestic art and manufacturing.

Cox's personal views were relatively simple. "Make importation free, then let art alone to take care of itself," he wrote one inquirer in March 1889. "Travelling scholarships might do good if we could be certain to keep them apart from politics." He elaborated his views with the usual vigor in a series of articles for the *Nation*. He realized that artists were in the odd position of demanding an end to protection, but their case was special. The duty did not help them, because an artist's reputation at a given moment determined the cost of a work. Sometimes the tariff ironically benefitted dealers, who cited it as proof that foreign art was more valuable than American work. The charge that eliminating the tax would benefit the rich was specious. Government did not support the arts; repealing the duty would simply leave individuals more money for collections they meant to give the public. In the end, the great question was one of culture's value. "No, art is not a luxury," he insisted, "it is civilization." The public could not raise its standards of taste without an expanding body of art to see.

Cox was equally forceful in dealing with powerful individuals, such as Senator John Sherman of Ohio, whose Finance Committee managed the tariff bill in the upper house. Cox rehearsed the intellectual arguments for Sherman, then shrewdly focused on material gains likely to follow repeal. "We believe that the cultivation of art in a country is not only elevating, refining and civilizing, but is worth vast sums of money to that country through its reflexive action on manufacturers." France, which supported its arts lavishly, proved this with lucrative art exports. Repealing the measure also would please artists and patrons, who "consider the tax at present imposed a barbarism unworthy of a civilized country, and we loathe and detest it in consequence. May we hope that its days are numbered?" Elsewhere, he insisted that a free flow of art would elevate public taste and foster support of American art, as protectionists allegedly hoped. The House finally favored free art, the Senate retained the 30 percent rate, and the conference adopted 15 percent. The reformers literally won half the loaf in the McKinley Act of 1890.[15]

Cox spent a good deal of time and energy on this first effort to remove the duty, and his interest somewhat subsided with partial victory. But he continued to send out literature and to answer questions as secretary of the league. "There is no demand for a tax on art and no excuse for it," he wrote one correspondent in 1892. The reelection of the tariff reformer Grover Cleveland in that year with a Democratic Congress gave reformers fresh hope of total victory. Early in 1893 Cox asked Gilder the "most delicate and proper way to approach Mr. Cleveland on the Free Art business." Though very busy, he undertook another letter-writing effort before Congress assembled in special session that fall. He wrote Cleveland that "the abolition of this special tax would be of great service to the cause of art and of civilization and would be highly gratifying not only to the artists of this country but to all who are interested in the advance of culture in America and in the world at large." This time the reformers succeeded, and the Wilson-Gorman Act of 1894 repealed the duty. The National Free Art League disbanded on March 21, 1895. It had raised a total of $624.55 and had a cash balance of $187.54, which it gave to the Municipal Art Society of New York. Cox had given twenty dollars.

The celebration was premature. The Dingley Act of 1897 restored a rate of 20 percent. Cox was busy with other interests thereafter but attacked the tax whenever possible, and often reminded people of what an odd policy it was for the United States. In 1904 he thanked Isabella Stewart Gardner for a tour of her collection in Boston. "To have got such things together, and to let others see them now and then, is to be a public benefactor who would be decorated, not taxed, by the government if we lived in a truly civilized country." The struggle went on into Cox's later years, and in 1913 he attempted to lobby President Woodrow Wilson, a summer neighbor in Cornish. The Underwood Act of that year finally repealed the duty.[16] The long effort had gained Cox considerable reputation in the art community, tested his organizational skills, and added to his general reputation.

Amid all these duties, Cox decided to visit the Paris Universal Exposition of 1889. He occasionally talked of returning to Europe, usually for only a brief time. He did not wish to become an expatriate or to shuttle between the continents, as so many friends did. "I expect to make New York my permanent home as far as I can see now," he wrote his mother in 1885. But with the passage of each year, narrowly focused on daily work, he realized the need for a study trip, especially to see art outside of France. "I suppose it is hard for you to understand my intense longing to see some really great and beautiful art again," he wrote his father in 1886. "If you can imagine yourself deprived of all good books for three years perhaps you can understand."[17] The exposition was to be a major international event and would have a good cross-section of current art as well as strong retrospective exhibitions.

In the fall of 1888, Rush C. Hawkins, who was in charge of the American fine arts exhibits, began to select a jury for American entries. Another group in Paris chose works from Americans who lived abroad. The NAD named twelve artists, including Worthington Whittredge, who became president. The SAA offered another five, including Beckwith, Coffin, Cox, Saint Gaudens, and Weir. Almost predictably, Cox became secretary. The effort was thankless, with the usual disappointment and outrage among the refused, but the chosen works were ready to ship to Paris by late March 1889. The American was the largest foreign exhibit, with 572 works, including 336 paintings by 189 artists; 117 drawings by 32 artists; 16 sculptures by 11 sculptors; and 102 assorted engravings, lithographs, and etchings by 21 artists.

The jury selected four of Cox's paintings and six drawings, which attested to his stature and to the appropriateness of these works for showing abroad. *Painting and Poetry* was a natural choice for a French exposition, with its classical allusions, complexity, and elegant figures. The portrait of Saint Gaudens was equally logical as an elegant statement of large ideas in a realistic vein. *Flying Shadows* was a good example of American landscape. And *Jacob Wrestling with the Angel* (1887), was an allegorical figure work on a familiar theme, bound to interest foreign viewers. The drawings were more intimate genre work, but in general Cox spoke for the cosmopolitan, classical element in American painting. The international jury announced awards late in June. Cox received a third-class bronze medal in each category, one of only four artists with such dual honors.[18]

On July 20, Cox followed the pictures across the Atlantic on the French steamer *La Champagne*. The voyage was uneventful, and he read, played deck games, and mingled with the passengers. For once he had adequate funds, from illustrations, the sale of a picture, and from the Hallgarten Prize and the sale of its winner *November*. He proposed to have fun, study art, and paint nothing. "I do not mean to do any work of any kind while over here," he wrote his mother upon arriving. [19]

He went immediately to the huge art exhibition at the elaborate fairgrounds. Contemporary French work showed a high average, but he saw no striking newcomers. "The best men are the same ones I admired seven years ago," he wrote home. He liked most the one-hundred-year retrospective of French paintings and thought its Millets and Corots were especially fine for the mood they evoked and the superb talent they revealed. The foreign work was not particularly striking and seemed derivative and thin. The American exhibition was in a large square room, poorly lit and indifferently hung, but showed "a larger proportion of work in the direction of the fine old things than any other." His own canvases looked good. "I have nothing to complain of personally." *Painting and Poetry* was hung at eye level amid other large works but dominated the area. Its "two large figures of noble bearing" attracted some attention from the French. Visiting American critics clearly preferred what the writer Harold Frederic called "Kenyon Cox's felicitous portrait of the sculptor, 'St. Gaudens at Work.' " *Flying Shadows* also gained approval as an excellent landscape. [20]

Of course, there was a great deal more to the exposition than art. The controversial Eiffel Tower that loomed over the grounds was impressive, though hardly pretty, and seemed smaller than it did in photographs. Various groups and nations displayed their wares and acted out their customs for tourists. Cox liked the Javanese dancers, whose brilliant costumes and stylized motions were impressive and artistic. A corps of male Sudanese dancers attracted onlookers with their bold maneuvers and rich costumes, which included rattles and strings of goats' feet. Cox thought the French did such expositions very well and liked the basic architecture, but he found a good deal of the scene tiresome. "There must be no end to study in any direction, but one must take his choice. Machinery, etc., is unintelligible to me and what should I get from gaping at it?" [21] He did the old rounds in the city and saw several friends, including Coffin.

He went on to visit the principal cities and galleries in Belgium and the Netherlands. Ghent and Bruges seemed quaint but somnolent. Brussels by contrast was a bustling modern city with new commercial architecture that looked alike but was impressive. Many of the medieval streets and squares remained and appealed to his artist's eye. He wanted to see the works of the Flemish school and began to revise his opinion of Rubens. Critics depicted this master as somewhat vulgar in his lavish use of color, loose drawing, and sumptuous nudes. Cox thought some of this criticism was fair, but on looking at the actual pictures in the Royal Museum and elsewhere, began to see classicism and grand effects in Rubens that he liked. He went on to Antwerp by train, arriving just as a huge fire in a suburban cartridge factory covered the area in smoke. The city was not very interesting, but once again he paused over Rubens's paintings. "On the whole, the only thing worth coming for is the number of pictures by Rubens, and I don't much care for Rubens, though I like him better than I expected to." Whatever his doubts, he needed to know this work better. "His is one of the big names and one wants to know for himself what one thinks of him, not take him on trust."[22]

The Netherlands was captivating. The country was hardly larger than an American county but was neat and well ordered, with an almost man-made landscape, filled with trees, flowers, and carefully tended plots of land. It was heavily populated, but the people remained polite and picturesque. Many wore traditional costumes, which Cox sketched in letters home. The cultural atmosphere was relaxed. "I think if I had to be a king, I should like to be the king of Holland." And there were other attractions. He spent a good deal of time in every city's museum. He admired Rembrandt and knew his greatest works from popular illustrations. "I could swear that I knew the very color of Rembrandt's 'Anatomy Lesson' before seeing it," he wrote from The Hague. He found a Vermeer landscape there, probably *View of Delft* (c. 1661), astonishing in its facility. Vermeer's elegant work was just beginning to gain appreciation. "I know and have long admired his figure pictures, and I knew he painted landscapes also, but I had no idea *how* he painted it," he wrote home. "In fact, the picture is enigmatic to me now and I can't see how the dickens it is done. It is real sunlight and air and out-of-doors and makes all the other Dutch landscapes look like feeble, brown drawings." He studied the works of Franz Hals in Haarlem with care, for he admired but did not really like this master's realism. "An astonishing talent, an overwhelming brilliancy and cleverness, but lacking something of a great artist," he noted. "Nothing but wonderful eyes and a wonderful hand. If the man had a soul he kept it out of his painting. Not that I want 'ideas' or 'sentiment' in a picture, but the great men show in the way they put two colors together something, mind or what you like—art, perhaps—, that Hals hasn't." Hals depicted reality with considerable expression, but remained mundane for Cox, never equal to Rembrandt or Velázquez. Large ideas and a reflective mood seemed missing in his work. In Amsterdam, Cox saw the collections of familiar Dutch realism, which was all admirable but uninteresting, at least after seeing a great many Cuyp and Ruysdael works. "Most of the school are a weariness to the flesh. I always thought that of them, but now I know it, and that is perhaps worth voyaging for."[23]

By late September, Cox had tired of living in hotels and riding in trains. He was more domesticated than he thought. Though he had no deep interest in German art or culture, he took a side trip to Berlin and Dresden to see their collections. The train ride was uncomfortable, to say the least. He missed connections and had to sit up all night, wrapped in his grandfather's old shawl, which he carried for just such emergencies. He complained of

German train service, only to have another passenger firmly reply that everything in Germany was done well. To make matters worse, he caught a chill, took quinine, and became deathly ill, but recovered enough at least to see the basic things in the German capital. The collections were interesting but not striking, contrary to the natives' beliefs. The dreary weather matched the popular temper. "Berlin is the most coldly pompous and disagreeable place I ever saw. German art and German architecture are abominable, and I find I don't like German nature much better," he wrote home. "They not only rob you, which is the nature of hotel keepers and which one expects, but they aren't polite about it. They strike me as disagreeable brutes." Dresden was interesting, but its galleries were not striking. He was glad to have seen Germany but longed for France and the United States.[24]

He spent a few final days in Paris, attending the theater and seeing friends, then boarded *La Champagne* again for an uneventful return voyage. Frank Duveneck was aboard, and they talked art when not playing the usual games and socializing with passengers. Cox designed and drew the program for a musicale that netted thirteen hundred francs for a fund to help widows and orphans of sailors lost at sea. On October 6, 1889, he was back in New York, ready for the fall term at the Art Students League, and another season of art activities.[25]

In some ways the trip resembled Cox's tour of northern Italy in 1878. He saw a lot of great art that he knew only from illustrations. He began to sharpen his estimates of famous talents, such as Rubens, and to analyze the achievements and limitations of others, such as Hals. First-hand knowledge made him more thoughtful and reflective, a sign of maturity. He had gathered impressions and information that would fuel his career as an art writer and painter in the years ahead.

Cox was intellectually richer for the European trip, and was also gaining emotional maturity and certainty in dealing with people and the world. This helped him face the most important emotional challenge of his life to date, which ended in matrimony. The lady's name was Louise Howland King. She always remembered her excitement on first entering the NAD building as a student in 1881. It was a variation of the Doge's palace in Venice and fulfilled her ideal of what high architecture should look like. She was sixteen then, having been born in San Francisco in 1865. She lived simply with her mother and sister Pauline, and an aunt in Boston helped with expenses. She was bright and engaging, with a strong ambition to succeed in art (fig. 22). She loved classical music, but knew she could not compose, "whereas painting was more stimulating, as I knew I could create in that medium." She profited from studying at the academy, but like so many of the new generation of students soon wanted a freer course. "For many months I had been attracted by the sturdy, progressive atmosphere of the Art Students League, and after two years at the N.A.D., I decided to make a change." A friend of

FIG. 22. Louise King in her youth.
Allyn Cox Papers, Archives of American Art, Smithsonian Institution.

her mother's helped with the higher fees, and she readily settled into the League's routine. The students were easygoing, but worked hard, which satisfied her emotional need for both companionship and a sense of purpose. She naturally wanted to be modern, but also hoped to master traditional skills and had a certain classical taste. She remembered fondly the times when the students dressed as their favorite historical or mythological characters to form living paintings.

Cox joined the staff in the fall of 1884, and quickly became something of a legend for his masterful draftsmanship. He appeared straight laced, but was also somewhat risqué to students because of his interest in the nude. "The male students very condescendingly permitted us to see the superb life drawings and starkly realistic life paintings that Cox had done at the Beaux Arts," she recalled. They also knew of his poems on the fool's May-day and to the Unknown Lady, both of which in different ways seemed bold to a generation that simply did not discuss sex or basic romantic emotions. At the same time, he was apparently a loner and a hard critic. "We also heard tales of severe criticism and that he was a confirmed mysoginist." In due course, he transferred to the women's life drawing class, and the group awaited his first appearance with curiosity and trepidation. Louise perceived at once that his gruff manner and caustic tongue hid a basic shyness and insecurity in dealing with people. His criticism often unwittingly reduced students to tears. Some of the girls dramatically sniveled to "get even" as they passed him in the halls. Louise found him interesting, and thought she saw a personality that needed more human relationships.[26]

Louise's art education was lengthy, and she had ample time to benefit from Cox's instruction and to observe him as a person. By June 1886, she felt confident enough to make an appointment outside class hours to show him some sketches. He had already noticed her among the students but was doubtless simply too insecure and inexperienced to act. Years later, he told mutual friends that he had fallen in love with her at age thirty, which was in 1886. Their relationship unfolded with all the solemnity of a Trollope novel, which was not unusual in their class and circumstances. By the fall of 1887, Cox praised her as his best pupil. He then wrote a recommendation for possible employment, which attested to her abilities and to his regard for her as a person.[27] The courtship by correspondence continued. Writing mediated the emotions involved and allowed Cox to express feelings he would never have spoken. By late 1888, Louise had become a real woman to whom he could pour out his idealized feelings. His letters to her involved intense discussion of art, which was a form of passion. He was also doubtless warning her that he was not an easy person to live with, if it came to that.

He visited Ohio that fall before the League term began and wrote her a lengthy letter in September from Wooster, where he stayed with his sister Helen and her husband John Black. Louise had a teaching job in Toledo, and her isolation must have reminded him of the years in Cincinnati. He urged her not to turn inward. "I know well the difficulty and discouragement of trying to work in a small place away from companionship and help, but do not lose heart. You have talent, and work and perseverance will develop it.

Only *work*!" She should do still life, portraits of friends, landscapes, anything that would keep her painting while teaching. "I know your temperament and your desire to do something in a higher kind of art, but believe me, your principal danger is that you may be tempted to despise too much the homely qualities of sound and simple painting," he wrote in a voice of both an instructor and a friend. "It is more interesting to try to realize one's dreams on canvas than humbly to spend one's efforts in trying to represent a jug and an apple, but until one can paint everyday realities, one has little chance with dreams." Above all, she must cling to ideals. "Fill yourself with a passion for *truth* no less than with a passion for beauty. If you are a true painter you will find delight in the humblest bit of true work, and then, whether you succeed or fail, you have had your reward. The *work* pays for itself." Later in November he spelled out his own credo in an equally dramatic and intimate vein. "We must work for the work's sake. You say you almost forget why you paint at all; well, I have long since satisfied myself that I paint because I cannot help it—because I love the work itself and would rather be a miserably bad painter than a successful man in any other work—because the mere joy of trying and even the excitement of failure are the only true pleasures for me." Ideals were always receding; the unsatisfied personality was fulfilled in the pursuit. "We are all chasing a vision which we can never catch, but who would give up the excitement of the chase? It is always just so far ahead—our ideal—but we grit our teeth and pound ahead, and, if we are worth our salt, we will *never* give in till we drop." He commended to her Robert Louis Stevenson's poem to Will Low, which concluded that for artists, no matter what happened, "we have come the primrose way." His signature marked a modest step toward intimacy: "Faithfully yours, Kenyon Cox."[28]

Cox had spent his life in masculine contexts. His art-student friends were men, and he had developed a circle of male friends in the New York art world. He socialized in essentially masculine circumstances, whether at Saint Gaudens's musicales or in taking visiting friends to the theater or opera. His view of women was obviously idealistic, and he had sublimated romantic and erotic interests into painting. He had not developed the social skills or self-confidence to deal well with women, who were also depicted as superior beings in his family and circle. But for all of that, he knew that falling in love was involuntary, as he had written his mother from Paris in 1880. He also insisted in 1885 that he was "a great believer in marriage." He saw in Louise a kindred spirit who understood his idealism and intense interest in art. She was intelligent and attractive, one of that "lady-hood" he had promised to marry when the time came. He also saw in her a streak of independence that was distilled in a story their friends often told later. At some point early in the courtship, he criticized her classwork harshly. "What in hell did you do that for?" Her answer was swift. "None of your damned business!" There was a good deal of truth in the later observation of Will Cochran's daughter that "he married the student who failed to hold him in awe." For her part, Louise doubtless saw in him a steadiness that she needed, and she admired his artistic talents. But as they both might have said, the attractions were simply right.[29]

Cox spent much of the summer of 1891 in Magnolia, Massachusetts, with his family and reported his daily activities to Louise in numerous letters. He sometimes talked about art, but more often about likes and dislikes, eating and sleeping habits, and other personal matters. The tone was breezy and confident at last. He entertained his younger sister Hope and her friends there, and feared that his genial conviviality had "punched holes through and through and irretrievably damaged the legendary K.C." One of the girls studied art in Brooklyn, and he mockingly hated to think what she would tell other students. "What shreds of my character as an austere and girl-despising melancholy genius, were left me after that Virginia Reel into which you [earlier] tempted me, will not be enough to hide my shame!" That fall the seriousness returned in the different setting of the League, when he advised her against seeking a five-year fellowship to study in Paris. She was beyond that, he thought, and should stop being a student and become a real artist at home. Of course, he also clearly did not want her gone that long. He took the visiting Hope, infamous for flighty gossip and scheming, to see Louise that fall, which was akin to buying a newspaper ad about their relationship. Hope liked Louise and spread the word among the family. Early in 1892 Louise finally took the last step and nudged Cox into proposing.[30]

News of the engagement flabbergasted the family in Ohio. Hope had prepared the way and insisted that Louise would be a perfect daughter-in-law, but still they were unprepared. "Of course, you know your letter takes my breath away," Mrs. Cox wrote on March 31. "I imagined you would never marry unless indeed one day you should happen to meet some rich girl who was romantic enough to exchange her riches for your fame." There must be plenty of such women, "but where to look for them, how to find them, of course that is the question." His father soon weighed in with some portentous advice. He naturally wanted Kenyon to be happy, and heard only good things of Louise, but marriage and romance were different things. "You have been training yourself to be a celibate," he observed. "Your doctrine, in practice, has been that if you were content with poverty, no one else should complain at your devoting your life and strength to unmerchantable productions." This now must yield to supporting a wife and family. "I do not mean to croak," he insisted. "I hope you won't think I do." He was simply being practical, as usual. "You have been chasing an ideal in art, and now you are laid under a necessity of striving for an ideal in conduct."[31]

The engagement released all of Cox's pent-up romanticism, and parental doubts seemed irrelevant. "We are immensely, superlatively happy, mammy dear," he wrote early in April. "I had no notion how much I loved her until since we have spoken." They were the center of attention at an Academy reception. "As everybody has been talking about us for so long, we just frankly accept the situation and almost demand congratulations." They planned to keep two studios, and to live in Louise's small walk-up apartment at 75 West Fifty-fifth Street. Her mother and sister would move elsewhere. He realized how surprising all this must seem to the family who were unaware of how long he and Louise had known each other. "Long before I felt the thrill of love, I knew that she would make the best wife in the world for me if I should love her," he insisted. "When love came to add to the friendship and confidence, I felt *safe* and so we mean to marry as soon as we can." Mrs. Cox thought he was "taking leave of your senses" for wanting to marry that summer, but if they insisted she hoped for a date when the family could all come. Cox reassured her that he and Louise were mature, knew each other well, and "having discovered our love for each other, we should be married as soon as may be." His finances were better than usual, and Louise's aunt, Mrs. B. M. Jones would arrange the ceremony in Belmont, Massachusetts.[32]

The family knew it was hopeless to argue. "Do not fear that we shall not love each other," Mrs. Cox wrote Louise and then displayed some shrewd motherly insight. "The fact that you have been able to find beneath the husk with which Ken surrounds himself, the sweet kernel underneath, the delicacy of refinement, the tender gentleness of the man, shows to me a nature that cannot but command my warmest love." His father wished them well, with a final comment on income. And his mother could not forbear reminding Louise that her son was "a great and distinguished man." Dolson, as usual, was more forthright. He had married in 1878 while Kenyon was in Paris, and it was "the only way to live." He hoped they would not spend a lot of money on a big wedding and should accept a period of retrenchment. He thought he knew Louise, and recalled hearing that Kenyon had been eating Sunday dinners with her family. "Is this the one? I bet it is, for I know what a powerful influence a good Sunday dinner is—especially when accompanied by the warm friendship and esteem of a lady with a daughter. I've been there—and I got the dinners and the daughter too!"[33]

Wedding preparations got underway in Belmont, and Cox became the momentary center of attention in New York. His friends arranged a farewell bachelor dinner for May 23, 1892, at the Hotel Martin, University Place and Ninth Street. Thirty-eight people appeared, the food was good and the speeches clever. The guests, who included many famous artists, signed a souvenir for Louise. Cox was flattered and drank everyone's health so often that he could hardly meet his class the next day.[34]

In the meantime, Cox began a portrait of Louise as a wedding present. He posed her standing against a door, right foot slightly forward, arms crossed holding an elaborate fan. She looked at the observer with a firm gaze, and the face was realistic, a good contrast to the smoothly painted ruffled blouse and

FIG. 23. Kenyon Cox, *Louise Howland King*
(Mrs. Kenyon Cox) (1892). Oil on canvas, 38⅝ × 18 ins.
Courtesy of the National Museum of American Art,
Smithsonian Institution, bequest of Allyn Cox.

dress. The background colors were muted gray, blue, and yellow, the dress rose. The background was cropped for effect and the space compressed. The work echoed Whistler in its lightly painted, modulated tones, but also recalled somewhat the portrait of Henry Fry that Cox painted in 1883. He carefully lettered the upper left-hand corner, L.H.K. AET. XXVII, and signed the lower right-hand corner KENYON COX 1892 (fig. 23). The painting was realistic, but he had idealized Louise's appearance and captured what she meant to him.[35]

Cox went on to Belmont about a week before the wedding, chiefly to calm Louise. On the appointed day, June 30, his parents arrived to see their new daughter-in-law for the first time. They first encountered Kenyon, dressed in a black Prince Albert coat with matching trousers, formal shirt and patent pumps. He seemed relaxed and unconcerned, "docile to the last degree." Mrs. Cox asked if he would go upstairs and kiss the bride. "I'm not allowed," he answered. "This is the one day in a man's life when he can do nothing but what he is told to do." Mrs. Cox proceeded upstairs and encountered Louise's sister Pauline, or Polly, who she frankly thought was plain. On entering the dressing room, she saw Louise resplendent in her gown, and "I loved her at once. There was no need of words. I went up and put my arms around her and claimed her for mine at once." But in reporting to her daughter Helen in Wooster, she could not omit saying: "She is so much prettier than her picture." After the ceremony the couple went to a hotel in Monadnock, New Hampshire, for a honeymoon. Kenyon dutifully wrote home, and could not help being a Cox, telling his mother: "I'm so glad you think her pretty, though that you should not have expected it is hardly a compliment to my little portrait of her, which everyone seems to consider very like [her]."[36] And so the long courtship ended, on a happy and fulfilling note, with both partners ready for a dual life in art.

V

❧

MURAL PAINTER

K ENYON AND LOUISE WERE
hardly the typical newlyweds. As he had told his mother on announcing their
engagement, they were mature people who understood each other's needs
and habits. They took to domesticity quickly, enjoying each other's company
and settling into Louise's cramped but familiar apartment. Their careers and
interests were a major bond, and they exchanged news on progress in various
works, shared hopes and hesitations, and circulated among mutual friends.
Cox was happy, and a year later wrote Leonard Opdycke on his own engagement: "I do congratulate you with all my heart, for my own experience shows
me that marriage may be and is the only happy state. A single life is a very
incomplete one."[1]

The new couple anticipated a leisurely summer together before beginning
the regular winter art season. Fate intervened in the form of a commission to
decorate a building at the World's Columbian Exposition in Chicago. The
event was meant to celebrate the four-hundredth anniversary of Columbus's
contact, and to symbolize America's progress and future directions. The
planners decided to emphasize the vitality and variety of American art. For
artists who wanted to make a grand statement in painting, the fair was the
first opportunity to work on a large scale in public decoration. This appealed
to many painters who thought the time had come to display their talents
outside the galleries and exhibition halls, and who believed that the public
was ready for an art that celebrated civic virtues. Cox's friend Edwin H.
Blashfield remembered receiving a cablegram while in Italy inviting him to
join the project. "Would I?" he answered. "Would a duck swim?" The
painter Frank Millet, an impresario of this effort, knew of Cox's large-scale
works and asked him to join the project. Almost every important or rising
American artist was involved and was excited at the prospect of creating a
white city that celebrated the arts. At one gathering, Saint Gaudens summed

up their feelings with emotion: "It has been the greatest meeting of artists since the fifteenth century."[2]

By late August, the Coxes were at the fairgrounds, which were emerging from mud flats near downtown Chicago. There was an artificial lagoon, amid large temporary buildings made of material that looked like white marble. The artist Charles Yardley Turner had devised a spray paint apparatus that reduced the number of house painters needed, and these savings paid for the decorations. The artists had about two and a half months to complete their work. Married people lived in boarding houses and single men in dormitories. At lunchtime a whistle blew and a steam launch took them across the lagoon to eat with local navy personnel, or they could eat on the grounds or at a local restaurant. The site was dusty or muddy as the weather decreed, and confusion and haste reigned, but it was all very exotic and exciting. The artists talked ceaselessly of their work, and ended the day happy though covered with plaster dust, grime, and paint.

Louise thought "it is so funny and larky here." At first she believed that Kenyon missed working with the single men. But as friends arrived they had as much socializing as they wanted. The work was demanding and intense, but everyone seemed to like Kenyon and to approve of his ideas and methods. They went into Chicago to buy supplies once and disliked the noise, dirt, and confusion. "We escaped as rapidly as possible and will not return there unless obliged by dire necessity," she wrote her mother-in-law. The generally ragged look of the city prompted a tart poem from Kenyon:

> *Fair Game*
> Of all the ills that flesh is heir to
> Chicago Ills. is one I'll swear to
> Chicago ills are very many
> Chicago Ills. is the worst of any
> N.Y. Body[3]

The painters had not been formally trained as muralists but had studied the figure and knew the grand tradition from their European training. Cox was assigned space in the east portal of the huge Manufactures and Liberal Arts Building. Each of its four entrances had two vestibules with domes that formed four pendentives. Painters chose their subjects but agreed to unify the various domes with figures that symbolized the activities in the building. The domes were some fifty feet above the floor, with only reflected light. As Cox wrote later, the painters had to "discover a treatment that should not too grossly deny structure, that should be visible in such light and at such distance, and that should give scope to their pictorial training." Each artist had a model of his vestibule. Cox studied his and slightly altered an original conception in favor of lower, small figures, with strong perspective and color. The domes were so high that viewers really would see only the pendentives, and the focus had to be on the figures. He probably worked from models, then used enlargements to see how the drawings fitted their spaces. He and assistants then painted directly onto the dome, which was covered in a neutral blue ground. The works were enclosed in plaster moldings that ran down to Corinthian columns. The space was defined and attractive, given the building's size.[4]

Cox settled on a decorative scheme that reflected his own interests and talents. The subjects were *Metal Work, Building, Textiles,* and *Ceramics.* Each was an idealized female figure in antique drapery, holding symbolic evidence of the craft involved. They stood before balustrades, and elegant banderoles bore the titles above their heads. These enclosed the figures in large V-shaped, shieldlike forms, and also outlined a circle in the dome's middle. The composition enhanced the space and was easily understandable while being symbolic (fig. 24).

The color scheme was rich. The figure for *Metal Work* held a flexed sword and was clad in yellow, lilac, and orange draperies, with flowers and greenery behind her balustrade. A calmly poised *Building* bore a barlike implement and wore dark and light green drapery. The corner of a building was behind her. The figure for *Textiles* was in a classical full-front pose, with a spinning staff in one hand and a winding spool in the other. Her chemise top was pink, and the falling drapery was carmine. There was a rich floral background with her balustrade. *Ceramics* stood full-front, with her right knee bent and her head turned to the left. An outstretched right hand held a paintbrush, and her left an urn. The left breast was bare, and the dress was white, with purple and blue drapery below the hips. The figures were about ten feet tall, well drawn and richly painted, and the parts of the designs flowed together. The high colors must have been clearly visible and striking from the floor.[5]

The commission completed, the Coxes returned to New York. Both exhibited paintings at the exposition when it opened in 1893. Kenyon showed a dozen, including *Painting and Poetry, An Eclogue,* and *Vision of Moonrise,* as well as nudes and the portraits of Saint Gaudens and Louise. Louise showed two recent works, *A Rondel* and *The Lotus Eaters.* Kenyon won a medal, and both it and the number of works attested to his stature in the art community, chiefly as a representative for ideal painting. The principal result of the experience for him, however, was to sharpen a growing interest in formal decoration. The fair offered an impressive display of art in its exhibitions, and in the buildings. He had enjoyed working with so many artists of like mind, who were now trained to do such painting. And perhaps the public was at last ready to appreciate murals, which had never figured significantly in America, though they were a major aspect of European art. Blashfield recalled that "Cox talked Venetian decoration tirelessly and entertainingly." He

FIG. 24. Kenyon Cox, *Metal Work, Building, Ceramics, Textiles* (1893),
Manufactures Building, World's Columbian Exposition, Chicago. Original work,
now destroyed, was oil on plaster, dimensions unknown. Photograph, source
unknown, gift of Allyn Cox, 1959-69-129. Photo by Ken Pelka.
Courtesy of Cooper-Hewitt, Museum of National Design,
Smithsonian Institution/Art Resources, New York.

was clearly trying to develop a suitable decorative ideal and to refine the
methods used at the fair, for mural painting had special rules and
conventions.[6]

The 1892–93 art season was especially hectic, because Louise was pregnant. The outcome was not happy; she gave birth to a stillborn girl early in
April. Kenyon understandably was distraught. "I shall never forget the long
night I spent, nearly two years ago now, in suspense," he wrote Leonard Opdycke in 1895, "and the relief of knowing that my dear wife was safe, even

if the little girl never lived." Louise recovered slowly and became depressed. By mid-May she was still seeing the doctor regularly and tried electricity treatments to restore her energy and spirits. Kenyon remained calm, at least on the surface. "Kenyon is so good, so patient," Louise wrote his mother. "Sometimes it seems as if I must try him—but he is always loving and tactful, comforting me with his hopes for the future and his dear love."[7]

These hopes for the future centered more and more on mural painting. They were clarified in the midst of the family crisis when the architect Charles F. McKim asked Cox to consider doing a major decoration for the new Walker Art Museum he was completing at Bowdoin College in Brunswick, Maine. This small elegant building had a central dome with spaces for four large lunettes. Each would depict an allegory of a major city in the European art tradition. This would decorate the building and prompt study and reflection among students and visitors. John La Farge would do Athens; Elihu Vedder, Rome; Abbott H. Thayer, Florence; and Cox, Venice. Here was a chance to do a major work, enshrined forever in a public building, that drew on the great tradition and tested each artist's skill both as a painter and as a thinker. Though worried about Louise's health, Cox quickly agreed, "principally on account of the opportunity for serious and permanent decorative work, which is what I have long wished." Cox's preliminary ideas for the work pleased McKim, and the details would be settled later. In the meantime, the Coxes decided to go to Europe, chiefly to "make some notes for Kenyon's decoration." The trip would also help Louise, introduce her to a range of European art, and be a real honeymoon.[8]

They sailed on June 10, 1893, on the Dutch ship *Maasdam*. The departure was somewhat dramatic, with Louise's mother crying on the dock to the mixed strains of a brass band. They were determined to relax and mixed freely with the passengers. Kenyon smoked and read, and often behaved like a swain, holding Louise's hand under the rugs when they sat in deck chairs. He had brought a new Kodak camera, then all the rage in America, and made a great many snapshots. One of the subjects took umbrage and challenged him to a duel. Cox was startled, but loftily ignored the man.

In Paris they encountered old friends, including the Dyers and the Stotts. They moved on quickly to Italy, the trip's focus. Cox sketched scenes and works that might help with the Bowdoin mural and studied the ideas and techniques of the great northern Italian muralists. Both he and Louise especially liked Veronese's *Martyrdom of St. George* (1568) at the Church of St. George in Verona. The breadth of style, rich coloration, and elevated mood in this and other Veronese works were striking and became examples for Cox. By mid-September they had seen all they could digest and returned home. The trip turned out to be a rare break in their hectic lives, and they both discussed it for years. Cox remembered many of the scenes from his trip of

1878, but this journey helped clarify his ideas about traditional art and offered many examples for his mural work.[9]

Cox signed the agreement for the Bowdoin commission on October 25, 1893. He would receive three thousand dollars in installments as the work progressed, and it was due May 1, 1894. Given his other duties, he faced an arduous winter and spring schedule, but this was really nothing new. He immediately worked up the notes he made on the trip and did a broad oil sketch that the Walker sisters approved. He then did studies of the mural's components, squared them onto a cartoon, and painted the finished work.

Each of the four muralists worked in his own style, which McKim hoped would add variety to the rather small building, done in the firm's modified Italian renaissance style. Cox chose a design derived directly from Venetian art, whose formality matched his conception of what the building and its art symbolized. A female figure of rather haughty mien representing Venice enthroned divided the lunette into two halves. She held a scepter and wore a diadem to symbolize authority, and a laurel wreath at her feet represented glory. At the left the god Mercury, patron of commerce, sat in a relaxed and confident pose. Behind him, dramatic sails spoke for Venetian commerce, and their curve paralleled the picture's edge. At the right sat a seminude female figure representing painting, armed with brushes and palette. Behind her was the famous lion of St. Mark, whose wings also complemented the picture's curve to complete its symmetrical composition. There was a glimpse of the Campanile and the Ducal Palace in the blue background of sea and sky (fig. 25).

Cox followed a sumptuous color scheme. The dominant tone was a deep red in the draperies of all the figures and in Venice's chair. The ship sails were light brown, with red tops, and the lion was in rich buff. The blue sea and sky and the green laurel were other brilliant touches. An elaborate gold border added to the lunette's elegance. The composition's rich coloration and dignity symbolized the wealth and cultural authority of Venice at its height. The lunette was an appropriate and satisfying work for the place, which was always the decorator's goal. Cox had demonstrated his ability in draftsmanship, color, and composition and was beginning to establish a personal style for mural work.[10]

Cox demonstrated again, as he had in 1886 with the illustrations for *The Blessed Damozel,* that he could meet deadlines, always a major consideration among the architects who chose muralists. By March 1, 1894, he invited Weir and Robinson to see the half-completed work. On April 25 and 26, he asked friends to view the finished painting at a studio reception. "It is generally considered by those who have seen it, I think, the best thing I have done and some partial friends give it even higher praise," he wrote Leonard Opdycke. He shipped the canvas to Bowdoin, then followed to oversee its

FIG. 25. Kenyon Cox, *Venice* (1894), Walker Art Building rotunda, Bowdoin College. Oil on canvas mural, 144 × 288 ins. Courtesy of Bowdoin College Museum of Art, Brunswick, Maine. Gift of the Misses Harriet and Sophia Walker (1893.38).

installation. He had some doubts on seeing it set up, but retouched the color scheme until satisfied. The Walker sisters sent a special note of thanks with the final payment, which pleased him.[11]

The Bowdoin murals symptomized growing concern for the decoration of public buildings. The murals at the Columbian Exposition were attractive and widely discussed, yet were temporary and seldom the product of careful analysis. But the event marked growing interest in decoration within the art world and among the art public. There was no grand tradition of mural painting in America, as there was in Europe, where it had long enjoyed ecclesiastical and governmental patronage. But there were some antecedents by the time Cox began to do such work. William Morris Hunt had decorated the assembly and senate chambers of the new state capitol in Albany with allegorical murals in 1878. John La Farge did the same for Trinity Church in Boston in the 1870s. He also produced a major decoration, *The Ascension,* in 1886–88 for the church of that name in New York City. The country was economically depressed when Cox did the Bowdoin commission, but recovery after 1898 brought a long building boom that included many public edifices, such as state capitols, courthouses, and federal offices, as well as apartment houses, hotels, and office buildings that were suitable for decoration. Modified classical and Renaissance architectural styles also made such decorations logical and even necessary. From about 1895 to 1925 painters decorated some four hundred major buildings in the United States.[12]

This movement reflected and represented several large civic beliefs. The nation emerged onto the world stage after the Spanish-American War of 1898 and felt at last that its history and energy were those of a great power that architecture and the arts could help make tangible. The industrial system was clearly triumphant, and it generated wealth that supported this sense of national power. Despite some anxieties and uncertainties of direction, the country's spokesmen believed that the varied American people constituted a great polity that needed cultural expression and direction. These in turn could only come from the European tradition. As Cox and others had long held, the nation needed to assert itself as part of a vital world culture. It should not copy European examples but could express its own ideals and desires in terms that were well understood in that context. Muralism was one way to state these aspirations, to remind people of their roles in larger processes, to soften the impact of materialism, and to help beautify the country, especially its cities. It was a time of confidence and large plans, and the expansive ambitions behind muralism seemed reasonable.[13]

Murals enlivened ballrooms and foyers in hotels and apartment houses. They dignified office buildings or added a sense of drama to rail and ship terminals. But they were most important in public buildings where their ideas were complex. Murals were the grand opera of painting and required a willing suspension of disbelief in the viewer, who must transcend the mundane and real. Their themes were larger than life, grander than living, and were cast as allegories whether the form was realistic or idealistic. Muralists meant these works to speak broadly to a tradition that viewers could comprehend, and which would enlarge their sense of importance as citizens.

Cox filled his own murals with idealism. His work in official buildings naturally emphasized aspects of government, but he did not intend to exalt the power of the state over the individual. He sought to stress where possible the common aspects of a polity to which all people could subscribe. This involved order, but it rested on the attachment of society and individuals to a tradition that tempered both disorder and authority. Ever the idealist, Cox emphasized Law, not current laws or judicial procedures; Government, not politics; and Custom, not reigning taste. As a classicist, his doctrines were cohesive, but he hoped to expand the individual's consciousness always within a tradition that emphasized order and harmony. Like his friend Will Low, who also became a muralist, he wanted uplifting, complex compositions to temper atomized individualism and materialism. "From a work of this character, a cursory glance may carry away, if not its full import, enough at least to impart a leaven of spirituality to a day of material preoccupation," Low wrote in 1907. It seemed possible to fulfill these hopes, now that a generation of painters had been trained in the techniques and ideas required for such expression. The architectural profession also took on greater authority with cosmopolitan training, and architects wanted their buildings to be sophisticated and visually impressive, to express the unity and importance of all the arts. They were the chief sponsors of mural painting in the generation to come. For themselves, muralists sought the unifying experience, so necessary to classicists and idealists, of working with other artists on projects that would affect the public. And they wished to make statements that would transcend the momentary realism of the model and the easel. [14]

When he began to paint murals, Cox was well versed in the general precedents of the ancient world and of the Italian Renaissance. One modern example, that of the French decorator Puvis de Chavannes, caught his attention for a time in the mid-1890s and influenced his thinking about murals. Puvis de Chavannes began painting large decorations in the mid-1860s. He sought a fresh style to express ideas in abstract but recognizable forms. He progressively eliminated realistic details in favor of large, balanced compositions with abstracted figures and scenes set in flat contexts that emphasized their symbolism. His figures were stylized, caught in important actions, and represented grand ideals. Puvis used pale, understated colors, often gray, blue, green, or brown, in a matte finish that complemented the sobriety of these works. These compositions were clearly the product of the decorator's mind rather than depictions of nature. They dealt with eternal themes, such as war and peace, labor and family, patriotism and religion, and historical processes relevant to modern man. Though surprising to some critics, these grave works were powerful and fascinating. Puvis decorated institutions such as the museums at Amiens and at Marseilles, the Sorbonne and Panthéon in Paris, and the Boston Public Library. [15]

Cox saw Puvis as a bridge between the familiar grandeur of traditional decorative work and the modern demand for fresh and unusual allegory. The Puvis works at Amiens and at the Sorbonne in Paris especially impressed him during the trip of 1893. "Of the men of today, it is Puvis first and the rest nowhere," he wrote his mother. Three years later he did an important essay on Puvis that reflected many of his emerging ideas about decoration's role in modern art. He thought that Puvis was grave, detached, and grand, as befitted decorations meant to last the ages. Puvis avoided transitory realism in favor of enduring ideals that were beyond time and place. He suppressed details until only symbolic essentials remained, which could speak to any viewer. He had blended many styles and was a "classicist of the classicists, a primitive of the primitives, a modern of the moderns." [16]

Cox continued to admire Puvis's sense of gravity and elevated style. He later used some of the flatness in Puvis's work and employed similar floating figures, but he came to believe that modern man, especially Americans, required more boldness of form and tone than were in the Frenchman's style. As time passed and he gained experience as a muralist, Cox drew on the large Italian Renaissance tradition in general, and on the works of Titian, Giorgione, and especially Veronese, in particular. Their rich coloration, realized figures, and varied accessories seemed more appropriate for an expansive American society.[17]

Cox and other muralists sought to influence a modern democratic society that had no tradition of decorative art. The muralist for a public building often dealt with people who wanted to celebrate an area's history or alleged uniqueness rather than large ideas. Painters compromised and used historical subjects that neutralized local differences and complexities and afforded some chance to paint sumptuously, with the hope of at least echoing larger ideas. Such work was sometimes impressive but more often was hackneyed. A typical courthouse mural might show an allegorical figure leading settlers in covered wagons under the title *Hope Leading Pioneers West.* A variant of this approach might involve a famous local event that illustrated a larger process, such as economic development.

Cox understood the appeals of historicism in reconciling realistic treatment and classical idealism. He thought that a mixture of allegory and fact could succeed in the hands of a master painter like his friend Edwin H. Blashfield. He praised Blashfield's elaborate decoration for the Baltimore Courthouse, *Washington Laying Down His Commission* (1902). In it a classical female figure was enthroned above the legend *Patriae,* with figures on each side holding symbols of war and peace, power, and responsibility. Washington, dressed realistically in his general's uniform, surrendered his commission to the new republic. The figures were beautifully drawn, and the scene was sumptuously painted. The theme was clearly the wisdom of Washington's refusal to turn military command into personal power, and his consciousness of history and idealism.

This particular blend of allegory and fact did not offend Cox because it was well done and logical. "So swiftly is time foreshortened as it recedes into the past that Washington, in blue and buff, seems naturally enough placed amid the half-medieval, half-ancient costumes of the symbolical figures about him," he wrote. "They are all removed from the present, which is, for us, the only reality, and seem equally to belong to an ideal world." He thought the same of Saint Gaudens's equestrian statue of General William T. Sherman, with its idealized Victory. In a few such instances, real people filled such important and familiar historical roles in national life that they were allegorical.

Cox believed this was seldom the case. America's history was not as lengthy or complex as Europe's. The religious dimension was also missing. Modern costumes and accoutrements were unattractive and inhibited dramatic, large effects that were appropriate to idealism. As he said bluntly: "The painter who cares greatly for the expressiveness of the body will feel little attraction to belt buckles and brass buttons." Above all, the historical story too easily became parochial.

These considerations, combined with his bent toward figure painting, made Cox a leading spokesman for the use of allegorical figures and designs in murals. The figure represented ideas, and formal compositions were in order for public buildings. Cox also wanted to emphasize timelessness in a democratic society that too often accepted change uncritically. "Again, mural painting is especially an art of formal and symmetrical composition, of monumental arrangements and balanced lines and masses," he held in 1911, "and such composition necessarily destroys all illusions of veracity in the depiction of historical incident." In the end, "we must admit the symbolical or we must give up monumental and decorative painting altogether.[18]

Cox's methods of work expressed these principles and reflected the special demands of decoration. He differentiated clearly between easel pictures and decorations. The former were portable, intimate, and suitable for many circumstances. The enlarged easel picture seldom worked as a decoration. The latter was fixed, needed special treatment for optimal viewing, had to express ideas simply, and above all, must be "designed for a special place." Decorations should complement a building's uses. He believed that the symbolism derived from familiar models such as the Italian Renaissance best resolved this problem of unifying form, content, and placement. Experience also taught him to study assigned spaces. The half-oval lunette was difficult to do because of the shape, and because it was often poorly lit and high above the viewer. Pendentives were equally hard to treat effectively. The best space was an uninterrupted wall, which architects usually reserved for marble or wood. The problem of placement thus determined much of the form and intellectual content in any decoration and required careful thought and attention to historical examples.[19]

After resolving these basic preliminaries, Cox proceeded to work. A successful composition resulted from study and thought. "If you are a true decorator, the first pencil sketch of three or four lines has determined your composition, placed the principal masses, and settled the principal lines," he wrote in 1906. "After that, study may be arduous and pushed very far, but unless the preliminary sketch suggests the beautiful disposition of the parts, no beauty in the details and no style of treatment will make of the whole a beautiful decoration." He then developed a sense of the whole composition with a scale drawing, to judge how the parts interacted. The result at this stage might be a color sketch.

He then drew the figures. "The making of a nude study for such a picture is an entirely different thing from the making of a school study, in which exact drawing of the model in the set pose is the aim," he cautioned. "The principal aims here are: first, the composition of the figure in its relation to all the other lines of the composition; second, the expression of life and movement or of repose in the attitude; third, the beauty or the desired character of the forms." This required steady refining of the figure drawing away from realism until it represented an ideal type.

Drapery posed special problems because it too could not be merely realistic. "The functions of drapery in monumental painting are three in number: to give color; to give dignity and mass to the figures and variety and richness of lines to the composition; to accent and intensify the action or the repose of the figures," he counselled. "A properly arranged drapery does not cover or hide the figure—it expresses it." A successful decorator had an indefinable feel for painting drapery, which came from experience and from sensing its role in accentuating figures and in enlivening a composition. In all of this, Cox's drawing was careful, elegant, and composed, as befitted an ideal, formal work.

In the meantime, he and assistants laid in parts of the work on smooth prepared canvas. They usually made outlines in chalk that was set with a fixative. He might then apply a wash of transparent color and paint rapidly while the canvas was on the floor or stretched, if size permitted. He mixed the paint with wax to create a flat finish and took care to avoid a glassy or spotty effect in areas of high color. The color scheme had to be complementary and effective when seen from a distance. If he had met the deadline, he invited friends to see the finished work at a studio reception. The canvas then went to the site rolled up and was affixed to the wall with white lead and varnished. If possible, he made necessary adjustments in shape and color there.[20]

Cox believed that the successful mural was more important than easel work, because it remained in place indefinitely and expressed lasting ideas. Such work was more creative than the realism usually involved in easel painting. Murals were the products of careful thought and knowledge, and could be a force for cohesion and idealism in a complex society like the United States. He sensed a turning away from the transitory to the enduring, "and as the highest aim of the painter will be to beautify the walls of the temples and palaces of the people, so the highest name he will give himself will be that of 'decorator.' "[21]

Cox worked out these views in a long series of murals after the mid-1890s. By then he was well known for idealistic painting and for figure work and attracted attention as a critic and writer on art history. His works at the Columbian Exposition and at Bowdoin College made him familiar to architects and decorators who wanted murals done in a classical style. In 1895 he became a founding member of The Mural Painters, a group that advertised the importance of decoration and whose members were available for mural work.

Cox's next commission was for the new Library of Congress building in Washington. The librarian naturally wanted a modern facility for the storage and use of printed matter. The architects hoped to combine this goal with a lavishly decorated structure that would symbolize the arts for the entire country, just as the Capitol and Washington Monument represented politics. The building was in a traditional French style, with inner courtyards and exterior plazas and fountains. The architects had saved enough money for a lavish array of external sculpture and various kinds of interior decorations. General Thomas L. Casey, the chief architect, first approached leading painters such as John Singer Sargent, James McNeill Whistler, and Edwin Austen Abbey to do decorations. All declined because of prior commitments. Bernard Green, the superintendent of construction, then asked Charles F. McKim to recommend artists. He drew up a list of suitable people, chiefly NAD members and those who had worked at the Columbia Exposition. In the end, some twenty-two sculptors and twenty painters worked on the building.[22]

The Southwest Gallery of the building was a long, well-lit room on the second floor, with a view of interior courtyards on one side and of the Capitol on the other. It was to be an exhibition hall, with display cases of artifacts relating to the library and to learning in general. The ceiling was an elliptical barrel vault. Its gold-bordered coffers contained white carved rosettes of various flowers, each set against a turquoise blue background. The walls were painted in regular areas of cream and a buff gold, with accents of russet and blue amid ornately carved white woodwork. The floor was done in regular patterns of light plum, blue, and white marble. The room was well proportioned, with a light, airy feeling, and managed to seem both impressive and comfortable. Each end contained a lunette space some 9½-by-34 feet. Any decorations would have to match both the decor and the mood.

Late in November 1894, Green offered Cox five thousand dollars to decorate these two spaces. Cox was intrigued at the prospect of doing works for a government building that many people would see. He hesitated only because most of the fee would go for materials, models, and assistants. He would have to forgo other work for several months, and the issue was simply how to live. He asked for more information on who approved the final designs, and on the color scheme and lighting in the room. He accepted the commission on January 1, 1895, not knowing "just how I am to get through the work, but the opportunity to do a fine thing for a public building is so tempting that I have decided to accept the commission and arrange as best I can about money for executing it." Two weeks later he wrote his father about the opportunity, and shrewdly enclosed an unnamed newspaper clipping that ranked him among the country's best artists. If his father could advance money at interest, Cox could do the work with reasonable comfort. The general agreed, but cautioned that government payments were slow and uncertain. Kenyon had better be prepared for financial stringencies. "If you can do enough besides to keep the pot boiling, so much the better," he wrote with the usual fatherly caution, "for the government pay, when it comes, will then be a little capital against a rainy day or to meet a similar exigency in the future." Dolson shortly repaid a loan, which the elder Cox sent Kenyon as the first of several advances. Cox reported the commission to Leonard Opdycke and brooded over the everlasting money problem. "I am beginning to think, however, that I shall get through all right. There are signs all about of jobs on the way, some of which seem likely to get here." Opdycke immediately offered a loan, but Cox declined again. His father's offer was firm, "and I had rather take it from him than anyone else."[23]

Cox proposed from the first that one panel would depict the arts and the other the sciences. He began preliminary work at once, but progress was slow, chiefly because there were so many figures. But by late February 1896, *The Arts* was nearing completion. The visiting Will Cochran "spoke of it with unusual enthusiasm when he came home from seeing it," his father reported. "It impressed him very strongly, both in drawing and color." At the same time, the general went out of his way to praise Kenyon's article on Puvis de Chavannes as a mature piece of criticism. "If your new panels shall give equal rank to your work with the brush, you will have good reason to be content." Kenyon sent a photograph of the work to the family, and his father enthused again. A show of the preparatory drawings for many of the building's murals at the Architectural League in New York City drew considerable attention. The *New York Tribune*'s traditionalist art critic Royal Cortissoz praised Cox's drawings as excellent academic works. He liked their certitude and control, while recognizing that they were not overly expressive. They suited the project and would succeed well.[24]

Cox designed the two lunettes to complement each other and to unite the long room. As usual, he used balanced, symmetrical compositions that suited the space and its symbolism. At the north end, a central figure representing poetry was enthroned in *The Arts*. Idealized female figures symbolized architecture and music to the left, and sculpture and painting to the right. Each held the symbols appropriate to her art. There were two nude, winged cherubs at poetry's feet, one writing down her words, the other moving to her song. Two burning braziers separated the groups from the central figure, and a blue sky and green treetops were visible beyond an elegant balustrade. *The Sciences* was at the south end of the room, in a similar composition. A female in billowing drapery represented astronomy. Two cherubs held a globe and a telescope. To the left were idealized figures of physics and mathematics. To the right were botany, in an elegant green and white figured dress, and zoology, who was nude and who reached out toward a magnificent peacock perched on the balustrade. Symbolic touches and accoutrements spoke for other sciences (fig. 26). These compositions had larger overtones. Science was increasingly important in modern life, and Cox's work suggested that it was more than experiments and discoveries. It had ancient roots in general culture, and the painting added a sense of emotion and breadth to the usual conception of science. He balanced this with a reminder that the arts had as great a lineage and were quite as central to life.

Cox corresponded with Green as the murals developed. He had a moment of panic in April, when it seemed that *The Arts* would not quite fit into the allotted space as Green now described it, because of a change in the molding. He had painted nearly to the edge of the canvas, with no room for accommodation. This reinforced his desire to see the murals put in place, and he arrived in Washington on Monday, May 25, 1896. The building was unfinished, though taking shape inside, and workmen were everywhere in a chaos of dust, scaffolds, and tools. William A. Coffin had visited the site earlier for an article on the library. He took one look at the bustling workmen and artists and saw "the spirit of art and labor." He threw his new silk hat into the air and cried: "*This* is the Renaissance!"[25]

The weather was hot and muggy, and Cox changed clothes at the Cosmos Club, where he stayed when not haunting the library site. He took an instant liking to the workmen and reported proudly that they approved of the paintings and invited him to share their fifteen-cent catered lunches. He drank beer while they drank tea. They even changed some color in the room that he did not like. By Tuesday evening, *The Sciences* was up and seemed perfect. His modesty faded. "Don't tell anyone I said so, but *my decorations are the best things in the place!*" he wrote Louise. "There! How's that for cheek? Really, though, I'm very proud of them and delighted with them in decorative character, in line and in color. They look as if they had grown on the wall by a law of nature, they *fit* so perfectly. For once, I think I have done something really charming as well as good." There was a steady stream of visitors, including Vice-President Adlai Stevenson, who simply said: "Beautiful, beautiful!" The next day Cox worked on *The Sciences,* then had the scaffolding pulled back for an unobstructed view. It needed a few changes, but looked "stunning." *The Arts* was a different matter. The workmen made it fit the space, but "the sky in the whole middle piece is darker than at the sides and must be repainted." He worked steadily until finally satisfied. Louise was supportive and amused from New York. "You certainly sound most conceited, but as it is the first time you have ever liked one of your things on first seeing, I think you've done it this time."[26]

It was an intense three days, and he had few relaxations beyond popular novels at bedtime. While scaffolding was being moved, he and Green visited Rock Creek Cemetery to see Saint Gaudens's celebrated *Adams Monument*

FIG. 26. Kenyon Cox, *The Sciences* (1896), Southwest Gallery, Library of Congress. Oil on canvas mural, 9.5 × 34 feet. Courtesy of the Library of Congress.

(1890). This enigmatic, brooding, seated figure had caused much comment in art circles, and Cox found it "wonderfully impressive and full of a strange majesty and sentiment."[27]

Cox returned to New York satisfied with the works and their placement. "They're *both* daisies!" he wrote Louise at one point. "Really, I think it's time I got away from them or I shall grow too conceited to live. At any rate, they absolutely and entirely belong to the place." The works differed from *Venice* at Bowdoin, with its solid figures and sumptuous colors, and in retrospect Cox regretted the "harmonization by paleness" in them that bespoke Puvis's momentary influence. But these lunettes were attractive and decorative, with a lightness and charm that did not diminish their dignity. They were a major commission well executed. The building and its art were immediately successful with both the public and politicians when it opened in 1897.[28]

The Library of Congress showed how well American artists could decorate public buildings and how popular such work was. In 1898 a similar project on a smaller scale developed in the new state appellate court building at the corner of Twenty-third Street and Madison Avenue in New York City. The building was based on Renaissance models, and its architect, James Brown Lord, wanted exterior sculpture and interior murals to intensify its impact and to illustrate the law's importance in civic affairs. He asked The Mural Painters to nominate artists, and by the spring of 1898 they had suggested ten people, including Cox.

The project quickly became lavish and complex. Richly painted friezes of allegorical figures and scenes ran around the top of the foyer. There were large murals in the stairways and elsewhere. Each artist worked in an individual style, with a general emphasis on the history and ideal functions of the law. The focus of the work was a central courtroom, whose rear wall was divided into three areas for different artists. Edwin H. Blashfield painted *The Power of the Law;* Edward O. Walker depicted *Wisdom;* and Edward Simmons did *The Justice of the Law.* All were in rich, high colors, and in a rather flowing style, filled with idealized figures and their accoutrements. A frieze devoted to Joseph Lauter's *The Judicial and Other Virtues* ran around the top of the back and sides of the room. A long, ornate judges' bench occupied the main wall, set against an elaborate carved screen that rose almost to the ceiling. A stained-glass dome admitted light and was a decoration in itself. The long, interrupted space above the judges bench was assigned to Cox, along with two smaller side areas at each end. The room's decoration would be the work of many hands, crowded into a relatively small area.[29]

The space allotted to Cox was the most difficult in the room. It was about four feet high and some thirty-five feet long, with the two additional smaller angled areas at each end. The high screen behind the judges' bench interrupted the frieze and meant that the work would have to be done in sections that complemented each other and made a coherent whole. Spectators faced the judges, who formed a black-clad frieze of their own against the dark wood screen. Cox's murals would cap and highlight this tableau and somehow must lighten the area, but with dignity.

This was his first work to deal with large civic virtues, and Cox decided to let figures symbolize law and the fruitful results of a just society, under the title *The Reign of Law*. He left the central panel above the bench blank, with an open background and a large scroll with the words "Law Reigns," which spectators would see clearly. The two side panels were about four by fourteen feet, with figures symbolizing law, tradition, enlightened justice, and responsible citizenry. They dealt with the common law and the statute law, and each figure held the accoutrements and symbols appropriate to its station. Tradition, for instance, carried an endless chain, while Equity balanced scales.

By April 1898, Cox was hard at work on preliminary sketches and offered to show them to Leonard Opdycke if he would stop by for a chat. He wanted the colors to be rich but not garish, and to highlight the room without being informal. He carefully complemented warm and cool tones and noted the effects of light and shade throughout the compositions. It was a very slow process, and he did some of the work that summer in Cornish. He continued in the New York studio that winter, and the visiting Dolson thought the result looked fine. As usual, Cox would not compromise about elaborate preliminary drawing and made many nude studies, which he then rendered with drapery.[30]

The final mural suited its place as well as possible, and was probably the most logical painting in the room, given its emphasis on the ancient origins and enduring values in the law. The look was naturally formal but had charm. The figures were suavely drawn, with excellent flesh tones and rich draperies. There were touches of color in the accoutrements and symbols, and an expansive blue sky. The male figures generally were seated in relaxed poses and expressed confidence and energy without being dominant. The female figures were idealized but real. The artists agreed that the room was much too busy, and should have been left to a single decorator. But despite its awkward shape, Cox's space seemed appropriate to the symbols and style he used. He had been unreservedly pleased with the Library of Congress works, but modestly expressed some doubts about this more dignified work. "I don't suppose the color of my Appellate Court work [is] perfectly successful," he wrote Blashfield. "It is an effort at what seemed to me the thing for the place, and I feel still that the *idea* was right. Alas! I am not a big enough man to do the trick. But the work *is* serious, and it is good to know that a few people like yourself know it for such. Perhaps I can better it someday, if I have another chance.[31]

Despite its frustrations and the necessary sieges of hard labor, Cox liked mural painting. It enabled him to express classical ideas and to paint with a breadth of style and largeness of purpose he did not find in easel work. By the turn of the century he was a leader in the mural movement, well known to the architects who selected decorators. His work was increasingly discussed in art journals, and in those for the literate middle class he hoped to impress. But his income was always precarious, especially with a new family and the effort to maintain a middle-class life-style that included a city apartment, maids and nannies, and summers in Cornish.

The family naturally consumed time and energy. Louise delivered a boy on July 5, 1894. "He weighs ten pounds and has a voice of prodigious strength," a relieved Cox reported to Leonard Opdycke. They named him "after a good friend and a fine fellow," and he became "Leo Minor." A second boy, almost as large, named Allyn, arrived on June 5, 1896. The last child, Caroline, named for her mother's aunt, was born on April 1, 1898.

Kenyon and Louise were good parents, but three small children reduced any household to chaos. The inevitable strain intensified Louise's tendency toward "the jiggles," as she called her nervousness. When possible, she visited relatives or simply went away to rest. She and Kenyon were close and compatible, but she inevitably sometimes resented his absorption in work and his seriousness. He was kind, attentive, and could be charming, but seldom engaged in light conversation. They corresponded when apart, and Kenyon sent Louise valentines, birthday greetings, and numerous poems, some whimsical, others affectionate. Like many husbands, he sometimes did not seem to take her seriously. She inevitably struggled to maintain an identity as both a person and a painter. Her will could show, as in reporting on a visit to Dolson and Nellie in Cleveland in 1903. "Nellie is a most reading person, and they have lots of books, and if you could hear me getting off fine literary opinions on things, I know it would amuse you highly, only you would contradict them all, I am afraid," she noted with a touch of sarcasm. "You have no idea how clever I am when I am away from your superior shadow."

Cox also sometimes had "the blues" and was lonely when Louise left town on family business or simply to escape the hubbub. He also resented having to teach, illustrate, and write essays and criticism to make ends meet. He had found his medium, but feared that he would not get enough mural commissions to drop other distracting work. The remuneration for murals was not great, especially given the expenses involved in making a decoration. Not every architect wanted his classical style, and the competition was strong. "I've had another nibble, like that of last year, about possible decorations, but don't think it will come to anything," he wrote Louise in 1900, while she vacationed in Belmont. "It's the old business of trying to get bids and sketches out of a number of artists. All it means, as far as I am concerned, is that such work is wanted, and that 'they've got me on their list.' " But he had to be optimistic. "More such work will come my way sooner or later."[32]

Commissions did indeed come his way as the national building boom developed. Late in 1900 the architect Henry Hardenburgh asked him to decorate an unusual space in the lobby of the new Hotel Manhattan at the northwest corner of Forty-second Street and Madison Avenue. The space was narrow and horizontal, at the top of an ornate elevator cage. The decoration had to balance across the upright elevator door and a matching standing clock, and complement ornate brasswork and wood carving in the cage and in the surrounding lobby. An elaborate symbolic composition was impossible in such a small space, and Cox opted for something decorative, entitled *Peace and Plenty*. To check the proportion, he pasted a small preliminary drawing on a blueprint of the cage, then did the final decoration with the usual care. The finished work showed two female figures floating horizontally in the space. Peace bore an olive branch, and Plenty had a shock of wheat, and they held a shield with the legend WELCOME. The figures were classically draped and the composition symmetrical. Yet the figures had an engaging presence and charm and seemed to float toward the viewers they welcomed (fig. 27). This was a minor work, but it showed that Cox could be effective in unusual circumstances.[33]

In 1903 he and Edwin H. Blashfield did large lunettes at the ends of a high-vaulted ceiling in the lobby of the Citizens Savings and Trust Company building in Cleveland. Blashfield's theme was *The Uses of Wealth,* and Cox's *The Sources of Wealth*. They knew each other from working at the Columbian Exposition and at the Library of Congress. Blashfield was an outstanding figure painter, with a sumptuous style very different from Cox's. The two were friends, but also inevitable competitors. They worked on the Cleveland lunettes in separate studios but regularly compared notes. Cox thought that Blashfield's first color sketches were better than his own, which seemed muddy; but his drawing was superior. He made careful sketches, as usual, and sold the final drawings to the architect Cass Gilbert for some three hundred dollars, then showed them at the Architectural League.

Cox's lunette was complex. At the left, a richly robed, seated female figure of Prudence leaned against a classical pillar. Behind her a large beehive symbolized the labor necessary to create wealth. She motioned to a nude cherub to take a bridle of self-control to three figures at the right who symbolized industries important to Cleveland. A kneeling Manufactures unrolled a green-and-gold tapestry. Fishery held a catch aloft. Agriculture carried the inevitable shock of wheat. As usual, Cox tried to use recognizable symbols for the functions of allegorical figures. To balance and unite the composition, Commerce floated between the two groups to symbolize their interconnections. The figures were set against a long, low wall, with treetops and sky beyond. Fishery was nude, and the others were in richly colored draperies. The formal composition had an impressive sense of harmony and a graceful appearance. In some ways it resembled the lunettes at the Library of Congress

FIG. 27. Kenyon Cox, *Peace and Plenty* (1901), above elevator bank, Hotel
Manhattan, New York City. Oil on canvas, dimensions unknown, location unknown.
Photo: *Pencil Points* 4 (January 1923), 31.

in openness and high coloration. The intellectual content was more subtle.
Cox was clearly saying that wealth came only from honest labor, not from
speculation; that an economy was made of interdependent parts and required
restraint to function; and that wealth had ideal as well as mundane responsibilities. This was a fit message for a bank.[34]

Cox usually thought that any completed project was his best work to date,
and he liked the Cleveland mural. A photograph of it in the studio reassured
him that "I too can do something. It *is* good! There are a few things I have
done that are (true?)," he wrote Louise. But he was seldom as confident as his
emotional armor indicated and was often depressed between commissions.
He realized that his work was respected but that the public probably liked
historical decorations better. "But I'm one of those men who hasn't the talent
for success. I *know* I do better stuff than some of the men who succeed twice
as well." And finishing any project made him realize just how precarious the
family finances always were.[35]

This characteristic mixture of gloom and certitude did not last long. Late
in June 1904, the architect Cass Gilbert conferred with Cox about a mural
commission in the new state capitol he was building in St. Paul, Minnesota.
Gilbert had designed a modernized Greco-Roman building and wanted substantial external statuary and interior decorations. The best painters would
be involved and could choose their subjects and styles. He wanted Cox to
paint a lunette above the entrance to the state supreme court chamber in the
east wing for twenty-five hundred dollars. Gilbert and Cox agreed that this
was hardly enough, but was the maximum available. Cox analyzed the cost
of materials and labor involved and finally accepted.[36]

Decorating any such building was a complex task. The styles and subjects
in paintings varied from area to area. Some were allegorical, other historical,
but each needed a cohesive theme. Cox thus focused on the supreme court
room, which John La Farge would decorate with four lunettes relating to the
origins of law, the citizen and law, morality and law, and the workings of law.
These would employ allegorical figures and scenes, done in La Farge's usual
subdued manner, which relied for effect on creating a contemplative mood.
The space assigned Cox was both awkward and impressive, at the top of a
steep flight of stairs. It was almost a half-circle under a barrel-vaulted ceiling
above the courtroom's entrance. The shape was somewhat constricted, but
the approach allowed for dramatic effect and clear visibility.

Cox worked hard on a suitable subject, and his preliminary drawings
showed considerable evolution of thought. He and Gilbert agreed on com-
plementing La Farge's work in the chamber, and given the supreme court's
role, wanted something grave but evocative of the power of thought and
higher ideals in law. "My idea has been to keep something of your idea of the
East as the country of stability and contemplation, while symbolizing abstract Justice, Law and Power," Cox wrote Gilbert. This view of Oriental

thought and culture was well established. It paralleled Cox's belief in Western classicism, which emphasized order, though it was more oriented to action in the world than was the Oriental thought of popular imagination.

Cox first placed an idealized female figure representing justice with scales in the center of a small pyramidal group. To the left a seated figure represented authority, and to the right another spoke for ideals in law and justice. This created a mood of rather authoritative introspection, but after sending the sketch to Gilbert, Cox thought it too formal. He changed this to a central figure with billowing robes, which he had first avoided "because it seemed to me to introduce too much restlessness and movement where I wanted immobility and stability." To the left an old man represented wisdom and caution, and to the right a female figure spoke for thought and justice. Cox then changed this to a scheme with a central figure with folded wings, seated on an exedra in deep contemplation. He was trying to show the enigmatic nature of justice and its cultural sources, and the figure resembled that of the *Adams Memorial*. A richly clad female on the left held a book that symbolized letters, and a half-clad woman on the right grasped the sceptre and bridle of authority. The general effect was of equipoise and calm, suggesting that the law rested more on thought and a sense of justice than on power. Cox knew that this was a formal, almost static composition, and hoped to enhance its presence with strong colors, especially a brilliant blue for the central figure. To emphasize its universal character, he titled the work *The East*, and later *The Contemplative Spirit of the East*, which complemented La Farge's approach, though in a very different style.[37]

Cox worked steadily on the preliminary drawings that summer in Cornish. By late October, he had sent the cartoon to New York and began painting when he returned for the school term. The canvas was enormous, and he wryly invited friends to see "an elephant in my studio." Gilbert thought the central figure's wings looked artificial, but Cox insisted that they added symbolic gravity and artistic balance to the work and retained them. He showed the finished canvas at an informal studio reception early in December, and placed the work at the year's end. Gilbert finally liked it, and complimented Cox, who gently suggested that the architect keep him in mind for future commissions.[38]

The final work was more impressive and grave than attractive. As usual, Cox painted the figures well, though the central winged one was almost overdone in the crowded composition. The color scheme was strong, partly to enliven the space. The central figure wore blue drapery and sat on a yellow-buff exedra. Her companions were dressed in dark, wine red draperies, and there were touches of strong color elsewhere. The blue sky offered a sense of depth and lightness. The rather constricted space, amid columns, a series of smaller decorations along the barrel vault, and an ornate skylit ceiling, all made the mural seem enclosed and formal.[39]

Cox visited St. Paul in 1906 and approached the completed capitol building with some trepidation, not knowing how his work would now look in place or how it compared to that of others, such as La Farge and Edward Simmons. Critics in New York had said La Farge's lunettes were weak when he showed them before they went to St. Paul. But Cox thought that, in place, they had great presence and rich coloration, even though he did not like them. Simmons had decorated the rotunda with four large panels depicting *The Civilization of the Northwest*. They employed classical figures and were painted with grace and high color, with a light, simplified modern effect that seemed appropriate to their spaces and themes. Cox wrote Louise that Simmons was "outrageously able and clever. The confounded things are too modern-French for my taste, and in lots of ways I don't *like* them at all, but they're humming bits of work, and altogether more complete and more powerful than anything he has done." His own lunette was disappointing. "It's designed and it's drawn, but in tone and color it is thin and papery when compared to what I have been doing, or compared to what La Farge and Simmons have been doing here." The ensemble looked cold and stiff, and the central blue color lifeless. He seldom spared self-criticism, however strong, and merely hoped to do better.[40]

Much of this strong reaction reflected corresponding satisfaction with works he had just seen installed at the Iowa state capitol in Des Moines. The commission in charge of refurbishing this building, which dated from the 1880s, decided to include appropriate decorations. The members visited New York in July 1905 to seek advice from artistic leaders and to interview prospective painters. They liked Cox, "on account of his experience, reputation as an artist of the highest type, and one who has a large number of similar pieces of work in several of the important public buildings of the United States." On July 15, 1905, Cox agreed to do eight lunettes around the bottom of the dome for a fee of eight thousand dollars.[41]

This was a welcome commission, since Cox would develop a scheme rather than place numerous ideas in a single canvas. He first thought of using Iowa's history and natural resources as a basic theme, which doubtless would please the public. But he could not abandon idealism and settled instead on the general title *The Progress of Civilization*. He thus hoped to put Iowa in historical context, above place and time, and show how culture developed and what its ideal purposes were. The eight works moved through *Hunting, Herding, Agriculture, Manufacturing*, and *Commerce*, to a final stage that emphasized *Education, Science*, and *Art*. The struggle for security thus should culminate in appreciation for the arts. The series emphasized continuity, interconnected development, and the elevation of sensibility and was Cox's best painted statement of traditional ideas.[42]

Cox designed each lunette as an independent scene, with a story that clearly fulfilled its title. The earlier ones were realistic, as with *Hunting*

FIG. 28. Kenyon Cox, *Hunting* (1906), Iowa State Capitol, Des Moines.
Oil on canvas mural, dimensions unknown.
Photo courtesy of the State Historical Society of Iowa—Des Moines.

(fig. 28), which showed an almost nude male with dress appropriate to a primitive hunter, amid weapons, dead game, and a companion dog. The pose was relaxed but assured, and the figure represented energy, authority, and the ability to face challenges as an individual. As the series progressed, the figures became more integrated into complex activities involving agriculture, then a modern economy. The last of the set used allegorical females to symbolize the ideals and culture that followed material development and social cohesion. The painting was of high quality throughout. The figures were superbly drawn and expressed energy or repose as their roles required. The color scheme was bold, partly to overcome the height of placement and the lighting in the dome, but also to enliven and energize the works. The landscapes and allegorical backgrounds were richly painted and complemented the dominant figures. Cox's emotional preferences were evident in the last paintings. He clothed the central female figure in *Art* in gold and crimson robes, and she wore a golden wreath in contrast to the substantial but more sober painting for *Science*. Science and economic development were important, but the arts clearly were central to a cohesive social order.

Cox worked hard at the elaborate preliminary sketches in Cornish that summer, then painted the canvases that winter in his New York studio. Numerous friends and critics stopped by to see their progress. "The figures are wonderfully drawn, as is usual with Mr. Cox's work, but artists say that these decorations are his best work," one reporter noted. By March 1906, he had finished six of the canvases, and sent photographs to his parents. Roger Fry, the new curator of painting at the Metropolitan Museum, soon to be a major modernist critic, called and seemed genuinely enthusiastic.[43]

By mid-April Cox was ready to supervise the installation in Des Moines. He checked into a hotel, then the reception committee whisked him to the capitol, where he "went at it" with the workmen and supervisors. The building was "pretty rummy," but the decorations would enliven it a good deal. Each canvas fitted into an ornate frame, with large baroque statues standing at the sides. He had feared that these would interrupt the view but was relieved to see that they did not. He had also worried that the high colors would look garish, but found them rather pale and flat in place because of the height and the lighting. They needed repainting only at the edges near the frames. "The things are not a bit too strong, and if I were to make any serious changes it would be to strengthen them," he wrote Louise. The almost orange flesh tones of the hunter were just right, and the dark black head of a dead goose was a nice contrasting gray, not the blank spot he had feared. "My greatest audacities, like the crimson and yellow draperies of Art, look quiet and gray." He clambered up and down the scaffolding for various views. "I thought the things were strong and brilliant, and so they are, but what tickles me is how restrained and refined they look. Of course, I counted on this result, but it is pleasant to be justified." Once more, as with the Library of Congress lunettes in 1896, the more he looked, the less modest he became. "I really think I've scored ten—which is most satisfying." He was even pleased enough to lecture at a local women's club, and promised Louise to behave. "As I'm trying to be excruciatingly affable, of course I said yes."[44]

On returning to New York, he was still excited, almost self-satisfied. He asked the commission secretary to send him any printed or photographic work on the paintings, which he could circulate among friends and critics. "As you have, in Des Moines, the best work I have ever done, I want to make what reputation I can out of it!" That fall he asked Saint Gaudens to look over photographs of the works. "They seem to me, at present, the only *real* things I ever did—the only things that I can conceive of as really counting with serious works of art." Of course, the old Cox ambivalence returned: "Probably it will not be long before I get over it and they relapse into the category of more or less respectable efforts with what I have done before!"[45]

There was some comment in Iowa that the series did not reflect the state's history or locale and was too abstract, but most response was favorable. Cox had painted elegant individual pieces in a coherent whole. They worked because of his ability in figure painting, which matched his ideas.

Cox turned at once to a different, complex commission for Cass Gilbert's new Essex County Courthouse in Newark, New Jersey. Early in April 1906, he accepted the job, which was due in eight months, for a five-thousand-dollar fee. The work was for the large supreme court room, which had a decorated ceiling and elaborate chandeliers. The panel would have to complement and compete with dark curved woodwork throughout the room, and with the judges bench, the bar, and chairs. It would be about twelve feet high and nine feet wide, some three feet above the floor, and would dominate a long side wall, set between painted pilasters and lightly decorated flanking areas. It would easily dominate the room.

Cox opted for a formal, allegorical composition, both to suit the space and to express complex ideas. He seated an idealized female figure of Law before a curved set of Grecian columns. There was an open statute book on her lap and a golden scepter in her left hand. A figure of Justice, with heavenly antecedents, floated above her with scales. Peace sat at the right with an olive branch. A group in the lower left, with a half-nude woman giving fruits to cherubs, symbolized the prosperity that flowed from just social law. One child represented the artistic and poetic senses and was picking flowers. Cox's usual well-designed sky and landscape gave the huge picture some contrast and depth, but the general effect was of flattened space, echoing Puvis de Chavannes, but in rich colors and with strong modeling for the figures. The floating figure of Justice wore blue and white robes to denote idealistic qualities. The central dominating figure of Law was in regal red. At her side, Peace was clad in dove gray and bright rose. The seated female figure who represented prosperity and plenty wore a crown of gold grain and red poppies, her lap covered in golden drapery. Colors for the background and accessories were equally rich and well modulated. Cox wanted a legend to summarize his idealistic view of the proper role of law in a cohesive society. There was no room on the picture, and he finally had it painted below: Under the Rule of the Law, Inspired by Justice, Peace and Prosperity Abide. He titled the work *The Beneficence of the Law* (fig. 29).

Shortly after returning from Des Moines, Cox went to Cornish for the summer as usual and began working on the preliminary drawings and cartoon. He enjoyed the theater and the popular Ethel Barrymore was one of his favorite actresses. She was recuperating from appendicitis with friends in Cornish that summer. She was an attractive woman of great presence with a no-

FIG. 29. Kenyon Cox, *The Beneficence of the Law* (1906),
Essex County Court House, Newark, N.J. Oil on canvas mural, 12 × 9 feet.
Photograph, gift of Allyn Cox, 1959-69-80. Photo by Scott Hyde.
Courtesy of Cooper-Hewitt, National Museum of Design,
Smithsonian Institution/Art Resource, New York.

ble visage, and Cox persuaded her to sit for the head of the floating figure of
Justice in the mural. She was patient and remembered the experience for
years. "I was fascinated by his enormous studio, and by his climbing up on

ladders to do his huge canvases." By mid-September he had blocked in the figures and was ready to start painting. A month later he sent the canvas to the New York City studio and followed to teach and to complete the mural.

The numerous city dailies needed a great deal of news to fill their columns, and public interest in art was strong. The commissions and workings of a well-known artist like Cox bore reporting. Early in November, he discussed the Newark decoration with a reporter from the *Tribune* and was "incautious enough" to mention Barrymore's role. Given her stardom, the reporter immediately wanted to include this in the story. The numerous controversies over nude models prompted Cox never to discuss his sitters. Nor did he want any sensationalism about Barrymore to obscure the inherent qualities of the Newark picture. Warning bells rang, and he specifically refused permission to mention her name, "conceiving that the personality of my sitters was no one's affair but my own, the public having no legitimate interest in anything but the result." The reporter defied Cox and published a brief description of the work, with a headline that proclaimed Barrymore's sittings. Leslie D. Ward, president of the Essex County Building Commission, sent a clipping of the story to Gilbert with a self-righteous covering letter, holding primly that actresses had no place in such dignified art. "It would have been just as well, it seems to me, if Mr. Cox had looked elsewhere for a subject," he intoned. "This is not said in disparagement of Miss Barrymore especially, but out of regard for the fitness of things."

Architects quickly learned to deal with unexpected reactions from clients, especially where public money and tastes were involved. Gilbert was circumspect and forwarded the clipping and letter to Cox for a response. Cox quickly explained his friendship with Barrymore, her posing that summer, and the circumstances of the newspaper interview, which he now thought was a breach of confidence. He insisted that Barrymore's portrait was not in fact in the picture, since he had merely used her as an ideal type. The resulting head was "one of the most beautiful I have ever painted," and he hoped the commission would see no sensationalism where none was intended.

Unhappily, a sharp minicontroversy followed among the parties involved. Cox continued to protest that the final head of Justice was not a portrait of Barrymore or anyone else. Of course, there was no appeal to artistic integrity; the commission could reject anything it did not like. Late in November, Gilbert directed Cox to change the head to a type, obviously reflecting the board's views. The Newark newspaper noted the affair, admonishing that "in making the change no criticism was meant either of the artist or the actress involved." Cox thought that everyone attached "too much importance to idle newspaper chatter" but agreed to make the changes. By early December, he had altered the head until he thought it resembled the *Venus de Milo* more than anything else. Whether Cox was dissimulating or actually tried to modify the head, it continued to resemble Barrymore's well-known profile. He finally asked Gilbert and anyone else he chose to see the revised work, approve it, and proceed to its installation. Gilbert and Ward visited the studio late in the afternoon of December 20 and accepted the result.[46]

Cox showed the panel briefly at the Fine Arts Building and dreaded potential newspaper coverage. "I have absolutely refused to give them any encouragement, and have kept my mouth shut," he wrote Gilbert. Nothing much happened, except that Gilbert was ecstatic about the picture. "Your Newark picture is superb," he wrote Cox on December 29. "I want to congratulate you on having created a distinguished and *beautiful* work of art. It is fine in color, drawing, composition and all that, as you know; but withal, it has a charm, a dignity, and a *serenity* that is not usual in modern work." As if this were not gratifying enough, he reported two days later that many of his friends had seen it and agreed. "You have painted a noble picture and have given the world a new work of natural beauty and great quality." Cox was overwhelmed, given the late debate. "I am particularly pleased with your choice of the word 'serenity' to express the sentiment of the work," he replied in January 1907. "A kind of serene and noble quality is the note I tried to strike." Cox spent Saturday and Sunday, December 29 and 30, on the site, revising some colors. He was satisfied with the painted legend and with the general architectural setting. The picture was "much handsomer in its permanent surroundings than it was apart from them." The style matched the setting and was pictorially effective. Cox was right in saying earlier that "I feel sure that the panel is a piece of work which will be an ornament to the Courthouse after all this rubbish is forgotten."[47]

These were busy years for Cox, as mural commissions developed in rapid sequence. He also taught, wrote, and was active in the art societies. The next large mural came in 1908. Pennsylvania's prosperous Luzerne County and its seat Wilkes-Barre decided to erect a new courthouse, almost on the scale of a state capitol building. It called for substantial interior decorations, and Low and Blashfield among others were involved. After consulting with the architect, Harry Livingstone French, and the building commissioners, Low recommended Cox to do an elaborate painting to fit behind and above the judges bench in courtroom number four. By midsummer 1908, Cox had agreed and was making preparatory sketches.[48]

The assigned space posed a considerable challenge. The picture's size alone, nearly nine feet high and fifteen feet long, was daunting. It would be clearly visible to spectators, but had to compete with and complement ornate woodwork throughout the room. The lower wainscoating was dark mahogany, as was the picture frame. The three-judge bench was dark and richly carved. Behind it there were two large wood panels and a central entryway that admitted judges to their chairs. An ornate carved shield was exactly above the central chair and provided a kind of footing for the painting's bottom frame. Strong wooden pillars flanked the bench and stood out slightly into the room at each end of this area. Two chandeliers hung just beyond them in the room. The viewer thus saw a set of strong horizontal lines in the judges bench, molding and picture frame, enclosed in equally strong vertical lines from the pillars, panelling behind the bench, and the chairs.

Cox carefully studied descriptions and plans of the room and his space and decided on an almost static composition. "The formal symmetry of the setting seemed to demand a grave and balanced composition, while the rich tone of the woodwork called for great fulness of color," he recalled, "and the depth of the moldings and the projection of columns required force of light and shade and strength of modelling if the painting were to hold its own." The figures involved were especially challenging. They "must be large enough not to be too greatly dwarfed by the columns on either side, yet not so large as to make the real figures of the judges below look like pigmies." He decided to make them about seven feet high and to use a rich color scheme that would let the painting stand out without being garish.[49]

The color plan was especially important. Exactly in the picture's center, under a canopy of gold and crimson, he placed a standing female figure of Rectitude. She held a builder's triangle and a plumb bob to symbolize impartiality and correct judgment. She wore a white dress with a striking black, off-shoulder, full-length robe to complement those of the judges below. Two standing nude cherubs flanked her, holding tablets proclaiming Fiat Justitia Ruat Coelum (Let justice be done though the heavens fall). At the right, an aged woman representing learning consulted the statute book while a female Wisdom offered to temper her findings. A seated, armed male figure symbolizing courage was at the left, under the influence of a female Moderation who carried the bridle of self-control. The figures at the left were done in crimson and red, those at the right in orange and brown. There was a line of richly painted white clouds just behind the figures, with green treetops and a blue sky that rose to the top of the painting. As Cox planned, the work was dignified and symmetrical, with a sense of authority and easily read symbols. The other muralists opted for different, lighter treatments, but Cox's was highly appropriate to his ideal of the law and to its space. Few of his works better illustrated an idealistic desire for justice under law that promoted harmony in a cohesive social order. He titled it *The Judicial Virtues*.

Cox worked on the usual complex preparatory drawings that summer and had settled on the final design by late November. In February 1909, he invited students to see the sketches in the studio, chiefly to illustrate how he worked. He completed the picture in April and had another reception. Cox liked the final painting and thought it appropriate to its setting and as an intellectual statement. To his surprise, on January 28, 1910, the Architectural League of New York awarded it their prestigious gold medal. Cox prized this honor because it testified to the painting's merits and to his general standing as a muralist.[50]

Cox worked on two other substantial commissions in 1909. One was an over-mantle picture to fit above the fireplace in a room assigned to the collector of customs in the new federal building in Cleveland. Blashfield, Low, and Alexander, among others, were decorating this typically lavish new public structure. Cox's space permitted a framed picture rather than a true mural. The chimney mantle was deep purple marble, and the woodwork along the lower part of the walls was an equally rich, dark Circassian walnut. The color scheme above this was light and neutral, with ornate gilded pillars and a decorated ceiling. The painting would occupy an elaborate carved frame, about six feet from the floor, within carved moldings. The area did not permit an elaborate composition, yet demanded something with rich color and dignity to enliven the room without being informal. "It seemed best to make the decoration a spot of brilliant color in its rich and quiet surroundings, while the shape of the panel and the deep frame at once suggested a certain Venetian air in the composition of the panel," he noted.

He adopted a 7-by-4½ foot oval design, titled *Passing Commerce Pays Tribute to Cleveland.* In its upper part a flying Mercury, god of commerce, nude except for flowing maroon drapery, dropped golden coins into the lap of a reclining female Cleveland. She wore a white dress and caught the coins in her lap with a rich red cloak. Both figures carried golden scepters, and Cleveland wore a gold crown. The subject was familiar, if not clichéd, but was understandable at a glance and made its point about commerce and custom duties without an elaborate scheme. The figures, especially Mercury, were well drawn, fully modelled, and richly painted. The composition was a logical, harmonious whole (fig. 30).

Cox showed the finished work in the annual exhibition of the Albright Art Gallery in Buffalo early in 1910, and it went to Cleveland in June. A year later he visited Dolson in Cleveland and saw the mural at the Citizens Savings and Trust Company and the painting at the federal building. *Passing Commerce* "struck me as rather bully."[51] It might lack the complex allegories of his other works, but as a decorative piece it was dignified and suited the room.

The next commission for 1909 was a familiar kind of work but was more complex than the custom house painting. In November 1908, Dolson reported that he could probably secure a contract for Kenyon to do a memorial lunette for Charlotte Prentiss Hayes in the public library of Winona, Minnesota. Mrs. Hayes was a cousin of Nellie's and had been married to a business friend of Dolson's, who made a fortune in lumbering. She had been a pillar of the library and cultural community in the area, and her husband sought to provide a suitable memorial. The family and friends wanted a lunette in the reading room, dedicated to learning. Mrs. Hayes had known of Cox's family connection and admired his work, which made him a logical choice for the painting.

FIG. 30. Kenyon Cox, *Passing Commerce Pays Tribute
to The Port of Cleveland* (1909), U.S. Custom House, Cleveland, Ohio.
Oil on canvas, 7 × 4.5 feet. Photograph, gift of Allyn Cox, 1959-69-83.
Photo by Ken Pelka. Courtesy of Cooper-Hewitt, National Museum of Design,
Smithsonian Institution/Art Resource, New York.

This offered Cox a chance to refine his allegorical style. He knew that the subject must please the Hayes family and the townspeople and reflect the public's conception of a library as a depository and disseminator of knowledge. Such a theme exactly suited his classical idealism. The space was large enough for groups of figures, and his final design was filled with allusions to Mrs. Hayes and to the general ideal of learning. He entitled it *The Light of Learning*.

In the center of the large work, a female Learning, clad in green to symbolize youth and vigor, sat on an elaborate marble Renaissance-style throne. A colorful band of flowers dipped below her feet to underline the memorial inscription to Mrs. Hayes. A cherub stood at each side, holding a flaming lamp to symbolize learning and its passage between the generations. To the right, there were female figures of Romance, Poetry, and Art. To the left, Philosophy, History, and Science held appropriate accoutrements and symbols. Each suggested that learning was vital and ongoing, that it shaped people's lives and reminded them of their lineage. Knowledge was a great force, and its parts, each symbolized in an ideal woman, were integrated and interdependent.

The composition was formal in its lines and masses, but the figures were clad in unusually rich and varied colors, which gave the ensemble a sense of life and vigor. The colors ranged from lime green to orange, crimson, blue, and buff. The drawing and modelling were very fine, and the painting graceful. Despite its formality, the work had a charm that somewhat resembled the Library of Congress lunettes of 1896. The painting was serious and about a serious subject, but would not inhibit anyone from seeking learning. It decorated the room well and offered an intelligible message.

The local committee dedicated the work on April 29, 1910, and the public response was enthusiastic. The lunette seemed perfectly suited to Mrs. Hayes's dignified and somewhat retiring nature, but represented her civic work and reminded people that Winona and learning were part of the wider world and greater heritage. Cox's technical skill was obvious, and his ideas were appropriate. "In his mural decorations, here as elsewhere, he is always dignified and one feels that the situation has been adequately met," the local newspaper reported. "He is never trivial and one realizes that art to him is a serious profession which requires culture and training." Cox was equally satisfied, and thought that this work and the one at Wilkes-Barre were among his best decorations, both as paintings and as expressions of ideas.[52]

Early in 1910, Cox's friend Francis Davis Millet wrote him about yet another kind of commission. Millet was a painter and was well known among artists as an organizer and overseer of artistic projects. He had supervised the mural work at the World's Fair of 1893 and was now planning decorations for the new Hudson County Courthouse in Jersey City, New Jersey. The best muralists would be involved, and he immediately thought of Cox for some unusual spaces. There were four small lobbies near elevators on the third level, each with a groined ceiling about seventeen feet from the floor. There was room for two small lunettes about four and a half feet high and six feet long, in each one, for a total of eight. The spaces were self-contained and Millet thought that some simple design would be best. There was not really enough room in them for figure compositions or to tell an elaborate story, and they should not clash with larger historical works nearby. He could pay three thousand dollars, and suggested that Cox take the train across the river, see the spaces, and suggest a plan. Cox did so, and Millet passed on the proposal to the contractor, then got an extra five hundred dollars in the fee, "which is better than a poke in the eye with a sharp stick." The contractor liked the proposal and gave Cox a free hand.

The designs were unlike Cox's previous work and showed his ability to deal in basic forms as well as in idealized figures and symbols. The eight lunettes were titled *Liberty* and *Law*, and the six virtues assigned to the law, *Justice, Rectitude, Courage, Moderation, Wisdom,* and *Learning.* Within a circle in midlunette, a stylized figured represented each idea. He surrounded these with abstracted vases, vines, and leaves. The works recalled the ancient Near East and the Bible, as well as Greek and Roman antecedents. Each lunette's story was recognizable through its title, and the concepts were all familiar and suitable to a courthouse and the law. They were done in a cameo style, and in attractive but subdued earth colors such as russet, green, and ivory. As he wrote his mother that June, they would be purely decorative, much like cameos (fig. 31). He completed the panels, and two well-known artistic assistants, Vincent Aderante and Alonzo E. Foringer, helped install them.[53]

After he finished the Hudson County work, Cox joined the family for a quick tour of Italy. They returned with slim financial resources, and he paid the bills with an occasional sale, articles and reviews, and lectures, though he had retired from the Art Students League in 1909. He survived a real financial crisis early in 1911. By September, fortune seemed to change in his favor. "But the big decoration has turned up!" he excitedly reported to the art publisher August Jaccaci. The architect George B. Post wanted him to do a major decoration in the new Wisconsin state capitol, then rising in stages in Madison. In January 1912, he signed a contract to do four large pendentives in the dome for twenty thousand dollars, payable in the usual installments.[54]

The building was in the form of a Greek cross, with four wings of equal height and length. The dome sat atop the point where they converged, and there were four large, semi-triangular spaces, between it and the arches of the corridors. This sort of space was classic for decorators, and here posed special challenges. The corridor ceilings were decorated, with the walls done in a soft yellow-toned stone. The space under the dome was huge and well lit. But the pillars and pilasters were dramatic dark green marble, and there

FIG. 31. Kenyon Cox, *Learning* (1910), Hudson County Court House, Jersey City,
N.J. Oil on canvas, dimensions unknown.
Photograph, gift of Allyn Cox, 1959-69-123. Photo by Scott Hyde.
Courtesy of Cooper-Hewitt, National Museum of Design,
Smithsonian Institution/Art Resource, New York.

was a frieze of deep rose marble. There were also numerous elaborately carved
cornices and frames. The colors and materials were rich, formal, and the entire Renaissance style harked back to a Greco-Roman world of wealth and
confidence. Cox wanted the pendentives to match this grandeur and solemnity in both materials and design. The four spaces should tell a simple story
in easily recognized terms and speak with authority through their materials.

Cox decided to do the works in colored-glass mosaic, the largest such effort in the country to date. The spaces were about twelve feet high and
twenty-four feet long. Allegorical figures in their centers would represent the
building's ideal function as a place of lawmaking and government. The
background of each pendentive was gold, with stylized green oak leaves, and
the figure was in a circle of fasces. An elaborate guilloche border of purple
and gold enclosed each composition, which gained added effect from the decorations in the dome and halls.

An aged male figure in a yellow gown and blue mantle, derived from popular conceptions of Moses, represented legislation, which needed the support of wisdom and cautious precedent. Government was a seated soldier figure, dressed in red. "His left hand rests upon a great sword, sheathed and bound, only to be drawn in case of necessity." A female Justice in red and purple weighed her scales with apparent detachment. Liberty, dressed in blue and green, rather dramatically guarded the ballot box and pointed upward with her right hand "as if to say that 'Under a republican form of government, the voice of the people is the voice of God's' " (fig. 32). Each pendentive was clearly labelled in the design and visible throughout the dome area. The figures, their draperies, and the accoutrements were firmly and broadly drawn and well integrated into the backgrounds. The viewer's eye and mind easily grasped the ensemble. "I tried to get into them something of the splendor of color and formality of design of the old mosaics, combined with a style of drawing in harmony with the Renaissance character of the building," Cox wrote later. "The avoidance of pictorial and realistic effect was, of course, intentional."[55]

Cox realized that this was likely to be his largest commission and the best chance for enduring fame. He worked over the preliminary drawings with special care in the summer of 1912 in Cornish, and by mid-July had finished them on a scale of three inches to the foot. The rate of progress was gratifying, for as he told Lew F. Porter, the capitol commission secretary, "it would be quite possible to carry out the work satisfactorily, under any competent supervision, if I were to die tomorrow." He then made color studies on the same scale. Post saw the work in progress, and "expressed to me a degree of satisfaction, and even enthusiasm, which was most gratifying to me." Cox continued that winter in New York and asked Leonard Opdycke to visit the studio "to see my designs for the great mosaics, which I am rather prouder of than anything I have done."[56]

Turning the drawings into small pieces of colored glass was yet another challenge. Cox proposed to supervise the work in New York, and on the advice of friends, selected the bid of the Decorative Stained Glass Company. He thought that a small firm with suitable experience would do better work with less trouble than would a large concern. Grace Edith Barnes, former secretary to John La Farge, who was famous for his stained glass, acquired the company shortly thereafter. This was a mixed blessing. She was "familiar with the trials and tribulations of artists" but had little capital and no experience in running a business. The original bid was too low and the company nearly closed while doing the work. This led to endless correspondence between Cox, Porter, and Barnes over minor expenditures that meant the difference between solvency and bankruptcy. Barnes was obviously under strain and was apprehensive in dealing with this inherited difficulty. "She is a

FIG. 32. Kenyon Cox, *Justice* (1913), Wisconsin State Capitol Rotunda, Madison.
Glass mosaic on plaster, 12 × 24 feet.
Photo courtesy of Mazur Design, Monona, Wisconsin.

prickly kind of person to deal with," Cox wrote Porter, "but I believe her to have been honest in this business, though unlucky."[57]

Somehow the work went on. By late May 1913, Cox assured Porter that the glass for Justice was almost done and that he took special pains not to render the title as *Just ice,* a common joke among artists. The dome was not completed, so the mosaics were glued to heavy canvas and shipped to Madison for storage as completed. The last went out on October 20. Cox cautioned the people there to store them flat and in perfect dryness. If the pieces came off the canvas, they might have to be redone. Once set in cement on the walls, they "should be as nearly indestructible as anything can be."[58]

By mid-May 1914, the masons and plasterers were almost finished in the dome and Cox prepared to go to Madison to watch the first stages of installation. "I am rather excited by the prospect of getting them up at last," he wrote Porter, "for I think they will form a more splendid piece of decoration than anyone can have any idea of from the studies." Once there, he had the men lay out the canvases on the floor. Some of the pieces had separated but were not damaged. He clambered up the scaffolding to check the spaces. After Cox returned to New York, Porter reported that a few areas needed reworking to accommodate the glass, and that some colors had bled through the border, which must be repaired. Porter did not like the company's work, or their men on the site. Everyone was irritated about money. The state could not always pay Cox on time, and he had to borrow at interest. The company was desperate for payments, and the commissioners challenged every charge for repairs or reworking. Cox wearied of the details. "I am sorry there should be so much trouble about these mosaics," he wrote Porter. "I have done all I can to satisfy the Commission, and am proud of the work, but I feel sorry, sometimes, that I ever undertook work needing the cooperation of subcontractors. When I undertake a piece of painting, I know where I am!" He became defensive about complaints against the company. "As to the actual work of making the mosaics, it was admirably done and *as I wanted it,* and I should not have got anything like so good a result from some of the larger firms." In the end, everything worked out. Post, who died in November 1913, had been enthusiastic about the designs. And for all the trouble involved, Porter liked the tympanums. "I agree with you that the mosaics are a splendid piece of work," he wrote Cox in October 1914. "They are head and shoulders above everything we have in the capitol, or will have, and everyone is much pleased with them."[59] Over the years, the building's users and tourists agreed that the works were attractive and impressive. They suited the space and made large statements with ease and remain among the country's best decorations.

The possibility of doing a second large commission for the Wisconsin capitol began to intrigue Cox as he finished the mosaics. Post had originally approached him to do a large tryptich for the senate chamber, but the work finally went to John White Alexander. At the end of October 1913, while visiting Post's office in New York City, Cox heard that Alexander had decided not to do the work. Cox immediately wrote the news to Porter, and cautiously suggested himself as a replacement. With the last of the mosaics just shipped to Madison for storage until the dome was completed, he had the time to do another project. "I have thought I might venture to suggest that, if you have no one else in view for this work, I should feel greatly honored if it were confided to me." He realized that the capitol commission wanted to have numerous artists represented in the building. But Blashfield already had two commissions, in the dome and in the assembly chamber, and "there would be no inconsistency in doing a similar thing in this case." Cox did not quite sing his own praises, but the commission did know his work and seemed to like the mosaics. "I believe it is unnecessary for me to say anything of my qualifications for the work, or to assure you that I should take pride in giving the best thought and effort I am capable of to the production of something worthy of such a splendid opportunity."

Porter was obviously surprised, but somewhat noncommittal. He would note the letter at the commission's next meeting. "I thank you for it, as possibly it may relieve an embarrassing situation." Cox continued to remind Porter of his availability. Porter did not think that Alexander would void the contract, which dated from 1911. "It would seem very strange and unbusinesslike if he should withdraw at this late date," he wrote Cox early in December. Cox immediately answered that he understood from Alexander that he would decide about doing the work before the capitol commission's next meeting, December 19, 1913. Cox was obviously anxious. He needed the work and also saw it as another chance for a major, enduring mural. Alexander did withdraw, and the commission turned to Cox for this elaborate painting.[60]

While in Madison in mid-May 1914 to check on the mosaics, Cox measured the allotted space in the unfinished senate chamber. The relatively small room was circular, with the senators' desks to be arranged in semicircles facing the president's chair and bench. The walls would be in a creamy yellow Italian marble, and an elaborate round stained-glass ceiling admitted light. The carpets would be dark red, and the plaster trimmed in gold. The three large paintings, each eleven feet six inches high, and seven feet two inches wide, would be framed in simple gold, recessed behind and between elaborate Corinthian columns done in a light, veined French marble. The room would require dignified and elegant decoration to complement its compactness and symbolic purposes.

Cox apparently had not settled on a subject. The evening after he measured the chamber, he suddenly decided to suggest a work to commemorate the completion of the Panama Canal. He had been "hankering" to do this, because of the event's importance and his belief that cultural symbols were universal and unifying. He proposed this to the commission with some trepidation. "It has so little to do with Wisconsin that I was afraid they would turn me down," he wrote Louise. "On the contrary, they were delighted. The importance of the event historically, and its neat coincidence in time, *dating* the building forever, appealed to them." He signed the contract that August, just after the canal opened, and would receive twelve thousand dollars in the usual installments as work was finished.[61]

Cox titled the triptych *The Marriage of the Atlantic and the Pacific,* and it was his most elaborate mural. In the central panel an enthroned America blessed the union of the two great oceans. Neptune represented the Atlantic and placed a ring on the finger of a female Pacific. Below this ensemble two cherubs held a shield of the American flag. To the right, a floating female Peace welcomed European nations to the ceremony. France bore a palette for art, Germany held a book for science, Great Britain had the symbols of power and authority. On the left, a female Commerce, with some resemblance to Mercury, beckoned to symbolic figures of Japan and China, while a figure representing the Semitic groups stood at the far edge of the canvas. Below these was a garlanded female Polynesia in a boat. Landscapes and skies behind the two side panels offered perspective and lightened the formal figures. The colors were rich maroons, reds, purple, and touches of green and yellow. The composition, as befitted its space and the purposes of the room, was formal, balanced, and the three parts were well integrated (fig. 33). Cox personified his and the public's perceptions of the various important cultures, but he treated them as equals and as ideals, significant to one another and to the world. As usual, female figures represented the unifying and softening power of ideas and culture. The basic message was optimistic. Culture triumphed over national differences because it dealt with universals. Unifying ideals as well as commerce would pass through the canal.

To avoid distractions, Cox spent much of the summer of 1914 at an artists' retreat in Croton-on-Hudson, New York. He worked steadily at preliminary drawings, and by the end of July offered to submit a basic sketch to the capitol commission. He followed the world news, and wryly commented on the outbreak of war in Europe. "Present European news gives an ironic aspect to my subject, but the canal will be there when the wars are over." That fall and winter he moved on to the cartoons and was about one-third finished before Christmas. By February 1915, he had completed the full-sized charcoal cartoon, which Otis Post of the architectural firm liked. "It has involved a great deal of hard work and intense study," he wrote Porter, "but I am pretty well satisfied with it, and Mr. Blashfield tells me it is the finest thing I have done." Assistants helped with the cartoons, but he would do all of the painting himself. In late May he asked that the delivery date be extended from August 1 to November 1. The work had been more complex and demanding than he had first thought. "Certainly no part of the delay is due to

FIG. 33. Kenyon Cox, *The Marriage of the Atlantic and the Pacific* (1915), Wisconsin State Capitol Building, Senate Chamber. Oil on canvas, triptych, each panel 11.6 × 7.2 feet. Photo courtesy of Mazur Design, Monona, Wisconsin.

laziness, as I have never worked so hard and so continuously for so long in my life as I have since last November." The commission readily granted the modest extension. By late July 1915, he promised Porter some photographs of the basic work, which only needed more coloring.[62]

On October 4, 1915, he triumphantly wrote Porter that the work was completed. The following day he wrote Louise, who was in Belmont, that he was finished, "and today have tinkered with everything I could find to tinker with." Blashfield suggested that he show the canvases and drawings at the Vanderbilt Fine Arts Gallery, which had a large exhibition hall. The public response seemed positive, at least among the people whose views he valued. "I am pleased with the result of exhibiting the pictures. Even as they are seen out of their proper surroundings, they have been much admired by the public, and by all artists and critics except the ultra- 'Moderns.' That they attack it is, I think, rather a compliment," he wrote Porter. He dispatched the works to Madison on October 17, 1915, and followed ten days later for their installation. The decorators and workmen were helpful, and he was satisfied. So was Porter. "Since your decoration was placed, I have had a number of the best informed of our local people in to see it, and they all admired it very much," he wrote shortly after Cox left Madison. "While personally I do not consider myself a judge of work of this character, I must say that it pleases me greatly, and I feel that the Commission was most fortunate in the selection of yourself as the artist." Cox took the praise in stride. "I am, at least, sure that I have done everything in my power to produce an adequate piece of work."[63]

The Wisconsin decorations pleased Cox, and he did one other commission at the same time that had special significance for him and the family. Dolson wished to endow a new administration building at Oberlin College in memory of his parents. The college had some funds, and Dolson added fifty thousand dollars. Cass Gilbert designed a Mediterranean-style building, which with furnishings ultimately cost seventy-nine thousand dollars.[64]

As the design progressed, Dolson decided to include a bronze tablet noting the accomplishments of his father, who had died in 1900. Like many others, he thought General Cox an unusual combination of practical and reflective personalities, who had pursued careers in warfare, politics, and business without abandoning his idealism or interests in education, science, and philosophy. In late 1913, he suggested that Kenyon design such a tablet for a small vestibule on one side of the building. He did not want anything "*extravagantly* expensive," but agreed to pay the sculptress Frances Grimes $450 to cast the work. The tablet would be about twenty-two inches high and eighteen inches wide, and would list the general's career in a kind of free verse that he and Will Cochran would provide. Kenyon duly finished a simple but elegant design with crossed swords, shields, and olive branches.[65]

By January 1914 this did not seem enough, and Dolson proposed that Kenyon do a painting to go above the tablet. He would pay him a thousand dollars, and "let it be understood by all parties that the painting is your contribution to the memorial building." Dolson had in mind some kind of picture, "and not a decoration." But he would "leave the entire suggestion and execution to you believing that you will do the very best you can and 'then some.' " In May 1914, when Kenyon went to Madison for the first installation of the mosaics, he stopped in Cleveland to show the family pictures of the decoration for his father. He had decided to do a small lunette-shaped painting, and his brothers knew enough not to argue. They all agreed that to balance the foyer area, and for their own reasons, a second lunette was in order for their mother who had died in 1911. Cochran and Dolson "seemed delighted with the decoration, and with the prospect of the decoration in memory of mother, though I don't think they understood the rough sketch very well," he reported to Louise.[66]

The space involved was a small foyer, leading into the building. It would be done in neutral tones and had a fairly high ceiling. The art works would be at about eye level and were only some three feet high and five feet wide. Any allegory would have to avoid overwhelming the viewer. Cox settled on designs that reflected the family's view of their parents. They also symbolized the power of large civic ideals worked out in individual lives, a theme which Oberlin always emphasized. The lunette for his father, *The Active and the Contemplative Life,* showed a figure derived from Pallas Athene and Hermes that represented public activities and practical wisdom. It was seated but seemed ready to rise and act. A second seated figure represented thought and contemplation. Attributes of the two obviously represented General Cox, whose deeds were recorded in the tablet below. The modelling was strong, and the colors were rich, in broad masses of maroon, brown, and red.

The lunette to Cox's mother, *The Spirit of Self Sacrificing Love,* was a few feet across from this space. Kenyon saw her as a true helper to his father and as a sustaining force to her children. But she was an independent personality. He thought that "the great principle of her character was that of love, of self-sacrificing love, of something like the Biblical charity." But he did not wish to depict the usual allegory of charity, instead inventing "a Charity of my own—a robust angel, holding in the hand a burning heart, and crowned with a crown of thorns—the Spirit of Love which 'suffereth long and is kind' " (fig. 34). This figure had brilliant blue wings and was clothed in red and yellow-buff. Both lunettes were striking, with great immediacy because of their placement and size. Cox had caught his own view of his father as reserved, dignified, and important, yet thoughtful and caring. And his mother was a personal symbol of the values he attributed to idealized women. He successfully depicted these large ideals in an intimate manner.

FIG. 34. Kenyon Cox, *The Spirit of Self-Sacrificing Love* (1914),
Administration Building foyer, Oberlin College, Oberlin, Ohio.
Oil on canvas mural, 3.2 × 5.7 feet. Courtesy of Oberlin College.
Photo: Geoffrey Blodgett, Oberlin, Ohio.

Cox exhibited the works at the Fine Arts Club in New York City in November 1914, and an unnamed reviewer for the *New York Times* praised them lavishly both as painting and as symbolism. He thought the drawing, modelling, and color were outstanding. Cox had imbued the figures with a strong sense of both vitality and reflection. The decorations were "eloquent of that passion for rightness which lifts his paintings to their high place in modern decoration." The Oberlin community liked the works. The college administration later adopted the lunette to Cox's mother as the official alma mater symbol on its publications.[67]

By Christmas 1914, the building was nearing completion. Cox corresponded with the contractors and furnished sketches and paint samples. "Please have the painter match the tone as accurately as possible," he wrote President Henry Churchill King's secretary. "The paint should be stippled and with a dead surface as like stone as possible." He wanted the decorations in neutral surroundings in the small space. King invited Kenyon, Dolson, and Will Cochran to speak at the formal dedication on February 10, 1915. Kenyon arrived at Dolson's early and took the trolley to Oberlin on February 8. One decoration was up and the other was nearly ready. They did not require much work, and he had painted the edges by one o'clock. He was not expected back at Dolson's until dinner time, and spent the afternoon in the college's small art museum. "I expected to be bored to death," he wrote Louise, "but, of all things, found a lot of little Japanese ivories that I was allowed to take out of their cases and study at leisure and make notes of. So now I know how the Japanese ladies do their hair and understand what the prints and drawings had left rather vague to me." He must have recalled his strong youthful interest in things Japanese. At the ceremonies, Cochran spoke on their father as "the Scholar in Action," Kenyon described the decorations, and Dolson made perfunctory remarks.[68]

Cox was proud of the Wisconsin and Oberlin murals, and the public response was positive. He was treated as an important painter whose dignified compositions were suitable to civic buildings. Nearly twenty-five years of work had allowed him to express classical ideals, to paint the figure, and to make a decent, if often precarious, living. As he told fellow painter Philip L. Hale in 1914, "I haven't painted many pictures of late years—too hard at work making the semblance of a living out of mural painting."[69]

The ideas in the murals were similar, but Cox varied their style as the occasion demanded. He worked in a large allegorical manner for the Essex County Courthouse and the Wisconsin capitol. But he was a fine figure painter in the elegant decorations for the Iowa capitol. He could be intimate, as in the Oberlin works, and purely decorative within the grand tradition, as at the Hudson County Courthouse. His works were always recognizable, but he was never a mere realist. His drawing was firm, the modelling strong, and the coloration rich, as befitted decorations meant to endure and to be seen as part of larger complexes. With considerable justice, he could hold that these works were appropriate to the symbolism of the buildings involved and were decorative as paintings.

Cox employed classical symbols because they condensed and expressed important ideas; they could and should become common currency for the people likely to see the murals. They were universal, rising above place and time, and were thus quite suitable to a modern nation like the United States. These symbols also were reminders that the country was part of great traditions. For Cox, the fundamental cohesive power in any society was cultural, rather than political or material. Every institution, such as law or government, was obliged to balance personal and civic needs within that tradition. Government was power, but should reflect the will of a thoughtful people. Law was a restraining influence and a balancing force in society, but must involve wisdom, learning, and a concern for justice. The arts could be central to society, creating civic pride and a sense that individuals had obligations beyond their immediate interests. He tempered the authority figures in his murals with cultural symbols of restraint. Justice was more important than law, governance than politics, wisdom than facts.

These and similar ideas had motivated Cox most of his life and found their best expression in his murals. In them, he stated formal ideas in a coherent view of intellectual and emotional life, never forgetting his separate role as a decorator. But he had also expressed his need for romance and expansive statement in the use of rich and unusual colors, applied in broad masses and in effective lines, and in suave drawing and strong modelling. The murals were also his major statement of idealized womanhood and of controlled and harmonious emotion.

Cox had good reason to be proud of this body of work. But by 1914 there was a sense that the cycle of interest in such elaborate decorations was coming to a close. Architects' tastes had changed, fewer large public buildings were being planned, and the interest in elaborate murals, whether historical or classical, appeared to be yielding to more personal forms of artistic statement. But as a good traditionalist, Cox doubtless knew that ideas and ideals survived events, and that art endured changes of taste. The murals spoke his thoughts and would affect those of like mind.

VI

AN ESTABLISHED ARTIST

THE NEW CENTURY MARKED THE beginning of Cox's busiest years. His reputation as a major critic continued to develop from a steady stream of reviews and magazine articles that reached an influential and cultured audience. He was active in various art associations, such as the SAA, and was on the special committee that negotiated its merger with the NAD in 1906. The production of easel pictures declined as his work on murals increased, but he frequently exhibited in major shows, such as those for the Academy, the Carnegie Institution, and the Pennsylvania Academy of Fine Arts. He worked hard, lived with the anxiety that followed a periodic lack of mural commissions, yet managed to make a reasonable living, though there was seldom any cash to spare.

The family members had matured and led their own lives, but the Coxes maintained a strong sense of their special character. General Cox had been dean of the Cincinnati Law School since 1880, with a concurrent term as president of the University of Cincinnati from 1885 to 1889. He remained in the public eye as a distinguished liberal Republican and wrote an occasional article on public affairs. He also produced several volumes of memoirs about his role in the Civil War, which brought fresh attention, especially from old comrades who disagreed with his recollections of events. In 1897 he refused President William McKinley's offer of the ministry to Madrid. Cox assumed that only a war with Spain, which he opposed, could solve the Cuban problem and did not wish to be involved. The offer showed that he remained in the public consciousness. For all of that, a distinguished military, political, and educational career left him dissatisfied. A search for unattainable goals motivated him: for politics conducted for the public good rather than personal gain, for abstract truth in religion and thought, and for a harmonious world in which every idea had its day without penalty. A reserved stoicism covered his disappointments with the world. "Few people know better than I do how many of the dreams of youth vanish," he wrote Kenyon in 1892, while advising on matrimony, "but few have a more cheerful faith that pre-thought and wisdom and will may compel almost any circumstance." Kenyon had adopted much of this attitude in seeking the ideal statement in art. Dolson thought that this sober, almost melancholy view of life, even in success, was a family trait. Late in life, he noted that Louise's portrait of his daughter Jeannette looked a little sad, "but isn't that a characteristic of the Cox family when not stirred up?"[1]

After declining the Spanish mission in 1897, General Cox decided that his various careers were over. He was almost seventy, was weary of the usual dissension among the law school faculty, and disliked the trustees. It was time for both him and the institution to change. He was not wealthy but had saved enough for a reasonable retirement and wrote Kenyon of his decision that summer. The lengthy letter was a gentle way of saying that he could not lend any more money, as he had done recently to help with the Library of Congress mural commission. He and Helen moved to Oberlin to be among friends and in a collegiate setting. The general's health was not good, and he kept a serious heart condition from Helen. They visited friends and family regularly and enjoyed a lavish fiftieth wedding anniversary party on Thanksgiving Day 1899 at Dolson's new home in Cleveland. The children gave them a large gold loving cup, and the honorees led the group in dancing the Virginia reel. In the summer of 1900, while visiting at Dolson's place in Magnolia, Massachusetts, the elder Cox suffered a series of heart attacks and died on August 4. He was buried in Spring Grove cemetery in Cincinnati.[2]

Helen remained in Oberlin with her sister Julia Finney Monroe. She continued to watch the affairs of her children and grandchildren and expected them to respond to her frequent lengthy missives. As always, the family was her life. She followed Kenyon's career closely, and he kept her informed about commissions and honors and sent her copies of his articles and books. "Although late, your full recognition by the public has come," she wrote him in 1908. She suffered the inevitable infirmities of old age and was not well a good deal of the time. In 1908 she filled out a form requesting information for use in celebrating Oberlin's seventy-fifth anniversary. Under the question concerning recent occupation she wryly noted: "Sickness." Still, her days in the little community were busy and her mind never failed.[3]

Cox seldom saw his older sister Helen, whose husband John Black taught at the College of Wooster in Ohio. He met Will Cochran occasionally when legal business brought him to New York City. Their youngest brother Charles died young in 1907 after pursuing several unsuccessful business enterprises in Colorado.

Cox was actually closest to his brother Dolson, which was somewhat surprising given their divergent personalities. Kenyon was high-minded, introspective, and absorbed in his art. Dolson was the stereotypical self-made businessman, forceful, utterly practical, and rather naïvely blunt. After many vicissitudes, his Cleveland Twist Drill Company was so widely noted for high quality machine tools that it often could not fill all its orders. Dolson took no salary, and his financial fortunes rose and fell with the company's through the stock he owned. By the time he retired from management in 1905, he was wealthy and the company was worth millions. Dolson was a hard taskmaster, but did not forget that he had once been a common laborer. He shared the company's success with the workers in the form of safety equipment, cafeterias, and locker rooms, health services, night classes in English and engineering, and rewards for study and training. He also took great pride in the quality of the tools. "In these later days when manufacturing tools it has been a constant pleasure to know that every day the world was better off for the good, serviceable tools I was pouring into it," he wrote Kenyon in 1913. "As for money, I have never taken any pleasure in it, but it is a 'comfy' feeling to have all you need for a rainy day laid away."[4]

Hope, the youngest sibling, continued to travel with her engineer husband John Pope. They were sometimes separated when large projects took him to exotic places in Central America, and she missed the family connections. Her mother kept Hope current with family news. She remained the charming girl who older siblings had tolerated with good humor. Dolson was shocked at her spending. In 1913 he sent on a long letter from her, which Kenyon was to send to sister Helen. "Gee, isn't she a money spender," he could not help noting. "If I had squandered my income as she does, I should expect to fill a pauper's grave."[5]

Closer to home, Kenyon and Louise attended to growing children. Leonard developed into a sensitive, somewhat undisciplined youngster. By 1907, when he was thirteen, the family began to think about preparatory school and college. Dolson was willing to help financially, but thought it unwise to have either Leonard or Allyn enter his business. This would be favoritism, and he doubted that either one liked manual labor, which they would have to do before even thinking of management. If they could not make up their minds, their parents should do it for them. He wrote Kenyon a marvelous explanation of his skepticism about the value of college, except for truly scholarly boys. The typical youth would simply "learn to play a good game of billiards, be a good judge of cocktails and tobacco, know all the actors and actresses by sight, have a holy horror of dirty hands and old clothes, and tell you there is a lot more in life than earning a living," he cautioned, "[and] that the working man has a hard lot and gets none of the good things in life, learn to breakfast at 9 to 11, and supper at 11:30 p.m., and never look for a job where he *has* to work and give good value for his salary." In fairness to Dolson, college was pretty much restricted to the sons of middle- and upper-class parents, with little emphasis on business preparation.

Two years later, Cox wrote President Woodrow Wilson of Princeton University for advice on that school's science program. Dolson was paying for

Leonard's education at the prestigious Taft School in Watertown, Connecticut, and could help with Princeton's tuition. Leonard apparently was interested in electrical engineering but was immature and subject to the leadership of others. Cox had heard of Yale's offerings but feared that its social scene would ensnare the boy. He hoped that Princeton's program would focus his son's native abilities. Leonard did graduate in 1915 and became a decorated hero in the world war.[6]

Allyn, the middle child, was calm and cooperative, with considerable natural skill in draftsmanship. In the summer of 1910, he accompanied Louise, her mother, and sister Caroline on a tour of Italy; Leonard and Kenyon joined them later in the summer. In Ravello, near Salerno, Allyn's art interests became clear. Though only fourteen, he seriously studied churches, castles, and art works. "Allyn is painting watercolors and *selling* them to tourists," Louise wrote home proudly. In Fiesole he behaved like a mature artist, daily taking paintbox and brushes to historic sites. "I think he is going to be a painter unless some other influence comes in very strongly," Louise noted. "He simply is perfectly happy doing his sketching." He even shopped for her in Florence "as if it were New York."[7] Allyn studied with his father, and at the National Academy and the Art Students League, then won a fellowship to the American Academy in Rome between 1916 and 1920.

Caroline, the youngest child, born in 1898, fulfilled several roles. Louise developed a considerable reputation for portraits of children, and she often helped amuse these restless sitters. Louise had periodic bouts of depression and sometimes stayed in the apartment for extended periods of time, when Caroline read to her. Caroline retained fond memories of her father. For all his formidable public demeanor, he was a lamb at home. Artists and critics who felt his lash would have been surprised at his domesticity. He played many games with her, supervised her reading, and spent time every day in serious conversation about books and ideas. He encouraged her to ask questions, and helped to look up the answers in various sources. His controlled sense of whimsy found an outlet in loose, fanciful drawings for all of the children, but especially for her. He drew mythical and fantastic animals that matched amusing poems and published them in book form as *Mixed Beasts* in 1904. In later years Caroline drove him around the environs of Cornish in their Model T Ford automobile "Fido," conversing all the while about art, life, and the world. Caroline was interested in painting, and although she loved her parents, apparently resented their refusal to give her the same level of education they gave the boys.[8]

The Coxes followed a fairly predictable routine. Louise's reputation as a painter of children, and of other kinds of art, grew steadily and kept her busy. She shared the old studio space at 145 West Fifty-fifth Street with Kenyon and worked at home in the small apartment at 75 West Fifty-fifth

Street. The normal pressures of rearing children, concern over finances, and attending to Kenyon's health and emotional needs were exhausting, and she sometimes spent time alone at a resort outside New York City, or with her family in Massachusetts. Louise was often depressed or anxious, but was also trying to maintain her individuality and her role as an artist of some note.

Cox worried constantly about their income. He continued to illustrate for magazine and book publishers, as he had done since coming to New York in 1883. This was the typical artist's lot, but the uncertainty and the uninteresting work often got on his nerves. "Oh, if one only had a little money!" he exclaimed to Louise in 1901. "I should so like to rest from pot boiling, and wait until I wanted to paint something, and do a little landscape work again." But the dark moods passed, and he tried not to be negative very long to avoid affecting her. "I mustn't be too silly," he quickly reassured her. "I daresay I shall feel better tomorrow." Mural commissions were his main source of income after about 1904, but he never entirely stopped the pot-boiling. He continued to do illustrations, magazine covers, posters, and advertisements for a variety of products. He also taught at the Art Students League until 1909, lectured when possible, and wrote many articles, which he then collected in books that enhanced his reputation and sold modestly. He sold a few easel works. Dolson bought several pictures and was usually available for small loans. On this piecemeal income, Cox supported the family, retained a maid and nanny, kept a summer home in Cornish, and even traveled to Europe in the summer of 1910.[9]

Cox naturally wanted to improve the family's living situation, which was especially crowded with three small children and two full-time painters. Early in 1907 he investigated the idea of buying an apartment in a new co-operative building at 130 East Sixty-seventh Street. The price was twenty-four thousand dollars, which was not overly expensive in this fashionable neighborhood, and in a well-designed building whose value was bound to appreciate. The sum was beyond his means, and he turned to Dolson for advice and help. For all his brusqueness, Dolson had a deep affection for his younger brother and worried about Kenyon's ability to survive in the uncertain art world. In 1906 he canceled all of Kenyon's debts due him. When first approached about the apartment, he lectured Kenyon and Louise about living beyond their means. This was a way of showing concern, of trying to change their habits, and of expressing his own sense of importance as a success in the hard world of business. He cautioned against buying too large an apartment; the children would soon be gone, and Kenyon and Louise did not need a lot of overhead. He also did not want the rest of the family to know of his past help to Kenyon, or about his underwriting the apartment. "There will be a day sometime, sure as fate, when hard feelings will be created between our families because of this transaction," he cautioned. "I only hope I won't live long enough to see it." Times were hard in the wake of the Panic of 1907, and Dolson's income was down, but in the end, he loaned Kenyon the money at five percent interest, with a monthly payment of one hundred dollars.[10]

The Coxes continued their routine as the new building rose in late 1907 and early 1908. They chose an apartment with fourteen rooms on two floors. The rooms were small, but there was studio space for the parents, and the children had some privacy. Early in 1908 they stayed briefly at the Stirling Hotel on West Fifty-sixth Street, then moved into the new quarters on March 1. "I have been here about six weeks," Cox wrote the publisher August Jaccaci in April, "and am finally out of 145 W. 55th, after 25 years of occupancy!"[11]

The anxieties about finances affected Kenyon's health, usually in digestive troubles and a sense of exhaustion. But the family was no sooner settled in the new apartment than he suffered a serious illness. He reported an attack of disabling neuritis in his right arm to Helen Cox, but he may have suffered a mild stroke. He was careful not to discuss many details lest this cost him some mural work. Helen was momentarily outraged. "How can I bear it that you should have rheumatism in your *right arm,* now when the environment is so suitable to your work, when orders are pouring in, when you fame is spreading throughout the country!" She thought for a moment that an evil spirit was at work. "It *must* be true, as I have often thought, that the spirit of *evil rules* the world, and that the *good* spirit, try as he will, only now and then gains the ascendancy." In more practical motherly terms, she urged rest, good food, and a change of pace. From Costa Rica, Hope testified to the benefits of massage. Cox worked on as best he could and assured correspondents that the ailment would pass. He had to forego some speaking engagements and missed some deadlines, but he lost no significant work. By November he felt better, and seemed almost well a month later. "There is plenty of work on hand and in prospect," he wrote Leonard Opdycke in December, "and my right arm seems to be really getting well."[12]

Despite all the pressures and inconveniences involved, Louise and Kenyon enjoyed living in New York City. It was the center of the country's art life, and in the season from October to May there were always exhibitions, parties, and cultural events of interest to artists. This all helped keep their special identities as artists and encouraged them to work, however financially lean the season might be. But they both also liked the country. For all his emphasis on formal, classical painting, Kenyon appreciated landscape and genre, which he associated with leisure and informality. He was also especially sensitive to the heat, which was intense in New York City. As soon as he could afford it, he spent at least part of every summer in cooler climes. He long remembered the broiling studio during the summer of 1886, when he worked remorselessly at *The Blessed Damozel* illustrations. In 1890, while still single, he rented summer quarters at Sheldon Springs, Vermont. He spent several summers with the family in Magnolia, Massachusetts, and elsewhere along the upper East Coast. In 1894 he spent some time at Riverside Farm in Tyringham, Massachusetts, presumably with Louise.[13]

Cornish, New Hampshire, became the family's favorite summer retreat. It was an era of artists colonies, which testified to the growing importance of art. France boasted many such places in Brittany, Normandy, and especially south and west of Paris. Cox and other students had sampled the picturesque and charming life of the Fontainebleau Forest, Barbizon, and Grez-sur-Loing. There was a famous colony at St. Ives, on the Cornwall coast in England. In the United States, there were such settlements at Old Lyme, Connecticut; Magnolia, Massachusetts; and even in faraway Santa Fe and Taos, New Mexico.

But Cornish was the country's most famous art colony. It was actually not so much a defined colony as a collection of artists who lived within visiting distance of one another. Their houses were generally situated on large acreages amid tree-covered hills and running brooks. Residents usually left nature alone and planted fruit trees, flowers, and perhaps a grape arbor. For limited shopping and to get the mail, they crossed a covered bridge over the Connecticut River into the tiny hamlet of Windsor, Vermont.

The colonists doubtless seemed odd to the locals but were never radical or bohemian. They were not students but established figures in the profession. Augustus Saint Gaudens more or less founded the settlement in the mid-1880s and was hardly radical. Nor were Thomas Wilmer Dewing, or the illustrator Maxfield Parrish, friends of Cox's. Most of these residents were trying to create an Arcadian setting to reinforce their view of art as an expression of harmonious and positive ideals. The mountainous terrain exactly suited their emotions. It was dramatic enough, especially to city dwellers, to create a strong sense of natural power, but was not overwhelming or disorderly, as in the Far West. The artists basically saw art as a special calling, which they wished to explore within the context of a beautiful and beneficent nature. They were hardly alienated from society. As one reporter noted in 1907, the place had "an atmosphere of modern antiquity, yet [was] not dangerously distant from intellectual Boston, nor more than a day's ride from commercial New York."[14] The artists worked hard, enjoyed each other's company, debated cultural issues, but were not likely to disturb the world's sleep with strange new forms or theories.

Cornish was well known among artists, and Cox knew how much Saint Gaudens enjoyed it. Early in 1896, Louise wrote for details about boarding with a local farmer from mid-July to October 1. She wanted at least two rooms, one with a fire, and fare for two adults, young Leonard, and a nursemaid. Shortly after this, Kenyon concluded the arrangement, with an added request for wholesome food. They enjoyed the sojourn, and a year later spent some of Louise's money on three acres near Blow-Me-Down Brook. They built a rambling wooden house called "Monorado," after the botanical name for the beebalm flower, *Monardo,* which grew on the lot. They did not have much money to spend and the house was poorly constructed, though suitable enough for summer living. Allyn Cox, who spent many happy days there as a child, thought later that it "has done well to have stood for more than 80 years." The furnishings were scavenged from the family. The elder Coxes gave excess pieces after their retirement in 1897–98. Kenyon sent his father a snapshot of the place, which the general approved. He presumed, correctly, that the house had a fine view of the western mountains.[15]

Summers in Cornish were filled with hard, steady work, because most artists had projects to finish on deadlines or to prepare for fall and winter exhibitions in New York City. There was an understanding that no one called before 4:00 P.M., unless an artist requested another to see or criticize work, or in case of emergency. Cox worked hard, usually on murals. Louise was well liked, genial and sociable, and the children visited other children and played in the wilds. But Kenyon was noted for an unyielding seriousness and a rather crotchety demeanor. If someone appeared and Louise said "Kenyon isn't feeling well today," the potential guest fled. He finally built a studio behind the house, with a tall door to accommodate large works on stretchers. But when time permitted, he also donned old clothes and painted the landscape, often in an easy style that testified to some degree of modern influence on his work[16] (fig. 35).

But even Kenyon was not serious all of the time. Louise bought a horse, which amused him, and both wondered what the new automobiles would do to the community. After lunch he usually read to the children, supervised their lessons, or played games. If he had time, he would even visit a friend for tennis, go for a picnic, or walk. He liked the neighbors and got along well in the community despite his gruffness. Perhaps everyone agreed with the young Homer Saint Gaudens: "A more kindly grouch I never met." His dry sense of humor occasionally showed through, as when he asked his neighbor, the novelist Winston Churchill, to remove the bell from the lead cow in his herd. "Its tintinnabulation in the early morning is somewhat insistent and very close at hand as, at that hour, the gentle ruminants like the shade of the trees along the line fence. I don't object to it, but the ladies seem to feel it is an interruption to their beauty sleep." Churchill obliged.[17]

Augustus Saint Gaudens was the central figure in Cornish, and his studio and house "Aspet" were the center of much discussion and entertaining. Cox continued to admire the sculptor, both as a man and as an artist. In 1904 Saint Gaudens made a medal of the portrait medallion of Cox, who was pleased with both the gesture and the work. "It is one of the encouragements, in a world where there are not too many, to think that my work is liked by an artist like you, and that a man I greatly admire and like returns

FIG. 35. Kenyon Cox painting in Cornish, New Hampshire, ca. 1896.
Original photo in Cox Collection, Dartmouth College, Hanover, N.H.
Gift of Dr. Cornelius Lansing. Courtesy of the Dartmouth College Library and
the Saint Gaudens National Historic Site, Cornish, N.H.

the liking." He expatiated on the high quality of Saint Gaudens's work to anyone who would listen and thought that with age, the sculptor moved from elegant to powerful presentations, best typified in his *Shaw Memorial* (1884–97) in Boston.[18]

Cox was pleased to help honor Saint Gaudens in an elaborate pageant that became famous in local lore, staged in 1905 to note the twentieth anniversary of the sculptor's arrival in Cornish. Such pageants, charades, and *tableaux vivant* were commonplace among the artists, but this was to be a true outdoor spectacle. Early in June 1905, the community was alive with preparations. Women made classical costumes, and friends of Saint Gaudens practiced their lines and gestures. Cox was Pluto, complete with false beard, staff, and classical garb. The weather did not cooperate and forced a delay until June 22. The actors read speeches filled with allusions that only artists could understand. They finally presented Saint Gaudens and his wife with a bronze bowl, copied from an antique work found in Italy, with the dates of the anniversary. The central acts completed, they formed a procession, complete with chariot, and paid homage to the classical ideal. The evening concluded with a dance, after which the weary gods and goddesses went home for a good night's sleep. Like so many pageants staged elsewhere in the country, this one celebrated the classical ideal of harmony. The actors effectively created living murals meant to uplift the senses. The pageants were genial fantasies combined with high art and serious purpose. Saint Gaudens died two years later, and in some ways the pageant was the high point of orderly, cohesive art life in Cornish. The colony continued but increasingly attracted well-to-do visitors and nonartists. The artistic tone, which depended in good measure on the reinforcement of isolation, weakened.[19]

In later years Cox spent some summer time at Calder House, a small complex of cabins built for artists and writers in Croton-on-Hudson, New York. There he was free from interruptions and focused entirely on work he had to complete on deadline. But he remained deeply attached to Cornish. By 1918 Louise or Caroline often drove him around the countryside in Fido, the Ford car. "As Fido makes us foot-loose and able to get about over the country easily within a radius of 30 or 40 miles, I find the wonderful beauty of the region growing upon me all the while," he wrote Allyn in 1918. "I really think it *the* loveliest country going. The subtlety of line, the flow and variety are incomparable."[20] At such times, his classical idealism and reality seemed to fuse.

Whether in New York City or Cornish, Cox spent most of his time and energy during these years working on murals. But he did other commissions, both for the income and to broaden his artistic range. He had considerable reputation as a portraitist and sometimes did one for friends and family members. He also occasionally painted a prominent person. These commissions came through his NAD connection or from artist friends.[21]

New associate members of the Academy had to present their portraits to its collection. A current member often either volunteered or was asked to do such works as a professional courtesy or for a modest honorarium. Cox volunteered for several of these, usually of people he helped elect. These included the painter Emil Carlson and the architects Charles F. McKim and C. Grant La Farge. He could show these in major exhibitions before sending them to the Academy. He tended to employ masses of color, good shading, and careful drawing in these works, while trying to catch the sitter's personality. But most such portraits were sober likenesses, done as a record and a kind of memorial.[22]

Many of these, of course, were routine or unexciting, however gratifying the results, but he enjoyed doing several. Maxfield Parrish, a Cornish neighbor, was gaining prominence as an illustrator noted for a dreamy, allegorical style that emphasized youth and escape from worldly cares. He often used Cornish backgrounds for idealized people in fairytale landscapes. He was a charming personality. He was elected an associate of the NAD in 1905, and Cox offered to do the necessary portrait. Parrish was busy and somewhat disorganized but accepted in mid-May 1905. "It is very good indeed of you to want to take my likeness for the Academy, and out of the 407 applicants, I accept you," he wrote with characteristic whimsy. "It says that I must comply with the requirements of Article 4, Section 5, of the constitution; the latter has not arrived yet, but I don't suppose it is anything very dreadful; they probably knock out your front teeth and tattoo A.N.A. on your bosom, but maybe it won't hurt too much." Cox probably got Parrish to pose that summer in Cornish, and the result was striking. He placed the youthful illustrator in left profile, arms across his chest, wearing shirtsleeves. The tones were light, with fine flesh color and brown highlight for Parrish's hair. Cox caught the sitter's youthful charm, which hinted at energy and calm self-assurance. It was realistic, academically depicted, yet informal and pleasant (fig. 36). Parrish liked the picture and promised to frame it well. It went off to the NAD that November, and he avoided losing teeth or being tattooed.[23]

Cox was equally quick to volunteer for a portrait of another acquaintance, the architect Cass Gilbert. Cox lobbied strenuously to admit more architects to the NAD and had supported Gilbert's nomination. He was also just finishing the large mural *The Beneficence of the Law* for Gilbert's Essex County Courthouse in Newark, New Jersey. Gilbert liked Cox, thought the finished mural was superb, and readily consented. Gilbert was very busy, but Cox assured him that he could do a finished portrait in one day if they were not interrupted. He wanted to complete the picture at once so that Gilbert would be eligible for full membership in the NAD at the next election. The architect made time for the sitting, and the work was done by February 1907, when Cox sent Mrs. Gilbert a photograph of it. It was a more solemn likeness than Parrish's but suited both Gilbert's personality and the Academy.[24]

The most unusual of these commissions involved Cox's old friend Saint Gaudens. Cox's 1887 portrait of the sculptor had caused much favorable comment in American art circles and at the Paris Universal Exposition of 1889. It had burned in the fire that consumed Saint Gauden's Cornish studio in 1904. The sculptor's friends now wanted Cox to reproduce it as a memorial. The energetic August Jaccaci talked to him about making a replica and then tried to get a single donor to pay the targeted fee of fifteen hundred dollars. He failed at this but quickly circularized the art community for donations, payable to Cox, and the project got underway late in 1907.

FIG. 36. Kenyon Cox, *Maxfield Parrish A.N.A.* (1905). Oil on canvas, 30 × 25 ins.
Courtesy of the National Academy of Design, New York.

Cox was enthusiastic. Making such a replica from memory was an interesting challenge, and he wanted to memorialize his old friend. As it happened, he had an excellent photograph of the original work. He knew of only one other print, and the negative had been ruined. This and memory should suffice for an accurate copy and good likeness. By early January 1908, he had drawn the picture and rubbed in transparent color, which he jokingly said made it look like one of the fashionable, loosely painted works of the English artist William Quiller Orchardson. "I really believe I can make a finer thing of it than the original," he wrote Jaccaci, "however, it must lack the *documentary* character of a thing done from life." He finished the picture in April 1908. It pleased Jaccaci and others, and Cox liked it, though it seemed a trifle more formal than the original. "I'm glad you liked the portrait, which, I think myself, a work that I may be content to rest my reputation on as far as that side of my art is concerned," he wrote Jaccaci. The replica went to the Metropolitan Museum, and was one of the best modern American academic portraits.[25]

Cox's interest in classical ideals and in the formal qualities of mural painting underlay his increasing fascination with another medium, stained glass. A window, like a mural, could express traditional ideas in dignified and enduring ways, with strong emotional attachments to history and to cohesive symbolic values. Windows were always suitable for churches, but were increasingly popular for secular buildings and homes as pure decoration. The medium underwent a considerable revival in the late nineteenth century, with most attention focused on the innovations of the famous painter John La Farge.[26]

Many of the qualities in stained glass satisfied Cox's interest in strong design and thoughtful composition. As early as 1891 he noted differences between European and American glass craftsmen. The former generally had a strong sense of design based on mass and line but used leading and painting that weakened the general effects. American designs were usually less bold but achieved better color and light effects through layering small pieces of multicolored, often imperfect, glass rather than using flat glass of uniform color. The strengths of both approaches could join in an emphasis on the flow of a line that defined its subject matter. "We have seen that the lead is an essential part of the window, and that its firm black line is of the greatest decorative as well as structural value," Cox wrote in 1897. "Why should not this inevitable black line become the natural unity of the design?" Such defined lines would clarify the subject of the glass, like modelling in a mural, and would complement the colors.[27]

Cox's first chance to work in stained glass came when the family asked him to do a memorial window for his father at Christ Episcopal Church in Oberlin. The small church was intimate, on the edge of town beyond the college quadrangle. The window space was eight feet tall and two feet wide, which allowed for a dramatic statement. Cox could have done a realistic likeness but decided to emphasize the abstract and universal qualities in his father's life and personality. He placed a standing medieval warrior in armor, grasping a shield, against a background of stylized oak foliage that symbolized strength and fortitude. The title, *Courage,* was above the figure, and the simple inscription "In Memory of Jacob Dolson Cox 1828–1900" was below his feet (fig. 37). The colors were strong and the formal composition deliberately echoed Donatello's famous statue *St. George* (ca. 1415).

Cox took considerable care with the window, both because of its emotional meaning for him and the family and to demonstrate that he could create in stained glass. After settling on the design, he drew cartoons then made a color study. The leading outlined each form in the glass, which added to its sense of authority and power. He used mineral paints for the flesh tones, then fired the glass, but avoided painting as much as possible. Following the lead of La Farge, he put small pieces of multicolored glass behind the first layer to produce rich effects. The resulting work was a little stiff, but its gravity and formality emphasized the qualities in his father that Cox best remembered.[28]

He exhibited the window in New York City in March 1901 before sending it to Oberlin. He had some hesitation about the critical response, because this was a new medium for him, but friends at least were enthusiastic. "It seems to me extremely dignified and well drawn, a quality, alas, somewhat rare in that field of art," one wrote. Wendell Garrison, publisher of the *Nation,* for which Cox often wrote, was also gratified. He liked the "Donatello effect" and thought the work exactly symbolized General Cox's personality and contributions. The painter J. Alden Weir, who had done some stained glass, was enthusiastic. "I must write you about your splendid window. It is [illegible] full of beauty and strength." The work's effects lasted longer than Weir wished. "I was awake at four o'clock this A.M., and that window was what filled my brain!" Later that summer Weir took Cox to dinner and again enthused about the window.[29]

Cox shortly followed the work to Oberlin, for rather elaborate dedication ceremonies. He was a celebrity to the college community and had to perform, both intellectually and socially. On Friday evening, April 5, he lectured on Michelangelo to a large crowd of students, faculty, and townspeople in the chapel. He hoped that his somewhat stylish dress drew attention away from a sore throat. "My 'yaller weskit' [yellow waistcoat] seems to be considered a great sensation!" he wrote Louise. "I had managed my tie beautifully, and on the whole looked the 'swell from New York' to perfection." He thought the speech too long and complicated for the students, but perhaps the faculty benefitted. He was determined to be charming, and at a Saturday night reception "the lion dutifully stood on his hind legs and roared as gently

FIG. 37. Kenyon Cox, *Courage* (1900), Christ Episcopal Church, Oberlin, Ohio.
Stained glass, 8 × 2 feet. Courtesy of Christ Episcopal Church.
Photo: Geoffrey Blodgett, Oberlin, Ohio.

as a [sucking?] dove for their delectation." He could not resist a moment of humor that entered Oberlin's lore. A faculty member asked which college he had attended. Standing nearby, Dolson saw a twinkle in his brother's eyes as Kenyon answered: "I regret to say, Professor, that I belong to the uneducated class." The window was formally dedicated on Sunday, April 7, 1901. The Right Reverend William Leonard, Episcopal bishop of Ohio, spoke on General Cox's life, and musicians played two compositions of Will Gilchrist's, the general's nephew. Cox enjoyed the event and thought that Oberlin had improved a great deal since his youth.[30]

Cox knew that he was not a leader in the stained-glass movement but hoped to get other commissions. The medium suited his formal thinking and interest in design. "The difficulty is to get in touch with people who have glass to do in a dignified way, and to get it known that I can do such work," he wrote his mother. "I believe firmly that I can do it better than anyone now working in that line except La Farge, and I think I can design better than he, though he is wonderful in color." Cox did some designs, and finished a window for the Second Presbyterian Church in Pittsburgh in 1908. In that same year, Cass Gilbert approached him to do a large rose window for a memorial chapel that Cox's Uncle Norton Finney gave to Oberlin College. But Cox's designs did not please the Finneys, and financial reverses left the chapel unfinished and the window space boarded up.[31]

Cox completed two other significant glass works. In 1908 the architect James Gamble Rogers finished the elaborate Harkness family mansion on East Seventy-fifth Street in New York City. He asked Cox to create a pair of windows for the dining room area, which was dark and needed a dramatic touch. They would be about seven feet tall and four feet wide, with an ornamental wooden divider near their tops. They would flank a large fireplace, above which stood an elaborately framed picture. The space called for dignity and elegance, though in the dining room.

Cox decided on two complementary subjects, *Abundantia Maris,* Abundance of the Sea, and *Abundantia Terrae,* Abundance of the Earth. Both were female figures in classical garb outlined in leading in clear glass, amid appropriate accoutrements and symbols. But Cox focused less on symbolism or a story than on the abstract possibilities in the designs. He treated both windows as puzzles, trying to make elaborate lines define the subject matter but be independent and create a sense of strength and be visually unusual. He derived the designs from Italian Renaissance book decorations. He plotted out these sinuous, flowing lines in several drawings, so that none touched or overlapped. The leading, which was actually copper, became a dramatic and powerful design of its own, as he had theorized. He built up the figures with small pieces of glass "in the American manner" and set the finished works against solid sheets of glass for tensile strength. The window glass was slightly bubbly and whitish to make the light opalescent. There was no color, which would have seemed busy in the elaborate room. He painted only where absolutely necessary, as in the divisions of the fingers and other hard-to-see spots, where he used black paint to complement the leading. The result was a striking pair of works, which dominated their situation without being overly strong. Their unusual visual effects complemented the basic classical message about the relationship of people to the earth and to their history[32] (fig. 38).

Another unusual commission came to Cox at this time. The planned external decorations for the new Brooklyn Institute of Arts and Sciences building included a frieze of about thirty monumental figures just below the roofline. The works were not portraits of individuals, even if they bore names. Justinian was to summarize Roman law; Confucius would symbolize Chinese thought. All thus typified the stages of development in human thought and culture, with a strong emphasis on Greco-Roman tradition. This thoughtful and comprehensive program reflected the era's belief in linear progress, of which it hoped to be a major part. The approach also suited Cox's own belief in the power of cumulative tradition and in the universality of basic ideals, which he attempted to express in murals.[33]

Daniel Chester French was put in charge of the project in January 1907 and moved quickly to enroll leading sculptors. The deadlines were remorseless. The artists had to submit nine-inch drawings for French's approval. By the fall of 1907, they had to furnish three-foot plaster models, to be exhibited at the Vanderbilt Galleries. The last step was a six-foot clay model, to be ready in the spring of 1908 for the Piccirilli Brothers foundry to carve into twelve-foot statues from Indiana limestone. The fee was fifteen hundred dollars. Cox was not known as a sculptor. French apparently included him as a gesture to painters, because they were acquaintances, or most likely after someone dropped out and Cox seemed logical because of his ideas and talents.[34]

Cox was reasonably knowledgeable about the history of sculpture. As a student in Paris, he greatly admired the work of Paul Dubois, which combined Renaissance Florentine elegance and poise with a certain modernistic realism and spareness. He almost literally fell in love with the small Renaissance bust in the Louvre, *Femme inconnue,* which occasioned his famous poem to her virtues. The sculptural works of old masters such as Michelangelo figured in his writings, and he drew on Donatello's *St. George* for the memorial window to his father in 1901. He greatly admired the work of Augustus Saint Gaudens, which wedded classical order and elegance to a modern desire for action and realism. He disliked the modern sculpture of Auguste Rodin, which seemed too rough and impressionistic. A desire for simplicity, symbolic realism, and elegant execution unified his modest taste in sculpture. Yet he had not shown much interest in the form, and the Brooklyn project was unexpected.[35]

FIG. 38. Kenyon Cox, *Abundantia Maris* (Abundance of the Sea),
Harkness House, New York (1909). Leaded glass, 84½ × 44¾ ins.
Courtesy of the Commonwealth Fund, Harkness House, New York.
Photo: *Architectural Record* 26 (December 1909), 453–54.

Cox's subject was *Greek Science,* and he began to make studies in the spring of 1907. Whatever his hesitations, he found the project "enormously fascinating work." He expressed the usual uncertainty in a kind of diffidence, telling August Jaccaci that, after all, he would lose money on the statue. "The price is not high, and I must do my best to justify French in giving me the commission, and it will cost me more work than would be required of one [who is] used to the business. I have a moderate confidence in the result, but I don't expect to make anything out of it." He dutifully reported to his mother on the progress of the designs. She too thought the project odd. "But if it affords you amusement, and you have nothing else to do, of course, I have nothing to say."[36]

Cox adopted a rather curious and unexpected design. No details would show at street level, and all the sculptors used abstracted forms. Cox depicted Greek scientific thought as an idealized female, with elaborate folds in her heavy cloak and drapery. She was realistic, but he emphasized the masses and rounded curves of both her form and the drapery, rather than the details. This approach naturally complemented his murals. He had "directed his attention in all his pictures to form and decorative composition," he told an interviewer, "so that the rounded form instead of the suggestion of it might be taken as simply a further step in the same direction." He wrote August Jaccaci that "it is rather an architectural design than a piece of sculpture. I haven't tried for the qualities of modeling that are desirable for an independent statue to be seen close at hand—only for such arrangement of mass and line and light and shade as will tell at a great height."[37]

Although the stylistic problem naturally interested him, Cox focused on the work's larger symbolism. Like most traditionalist thinkers, he was suspicious of modern science, which he thought separated man from nature and atomized large ideas into experimental procedures. He saw science as a body of thought designed to explain the world rather than as a way of solving problems. In his 1896 mural *The Sciences* at the Library of Congress, Cox treated science as part of the classical tradition, with broad cultural values and purposes. In the 1906 murals for the Iowa state capitol, which dealt with the development of civilization, he used idealized females to depict science and art, with art clearly superior to science in both its lineage and cultural value. Once again he chose an idealized female form for the Brooklyn statue, doubtless to soften the complexities of science through familiar symbolism, and to emphasize its potential power as a body of unifying thought (fig. 39).

Though busy, Cox met the deadlines. Early in March 1908, he invited his women's life class to see the newly completed clay model of the statue. It went to the carvers on schedule and by mid-1909 was in place on the northwestern facade of the Brooklyn building.[38] Whatever his customary ambivalence about his ability to do the work, which was typical with any commission, Cox had enjoyed the project. It challenged his abilities as a

FIG. 39. Kenyon Cox, *Greek Science* (1907), Brooklyn Museum
facade. Plaster model of limestone statue, 6 feet.
Photograph courtesy of the Art Commission
of the City of New York.

designer, and as with stained glass, allowed him to make a mark in a new
medium that suited his talents and ideas.

The fall of 1912 brought Cox's most unusual commission, in yet another
unexpected medium. The U.S. Treasury Department had hoped for some

time to reorder its chaotic currency. Saint Gaudens had helped produce an impressive new gold coinage, and the currency deserved equal treatment. Bills were crowded with information, and bore the faces of politicians, fussy scrollwork and lettering, and ornate allegorical scenes. This may have given counterfeiters pause but did not result in attractive or easily recognizable currency. The department thought it time for simple new designs of high artistic quality. Secretary of the Treasury Franklin MacVeagh sought the best advice and spoke at some length with Edwin H. Blashfield, a member of the National Fine Arts Commission. Blashfield's murals emphasized traditional ideals, and he naturally believed that any new currency should incorporate such ideas and represent America's greatness. He apparently recommended Cox to MacVeagh, certain that he would produce an elegant classical design. Early in October 1912, Cox contracted to present the necessary design by January 15, 1913, if possible, and no later than February 1, for a fee of three thousand dollars.[39]

The law required a good deal of information on the face of bills, and Cox's design was only for the back. It was to be simple, of high artistic quality, and suitable for a new, reduced size of bills 6-by-2½ inches. Cox decided to group three seated female figures representing peace, plenty, and prosperity. They were clad in flowing draperies in a balanced, pyramidal composition. At the left of the group, a classical male held a sheaf of wheat to symbolize plenty, and at the right an almost nude Mercury represented commerce. Cox thought that Allyn might as well pose as draw and pressed him into service for Mercury. The result was "an idealized view of my face as a *very* young man on the figure of 'Commerce' in this design." The open background created a good sense of scope in such a small work. The necessary numbering and printed information ran along the outside edges of a firm line that enclosed the scene. As he worked, Cox was amused at the difference in scale between the banknote and the huge pendentives for the Wisconsin state capitol, whose drawings he had just finished. The currency's figures were two inches high; those for Madison were ten feet high seated.[40] Cox produced a small mural for the bill, elegantly composed, and drawn with a suave but energetic line. Its symbolism reflected what most Americans probably thought about their country as a place of peace and plenty, in the vanguard of progress, but in harmony with traditional ideals.

Cox worked steadily and presented MacVeagh with a preliminary sketch early in December 1912. The secretary thought it had "delightful promise" and accepted it with "the greatest pleasure and without the slightest hesitation." Cox completed the studies, "on which I had worked myself dead tired," as he wrote Leonard Opdycke just before Christmas. At the end of January 1913, he showed the finished design to friends, who "consider it perhaps the best thing I have done," as he wrote Will Cochran. He took it to MacVeagh in Washington, where officials of the Treasury Department and the Bureau of Printing and Engraving fairly showered him with praise. The design was exactly right. "I more than ever congratulate myself on my good fortune in finding you sufficiently disengaged to take up this important work," MacVeagh wrote him after Cox had returned to New York City, "and it assures me of my good fortune in having been able to clear the entire back of the note for your design, giving, in this way, the finest opportunity that a currency note has ever furnished to an artist." The enthusiasm reassured and gratified Cox. "If the new administration doesn't upset things, I think we shall have, at last, a paper currency of artistic merit worthy to compare with the French," he wrote Cochran. "It is understood that, if other designs are to be done, later, for the backs of different denominations, mine will remain that of the one dollar bills, the commonest."[41]

These great expectations were only partially fulfilled. The incoming Wilson administration did not adopt either the new design or the reduced-sized currency. Cox had hoped that a new dollar bill would take the design's intellectual message to the masses, but instead it went on a 1914 issue of the new Federal Reserve hundred dollar bill, with modest circulation. None of this, of course, detracted from the merits of the work. Dolson liked the drawings so much that he bought them for three hundred dollars and had them displayed in the lobby of the Cleveland Trust Company. They finally went to the Cleveland Museum of Art.[42]

These same years, so busy with varied commissions and other work, also brought Cox considerable recognition. He was elected an associate of the NAD in 1900, and a full member in 1903. This latter selection produced wry congratulations from his old friend William A. Coffin. "The election surprised me, for I thought they were afraid of you," he noted. "You will next be going into the Century [Club] and then you will be as bad as any of 'em. I'm glad you are in the Academy. Stir 'em up." Cox was somewhat anomalous an academician. His ideas and work certainly fitted that body's canons, but he was not always a good establishmentarian. His bluntness was still legendary within the art world, and he usually told the truth as he saw it, no matter how dignified or certified the person or subject at hand. He also challenged the status quo in wanting to include more architects and other nonpainters and more people from outside New York City and the East. Still, he was a faithful member of the academy as his inscription of a copy of The Classic Point of View (1911) for its library showed: "To the National Academy of Design, which should stand for the doctrine here preached if any body of artists can, from its loyal member, Kenyon Cox." He was elected to the American Institute of Arts and Letters in 1898 and to the American Academy of Arts and Letters in 1908. He helped found the National Society of Mural Painters in 1895 and was its president from 1915 to 1919. This group included the most prestigious muralists and helped secure commissions and promoted the cause of decoration. He was a charter member of the Municipal Art Society of New York in 1898, which tried to beautify the city in classical taste.[43]

His painting also won honors. He had received the Second Hallgarten Prize at the Academy and two bronze medals for painting and drawing at the Paris Universal Exposition in 1889. He won the Temple Silver Medal from the Pennsylvania Academy in 1891 and a medal for his group of paintings at the World's Columbian Exposition in 1893. At the Louisiana Purchase Exposition in 1904 he received a gold medal for the murals at Bowdoin College, *Venice* (1894), and at the Citizens Savings and Trust Company in Cleveland, *The Sources of Wealth* (1903). Both were shown in photographs. In 1910 the NAD awarded him its Isidor Medal for *A Book of Pictures*, the best figure composition of the year. The most personally satisfying such recognition, "the greatest honor I have received," came in 1910, when the Architectural League of New York awarded him its gold medal. Technically it was for the mural at the Luzerne County Courthouse in Wilkes-Barre, *The Judicial Virtues* (1909), but really recognized his ideas and life's work. La Farge had won the first such medal, and Blashfield followed, which added to Cox's sense of being in superior company.[44]

Of course, there were some interruptions in the procession of honors. Contrary to Coffin's cheerful prediction, the Century Club, composed of varied prestigious New Yorkers, did not elect him. Leonard Opdycke reported rumors that his name was under consideration in 1906. "I am informed that there is considerable opposition to me in the Club, and I shall not be especially disappointed if it prevails," Cox responded. "It's the penalty of speaking one's mind on occasion!" He did sometimes dine there as a guest but was never comfortable in the rather pretentious atmosphere. He preferred the Players Club. "I don't like meeting at the Century Club anyway," he wrote Blashfield. "Since they won't have me as a member it is not pleasant to go there."[45] Cox also had a considerable reputation as a teacher at the Art Students League before his retirement in 1909 and was well known through lectures at colleges and universities. It was not surprising that Yale honored him with an M.A. in 1910, which he recognized was "given to me more as a critic and teacher than as an artist." Oberlin offered him a similar degree in 1908, but he could not appear at the commencement because of his painful arm. He accepted a Litt. D. in 1912. "The long connection of my family with Oberlin makes this honor particularly grateful [sic] to me," he wrote President King. Dartmouth College awarded him the same degree in 1915, with a citation that strongly emphasized his authority as a critic with "a clear and cogent style" and as a thoughtful classicist engaged in "the beautiful, dignified and creative adornment of our public buildings."[46]

VII

CLASSICS

&

MODERNS

COX'S ACTIVITIES AS AN ART CRI-
tic and as a spokesman for idealistic cultural values, which the Dartmouth
citation recognized, were as natural to him as breathing. Year in and year
out, he articulated a coherent view of the role of art in individual lives and
in society, which he termed *classicism*. First and foremost, he believed that
art was a high calling for both the creator and the appreciator. Art was not
something merely to see but also to feel. It extended the sensibilities and
imagination and changed perceptions of the world. Art appreciation and production required study and analysis as well as sensory response. He knew
from his own student days that fledgling artists were usually obsessed with
acquiring formulas and techniques that would permit them to reproduce reality. This was certainly basic to any artist's career; no one had worked harder
than he to master basic skills. Such skills allowed artists to use draftsmanship, design, shading, and coloration, to make a picture that was more than
mere reality. But too many artists lacked an appropriate context. Once
trained, the eye had to see and the hand had to express something special.
This required understanding of the great cultural traditions that culminated
in the present and would continue into the future. Too many people over-
valued the here and now. "No one can be said to be thoroughly educated in
art who has not seen and studied the best that the world has produced," he
wrote in 1889. "A man who has not seen the old masters, for instance, is no
more thoroughly educated in art than is one thoroughly educated in literature
who has not read the Greeks.[1]

The artist was thus a special personality, whose interpretations of nature
expanded the sensibilities. "All the arts are fine in the degree in which they

represent nature and at the same time express the human mind," he wrote in 1894. "Nature furnishes the form while the mind furnishes the significance." His heroes among artists had combined personal perceptions with reality to create something that transcended the present with a sense of expanded, harmonious imagination. Old masters deserved that title because their works expressed unusual personalities without mere egotism. Cox realized that each generation had different tastes and needs but doubted that circumstances provided more than context for an artist. Individual genius and unusual perceptions made great art. Botticelli, Ter Borch, and Zurbarán represented many aspects of their times, but Michelangelo, Rembrandt, and Velázquez were truly great because their statements spoke above present time and circumstances.[2]

Cox realized that the nineteenth century marked a shift in tastes and attitudes. People were interested more than ever in the unusual and the dramatic. There was a growing emphasis on the realistic, which most people could understand. The times had a "preoccupation with the direct representation of facts." Even so, he thought some moderns had continued to focus on harmonious and cohesive work, with insightful statements from special personalities. One of them was Corot, whose work had fascinated him since youth. "Take Corot as an instance: he thinks in pictures and creates a harmony of tones and forms as his first business," he wrote in 1902. "[He] can stick pretty close to the facts of a given scene, and yet his subtle modulations and modifications produce something which is really entirely independent of the facts, and even of nature itself, for its essential quality." He always admired Jean-François Millet, whose scenes of peasant life and human relations tied the present to the past. Modern life was special, of course, but had ongoing relationships with nature and cultural ideas. "It is the permanent, the essential, the eternally significant that he paints," Cox noted of Millet in 1908.[3]

Cox was not a reactionary in opposing change; nor did he want Americans to copy examples from Europe or anywhere else. He wanted an art that suited his personal need for ideals and that tied the present to a vital tradition. There was too much emphasis on isolated facts in modern art and on atypical personal expression that threatened to make the artist marginal in social affairs. Art had to speak to reality but be more than mundane. "All plastic art is both realistic and idealistic, and the highest art is *both* in the highest degree," he wrote in 1894. "When art becomes too exclusively realistic, it ceases to be art and tends to become science. When art ceases to be realistic, it tends to become pure decoration."

He never liked impressionism because it was perceptual rather than conceptual. To some degree, he appreciated its emphasis on light and color but thought it shallow, dealing with surfaces and effects rather than with integrative ideas. Yet he knew that both artist and viewer had to recognize what they saw; this needed only to be elevated into an ideal or harmonious mood.

"The truth seems to be that the art impulse—the love of harmony—has molded the material of art into various and strange shapes," he noted in 1898, "but that material has always been the representation of observed natural facts." In his large view, art was one way of explaining the world, of reducing its disorder, and of making sense of its energies. The artist had to deal with recognizable nature, yet present an extraordinary emotional message.[4]

Cox now saw a developing cyclical return of the romantic emphasis on self in the arts, which would gain added force from the modern tendency to focus on the unusual. This in turn would make the artist seem a dangerous eccentric, separate from society, which threatened the painful work of making American art part of Western culture and a force for social cohesion. "The romantic artist is intensely personal, intensely poetic, occupied solely with self-expression. The virtue of his work is something that he alone can give it, and he has no use for the hand of another," he wrote in 1899. "The classic artist is engaged in the clear and perfect expression of the ideals of all the world. His work is not so much different from [that of] others as it is better."[5] In discussing this approach, Cox employed terms such as order, harmony, self-control, continuity, and eternal.

Cox's learned and dogmatic tone often obscured his passionate belief in the emotional power of classical art to transform the individual and enrich society. His classicism was not a detached doctrine aimed at social control or at simply refurbishing past conventions. It expressed intense emotion in controlled ways and was more consistently enriching than was dramatic but ephemeral innovation that ignored tradition. In the end, his classicism rested on the belief that art could and should be central to society and the artist a major influence in affairs. Art represented past achievements and charted future directions. It helped unify society and enlarged individual feelings. It reminded people of society's scope and complexity and of their role in large processes. In short, it was, or should be, quite as important in the scheme of things as politics, business, or diplomacy. Such a role could only come from an art founded on continuity and order, and not from a romanticism based on eccentricity, the unusual or bizarre, and mere personal expression without regard for social context.

Cox expressed these ideas in a steady flow of reviews and essays. Writing took time and energy from painting and often made him irritable and distracted. He wrote evenings and on weekends and sometimes went out of town to finish a piece on deadline. He did a lot of reviewing for the *Nation* and wrote many longer pieces for magazines such as *Century* and *Scribner's,* which reached important audiences. He also often wrote for the art press. And he was a voracious reader, always acquiring background and keeping abreast of new publications. He used print to promote his ideas, but he also needed the income. He typically wrote a magazine essay, incorporated it in a book, and often used it as a lecture, for a triple fee.

His writing was distinctive and popular. "I hate writing," he told Robert Underwood Johnson of the Century Company in 1897. At the same time, he appreciated the challenge in writing well and opted for a clear, unadorned, personal style. "I do hate fuzziness!" he wrote a friend in 1898. He also had the great gift of brevity. "I *never* write as long a thing as I set out to do," he told Johnson. "I am an invincible writer-down." He sometimes seemed brusque or arrogant in guarding against editorial control. Much of this touchiness doubtless came from his long-standing difficulties in writing on the nude, but he was also simply blunt in judgments. In 1903 he was willing to help August Jaccaci with analyses of private collections for a special art book. But if a work seemed worthless or inferior, he proposed to say so and expected to be paid whether or not Jaccaci used the material. "I am a little jealous of my reputation as a writer who says clearly what he means, and I could not consent to the publication of anything that did not satisfy myself as well as you." For once, he met an equally strong personality. Jaccaci suggested that his ethics were not involved, and that in any event they had best wait to see what Cox produced before making judgments. Nor did Cox spare friends, at least in private. He liked Edwin H. Blashfield, a fellow muralist and traditional art thinker, but found his book *Mural Painting in America* (1913) bloated. "It has, of course, a lot that is true in it, but I have been surprised to see how repetitious it is," he wrote Louise, "and how many words he takes to say rather little."[6]

For the most part, Cox wrote concisely in a rather genial style, acting as a guide to works and artists. He generally focused on personalities and saw their works as expressions of their tastes and ideals. This was in keeping with a new art criticism that emphasized correct attributions, biography, and discussions of artistic techniques and styles in cultural contexts. He could be complex, but was never obscure. He also knew something about his audience. He hoped, as he wrote in 1910, to reach the expert and the knowledgeable, but also to "interest the 'schoolteacher at Oshkosh,' who may see, or hope to see, pictures by the artists spoken of."[7]

Cox became equally well known as a lecturer. Most of his teaching at the Art Students League consisted of supervising large classes in drawing, and he sometimes directed a special painting student. But he also lectured on anatomy and special topics. He was not an instructor at the NAD school, but lectured there occasionally on art history and mural decoration from 1900 to 1917. In 1908 Columbia University asked the NAD to recommend professors of sculpture, painting, and decoration. The positions went to Daniel Chester French, John La Farge, and Cox, but apparently were merely nominal. He taught no regular classes and received no stipends between then and

1914, when the arrangement ended. In the first decade of the century, Cox began to lecture more often at universities and museums and to cultural clubs. He became reasonably adept at working a transparency projector, but always preferred an assistant for the machine, to avoid fumbling with the transparencies or losing his train of thought. He maintained a good collection of slides but often asked host institutions to make special ones from their collections. He seldom spoke spontaneously and preferred to read a text but answered questions from the audience. He was not dramatic on the platform but radiated the seriousness and idealism that permeated the material. He was often subtle and moving in describing the emotions and ideals in the work of a Millet or Rembrandt. William A. Goodyear, curator of fine arts at the Brooklyn Institute, complimented Cox in 1906 for a presentation on Rembrandt. He had analyzed a complex subject with ease, showed a good deal of quality art, and kept Rembrandt's persona to the fore. He thought Cox had a good sense of timing and voice inflection, and that the transparencies were integrated with the text.[8]

Given his stature as a muralist and a spokesman of traditional ideals, Cox was a logical choice to deliver the Scammon Lectures at the Art Institute of Chicago in the spring of 1911. The lectures were an important platform within the art community and offered a chance to reach the literate public as well as artists and students. John La Farge gave the talks in 1903, and the noted critic of design, Russell Sturgis, did in 1904. Cox's good friend Will Low did so in 1910, and published the lectures as A Painter's Progress. Time had mellowed Cox's adverse impression of the city, gained while doing the mural at the Columbian Exposition in 1892. He had surveyed the city's chief private collections for Jaccaci in 1903 and rather liked the bustling, dynamic atmosphere. And he had just finished the decorations for the Cleveland customhouse, the Winona public library, and the Hudson County Courthouse, with no commissions in sight. Given this, "the lectures were a godsend." He would received six hundred dollars for six lectures delivered each Thursday afternoon at four o'clock and would teach art classes for about a month after that.[9]

The invitation came after the family returned from a somewhat hectic European tour in the late summer of 1910. Much of the art that Cox saw on the trip reinforced his determination to speak out for tradition, even if it made him a target in the growing debate over modernism. He had followed developments in the arts, chiefly in illustrated books and periodicals, but also in some exhibitions. By 1910 he was profoundly disturbed at the gathering wave of modernism. Its emphasis on the artist's personal view of life and nature at the expense of inherited ideals and forms threatened his own views. He had tried to be open-minded, and as he later wrote Low, did not think he was "merely growing old and stiff." He simply did not see the new work as progressive change. And "the latest developments—Matisse and his unspeakable followers—leave me *no* doubts. This *cannot* be healthy art. At any rate, I must speak out—others may settle the value of what I have to say." He had written about traditional ideas most of his adult life, but the time had come "to make a definite statement of the doctrines I have been teaching and preaching, piecemeal, for many years," he wrote his old Toledo friend James Henry Moser. He would make the book, as he said in its preface, "a definite *credo*—a detailed and explicit confession of artistic faith." The lectures were think-pieces rather than monographs, and would be concise, pithy, aimed at the literate public as well as at students and critics. He drew on previous work and simply thought about the subject. Once the themes were set, he wrote rapidly during the winter of 1910–11. Allyn counted the words, checked references, and offered occasional additions, as in suggesting that, like the celebrated emperor, the moderns really wore no clothes. *Scribner's Magazine* would print the first three lectures as articles, and all six would appear as a book, *The Classic Point of View,* which was printed and ready for the fall market when Cox left for Chicago.[10]

As the departure date approached in March, Cox was somewhat apprehensive. He looked forward to the experience but was always prone to "the blues" when separated from the family. He had no friends in Chicago, though the institute staff was cooperative and generous in helping him move. Living accommodations were important, because he wanted to be comfortable while alone. The institute secretary first suggested that he take a room in a hotel or boardinghouse. There were cheap ones, but he would have to walk or ride the trolley some distance. Then someone had a happy inspiration. He could stay at the Illinois Athletic Club, "a fine modern building," just across the street from the Institute. A room was twenty-five dollars a month, and he could get a reasonable thirty-five-cent lunch or sixty-cent dinner at one of several nearby restaurants. He agreed, and on arriving found the local art community cordial and cooperative. He was soon a member of the Cliff Dwellers Club, which sat atop the Orchestra Building across the street from the Athletic Club. Cox instantly liked its view of the lake and city, the members, and the group's large purposes. The club offered lunch and dinner, but no sleeping accommodations, and attracted "almost everyone who is anyone in Chicago" every day except Sunday. He especially liked the interesting mixture of people. "There come the painters, the sculptors, and the architects, the writers and the musicians, and there come also the bankers and the officials of the Institute," he wrote the *Nation.* The club typified Chicago's energy and interest in getting things done. "There, over the coffee-cups, many a scheme is discussed, and those schemes which survive such discussions are finally launched."[11] The club helped to alleviate Cox's loneliness and added a great deal to his knowledge of art outside of New York. It rained, the wind blew, and the temperature varied, but the Cliff Dwellers was a true refuge.

Cox especially liked Charles Lawrence Hutchinson, a prime mover in the city's financial and cultural affairs. Hutchinson began his career as a grain merchant, then became a banker with many interests. He had chaired the local fine arts committee for the World's Columbian Exposition in 1893, and was a founder and first president of the Art Institute. Genial and suave, he was determined to show the world that energy could produce more than money. He was thoughtful in dealing with Cox, who found him "one of the finest men going." Cox also liked the results of Hutchinson's labor. He helped make the institute comprehensive, with collections, an art school, and a lecture bureau for the community at large. He also organized the Friends of American Art in 1910, whose 165 members pledged two hundred dollars a year to buy contemporary American art. The purchases included works of Robert Henri, George Bellows, and J. Francis Murphy, among others, as well as those of well-known figures such as James A. MacNeil Whistler. The results were not daring, but the new additions gave the collection a sense of being current and helped support American artists. Cox also surveyed the institute's core collection, which was somewhat uneven but was a sound foundation for future growth. Chicagoans had spent a good deal of money on art, generally well, and had numerous private collections that should come to the institute in the future. Among other recent acquisitions, the institute had Millet's *Bringing Home the Newborn Calf* (1862–64), which Cox genially wanted to take home. It was always hard to judge the depth of interest in art, but Cox saw a growing network of support for the institute, the symphony, new architecture, and cultural education in both public and private schools. More to the point, for his present mission, he saw that the city liked a certain kind of sensible modernism but basically believed in his ideal of art that helped unify and stabilize society through attachments to tradition. Somewhat to his surprise, the West could teach the East something about the role of art in society.[12]

Cox began his lectures on schedule and aimed the first one, "The Classic Spirit," at both artists and the general public. Cox naturally thought that classicism should form and shape both art and society. He defined it, as he had before, as a quality of mind, of tone, of appreciation, that recognized the artist's personal statements within the context of a search for order, harmony, and understandable beauty in life and nature. Such art focused on the essential truths in a subject that transcended the moment, always expressed in comprehensible ways, and was done with a breadth of taste and quality of execution that linked it to greatness. This underlay its power to move. Classicism was not opposed to innovation, or even to the unusual. "But it desires that each new presentation of truth and beauty shall show us the old truth and the old beauty, seen only from a different angle and colored by a different medium. It wishes to add link by link to the chain of tradition, but it does not wish to break the chain."

Cox was known as a critic of recent art innovations, but this lecture marked his emergence as a fierce opponent of the moderns. He thought that most of the new work was inept and ugly, a conscious rejection of skills that had produced harmonious and elevating art. Nor did he think that the moderns' personal views of life and nature matched those of society. He also saw a streak of mental imbalance in many of these artists, such as Vincent van Gogh and Paul Gauguin, who seemed to reject broad social values. Above all, he feared that the new modernism would separate the artist from society and undo the work of his generation in bringing American art into the world's cultural mainstream. As an antidote, he suggested public discussion to counter critics who praised the new, a return to proven principles of performance and appreciation, and he counseled Americans to "patronize our own art."

The succeeding lectures were more technical, aimed at artists and connoisseurs, but they remained within this classical context. He urged students to choose subjects that symbolized something elevating and enduring. He emphasized the central importance of design in painting, which permitted individual expression within an orderly context. "Design is arrangement, design is order, is selection," he noted. "Design is the thing that makes [a work] a whole rather than a hap-hazard collection of unrelated things or a slice of unassimilated nature." As usual, he stressed the central importance of drawing as a way to depict interpreted reality and as a means to express controlled power through lines, which contain energy, emotion, beauty. He especially criticized the moderns for distorting the figure, which was always his standard of artistic challenge. He disliked any focus on light or noncomplementary color, which weakened the substance and resonance in a work. Light and shade, as well as modulated color, should create mood, mystery, reflection, not be ends in themselves. The interpreted subject, not transitory effects, was the basis of enduring work. Skill coupled with taste and ideals would allow the students to express truly important points with economy of means that summarized lasting values. The powerful idealism of his youth had not faded, as he said in valediction: "To the serious young artist I would say: Fix your eye on the highest, gird yourself for the journey, and God speed! If you fall by the way, you may at least fall face forward. And it may be that even you may reach the goal. It may be that you, too, may find yourself, in the end, among that small but glorious company whose work the world will cherish and whose memory the world will not let die."[13]

Although Cox was sharply critical of the moderns, he focused on his own positive message and spoke with measured and thoughtful tones. He wished to be blunt, even cutting, but not to be sensational, as he thought the moderns were. He employed familiar and human examples, as in the work of Millet or Rembrandt, to show the values in traditional art and the dangers in modernism. He took a broad sociological view, and his style was brief, concise, and filled with memorable phrases and examples. Cox did not expect to convert the moderns but hoped to influence the bewildered or uncertain. The lectures were an impressive performance, and in book form were the clearest statement of classical ideals in American art-thought.

Cox could not judge the impact of his words. A great deal was always going on, and few people could attend every cultural event, even if they were interested. He wrote Louise that some two hundred persons braved a stunning rainstorm to attend one presentation, and he probably reached most of the available audience. "I may be doing some good to someone by the lectures—certainly not to many," he wrote Will Low. In any event, he knew that the printed articles and final book would reach a larger, more important audience. "And whatever happens, I shall have spoken out on a good many things and relieved the pressure. Indeed, I have felt it almost a matter of conscience to say plainly my deepest thoughts, as I have never said [them] before." Louise reported that people were discussing the first article, "The Classic Spirit in Painting," in the May issue of Scribner's Magazine, which appeared in late April. He thought it "splendid to know that the thing is being talked about in New York." He always dreaded reading over his own work, fearing that it was not clear or that errors had crept in. But "it strikes me, when I read it over, as real stuff." Inevitably, the Cox doubt was there. "And now, of course, I am wondering if the rest of the series are anything like so good. I hope so."[14]

Cox came to Chicago not only to speak for classical ideals but to champion American art. The belief that the country would produce a distinctive and technically skillful art was one aspect of his idealism. By the late 1880s, he thought the nation would develop a great art, as its self-confidence and world roles increased. "He maintains that its ultimate supremacy is inevitable, and to do what he can to hasten the day when it shall be acknowledged second to none is his constant thought," William A. Coffin noted in 1891. Year after year, as a reviewer and painter, he saw steady growth. By the early 1890s he thought the United States ranked just after France as a producer of sound art. Most European art was stagnant. The same formulas, whether realistic or symbolic, appeared in it over and over. Though technically smart, the work was empty and formulaic.

Meanwhile, the quality of American art in exhibitions and galleries rose steadily. By 1907 he thought that the "best and most hopeful work being done anywhere today is being done by Americans, and largely in America." The breadth of it in genre, figure painting, and landscape was impressive. Modernism would not likely find a mass audience, and so American art could gain stature as European art declined. "The general level of attainment has never been so high or so uniform," he noted of the academy exhibition in 1907. Americans were not copying Europeans, had mastered technical demands, and were treating sound subject matter in integrated pictures. There were many artists to choose from, and he predictably liked the younger people who were in the grand tradition. But he also saw the individualist Winslow Homer as "our most original painter" for his sheer power and grandeur. He generally disliked the roughness and broad painting in the so-called Ashcan school, but had a reasonably good word for Robert Henri, who "has an unmistakable personality of his own, rude at times, but vigorous and capable of subtlety." Of course, he saw in such artists the qualities he favored, "the old fashion of thoughtful composition, the old fashion of good drawing, the old fashion of lovely color, and the old fashion of sound and beautiful workmanship," as he wrote in the winter after leaving Chicago.

Cox assumed that Americans would use European tradition, not copy it. He had enjoyed and benefitted from his own Paris training, showed in the Salon as a student, and welcomed recognition at the Universal Exposition in 1889. He used European ideas and techniques but saw these as adaptable universals. He was never overly impressed with modern European culture and remained basically American. "I have made my position *here* without any aid from foreign recognition," he wrote Will Cochran in 1913. But he understood the power of European examples in an essentially provincial society like America's. Collectors usually favored foreign works; critics overpraised European art. His fear that the new modernism's *cachet* would overwhelm the American school was a major factor in his attack on the moderns.[15]

Cox elaborated this theme in a lengthy, important interview published in the *New York Times* on April 30. He was generally suspicious of newspaper reporters, who emphasized the sensational and trivial. But he wanted as large a forum as possible and agreed to meet Edward Marshall at the Art Institute for a long talk. "He is a healthy though ascetic man," Marshall noted, "whose nervousness is energetic and not enervated. He talks fluently and logically, and has real things to say." Cox spoke easily and seriously, and the printed interview was really a long series of quotations.

Cox began with a reasoned criticism of the broad stream of nineteenth-century modernism. It had begun with a focus on appearances and seemed ready to end with eccentricity. "There has been too much personality, too; too much individual whim, due to lack of really competent education, and in general, to lack of discipline," he said. By contrast, he praised the American school, with homage to acknowledged masters such as Inness, Homer, and La Farge, whose works were realistic enough but dealt with varied powerful emotional themes rather than mere appearances. He thought that many American museums and private collections were outstanding. American students no longer needed to study abroad, because there were quality schools in every major city, and certainly in Chicago. Public interest in art, and the acceptance of artists was greater than ever, and the time had come to appreciate and support American art. "Foreign worship is mere caddism—caddism of the worst sort," he said. "This worship of foreign art is among our worst provincialisms."

He concluded with a somewhat unusual criticism of the thoughtless ugliness in the American scene, which art could help correct. He blamed most of this on advertising, which needed the grace and elegance of true art. He sensed that the maturity of formal art was part of a larger process that would make Americans conscious of their environment. In their haste to make money, most people simply did not see the charming or picturesque qualities of American life. He got a sense of this on returning from Europe in the fall of 1910. In late afternoon, the Gotham canyons of brick, stone, and mortar resembled Italian hill towns on a larger scale. Shaded colors and reflections on the harbor water caught his artist's eye. Then the lights began to come on and gave the scene an Arabian Nights quality. This brief vision simply reminded him that with a little effort, Americans could make art central to their hectic and often disordered existences. Art could provide cohesion, beauty, subtlety to an environment filled with energy and power. This clearly would not follow from a modernism based on mere personal expression and disregard for inherited ideals and methods.

Cox was anxious about the interview's dissemination and reception. He had tried to be temperate and measured, hoping again to affect the interested or uncertain public. Marshall promised to send him the text before publication, but did not do so. Cox finally asked Louise to send a copy. "I wondered sometimes if the whole thing wasn't a mistake!" He was reasonably satisfied when he finally saw the article. Marshall unfortunately entitled the interview "Our Art Has a Terrible Attack of Ugliness," which was misleading, because Cox was insisting that current American art was vital and could alleviate ugliness if supported. The language was generally his, though he had not used the word *caddism*. "It never occurred to me to call the worship of foreigners 'caddish,'" he wrote the painter Charles C. Curran. "I called it 'provincial.'" And he was somewhat amused at the attention. One had to leave town to get noticed. "The *Times* would never have thought of giving me a column as long as I stayed in New York."[16]

Cox began teaching in late March. The students were eager to learn but lacked basic skills and coherent ideas. "They were painting vast masses of heavy, chalky paint onto their canvases, with no drawing or light and shade," he wrote Louise. Whether because of prior instruction or examples in the art world, they emphasized expression over drawing and design. "They not only don't draw when they paint, but they try to paint when they draw, seeing nothing but effect and seeing that badly." He might not affect them much, but a good dose of academic discipline would not hurt. "But if I cannot actually teach these pupils much, perhaps I can give them a jog," he wrote Will Low.[17]

The institute asked Cox to choose a number of his own works for an exhibition. He selected twenty-three pieces, which were a good cross-section of his output and a fair statement of what he liked best. These included several female nudes and the group *Plenty*. He also used *Flying Shadows* to represent landscape and *The Harp Player* for genre. The portraits included those of Dolson, Louise, and of four NAD members, C. Grant La Farge, Cass Gilbert, Emil Carlsen, and Maxfield Parrish. There were also photographs and studies for the murals at Winona, Wilkes-Barre, Newark, Jersey City, Des Moines, and Cleveland, as well as a sketch for stained glass.[18]

In the midst of his varied duties, Louise reported a financial crisis. Paying the bills in mid-May, she realized that they had a mere three hundred dollars in the bank. After momentary panic, she showed considerable resourcefulness in painting a small picture of a little girl, which a collector promptly bought for five hundred dollars. She had to apply four hundred dollars to a debt, but they were that much safer for the moment. She cut down on every expense and even let the maids go, forcing Caroline to do most of their work. For the first time Caroline could remember, her mother simply filed unpaid bills, saying they would have to hope for the best.[19]

In Chicago, Cox did all he could to help. William French, the institute director, wanted the board to purchase the studies for the Winona mural for a thousand dollars. Cox thought this would see them through the crisis for the moment. But after weeks of indecision, nothing happened. He gave a few lectures in Chicago and the suburbs, but most clubs seemed unwilling or unable to pay the one-hundred-dollar fee. He got few inquiries even after cutting this to fifty dollars, but did send Louise a little money. He also hoped to do some portraits, and painted an excellent one of Ralph Clarkson, a local artist, which hung in the Cliff Dwellers Club. It elicited favorable comment but produced no inquiries. Portrait commissions were scarce, partly because the fashionable Spanish painter Joaquin Sorolla y Bastida had visited Chicago earlier in the year, with a large exhibition of his works, and painted many local people. Cox thought the Sorolla works he saw were weak, "with no construction in his heads, no bones, no flesh, no unity of tones—just splashes." It was another instance of Americans patronizing foreign artists. As so often in the past, he realized that the Scammon Lectures would bring prestige and pay few bills. "I don't doubt that this book will add to my reputation and influence," he wrote Will Low. "But I wish reputation and influence translated itself, in this country, more readily into dollars!" Maybe he could sell some books, perhaps even some art after he got back to New York City, and could turn to Dolson if things really got bad. In the meantime, he tried to keep his spirits high. "I *know* we must pull through somehow, as we always have," he wrote Louise, "but it gets harder after fifty to have these spells of hard times."[20]

With all his duties and worries, Cox took some time to socialize. He went for long walks, including one to the part of town where the wealthy "nobs" lived. He also saw Saint Gaudens's famous statue of Lincoln in the park of that name, "which is very impressive and noble in its setting." He went to a few plays, and to a performance of Elgar's *Dream of Gerontius* (1900), which he thought was dull. Hutchinson attended several of the lectures and was very sociable. He took Cox to his country place to meet the family, play tennis, and enjoy the woods, water, and flowers. Cox spent a lot of time at the Cliff Dwellers Club and with people at the institute. He suffered the predictable bouts of dyspepsia and "blues," but coped fairly well with anxiety about money and the general loneliness.[21]

He did have one unusual, not to say almost unique, experience in reading his own obituary. On March 15 the *New York Times* reported the death of Kenyon Cox. This, of course, was the uncle for whom he had been named, then eighty years old and living in Long Beach, California. Reporters called, only to find Cox very much alive. Leonard, away at school, was upset and could not figure out how his father had gotten to California. The story died, but not before the Washington *Star* printed a brief death notice. After discovering that Cox was alive, James Henry Moser sent a clipping of this and a genial letter. Fortunately for his self-esteem, Cox read that he had been a distinguished painter and art thinker, whose death left a large void in American art.[22]

By late May, Cox was finished at the institute. His last duty was to walk the class through the galleries, commenting on works. He was soon packed and ready to go home. Writing from Munich in April, his sister Hope had urged him to see their mother in Oberlin. "She is awfully proud of you, and loves you so dearly, that it would hurt her terribly if you didn't make the effort to see her when you are so near." Cox visited Dolson's family in Cleveland, and they all took the interurban train to visit Helen on Sunday, June 4. She was cheerful, full of questions about Louise and the children, and knew everything that had happened recently in the family. Cox went home, and to everyone's surprise, Helen died on the night of June 6. He was stoical in thanking Leonard Opdycke for his condolences. "My mother was eighty-three, I had just been to see her, and found her bright and happy and interested in everything, and she was unusually well the day before she died, passing away in the night. So we have to be thankful for the manner of her death and that she was spared all she most dreaded."[23]

Cox enjoyed the Chicago experience and thought that Chicago's commitment to culture boded well for the American art he praised and fostered. The city would be an example to others in offering a viable alternative to modern art. He was especially impressed at how movers and shakers in the business world worked closely with people in cultural affairs. "I found a good deal that interested me, and I thought we in New York might learn something from Chicago's spirit," he wrote Edwin H. Blashfield. He was realistic about his own labors. He had been blunt about modernism but did not see himself as merely negative or reactionary. He tried to set modernism in a large social context to show how it adversely affected many aspects of life. He analyzed and praised an American art that he believed could meet that modernism if Americans cared. And he spoke and wrote about intellectual themes and technical procedures that, from his vantage point, could vitalize art and culture. Back in New York, he heard the articles and book being discussed and would trust to luck and the judgments of those who cared to get results.[24]

The Scammon Lectures were a major step in Cox's emergence as the chief public spokesman for traditional art. Their dissemination as articles and a book reached an important audience. Together with the *New York Times* interview, they helped establish him as a thoughtful critic with a viable viewpoint. From now on, whatever else he did in the art world, he would be known as the chief opponent of modernism and a leading spokesman for classical ideals.

The reception of *The Classic Point of View* that fall was positive. The magazines and newspapers likely to review it sympathized with Cox's views and saw him as a leading cultural figure. The moderns had not quite developed a group of critics, or the necessary outlets, to make their case to any large public. And Cox's careful, lucid exposition, with familiar and easily understood art examples and literary metaphors, was bound to attract the interested public. An unnamed reviewer in the *New York Times* summarized the book at length and saw it as a basic antidote to modernism. He emphasized that Cox's message was positive, not reactionary. The book was "inspiring and corrective." The well-known literary critic Hamilton Wright Mabie praised the work in the widely read *Outlook Magazine*. He too saw it as a guide out of the "confusion of aim and practice which now reigns in all the arts." Frank Jewett Mather of Princeton generally agreed with Cox's views but was more genial about the moderns. He was gratified at the book's reception but privately cautioned that "most critics did not really get it as a doctrinal whole." Cox thought he was making some progress. He lectured in Baltimore in April 1912 and at dinner overheard the people at a nearby table talking about art. They were obviously part of his audience. One man said that something was "truly classic, in the sense of Kenyon Cox." He reported that he had two copies of *The Classic Point of View*, one in the city and another in a country place. Everyone at the table knew this Cox's name, "and I gathered they thought him an unusually intellectual man. So!" Kenyon wrote Louise.[25] This rather touching desire for approval and notice revealed a human side that most moderns would not have recognized.

To the family's relief, better financial times accompanied this fresh recognition. Cox received a small legacy from his mother's estate, and during the fall and winter of 1911 was able to write, lecture, and review enough to pay the bills. Then in January 1912, he contracted to do the pendentives for the Wisconsin state capitol, which produced a reasonably predictable income for more than a year. He then did the triptych for the senate chamber in Madison, which brought in payments for another year. He went from near poverty to modest affluence, and by the spring of 1913 he was asking Will Cochran for advice on investments.[26] Cox was never relieved of money worries, but the family continued its regular season in the city and summered in Cornish. Louise rehired her maid, and they had a few luxuries.

Cox's sense of the growing ability of modernism to attract attention and change the art debate accompanied his work on the elaborate decorations for Madison. He probably felt that he was coming to the height, perhaps the end, of his twenty-year career as a muralist. He was in his late fifties, a good age for most men, was overworked, and increasingly felt unwell. The long boom in monumental buildings that underlay the mural movement might not continue much longer. The number of commissions was likely to decline, whatever his or any other painter's abilities or reputation. But he believed that modernism's emphasis on the unusual and eccentric, and the transitory, boded ill for social stability and artistic growth in molds he favored. His increasingly biting criticism of the moderns was a kind of coda to a sense that his generation, with all its great achievements in art, was under siege from forces whose energy he recognized but did not understand.

Though very busy, he thus took opportunities after 1911 to speak in favor of traditional ideas when he could reach an influential audience. A major chance came in the winter of 1912, when the American Academy of Arts and Letters, and its sister body the National Institute of Arts and Letters, asked him to talk on current art at its December 13 meeting. This group represented established and respected writers, critics, artists, and others who agreed with his views, and who commanded attention in the press. Knowing this, Cox decided to analyze the current state of art briefly, bluntly, and in historical context. He titled the speech "The Illusion of Progress."

Cox reminded his audience that change was not always progress. But modern man, enamored of science and technology, believe that innovation was a step toward some kind of perfection. He cautioned not "to expect a similar pace in art and letters, to imagine that the art of the future must be far finer than that of the past, and that the art of one decade, or even of one year, must supersede that of the preceding decade or the preceding year, as the 1913 model in automobiles supersedes the model of 1912." The sudden pace of discussion about change in the arts, a product of modern communications, did not allow time for normal analysis. "It was scarce two years since we first heard of 'Cubism' when the 'Futurists' were calling the 'Cubists' reactionary. Even the gasping critics, pounding manfully in the rear, have thrown away all impedimenta of traditional standards in the desperate effort to keep up with what seems less a march than a stampede." Cox did not deny that every generation moved ahead. Advances in technical skills naturally affected all the arts. But the basic emotional impulses remained the same over time. The arts were outlets for the human urge to express something unusual in recognizable forms, to bring order out of disorder in nature, and to celebrate social cohesion while expanding the individual imagination.

Cox had always believed that the artist was a special personality, with insights above time and place, obliged to speak in intelligible terms. He did not believe that the ability to create or appreciate art belonged to any special group. None of this depended on class, status, wealth, or any other social value except thoughtful taste. Modernism and its agents threatened to overwhelm analysis and to overvalue the personal expression of many artists who lacked enduring merit. He thought that "detestable things" were being done and did not cavil to use words such as *insanity, degraded,* and *hideous.* But with normal caution, good taste would tell. The new that encompassed ideals and beauty, and that spoke to sympathetic minds, would survive. The rest was not worth discussing.

The audience applauded, and the lecture was certain to be printed. Cox apparently first offered it to the prestigious *Yale Review,* a natural outlet for traditional writing. But Robert Underwood Johnson, editor of the *Century Magazine,* asked to see it, and Cox retrieved the text. Johnson paid $150 for it and promised a wide readership.[27]

Cox continued to work on the stained glass pendentives for Madison and delivered the final design for the one-hundred-dollar bill late in January 1913. But he devoted energy and concern to the growing art debate, which he realized was reaching some kind of climax. The art world was full of discussion of the new Europeans, and many American painters had rejected what they called academicism in favor of more personal expression. Perhaps more to the point, the newspapers and popular periodicals had begun to discuss modernism, usually in sensationalistic terms. From Cox's point of view, there was a great deal of confusion and little hard criticism about modernism as it began to dominate the art debate.

The interest seemed to peak as both artists and the public anticipated the highly publicized International Exhibition of Modern Art, which the Association of American Painters and Sculptors installed in the New York Sixty-ninth Infantry Regiment armory on Lexington Avenue, between Twenty-fifth and Twenty-sixth streets. It would run for a month after February 17 and promised to be a major source of debate among artists and the interested or puzzled public. As the exhibition's opening drew near, *Harper's Weekly,* one of the most widely read periodicals in the country, asked Cox to review it. Though he had outlined his basic views in "The Illusion of Progress" the preceding December, he accepted, hoping to reach a large audience. He had not seen many of the foreign modern works, but knew of them and their styles from reproductions and descriptions. He had varied opinions about many of the artists, and treated modernism as a broad movement with central purposes and effects, whatever its individual variations in persons or schools.

He went to the armory certain in his own mind that he could be a fair, if harsh, critic. He accepted the show as a chance to clear the air and to render informed judgment. It was better that Americans actually see these works than merely read sensational reports about them. He did not see himself as a reactionary, opposed to change, and knew from art history that critics were often wrong in dealing with new art. Had not his old teachers Gérôme and Cabanel both attacked and misjudged Corot and Millet? He did not wish to join their company but would be blunt and thoughtful in his analysis.

Even with this perspective and good intentions, he spent "an appalling morning" at the exhibition. Royal Cortissoz, art critic for the *New York Tribune* and an equal foe of modernism, recalled meeting him there. They knew each other and talked about both individual works and the show's meaning. With his usual seriousness, Cox took the event personally, and looked stricken. "I meant to make a genuine effort to sort out these people, to distinguish their different aims and doctrines, to take notes and to analyze, to treat them seriously, if disapprovingly," he wrote in the *Harper's* review. "I cannot do it. Nor can I laugh. This thing is not amusing; it is heartrending and sickening. I was quoted the other day as saying that the human race is rapidly approaching insanity. I never said it, but if I were convinced that this is really 'modern art' and that these men are representative of our time, I should be constrained to believe it."

He thought that what Cortissoz called the "cubistic fantasticalities" were especially outrageous. Carried to its logical conclusion, that nature consisted of individual interpretations of abstracted forms, cubism was "nothing else than the total destruction of the art of painting." He did not doubt that colors, shapes, lines, forms, as in a turkish rug or tile, were interesting and attractive. But this was not his art of imagination and insight, which interpreted nature in recognizable terms to produce mood, reflection, and expanded imagination. The cubists "have abolished the representation of nature and all forms of recognized and traditional decoration."

He was especially harsh with Matisse, in whose work he saw a disturbing randomness, a lack of central purpose, and a love of idle decoration at the expense of harmony. Nature had no real relationships in it, and the artist was alone with artificial manipulations. As a classical figure painter, Cox disliked Matisse's distortions of the nude. Some of these were simply ugly, disjointed, insubstantial; others were frankly erotic and suggestive. Cox's nudes were always ideal in real forms; these seemed suggestive in unreal forms. They did violence to the sacred human body, especially that of women. "As to Matisse, I am no longer in doubt; it is not madness that stares at you from his canvases, but leering effrontery."

He thought Cézanne the most interesting of the postimpressionists, a term that the English critic Roger Fry had devised in 1911. "He seems always to have aimed at the great things. But he seems to me absolutely without talent and cut off from tradition. He could not learn to paint as others did, and he spent his life in the hopeless attempt to create a new art of painting for himself." Cézanne looked old masterish, and at least had the qualities of a sincere search for nature's meanings. Cox thought that Gauguin had a powerful sense of decoration but was "a decorator tinged with insanity." His works were simply too raw, too urgently personal to endure. "His arrangements of line are sometimes noble and graceful, but the things he represents are often hideous. His color is sometimes beautiful, but it is always unnecessarily false and often unpleasantly morbid." Van Gogh lacked the means to express his powerful urges and was clearly mad. Henri Rousseau was simply amusing, the sort of hanger-on Cox remembered from student days. "For a generation which demands *naïveté* and spontaneity above all other qualities, he is a valuable acquisition, for his *naïveté* is the real thing."

Cox generally liked the American section but wondered why it was included. Whatever their occasional excesses, these Americans retained a greater sense of traditional forms and ideals than the Europeans did. "Some of [their work] is silly, but little of it is dangerous." He did take Marsden Hartley to task for alleged drawings made of paper rectangles and random lines. This clearly pointed to abstraction, the end of art that could communicate.

Cox did not analyze every artist, nor individual pictures. He focused instead on the broad meanings in the works and closed the full-page review with some general thoughts. He hoped that critics would remain skeptical and that dealers would not raid "the pockets of the gullible." He admonished students not to see any shortcuts to enduring work or lasting fame in this modernism. They must always master classical techniques and know art history. He sent the public a final message, urging caution and good sense. After all, art was made for them. "You are not infallible, but your instincts are right in the main, and you are, after all, the final judges. If your stomach revolts against this rubbish, it is because it is not fit for human food. Let no man persuade you to stuff yourselves with it."[28]

The important *Harper's* review was dated Saturday, March 15. Cox added a codicil in a lengthy interview for the Sunday edition of the *New York Times*. It had been done in the preceding week and was timed to appear when the Armory Show closed. The unnamed reporter found Cox in his pleasant studio, wearing slippers and smoking a corncob pipe. He was calm, genial, and deadly serious. The two men sat, the reporter taking notes, but Cox periodically stood up and paced the room. He covered familiar ground again, knowing that he spoke to a large public. This individualism, he said, did not speak to a unifying tradition and was divorced from the society it needed to serve. The idea that modernism involved a new, special language was nonsense. If a writer announced "wigglety-wagglety-wigglety" to describe something, did he speak a new language that people must adopt? Cox thought that "the Cubists and the Futurists are giving us a 'wigglety-wagglety-wigglety' variety of art." He used this childish analogy to show the absurdity of the moderns' contention that they represented a new dispensation in art. He saw much of their work as simply pathological. Matisse, Rodin, and the Cubists and Futurists were products of modern culture. "These men have seized upon the modern engine of publicity and are making insanity pay." Bluntly stated, "Matisse has his tongue in his cheek and his eye on his pocket."

Personalities aside, the broad tendencies in modernism most concerned Cox. He thought these would bring public ridicule on the arts. Artist and public needed each other as part of an optimistic, cohesive, settled order. "The great traditions of the world are not here by accident. They exist because humanity found them to be for its own good." He naturally had to hope for a reaction in favor of classicism, but was uncertain. If not, art, as he knew it, was dead. Turning to a bookshelf, he took down a copy of *The Classic Point of View* and read the passage that depicted modern art as an emperor without clothes. A profile drawing of Cox, done from a photograph, was in the center of the full-page story, with illustrations of several modern works, including Marcel Duchamp's much-ridiculed *Nude Descending a Staircase* (1912). Opting for maximum attention, the reporter titled the story with a quotation from Cox: "Cubists and Futurists Are Making Insanity Pay."[29]

Cox's friends responded quickly. "Standing for clean, wholesome, sane, decent art, you have erected a standard that must and will be maintained," the architect Cass Gilbert wrote him. "And good citizens as well as honest artists must all feel that you have done a public service in speaking as plainly as you did." The painter Edmund C. Tarbell agreed. "I think every man who respects his profession and has spent his life trying to learn it owes you a debt of gratitude." Royal Cortissoz, responding to a message from Cox, lauded the interview. He appreciated Cox's intense feelings but suggested that modernism's worst excesses would pass with time and reflection. At any rate, people had seen the works. One could only hope the final judgment was sound.[30]

The Armory Show closed on March 15 and moved on to Chicago and Boston, where it caused more controversy and debate that spring. The contestants soon seemed exhausted, at least for the moment, but Cox hoped that he and other critics had made some impact on public thinking. Will Low had published *A Painter's Progress* in 1910, a combination memoir and survey of traditional art-thought. Edwin H. Blashfield produced *Mural Painting in America* in 1913, which dealt with the historical ideas and techniques involved in decoration. Cox, of course, had stated his position in *The Classic Point of View* in 1911. All three of these books had been Scammon Lectures. Together with numerous articles, reviews and speeches, they surely provided a reasonable alternative to the publicity for the moderns. But Cox understood that his message was complex and required some knowledge of esthetics and of art history. It was always easier to accept anything labeled modern or new. He wrote Blashfield that "our doctrine is very hard to drive into modern heads—whether because the doctrine is weak or the heads of too hard wood!"[31]

In the winter of 1913, Cox had finished his basic work on the glass mosaics for Wisconsin and had the time to make a final comprehensive statement against the moderns. He titled the essay "Artist and Public" and focused on that relationship while again summarizing his view of art history. Cox held that historically, the great artist had always produced for some supportive public. It at least understood the importance of the effort and could read his message, even if it did not always understand some of his ideas. Ecclesiastical and aristocratic patronage gave the artist a place in society. Leonardo, Michelangelo, Rubens, and many others had acquired fame, status, and even some wealth, but the main thing in all cases was appreciation of their work and ideas. Modern life had destroyed this web of relationships and set the artist adrift, seeking transitory support from self-advertisement and the pursuit of novelty. The idea of the artist as misunderstood genius, so dear to the moderns, was rather recent. Modern publicity, the need to be striking at exhibitions, detachment from craftsmanship rooted in history, all enhanced the artist's sense of separateness from society, which he then blamed for his predicament, in circular reasoning. Modern life had trivialized or atomized art production and experience, and steadily made the artist seem a free agent, feeling no obligations to society. The current moderns were theory-ridden, prone to bombastic and self-serving pronunciations, but had no real integrating ideals. They were "driven to the attempt at pure self-expression—to the exaltation of the great god Whim." Many were sincere, oblivious to the consequences of their work. But "an art cannot be improvised, and an artist must have some other guide than unregulated emotion." He appealed again for conscious links between artist and society. "Art is made for man and has a social function to perform. We have a right to demand that it shall be both human and humane," he insisted, "that it shall show some sympathy in the artist with our thoughts and feelings; that it shall interpret our ideals to us in that universal language which has grown up in the course of ages." Innovation and individualism were false if rootless. And in the end, the public had a basic responsibility. It must have strong ideals to depict, good taste to satisfy, and a willingness to support artists who wished to speak for more than self.[32]

Cox composed the essay in the usual clear, concise style, with an authoritative, dignified tone, and included familiar examples. He was sharp in dealing with the moderns, but was equally blunt in outlining society's responsibilities to support the arts. Late in December 1913, he read the essay to cultural groups in Lowell, Massachusetts, and in Philadelphia. The press took note and summarized his remarks, which seemed to find a responsive chord. Cox was a major figure in the art debate, and anything he said was newsworthy. There was considerable discussion of "Artist and Public" in some art journals and in cultural circles. Edward L. Burlingame of *Scribner's Magazine,* for whom the essay was destined, cautioned Cox to avoid reporters and to prevent quotations from the text. This would spoil its effect when printed as an article in the magazine in the coming spring. Cox tried to ward off reporters and promised not to read it again. The audiences were enthusiastic and wanted to read the lecture in print. The essay appeared in the magazine's April 1914 issue and provoked many letters of support. "I am still getting complimentary letters about that article more than a month and a half after it was printed," he wrote Burlingame in mid-May, "something the like of which has never happened to me before."[33]

The debate over modernism abated for the moment by the spring of 1914. Cox continued to work on *The Marriage of the Atlantic and the Pacific* for Madison, and made the usual rounds. He had become something of a celebrity in the preceding year, as a lightning rod for the modernists and a refuge for the traditionalists. He had spoken his mind, often in forceful, even shocking, terms. The moderns returned the favor, making him and his work the examples of what they disliked and hoped to replace in art. The moderns especially disliked Cox's murals for the very reasons that others praised them. They were allegedly based on historical precedents that had no present appeal, were civic rather than personal, stylistically academic, and instructive rather than expressive. Cox sought idealism, esthetic integration, and emotional harmony in art. The moderns pursued energy, expression, the unusual and unpredictable, wherever they might lead.

The shouting from all sides doubtless confused the interested or curious public. The popular press generally treated the Armory Show in sensational terms, but the country at least witnessed a debate over the role of art and culture in a modern democratic society. The press naturally reported Cox's most cutting remarks, and he was blunt in print. But he also wrote several major statements of his viewpoint in measured and reasonable tones. He emerged from this stage of the fray as a focus of modernist dislike. But he was also respected as a thinker and was the acknowledged spokesman of traditionalist ideas.

In calmer times, similarities as well as differences appeared among the combatants. Cox saw the modernists as agents of chaos. They saw themselves as trying to express intense feelings and large statements in new ways. The modernists sought grandeur and idealism in some of their work and hoped to revitalize more intimate and mundane subject matter. They seemed unperturbed at the prospect of separating artist and public, because they believed their message would change taste. Nor did they fear an emphasis on personal and individual interpretations of perceived reality, because they thought this was the distinctive core of modern life. Both groups faced formidable challenges in taking their views to the public. For all their energy and often striking works, the modernists were not likely to attract a significant public because they departed so much from familiar reality. At the same time, the traditionalists could not extend their vision in new forms that satisfied their own canons of thought or that appealed to the public's obvious need for some change within familiar work.

Cox was often a pessimist about people, and never fulfilled his own ideals, but he did not doubt the ability of art to transform the individual and society. He had no illusions about creating a broad public for any given approach, and hoped chiefly for the subtle effects of art as a civic enterprise. He knew that only a few people ever understood the heart of artistic insight. The public appreciated its forms, story, or superficial evocations. But art went on because artists had something important to say. Because idealism was the center of his personality, Cox often spoke intensely, sometimes thoughtlessly, about art's roles. But he could be realistic. "It is perhaps natural and inevitable that we who are artists or who are especially interested in art should seem to overrate the importance of art to the world at large," he wrote in an essay on Rembrandt in 1906. "We can hardly expect others to share our conviction that art is the only thing that really matters, the only expression of the human experience which endures." In more pithy terms, he was wont to say, as he did to Will Low: "The majority of Americans still feel that they can be 'fairly comfortable' without art."[34] By now he was wise enough to know that art and its appreciation would continue. He was grateful to be heard and viewed as a spokesman for whatever great tradition the American public wanted.

VIII

❧

LAST YEARS

The Art conflicts of the ban-
ner year of 1913 subsided as artists and the interested public digested the
challenge of the moderns and the defense of the traditionalists. Cox emerged
as a kind of culture hero to many people who disliked or feared a modernism
whose avowed aims and potential effects seemed to involve broad social beliefs as well as formal art. It was hard to say which side, if either, had won
the foray. But Cox at least had made a powerful, logical case for a body of
thought and art that could be dominant.

Cox continued his usual artistic work while speaking and writing. In May
1914 he oversaw the installation of the first glass mosaics in Madison. On the
way home, he conferred with Dolson and Will Cochran in Cleveland about
the memorial decorations to their parents for Oberlin College. About the
same time, an unnamed group, apparently including Leonard Opdycke,
wanted to stage a retrospective exhibition of Cox's work in New York. This
would honor him as a painter and thinker, and further advertise traditionalist
ideas. Cox was flattered but thought such a show would be hard to mount.
He had not painted many recent easel works and dreaded the expense and
bother of borrowing older works. He could supplement these with drawings
and photographs of murals, but had no idea how much this might interest
the public. He sent Opdycke a list of possible works, "the pick of the bas-
ket—each is in its own way one of my best things, and in different ways."
These almost duplicated the works shown in Chicago in 1911.

The Boston painter Philip Leslie Hale then took up the cause. Apparently
he first sought some of Cox's drawings for an exhibit at the St. Botolph's Club
but by July progressed to wanting a general show of Cox's works. Cox hesitated until the group in New York made up its mind. He could not realistically organize shows for both cities and reminded Hale that he had not
painted much easel work in some time, being "too hard at work making the
semblance of a living out of mural painting." Cox spent the summer of 1914

at Calder House in Croton-on-Hudson, which further complicated organizing a show at some distance. He was working on the Oberlin decorations and the preparatory drawings for *The Marriage of the Atlantic and the Pacific* for the Wisconsin senate chamber. By late August, they agreed on what to do, and the show was set for December 21, 1914–January 1, 1915.

The exhibition consisted of three figure studies; the portraits of Louise, C. Grant La Farge, Cass Gilbert, Maxfield Parrish, and Emil Carlsen done for the National Academy; the Oberlin panels, which he had shown in New York that November; and drawings and photographs of the murals for the Iowa and Wisconsin capitol domes, the Winona public library, and the courthouses in Jersey City and Wilkes-Barre. This was a good sampling of Cox's later works, though his earlier list to Opdycke was broader and included older works such as *Flying Shadows, Landscape,* and the portrait of Henry Fry, all of 1883, as well as *The Harp Player* and the portrait of Saint Gaudens. Given Cox's reputation as a muralist, the emphasis at St. Botolph's was on the decorations. A reviewer of the preview took Cox and the works very seriously. He cautioned that "Mr. Cox's work is essentially formal, and it is scholarly in character rather than spontaneous." He appreciated the figure studies and portraits. But the cameolike decorations dealing with justice for the Hudson County Courthouse in Jersey City and the monumental *Judicial Virtues* for the Luzerne County Courthouse in Wilkes-Barre were most impressive. "His is not the most original creative sort of imagination, but it is not commonplace," the reviewer noted. "His subjects are, for the most part, trite, but in the treatment of them he lends them dignity and a kind of formal nobility that is often highly impressive."[1] The show's sobriety and classicism was in stark contrast to the modern art Boston had seen in the spring of 1913.

War broke out in Europe early in August 1914. The United States was not involved, but Cox favored the Allies. He had never liked German art, and like many cultured Americans, saw Germany as authoritarian. He also favored France for its art, and because of his associations there as a student. He doubtless hoped the United States would remain neutral, but his sympathies were clear. He joined the American Artists' Committee of One Hundred, founded in the fall of 1914, to help French artists and their families who were caught up in the conflict. As the war continued, it seemed destined to alter basic Western ideals and beliefs. Cox, for one, remained militant in seeing modern art as one symptom of the chaos the war symbolized. He hoped that traditionalists would persist in upholding classical ideals and cultural order in the face of this destruction. And events might work in their favor. "It seems to me that if this war does nothing else it is bound to give the *coup de grâce* to the art of personal exploitation," he wrote Frank Mather in November 1915. "The world will be too seriously occupied to puzzle itself with any art that is not serious and comprehensive."[2]

The United States entered the conflict in April 1917, and Cox immediately joined a group of artists ready to do war work. Some designed printed matter, labels, and various articles, but most were illustrators and painters able to draw propaganda. President Wilson attempted to unify the country in a war for democracy and Western civilization, which suited Cox. His major assignment was a recruiting poster for the navy. Cox, of course, had spent years illustrating but saw the poster as a chance to use classical figure painting and mural composition for a popular audience. He drew on past work, especially a cover he did for *McClure's Magazine* at the time of the Spanish-American War in 1898. Such art was ephemeral, but he wanted a subject that people could understand, which was striking, and which spoke to idealism. He worked steadily in May 1917 and liked the result, with the usual Cox hesitations. "I rather wish you could see a Naval Recruiting Poster I have been doing," he wrote the art editor F. Wellington Ruckstuhl. "I think you would like it. Of course, it is a *poster,* therefore crude in color and modeling, but I think it has the right spirit."

The finished work was about 42-by-26 inches, lithographed on paper. It showed a classical female figure in a white robe, holding a partially seen sword in her right hand. She wore a breastplate with an eagle and flag, a crown of oak leaves, a red cap, and a flowing red cape. Behind her a ship sailed to unknown destinations in a deep blue background. Her left hand held a scroll with the legend: We Can Do No Other! The title below the picture space proclaimed: The Sword is Drawn/ The Navy Upholds It! The total effect was surprisingly modern. There were no realistic details and only broad modelling of the drapery and figure. The face looked past the viewer and was done in broad masses of color. A strong outline ran around the pictorial elements of the picture, which was flat in the best modern poster style. The work was not subtle or elegant, but it had a sense of dignity and of the ideals supposedly involved in the war.

Cox met the navy's deadline and it obliged with a rapidly finished product. Louise was out of town when the posters arrived. "The Navy Publicity Bureau has sent me about two million copies of my poster, with mailing tubes or wrappers for them. I'm sure I don't know what I shall do with them all," he wrote her. "It's very well reproduced, on the whole, by lithography. They've weakened and prettified the head a little, but it was either that or caricaturing it into a plug-ugly, and perhaps it's best as it is." A year later, Louise received a commission for a similar work as part of the campaign to save food and to recall the country's past sacrifices in wartime. "Most of yesterday morning I spent posing for a Grand Army veteran in a picture for the Food Administration which your mother is doing," Cox wrote Allyn in Rome. "She has made a beautiful old man out of me!"[3]

Of course, the war had more personal dimensions. Leonard graduated from Princeton in 1915, with an interest in architecture. But when America entered the conflict, he volunteered for the army and saw action in France and Belgium. His parents worried constantly about his safety, but he emerged unscathed, highly decorated with the Distinguished Service Medal, the French Croix de Guerre, and the Belgian Legion of Honor.

Allyn went to Italy in the fall of 1916 for a four-year fellowship at the American Academy in Rome. He became a first lieutenant in the American Red Cross in 1918, helping to move relief supplies, and worked with American servicemen. He also organized refugee lace workers.

His father wrote Allyn long letters about the home front and family affairs. They also discussed art history and theory and exchanged criticism on work in progress. Whatever the exigencies of daily living in wartime, Cox counselled his son to keep his eye on enduring values in art. He was wise enough now to reflect on what he had missed as a student and admonished Allyn to see and read as much as possible. "I hope you will become an all around painter," he urged as Allyn left for Rome in 1916. The son had good sense and serious purpose, but Cox hoped he would not succumb to the surface appeals of European civilization, even while learning what it had to offer any artist. "I am glad of all Rome is teaching you, but don't let it make you the kind of civilized and somewhat self-satisfied dilettante it has made of so many charming but somewhat futile people who have lost all touch with the real men and women who do the work of the world," he warned in April 1918. Allyn complained of the frivolity and lack of seriousness in the people around him, but Cox advised patience and discrimination. "Even the barbarous youth who drink and shout in cafes may have good stuff in them when it comes to serious things," he wrote. "Of course, what we most lack in life and art is discipline, but I think we are on the way to get it. Europe has been suffering from the reaction against excessive discipline for a long time," he thought, "now we, who have never had any, have been led into foolish imitation of a revolt which can mean nothing to us." Yet this would change as the war brought a higher idealism and showed the limits of individualism when social values were at stake. "But I think the general stiffening of character that I see going on is beginning to affect art as well as life, and I believe it is more the reaction against exaggerated individualism and whim than anything in the work itself that is bringing me, now, more praise for my work than I have ever had before." A thoughtful parent, he encouraged the impressionable Allyn to move beyond his own example. In retrospect, he realized that he had been too unyielding a personality, however right his ideals. "I have struggled against a bad education or none—against the tendency of the times," he reflected. "I have had to give myself the discipline I should have inherited and make out of nothing a *style* for myself. If I have got so far as to do something sound and solid, I have seldom been able to add that ease and charm which is the crown of effort. It is for you, who start, more or less, where I leave off, to achieve what I have only been able to foreshadow."[4]

Cox's painting changed as the war progressed. He completed *The Marriage of the Atlantic and the Pacific,* the elaborate triptych for the Wisconsin capitol's senate chamber, in the fall of 1915. He exhibited the work at the Vanderbilt Galleries in the Fine Arts Building before sending it west. Forbes Watson, then emerging as a reasonable promodern critic, took the occasion to summarize the opposition to Cox's work and ideas. He realized that Cox had a large reputation and that his painting appealed to those who wanted a serious, recognizable art with historical antecedents. He thus adopted a sarcastic tone, even when complimenting Cox for "his learning, his technical skill, and his indefatigable research." Watson recognized the enormous amount of thought and labor in the picture, but it was storytelling, designed to impress people who wanted serious, uplifting lessons rather than spontaneity or individualism in art. All in all, he thought it and similar works outdated. They would appeal primarily to schoolmarms and their charges, intent on learning lessons rather than on feeling energy.

Cox knew that the more he spoke out the more he would become the focus of modernist attacks. He did not answer Watson in public but was clearly irritated in writing to Frank Mather at Princeton. "I have never been able to make up my mind whether his determination to see nothing but illustration and preoccupation with subject in my work is unfairness or sheer stupidity," he wrote. Watson should realize that the picture was successful if it decorated the assigned space and made the building more impressive and beautiful. "As for the subject, it was chosen solely because I thought I saw a chance in it for beautification. *After* I chose it, I tried to express the thoughts that came to me, but the intellectual contents did not determine the choice." Watson could have his opinion but seemed narrow and intolerant. "But how theory-ridden these 'moderns' are. One would think they might see that even if what they admire is as good as they think it [is], it does not follow that everything else is bad."[5]

The Wisconsin decoration was Cox's last mural commission. His increasingly poor health might not have permitted another such large effort, but in any event, the war effectively stopped such art. With a sense of relief and challenge, Cox turned to more private efforts. At midsummer 1916, he was in Cornish, hard at work on "an important picture, 'Tradition.'" This elaborate easel composition was about 3½-by-5½ feet and was Cox's summary of his traditional ideals. He approached it with the usual care, making preliminary sketches and careful drawings. The picture contained four large female figures and three cherubs, each armed with the accoutrements of classicism in a balanced composition. The central female figure handed to the new generation a lamp that symbolized classicism. The work's themes were evident and matched its title, "the guarding and passing on of the light," as he told Edward Robinson of the Metropolitan Museum. But the style was modern in some ways. The figures' faces were realistic and broadly painted, the draperies were richly colored, and the small distant landscape was evocative. The general tone radiated Renaissance methods, elegance, and ideas, but a certain flatness dominated the picture, and its effect depended on masses and outlines rather than on realistic details in both the figures and their draperies. It was a small mural, with dignity and presence, but had some of the personal feeling of an easel work. "I have tried to combine in it the larger style of my mural work with the finish and tone of a small picture," he wrote Robinson (fig. 40).

That fall Cox tried to sell the work to the Metropolitan, but Robinson could not persuade the directors to agree. He was enthusiastic and helpful and sent along a list of potential museum buyers. As it turned out, Dolson bought the work for the Cleveland Museum of Art. He appreciated this kind of painting, and it complemented his *Hope and Memory,* but as usual he also wanted to assist Kenyon. "I have been carrying a picture in my mind's eye all the fall of the immense relief that spread itself not only over your face, but all over your whole body when I told you I would buy your picture of tradition, and I have been filled with gladness that I was able to relieve you of such a burden," Dolson wrote just before Christmas. He also bought one of the large sketches, to hang in his retirement home in Pasadena, California.

Cox exhibited *Tradition* in the regular winter NAD show. Visitors to such exhibitions doubtless knew what to expect from him, but the work must have looked unusual and old-fashioned even in those surroundings. Opponents of modernism welcomed any such work, and Cox's friend F. Wellington Ruckstuhl was enthusiastic. "It is stunningly drawn, beautifully composed, and a magnificent color-scheme," he wrote Cox. "Personally, I think it is one of your finest things, and in 200 or 300 years from now, when it shall have been 'patined' by time, it will be spoken of with as much respect as if it had been signed 'Veronese.'" Perhaps the operative term was *respect.* The unnamed reviewer for the *New York Times* merely noted "and there is the 'Tradition' of Kenyon Cox, steeped in Renaissance beauty."

Cox was "at present in one of those periods of suspension that come too often," as he wrote Will Low, with no commissions. He had to paint, both in hope of selling and to occupy his mind, "and we, who have been trained in decorative work, which we know to be wanted, find it, I think, increasingly difficult to work in the air—to paint merely for self-expression in the vague hope that someone may want the result." Because it codified his ideals and allowed him to work in a large manner, Cox considered *Tradition* to be "the most important easel picture I have ever done." It went from the NAD to the Pennsylvania Academy annual show, and he was relieved that it would teach its lessons permanently in a major museum. He even posed for a photograph in front of the work, seated with a palette, a frail, prematurely aged, serious figure.[6]

FIG. 40. Kenyon Cox, *Tradition* (1916). Oil on canvas, 41¾ × 65¼ ins.
Courtesy of The Cleveland Museum of Art, gift of J. D. Cox, 17.9.

Cox continued these personal efforts with a portrait of Leonard. He posed his son in a chair, facing the viewer, holding a book in his left hand. The face was realistic, though the clothing and background were more informal and loosely painted. Cox inevitably idealized his son, but caught a good deal of the young man's sensitive and nervous temperament. The picture attracted some notice at the spring 1917 NAD show. The ubiquitous Forbes Watson thought it "a marvel of rigid exactness, without color and without life." This was unfair. The work was an excellent likeness and a sound statement of academic methods. But Watson's remarks indicated how modernists now treated Cox. Most simply ignored his painting and writing, or dismissed him as a reactionary. A few like Watson doubtless believed that a serious tone would enhance their dismissal of him as both an old-fashioned realist in intimate works and an irrelevant classicist in larger ones.[7]

Leonard's portrait gained enough favorable comment to produce a surprise commission. Representative John J. Fitzgerald of New York was retiring from Congress in 1917, after serving since 1899. His colleagues wanted to honor him with a bust portrait to hang in the House Appropriations Committee room in the Capitol. They consulted Blashfield and the architect Thomas Hastings, both members of the Fine Arts Commission in Washington, who asked Cox to consider the commission. "Hastings didn't say so, but I imagine this comes from Leonard's portrait," Cox wrote Louise at the end of May. "I doubt if he would have thought of me as a portrait painter otherwise. And I shall never say anything against his architecture again!" The fee was a modest four hundred dollars, but as usual in Cox's career, the work was prestigious and would be displayed in a public place, presumably forever.

Cox dreaded dealing with sitters and was doubly unsure of how an important politician would behave. It did not occur to him that Fitzgerald might be equally nervous and uncertain in the presence of a well-known painter whose work would depict him for the future public. Cox's reflexive but superficial prejudices were evident when Fitzgerald arrived a trifle late for his first appointment early in June. "He looked like a horrible Tammany plug-ugly to me at first," he wrote Allyn, "but gradually I began to see a pleasant, human, Irish side to him, and also a certain real force." Both men were nervous. The first morning's work went badly, "and by lunchtime the canvas looked like the devil!" But Fitzgerald relaxed, stayed most of the afternoon, and the canvas began to take shape. Cox finally had three sittings, blocked in the black-and-white work, and spent a day on the coloring. "The Hon. Fitzgerald is not a thing of beauty, and either gets his face set like a bull-dog or goes to sleep," he wrote Louise in June. "When he gets up and talks and walks about, one is surprised to find that he has a nice human side, and rather a pleasant expression." Cox finally got considerable character into the face and did the final work predominantly in shades of gray-blue. Fitzgerald confessed to his original hesitations, especially after the first morning's work, but both he and his wife were enthusiastic about the final result. This "in spite of the fact that I haven't spared the realism of the thing," Cox wrote Allyn.[8]

Cox was also working on yet another unusual commission, this time for Dolson and Nellie. Late in 1915, they asked him to design a funerary monument for the Prentiss family plot in Cleveland's Lakeview Cemetery. Cox knew that they wanted something familiar and sober, and settled on a small temple with two idealized female figures. It would be about six feet tall and three feet wide on a base of four and a half feet. He titled it *Rectitude and Love* and thought it was "an interesting attempt to do a modern and original thing which is yet based upon an antique form." Late in 1915 he sent Dolson a drawing of the proposed work. His brother's reactions said volumes about his taste, which pretty well matched that of the middle class, who wanted serious and noncontroversial art. He would pay Kenyon for the work done thus far but had to say honestly that neither Nellie nor her sister thought the design entirely appropriate. He could not really say why, and then did so: "The figure of Love is too 'robustus' or chesty. She seems to dominate the attention in a not pleasant way. The drapery is drawn across the right leg so tightly that it gives one the feeling it may rip." Such comments must have taken Kenyon back to his youth and the endless controversies over idealized nudes. But he was patient and produced other drawings that with further modifications seemed to please the family.

The work progressed slowly, but by the spring of 1917, a promising young sculptor named H. D. Thrasher had made a clay model. "It's difficult for me to tell how successful it is [because] I've had so much trouble getting anything as I felt it, but I think it is rather handsome in the larger things," he wrote Allyn. "A little suppleness in the details would help, but I've pretty nearly concluded that that is not to be had." He and Louise visited the studio, and she liked the model. Dolson sent payments as the work progressed, and Nellie asked that her parents' names be carved on the back of the final work. The finished marble was set up early in November 1917.

Funerary monuments almost inevitably lent themselves to sentiment or to excessive formality. The final work was a trifle stiff and crowded, and the two figures seemed detached and unhappy without projecting any strong sense of either grief or hope. The work was more realistic and conventional than the Brooklyn Institute statue of 1907–8, but it had a good sense of power. The monument was appropriate enough for its setting and purpose and clearly spoke to the verities Cox emphasized (fig. 41).

Dolson was always unpredictable, and his reaction to the work was mixed. He and Nellie both liked the design a great deal, with a litany of exceptions. They thought the marble too roughly cut but assumed it would weather. They now wished the name Prentiss was on the front rather than the back. And the monument seemed too small. Dolson suggested putting it on a

FIG. 41. Kenyon Cox, *Rectitude and Love* (1916–17), Prentiss Family Memorial, Lakeview Cemetery, Cleveland, Ohio. Marble on granite base, ca. 6 × 3.5 feet. Courtesy of the Oberlin College Archives.

larger plinth, "a good big heavy granite slab on top of the foundation, and the present monument with its base imposed on top of that." The final placement of the work did not ruin its good proportions. Dolson quickly accepted it and promised to make photographs for Kenyon. "I have no doubt the work on the monument is as it should be," he wrote. "One frequently imagines how a thing is going to look, and has a feeling of disappointment when it doesn't look as expected."

Dolson offered to buy the plaster model, warning that he could not pay much. The government took 60 percent of the company's profits, and 50 percent of his dividends, "thus sawing off both ends of the log pretty near the middle." He had also spent some capital on the Pasadena home. If he could not buy the model, he suggested giving it to Oberlin. Kenyon showed the work in the Architectural League's annual, and then it went to the Allen Museum.[9]

Despite the lack of public commissions, Cox was about as busy as his energy permitted and did some unusual works. Cox saw his classicism as an exciting attitude of mind that enriched the individual's emotional experience. But he realized that other people thought it severe and demanding. His murals and most of the large easel works relied for effect on dignity and seriousness as well as rich coloration and strong composition. Cox was seldom whimsical, except in drawing for his children, but occasionally expressed a lighter side in a modified classicism. The living murals of the Cornish pageant in 1905 at one level were a way of showing that classical ideals could be personal and even amusing. In 1910 he extracted a small picture titled *Plenty* from the large mural for the Essex County Courthouse. It showed a semiclad female tending to three cherubs who represented in a bucolic setting such values as innocence, imagination, and hope. In the same year he painted *A Book of Pictures,* which won the National Academy's Isidor Medal for figure work. It showed another idealized female instructing a cherub from a large picture book. Like his more serious efforts, these works expressed his idealistic views of life's possibilities. They were richly colored, broadly executed, and relaxed in tone. They skirted sentimentality, yet showed some aspects of classicism in a genial way.

Early in the summer of 1917, Cox sent Allyn a drawing of another of these efforts, titled *The Education of Cupid.* It was an elongated composition, showing Venus teaching Cupid to shoot a bow and arrow at a target on the bust of a bearded philosopher. The setting was a classical terrace with a composite Cornish background. Cox realized that the subject was "light-minded," perhaps even trivial, but saw some challenges. "There's such a bully chance in it for serious study of action that even your mother doesn't object to the playfulness of the motive." The work also took his mind off serious matters. "To me it is a kind of relief from the horrid seriousness of reality just now." He then made a basic point about the passing era of confidence and expansion that had sustained his mural work. "It's only in pleasant and peaceful times that one wants to be ultra-serious in art." Caroline posed for Venus in white draperies and "a gorgeous piece of brilliant rose stuff, a brand new material which is the most glittery and amazing thing you can imagine." He refined the composition and, as usual, thought it the best thing he had ever done. "I have thought that so often of so many things and have found out afterwards how wrong I was! All the same, I don't think I am wrong this time."

He showed this pleasant work in the NAD winter exhibition. The nearby "shouting canvases" weakened its effect, and he redid the color after the show closed. Dolson immediately bought the picture, and Kenyon thought it was a good piece of painting but was realistic about its appeals. "I am greatly pleased with the effect it seems to produce on the outsider—the laymen, like your Uncle Dolson," he wrote Allyn in April 1918. "If it charms them, 'there must be a reason,' and I can answer, myself, for its possessing certain artistic merits which it might have without pleasing them."[10]

In odd hours Cox worked in yet another unusual form, the bookplate. He did several designs for family members and some for other patrons. The plate for Leonard showed a cherub leading a unicorn, which carried a woman attempting to escape from a seated satyr who faced away from the viewer. All were nude, and posed for simultaneous effect with the female's front and the male satyr's back and limbs. Firm lines depicted the figures, and there were swirling ones for hair, leaves, and classical devices, all enclosed within a strong rectangle. A small, parallel box below bore the legend: Leonard Cox—His Book. Other plates resembled tiny murals or Cox's allegorical easel works. He recycled *Plenty* into a plate for Edith Timken and included a fine pastoral view beyond the figures. In another he placed two female figures with cornucopias amid suavely drawn leaves and fruits. Others were abstract, some derived from Renaissance book models. One for himself boasted flowing, stylized foliage, a central device of circles and crossed lines in a square, and a ribbon with his apparent motto: As I Can. Another done for Warner Bishop in 1919 featured abstracted foliage, strong linear drawing, griffin heads, and other heraldic devices. Cox used these minor works to test his artistic skills on a very small scale. He took them as seriously as murals or easel pictures, carefully composed and drew each one, and saw that they were well printed. Their firm lines and stylized effects sometimes resembled the stained glass of 1909 for the Harkness House. They expressed his classical ideals and academic methods, but in eliminating details and in relying on lines and masses for effect, they were curiously modern.[11]

Cox also continued on the lecture circuit. He was well known to many kinds of audiences before the controversy over modernism. But after 1913 he was clearly the most vocal and best-known spokesman of classical ideals and methods and was a natural speaker for college art groups, museum programs for the general public, and cultural organizations. He drew on previous writings for these talks but continued to read widely. He also sharpened an already clear speaking style and used visual aids to good effect. Cox never spoke down to audiences and expected them to follow his often complex but easily expressed themes. A Cox lecture was noted for substance, simplicity, and thoughtful comparisons of art and artists across time.

He treated a variety of topics within a stated range of interests. He continued to believe in education as the basis of classical ideals and methods and spoke to a group of drawing teachers at the Metropolitan Museum in the spring of 1912. The museum authorities were eager to distribute the printed talk to interested people who could not attend because of a fierce thunderstorm. Cox also spoke on more familiar and substantive subjects at the Metropolitan. In 1914 he gained a good deal of publicity and public response for a series entitled "The Golden Age of Painting." It dealt with the high Renaissance masters, the chief Venetian painters, and the seventeenth-century Flemish and Dutch artists.[12]

He also lectured at several universities. He declined to speak at Yale in 1908 because of the pressure of mural commissions. "I have more to do than I see my way to accomplish just now," he pleaded to John Ferguson Weir, who was dean of the art school and a well-known painter of the previous generation. Yale honored Cox with an M.A. in 1910 and sounded him out in 1912 about succeeding Weir, whose retirement was overdue. The prospect was tempting in offering a reasonable steady income and a platform for his ideas, but he declined. "As this would amount to a decorous shelving of my career as an active artist, I don't think I should accept," he wrote Will Cochran, "but Weir kept on for another year and the decision was put off." Cox did not accept the position, but he gave several lectures at Yale between 1914 and 1916, some of which he repeated at the Metropolitan Museum and elsewhere. These included surveys of nineteenth-century realism and naturalism, traditionalists such as Ingres and Prud'hon, and mural painting in France and America.[13]

Cox spoke at numerous museums and colleges in the Northeast, where he was well known. But as late as 1917 he was on the lecture circuit in the Midwest. At the large Ohio State University in Columbus, he spoke to "the biggest audience of the season, who listened like mice," as he reported to Louise. He moved on to Gambier College and to Kenyon College, which had 150 students, by way of contrast to Ohio State. He found the members of these audiences attentive and polite, usually ready with thoughtful questions. Such talks were significant events on college campuses and in the cultural worlds of both small towns and urban centers, where they brought a taste of cosmopolitan Eastern culture and, in Cox's case, a glimpse of the world of great art.[14]

These lectures were necessarily eclectic. In discussing the Renaissance, Cox might analyze the style, techniques, and aims of Michelangelo, Leonardo, or Raphael, but he also tried to set them in cultural context. He knew how much detail or abstract analysis an audience would accept. He also realized his own limitations and seldom discussed British art, for instance. He appreciated some of it, but in general disliked what he saw as an emphasis on anecdote and incident, and a lack of integration or finish in drawing and color. Nor did he talk much about Oriental art, though he had appreciated Japanese work since his youth. He was good at explaining difference within a national or epochal style and between differing styles. He praised the similarities of manner and intent of Velázquez and Rubens but noted their marked emotional and imaginative differences. He celebrated Rembrandt's classical temper, as he saw it, which produced evocative and integrating moods, while noting other kinds of lesser power in the work of a realist like Hals. He always tried to show how art and society interacted. Breadth of treatment, idealistic purpose, and thoughtfulness in the arts were marks of mature and creative societies. And if it wished to, he thought the modern era could inherit the world's previous art ideals.

His own likes and dislikes were clear, and he embellished the themes that had made him a major critic. He reiterated the artist's need for discipline and order, founded on mastery of drawing, coloration, and design. Thus armed, the artist with something important to say became a special personality to people of like mind. He also showed the powerful emotional appeals of classicism to both the individual and society. Classicism was an attitude of mind, not a collection of skills or subjects. Successful expression expanded the imagination and heightened the sensibilities. "We feel ourselves, for the moment, possessed of clearer senses, of more lively emotions, of greater intellectual powers, than we had imagined." Classicism was emotional. "In all these ways, pictorial representation may be life-communicating and life-enhancing, and may therefore give us that highest of pleasures, the sense of superiority to our ordinary selves."[15]

These late lectures reflected Cox's integrated thought and a good degree of assurance about the validity of classicism in society. He was usually positive and revealed little of the combativeness and acerbity that had made him a famous foe of modernism. But he did not avoid the threat, as he saw it, that the new art posed. He relied on a rather gentle sarcasm instead of a frontal assault, as in the past, to note that mankind was not likely to reject its art heritage at the command of current modernists. At the same time, he attacked modernist pretensions and was unsympathetic with the complaint that artist and public had drifted apart, as he had said they would. Modernists had narrowed their appeals to a small circle of critics and commentators of like mind, "the still narrower interests of cliques and coteries in the exploitation of whims and extravagant theories. They have cultivated a contempt for the public, and have little right to complain if, in times like these, the public neglects them and what they do." He did not know whether or not classicism would triumph, but "if art cannot learn to express in the future, as it has done in the past, the highest aspirations and the deepest feelings of the age, then the age will learn to do with art."[16]

As in the past, Cox received the maximum exposure and income from the lectures. He gave them first as talks, then published them as articles, and finally gathered them into a book, *Concerning Painting,* in 1917. He probably received about one hundred dollars for each lecture, a little more than that for them as magazine articles, and then small royalties from book sales. These were not large sums individually but were a significant part of his total income at a time when a skilled worker often made one hundred dollars a month. Cox doubtless appreciated the lecture circuit as a forum for his ideas as well as a modest source of income, but it was a wearisome round. By early 1918 he had had his say and lacked the energy for more than occasional work. "I don't suppose I have entirely written myself out," he told H. W. Kent of the Metropolitan Museum, "but I have nothing waiting to be expressed at this moment."[17]

Cox managed to remain solvent, but just barely. Despite a lifetime of work and substantial reputations, he and Louise seemed as financially insecure as ever. Leonard and Allyn soon would be able to earn livings. He and Louise would educate Caroline, but like most parents of their circumstances, doubtless presumed that she would find economic security in marriage. This precarious situation did not alter their living habits. They still spent the art season in New York City and summers in Cornish, with domestic help. This was possible through close economy and occasional loans from Dolson, who for all his prickliness usually helped if asked, after suitable remonstrances and colorful candor. He bought a good many paintings, allowed Kenyon to borrow them for exhibitions, and let them be reproduced for modest sales that helped the finances a little. Kenyon dedicated *Artist and Public* to Dolson in 1914, with the note: "To J. D. C. In grateful recognition of unfailing kindness this book is inscribed."

In that year, Kenyon finally turned to Dolson with the only plan he could think of for financial security. He suggested that he sublet the apartment for a substantial rent, pay Dolson the usual monthly fee, and use the difference to live more cheaply in Croton-on-Hudson or Mount Kisco. Dolson replied after a brief period of "smothered thoughts," trusting that "you will forgive me if I speak plainly," as if he ever talked any other way. He first recalled the favor he had done Kenyon with the original low-interest loan. "I didn't go into it as a money-making investment, but to give you a home. If it is to be turned into a money-making investment to yield 10% or more, do you really feel you should receive the income, 'cause I don't." Kenyon and the family had lived practically rent free in the apartment. In addition, "I have bought, and paid you in cash, pictures that amount to more than the rent, and remitted rent unpaid to about the same amount." He would not continue this, "as we have about all the pictures from one artist that we want." His will provided that Kenyon and Louise could live rent free in the apartment for their lifetimes, but he did not think they should rent it. These remarks then led to a disquisition on their disregard for proper finance. They needed to economize and make the children self-supporting as soon as possible. He noted that Will Cochran had five self-supporting children. Kenyon and Louise had always lived "away beyond your means, and at your age, if ever, something should be provided for declining years." They could stay in the apartment or move to cheaper quarters as they wished, but the suggested scheme was unworkable and irritating. "In other words, you want to convert my capital, put up for your comfort, into your capital at my risk. This I decline to do. 'Nuff said.'"

Dolson was indeed generous to his younger brother. He thought that Kenyon and Louise were naïve about money, but that was part of being artists. His outburst of 1914 was harsh but reflected a mercurial mood and did not affect their relationship. Louise and Kenyon remained in the apartment and Dolson bought more art. But he knew that Kenyon was spending waning energy in lecturing, writing, and reviewing just to pay minimal bills. Their insecurity preyed on his mind because he loved them, but also because he always feared such an end in his own life. He outlined the solution to the problem in a surprise letter just before Christmas 1916. He was spending the winter in Pasadena and could not forebear introductory remarks on his own problems. An unpleasant operation had cost him an impacted wisdom tooth and a piece of jawbone. "This was done a week ago and I can't open my mouth wide enough to get a small cigar between my teeth," he reported. "I am living on soups, boiled eggs and milkshakes." Nor could he forgo the usual reminder of his humble beginnings and steep upward climb to affluence. He confessed to fearing that he might somehow lose everything and be impoverished in old age. "For years, I have suffered mental torment when I have thought of the uphill fight you and Louise were putting up to bring up your growing family, and [with] absolutely no assurance at any time that the necessary wherewithal would be forthcoming at the crucial time." He now proposed to give them the proceeds from a trust fund, whose principal would revert to his estate at their deaths. This surprise gift offered at least a basic income for Kenyon and Louise and came just in time. The war both ended mural commissions and caused a high inflation. The Coxes probably could not have survived without Dolson's help. "We would be completely swamped if it hadn't been for Uncle Dolson," Louise wrote Allyn in 1917. "Prices are so high too [that] even that isn't enough for us without the greatest care."[18]

Cox's health caused as much concern in the family as did the endless problem of finances. He was active enough but was never robust. He ate sparingly and became thinner with time, whereas Louise developed a matronly appearance. He still suffered from frequent colds and stomach trouble. Lack of commissions, money worries, or reflection on the danger to his ideals could trigger bouts of mild depression. Friends accepted his periodic ill health, which seemed to complement his reserved or dour demeanor. He submitted to periodic regimens designed to increase his strength and to provide relaxation, including special diets and trips to the masseur. At some point, he apparently contracted tuberculosis, which was among the era's health scourges. This disease could remain in remission for long periods, and he may have had it for some time. It also eroded energy and will, while always threatening a major recurrence, which may have explained much of his occasional lassitude. But through it all, he worked steadily and was remarkably disciplined.[19]

His circle of friends was never large and naturally dwindled with time. Saint Gaudens's death in 1907 was a special loss, but Cox retained many friends in the Cornish circle. Leonard Opdycke's death in 1915 cut ties that went back to boyhood. He corresponded with Will Low, who lived in Bronxville, both for old times' sake and to reaffirm their shared values. He meant to visit, but "one's feet are always in fly-paper." It was ironic that "when one has important work to do, one can't get away from it, and when one has no important work, one has to scrabble harder than ever at odds and ends in the effort to keep off the wolf," he wrote Low in 1916. There was some consolation that even if they all went to the poorhouse, which seemed likely on some days, "we have come the primrose way." They could also "hope that some of our own work will last; we can be sure that we have helped make things better for the next generation; and we have been able to help get our children into the way of doing for themselves." He naturally had some regrets, but in the end "one can only be one's self, and try to get the best out of one's own ideas and feelings—it is useless to try to do things as others see them." He still liked music and theater and managed an occasional evening out. Early in the summer of 1917 he took Caroline and some friends to see Ethyl Barrymore, "and had a few breathless and rapturous minutes in her dressing room," as he reported to Louise. He felt unwell, and being a Cox, had to add, "that is I suppose the minutes were rapturous for the others; they were mildly pleasant for me."[20]

By 1917 the bouts of feeling unwell came more frequently, and friends and family tried to make him comfortable. When he lectured at the Metropolitan Museum, the staff went out of their way to save his energy, gathering the necessary slides, standing by during the talks, and seeing him to and from the apartment in a cab. Part of the problem, of course, was circular. He needed work to maintain his spirits but lacked both the necessary strength and the commissions. He suffered a serious bout of illness in the winter and spring of 1918 but seemed to regain his spirits and some energy once in Cornish. "My life here is agreeing with me and I feel as if I were growing young again," he wrote Robert Underwood Johnson from there in October. "I have done no work to speak of, but shall get to whatever comes to my hand with renewed vigor." Caroline aided her mother as much as possible. Allyn felt helpless in Rome but had to retain his own emotional balance and continue his studies and war work. "I realize to the fullest possible extent your and Papa's troubles at the present time, but I don't think my remarks would cheer you up," he wrote Louise in June 1918. "I don't think that your sorrows are the light kind that can be dispelled by lengthy condolences. For the time being, there is a background of tragedy to all our lives, and the less we talk about it the better." By December 1918, Cox was spending a good deal of time in bed, able only to read or to work on small projects like bookplates.[21]

Cox tried to maintain his spirits, and the steady decline in energy and concentration did not diminish his interest in art affairs. In August 1918, Robert Underwood Johnson asked him to write the chapter on art for a proposed book on German culture for the American Academy of Arts and Letters. The idea that a lack of personal liberty in Germany's society had always shaped its arts would be the unifying theme. The summer in Cornish had restored some of Cox's vitality and spirits. He had never cared for German art but knew its masters reasonably well, had seen many examples of their work in European and American collections, and knew the basic literature. He felt competent to do the essay. But American troops, including Leonard, were fighting hard on the western front, and although victory over Germany seemed sure, no one could say when it would come. And an intense, often virulent, anti-German feeling accompanied the nation's war effort and clouded the judgments of many people, especially intellectuals who were overwhelmingly in favor of the Allies. Cox hesitated. "I own I am afraid of mixing patriotism and criticism," he confessed candidly to Johnson. He was too hardminded to think that anyone could escape the climate of the times in writing what should be an honest analysis of German culture, however harsh. "Would it be possible for the members of the Academy to write impartially, at this time, about German art and letters, and would anyone believe them impartial if they could be so?" That said, he outlined his thoughts. "I have a poor opinion of modern German art, but I think the worst of it is marked by anarchism and extreme individualism," he wrote Johnson. "German classicism and academicism is pompous and empty, but Secessionism seems to me even more deadly—delighting in hideousness and filth." This last was an extreme form of the "excessive individualism" he saw in all modern art. "German art has never understood idealism and has never cared for beauty. It has only been good when frankly realist (Holbein) or unimaginatively grotesque (Dürer)." German art swung between lifeless formalism and "brutal ugliness and morbid sensationalism. It has always lacked both Latin sensuousness and Latin lucidity. The drill-master government of modern Germany *may* have intensified the empty formalism of official art and the savagery of the art of revolt; but the trouble with German art is, at bottom, that the

Germans are not, and never were, an artistic people." These opinions were not unusual in his generation, and probably represented the general critical view of an art that was not well studied or understood outside of Germany. He was willing to write all this and more in like vein, "but I would much rather say it, or have it said, at a time when it would not seem merely an attack on our enemies." He disliked German culture but wanted to be fair. "And again, would condemnation of German art on any ground, at this moment, seem anything but a war measure? I wonder!"

Despite these hesitations and his obvious bias, Cox wrote about ten pages on German art that winter, for an address to the Academy slated for March 20, 1919. He refined the ideas he suggested to Johnson, and rated Holbein and Dürer as great artists, but thought that Germany's art ranked well behind that of Italy, France or Spain. The Germans had not produced enough secondary and tertiary figures to establish a strong tradition. Their view of nature appeared morbid and efforts to treat idealism seemed artificial and pompous. This in turn helped explain their regular violent artistic revolts.[22]

Cox enjoyed working on the German art piece and wanted to do it well, but his strength ebbed rapidly with the new year of 1919. For awhile Louise thought he was improving. "Papa is getting better," she wrote Allyn, "with six meals a day he should." The improvement was deceptive, and on March 10, Louise wrote Johnson that Cox could not deliver the address as scheduled because of pneumonia and heart complications. He had passed through a severe crisis, and another loomed. She returned the manuscript of the speech "for use as you see best." She obviously could not admit that Kenyon was dying but telegraphed family members about every change in his condition. Dolson thought the messages were reassuring and was shocked to hear otherwise on March 12. He knew that Kenyon was frail, with few reserves to meet any illness. "And when I recall how short of breath he seemed on the slightest occasion, I wonder how he can possibly survive an attack of pneumonia." Kenyon was "a dear fellow, one of the very few men I have always loved." He could only hope for recovery, but it was not to be. Cox died at the apartment on Monday, March 17, 1919, with Louise, Caroline, and Allyn in attendance. The funeral service was at St. George's Chapel at Stuyvesant Square and Sixteenth Street the following Thursday, March 20. The body was cremated and the ashes stored until Louise's death. On March 20, as a final act of homage, Johnson read the essay on German art and Blashfield gave a brief eulogy to a large group at the Chemists' Club on East Forty-first Street.[23]

The obituaries testified to Cox's public stature. Both the *New York Times* and the *New York Tribune* ran lengthy pieces, praising him as a muralist and critic. Letters of condolences flooded in to Louise. Blashfield's was typical in using the military metaphors that dominated the debate over modernism. "As for your husband, he has been a brave soldier who never fell back one step in the presence of the enemy," he wrote Louise, "and he has unceasingly done much to hold other men up to their artistic duty. I never knew a man who saw more clearly or affirmed more lucidly." Frank Mather wrote the best eulogy that June in a substantial piece for *Scribner's Magazine,* for which Cox had written so often. "He was an embodied conservative conscience, a stalwart and dreaded champion of the great traditions of painting," he wrote, "a dangerous critic of successive new schools and fads, a formidable foe of every sort of sloppiness. The times were fairly sloppy, so he was not popular." But Mather also realized that much of Cox's prickliness was defensive and reflected his deep belief in a threatened classicism. Nor was Cox unemotional. "There never was a greater error than to dismiss him as a cold person; he loved and scorned tremendously. Rightmindedness was a passion with him."[24]

The responses of close friends and family members comforted Louise. "I felt that he understood my husband better than almost anyone," Augusta Saint Gaudens wrote, "and I am always grateful to you both." Lucia Fuller, a good friend from Cornish, was more personal. "Yours was one of the few real, beautiful marriages. You upheld him. You made his life full of happiness. His pride in you and his love showed on his face." She remembered a dinner party in Cornish, when "we were all confessing our first loves, and it came Kenyon's turn to tell. 'My history is very simple,' he said. 'I fell in love when I was thirty with a woman who afterwards became my wife.'" Kenyon's death provoked a stream of memories from Dolson, who once again marvelled at his brother's long effort to support his family in an uncertain occupation. "I should have gone crazy," he wrote in admiration. "Surely this constant state of anxiety must have—whether he saw it or not—undermined his strength." But he had fond recollections and saw Kenyon as "a self-made and a self-educated man from his boyhood to his grave" who had triumphed against the odds.[25]

Louise carried on as best she could. Money was her first concern. Kenyon left no income due except royalties from his last book, *Concerning Painting,* which did not recover its modest advance. Once again Dolson came to the rescue, guaranteeing her the full income from the trust and the rent-free apartment. The sums involved were not great but kept her from penury in the years ahead.[26]

The children were adults, ready to follow their own lives. Leonard returned from France later in 1919 and became an architectural draftsman and editor, though he was only modestly successful. His apparent lack of discipline did not keep him from being a good soldier. When World War II came, he enlisted in the army and served as a colonel in the South Pacific.

Allyn returned from Italy in 1920 to find a changed world. His father was dead, and his mother seemed somewhat adrift. The home in Cornish was up for sale, and "earning a living [was] urgent." Allyn was a more stable and orderly personality than Leonard, and though reserved, became an astute observer of people and the world. He later recalled vowing to accommodate more to changes in art and in the world than his parents had done. He admired their lives as artists, and knew that both, especially his father, had faced large odds in adapting personal visions to worldly realities. He realized that his father's rigorous training had matched his emotional needs and ideals, but it had ill-equipped him for changing in life and art. Allyn went on to make a steady if often precarious living from decorating the homes of wealthy clients. He also decorated numerous public buildings in both allegorical and historical styles. He spent his last years working on murals in the U.S. Capitol in Washington. "When I was young and saw both our parents not doing work that was up to standard after the age of fifty, I swore I would stop at that age," he wrote Caroline in 1966. "Now I am pushing my seventy year old legs up the ladder, day after day, and I really think the quality of what I am doing is all right. At least there is a lively demand for it."[27]

Caroline worked hard to help her parents during the hectic war years. She had a brief bout with tuberculosis, apparently contracted from her father, then married the noted archeologist Ambrose Lansing in 1923. She had a recurrence of the tuberculosis, which also affected her son Cornelius. Dolson's son Jacob continued his father's support, paid her medical bills, and provided for basic needs. When she later suggested paying him back, he replied: "No, pay *ahead,* as you find young people in the same sort of difficulties."[28] She did so, to her great satisfaction. She also continued to paint.

Louise retained her modest reputation as a painter of children and women, had some commissions, and continued to exhibit at the National Academy. Her nervousness now found its outlet in travel. In the early 1920s she gave up the New York City apartment and moved to Italy. She apparently purchased and decorated two houses near Florence, which she sold at a profit to finance further travels. About 1929 she moved to Hawaii, built a house, and sold it for a profit in 1934. Though she displayed a somewhat surprising independence in traveling alone so much, her wanderlust naturally alarmed the children. "She was always settling down for her old age," Caroline recalled. And Louise once told her: "This is the nicest old age I ever settled down to." Allyn thought that she never overcame the marks of early poverty and the emotional strains in the family that shaped her. Louise did not complain or confide much, but he concluded, rightly or wrongly, that she was lonely and dissatisfied. "And so she was never happy, all those years from 53 to 80," he later wrote Caroline. Returning from Hawaii, she built a small home in Mount Kisco, near Caroline, who was in Chappaqua. Her health inevitably declined, but she loved the house and area and managed to travel short distances. Her heart began to fail, and she moved to a small nursing home in Windham, Connecticut, where she died on December 11, 1945. Her body was cremated, the ashes mixed with Kenyon's and scattered in

FIG. 42. Kenyon Cox, *Hope and Memory* (1900). Oil on canvas, 42 × 26¼ ins.
The Dixon Gallery and Gardens, Memphis, Tennessee, gift from Mrs. Lyle Bentzen.

Cornish.[29] The family story continued through the children's lives. Leonard died in 1963, after a stint as a city planner in Puerto Rico. Allyn worked on the Capitol decorations almost until his death in 1982. Caroline lived in Arizona until her death in 1986.

Kenyon Cox led an unusual and varied life in the art world. As a painter, he best expressed his idealistic vision in a long series of impressive classical murals. As a thinker, he spoke for classical order and civic harmony and found considerable response, even in a chaotic modern society. As a person, he had a successful family life that both love and shared ideals sustained. He probably thought that the murals as a whole were his best legacy, but he had favorite works at different stages of life. As a youth, he hoped to combine a fashionable realism with symbolic ideals. In middle age he painted complex allegorical canvases that radiated his ideal of life and a world infused with controlled beauty and imagination. Late in life he probably considered *Tradition* (1916) the best statement of his ideas. But in many ways, an earlier painting, *Hope and Memory* (1900), best summarized his persona (fig. 42). In it two idealized women stride toward the viewer. On the left, clad in rich red, Memory looks back over her shoulder to a rather somber but elegant landscape. She holds the hand of Hope, clad in the optimism of green, who looks ahead with expectation. Perhaps these were his two sides, reverence for traditions and the cautions of memory, and belief in the future.

NOTES

I. AN UNUSUAL YOUNG MAN

1. An older work, Alfred Matthews, *Ohio and Her Western Reserve* (New York: D. Appleton, 1902), still gives a good sense of the mood behind settling the Reserve. The same

is true of a later book, Harlan Hatcher, *The Western Reserve* (1949; reprint, Kent, Ohio: Kent State University Press, 1991).

2. See Robert S. Fletcher, *A History of Oberlin College,* 2 vols. (Oberlin, Ohio: Oberlin College, 1943).

3. The best biography is Keith J. Hardman, *Charles Grandison Finney, 1792–1875: Revivalist and Reformer* (Syracuse: Syracuse University Press, 1987).

4. JDC's family background is in "Cochran-Allen Family Record," William Cochran Papers, OCA. The basic family history is Eugene David Schmiel, "The Career of Jacob Dolson Cox, 1828–1900, Soldier, Scholar, Statesman" (Ph.D. diss., Ohio State University, 1969); on religion, see 19–21, 221–22. HFC's religion is discussed in Hardman, *Charles Grandison Finney,* 167–68, 397. KC recorded no church affiliation in a questionnaire he filled out for Oberlin College in 1915 (alumni file, OCA).

5. The first quotation is from Caroline Cox Lansing to the author, 8 October 1983. The epitaph comment is from KC to LEO, 9 August 1900, KC Papers, AAFAL.

6. HFC to KC, 24 October 1909, KC Papers, AAFAL.

7. "Cochran-Allen Family Record," 3–4, Cochran Papers, OCA.

8. Hatcher, *Western Reserve,* 120, 154–55, 191–93, 289–90; Matthews, *Ohio and Her Western Reserve,* 152, 190–211.

9. See Schmiel, "The Career of Jacob Dolson Cox," 23–34; and Harriett Taylor Upton, *A Twentieth Century History of Trumbull County, Ohio,* 2 vols. (Chicago: Lewis Pub., 1909), 1:293.

10. Trumbull County does not have birth certificates for that period and contemporary newspapers did not seem to record births. The place of residence for the year 1856 is mentioned in a work by KC's brother, Jacob Dolson Cox, *Building an American Industry: The Story of the Cleveland Twist Drill Co., and Its Founder: An Autobiography* (Cleveland: The Company, 1951), 12–47.

11. Upton, *Trumbull County,* 1:291–95; and the manuscript memoir by Will Cochran, AC Papers, AAA.

12. See William Cochran, "Political Experiences of Major General Jacob Dolson Cox," 1940, typescript, 2 vols., 2:1156, Western Reserve Historical Society, Cleveland.

13. Will Cochran memoir, AC Papers, AAA has the quotation; and Mary Rudd Cochran to author, 2 July 1971. Ms. Cochran was Will Cochran's daughter.

14. See the article by KC's good friend William A. Coffin, "Kenyon Cox," *Century Magazine* 41 (January 1891): 333–37 for relevant information, most of which he got from KC; and Cox, *Building an American Industry,* 43–44. The quotation is from DC to LKC, 17 March 1919, KC Papers, AAFAL.

15. The date is from Cox, *Building an American Industry,* 43–44. The quotation is from JDC to Charles Cox, 3 March 1869, JDC Papers, OCA. Whether the operation took place at home or in a hospital is not noted.

16. HFC to Will Cochran, 8 March 1869, and JDC to James Monroe, 17 May 1869, both in JDC Papers, OCA. See also Will Cochran memoir, AC Papers, AAA.

17. KC to DC, 26 September 1869, KC Papers, AAFAL; and Cox, *Building an American Industry,* 52–53.

18. JDC to Rutherford B. Hayes, 16 September 1869, Hayes Papers, Hayes Presidential Center, Fremont, Ohio.

19. KC to DC, 26 September 1869, KC Papers, AAFAL.

20. Ibid.

21. Mary Rudd Cochran interview with W. E. Bigglestone, 10 October 1975, OCA mentions the family views. The inscribed book was in the possession of Mrs. Katharine Smith, Wooster, Ohio, KC's grandniece.

22. JDC to James Monroe, 31 December 1870, JDC Papers, OCA notes the crisis of 1870. The aftereffects of the operation are discussed in AC to Henry Hope Reed, 10 January 1979, AC Papers, AAA; in an interview of the author with AC, 8 March 1982, Washington, D.C.; and in Caroline Cox Lansing to the author, 12 March 1984.

23. KC to LEO, 9 September and 29 October 1870, both in KC Papers, AAFAL.

24. The first quotation is from an undated fragment, the second from one dated July 1863, in KC Papers, AAFAL.

25. The recollection is from KC to Mrs. Lew F. Porter, 22 March 1914, typescript copy, Jersey City Museum. Mrs. Porter was the wife of the superintendent of the state capitol building in Madison, Wisconsin, where KC did major decorations, and he wrote this in response to her query about his career. A similar story is in Coffin, "Kenyon Cox," 334, which KC surely told Coffin. KC also approved his entry in *The National Cyclopedia of American Biography* (New York: James T. White, 1907), 5:321, which says: "The son at an early age announced his intention to become a painter." The quotation from Dolson is in Cox, *Building an American Industry*, 25. There is some information on Crawford in Upton, *Trumbull County*, 1:387.

26. JDC to James Monroe, 24 March 1872, enclosed some of KC's silhouettes; and JDC to T. H. Robinson, 11 June 1872, has the quotation; both in JDC Papers, OCA. After KC's death, DC recalled that "he took up his work and carried it on against the advice and without the approval of his father, just as I did, and I think this has been a tie between us. He lived to see his father proud of him as an artist and an author, and I know he thoroughly enjoyed it." DC to LKC, 17 March 1919, KC Papers, AAFAL.

27. There is an early sketchbook in the AC Papers, AAA, film roll 3976; and other sketches from the early 1870s in Box 1197, Folder 1, "Figures," KC collection, CHM.

28. KC mentions his health in his diary, 12, 23, 24, 31 January 1876 and many other times. The quotation about eating is from KC to JDC, 20 February 1876, KC Papers, AAFAL. He mentioned musical events often in his diary, and in KC to the Family, [18 December 1875?], ibid. KC recalled some reading matter in a letter to LEO, 28 June 1884, ibid. The U.C.D. is outlined in Mrs. William B. Davis, *A Historical Sketch of the U.C.D.* (Cincinnati: U.C.D., 1886).

29. The McMicken School's history is summarized in Robert C. Vitz, *The Queen and the Arts: Cultural Life in Nineteenth Century Cincinnati* (Kent, Ohio: Kent State University Press, 1989), 183–90. The quotation is from Cox's entry in the *National Cyclopedia of American Biography*, 5:321.

30. See *A Retrospective Exhibition. Robert F. Blum. 1857–1903* (Cincinnati: Cincinnati Art Museum, 1966); Bruce Weber, "Robert Frederic Blum (1857–1903) and His Milieu" (Ph.D. diss., City University of New York, 1985); and Charles A. Elliott, "Revolt in Old Art School Led By Famous Painters," *Cincinnati Commercial Tribune*, 21 March 1915, p. 8.

31. Bruce Weber, "Frank Duveneck and the Art Life of Cincinnati," in *The Golden Age: Cincinnati Painters of the Nineteenth Century* . . . (Cincinnati: Cincinnati Art Museum, 1979), 23–33; Vitz, *The Queen and the Arts*, 160–68; Michael Quick, *An American Painter Abroad: Frank Duveneck's European Years* (Cincinnati: Cincinnati Art Museum, 1987), 31; Josephine W. Duveneck, *Frank Duveneck, Painter-Teacher* (San Francisco: John Howell, 1970), 57.

32. Weber, "Robert Frederic Blum," 17–18; Elliott, "Revolt in Old Art School"; Will C. Cochran memoir, AC Papers, AAA.

33. Elliott, "Revolt in Old Art School"; and KC Diary, 26, 28 January 1876.

34. Elliott, "Revolt in Old Art School"; and KC Diary, 6 January 1876.

35. KC Diary, 8,9 January 1876; and KC to JDC, 18 January 1876, KC Papers, AAFAL. Many years later KC congratulated the Metropolitan Museum for acquiring this work. "I count on going to see it the very first thing on my return to town." KC to Edward Robinson, 17 September 1916, KC file, MMA. The engraving of *Salome* is in Paul Mantz, "Henri Regnault," *Gazette des Beaux-Arts*, ser. 2, vol. 5 (January 1872): opposite p. 78.

36. Despite his enormous vogue and influence, there is no biography of Fortuny. There is interesting information on him and a sense of his impact in Walther Fol, "Fortuny," *Gazette des Beaux-Arts*, ser. 2, vol. 11 (March 1875): 267–81, and ibid. (April 1875): 351–66. See also Baron Jean Charles Davillier, *Fortuny: sa vie, son oeuvre, sa correspondance* (Paris: Chez Auguste Aubry, 1875); *Mariano Fortuny et ses amis* (Castres, France: Castres Musée Goya, 1974); and Guillermo de Osma, *Mariano Fortuny* (New York: Rizzoli, 1980), which is a biography of Fortuny's son of the same name, but which has information on the family, esp. 14–29.

37. He noted the photograph in KC Diary, 8 January 1876. The quotation about the *Arquebusier* is in ibid., 29 January 1876. The letter to his father is dated 18 January 1876,

KC Papers, AAFAL. James Henry Moser to KC, 27 March [sent 2 April] 1911, James Henry Moser Papers, AAA, recalls youthful discussions of Fortuny. Weber, "Robert Frederic Blum," 22–27, 48 has the other information on Fortuny, including the stolen painting.

38. KC Diary, 2 January 1876.

39. The first remark on Corot is from ibid., 5 January 1876, the second from ibid., 12 February 1876. The comments of his development as an artist are from ibid., 16 March 1876.

40. Many such sketches are in sketchbooks number 1984-86-3, 1984-86-4, and 1985-86-7, and in Box 1197, Folder 2, "Figures, Nude Studies," KC collection, CHM. *The Whistler* (1875), oil on canvas, 14″ × 12″, was in the possession of Mrs. Katharine Smith, Wooster, Ohio. KC later disparaged the work. "It was not bad for me then but I expect to be rather horrified at beholding all my crude old efforts in places of honor when I get back." KC to JDC, 10 January 1880, in H. Wayne Morgan, ed., *An American Artist in Paris: The Letters of Kenyon Cox, 1877–1882* (Kent, Ohio: Kent State University Press, 1986), 188 (hereafter cited as KC, *Letters*).

41. The first quotation is from KC Diary, 6 February 1876; the second is from KC to JDC, 28 March 1876, KC Papers, AAFAL. The father used a variant with his son Dolson, trying to start a business: "Go slow and learn to paddle." See Cox, *Building an American Industry*, 96–97.

42. KC Diary, 10 February 1876.

43. KC to JDC, 20 February 1876, KC Papers, AAFAL, and KC Diary, 20 February 1876.

44. KC Diary, 29 April 1876.

45. KC to [Robert Blum?], 26 August 1876, KC Papers, AAA. This letter has no recipient but is logically to Blum.

46. KC to HFC, 18 October and 1 November 1876, KC Papers, AAFAL describe their routine. KC to U.C.D., undated but early 1877, KC file, OCA has the quotation and recounts their life for the friends who would read this long letter. KC to Will Cochran, 13 March 1877, KC Papers, AAFAL suggests that the family and friends wanted to hear striking reports of artist life. See also Weber, "Robert Frederic Blum," 45–46.

47. HFC to Will Cochran, 20 October [1876], JDC Papers, OCA.

48. Alfred Brennan to HFC, 26 January 1885, KC Papers, AAFAL. Brennan included here a small drawing of the young KC at Elbow Lane in the act of writing to his mother.

49. See David Sellin, *The First Pose, 1876. Turning Point in American Art. Howard Roberts, Thomas Eakins and a Century of Philadelphia Nudes* (New York: Norton, 1976). KC's desultory student habits are noted in a letter from Mary E. Mullen of the PAFA, 4 October 1984, to the author. The quotation is from KC to HFC, 18 October 1876, KC Papers, AAFAL. KC later admired Eakins's indifference to fashion but never cared much for his realism. See KC, "America's First Old Masters Exhibition," *Nation* 105 (29 November 1917): 614–15.

50. See Box 1197, Folder 1, "Figures," and Folder 2, "Nude Studies," KC collection, CHM. In the light of his later reputation as a superior figure painter, it is worth noting that he earlier wrote to JDC, 20 February 1876, KC Papers, AAFAL: "Here in Cincinnati one can at best see some Dutchman's head, never even a good nude figure, and how much of the world of beauty is in the figure?"

51. KC to HFC, 18 October 1876, KC Papers, AAFAL discusses his interest in Japanese art and describes the oil painting of the woman and cranes, which was in the possession of Katharine Smith, Wooster, Ohio. KC to HFC, 1 November 1876, ibid. has a drawing of another proposed oil, this time of a Japanese woman in a crimson gown, dancing amid swirling leaves. Drawing 1960-83-117, Box 38, KC collection, CHM is a good Japanese subject. His poem about a Japanese women is in several drafts in notebooks in KC Papers, AAFAL and is reprinted in KC to HFC, 11 August 1878, KC, *Letters*, 108. The Peruvian oil is noted in KC to HFC, 5 March 1877, KC Papers, AAFAL.

52. KC to James L. Claghorn, 8 December 1876, KC file, PAFA.

53. KC to JDC, 17 May 1877, KC Papers, AAFAL.

54. KC diary, 12 March 1876.

55. Ibid., 5–7 March 1876. Will Hicock Low, who later became a good friend, recalled that he went to Paris in 1871 with a cheap steamer ticket and five hundred dollars, which was almost the least of anyone he had heard about. See Low, "The Primrose Way," 15, typescript, Low Papers, AIAH.

56. KC to HFC, 7 February 1877, with the quotation; and KC to HFC, 5 March 1877, both in KC Papers, AAFAL.

57. KC to JDC, 10 March 1876 [1877], ibid.

58. KC to HFC, 13 March 1877, ibid.

59. KC to HFC, 17 March 1877, ibid.

60. KC to HFC, 24 March 1877, ibid.

61. KC to LEO, 17 July 1877, ibid.

62. KC mentioned the inheritance in a letter to HFC, 23 July 1878, in KC, *Letters,* 105. In a letter to JDC, 21 March 1886, KC Papers, AAFAL, he thanked his father for canceling debts due him and for the money spent on his Parisian education, and noted his mother's contribution to the expense. In a handwritten dedication of a copy of his book *Old Masters and New* (1905), he wrote: "This book owes everything to you, not only as I owe you everything, but especially as I owe you the artistic education which made it possible." The book was in the possession of Katharine Smith, Wooster, Ohio. KC did not, of course, go to college, and at this time betrayed considerable interest in that experience, which was then confined generally to sons of the well-to-do. His friend LEO was at Harvard, and on 17 July 1877, KC wrote: "I am going to try once more to get you to write to me. For I should enjoy hearing of college life much, I never having had such advantage." KC Papers, AAFAL.

63. KC to LEO, 17 September 1877, KC Papers, AAFAL; Will Cochran memoir, AC Papers, AAA.

II. PARIS

1. The basic story of KC's years in Paris is told in KC, *Letters.* The franc at this time was five to the dollar.

2. KC to HFC, 26 October 1877, KC, *Letters,* 38. Years later, KC wrote his son Allyn, who was studying in Rome and visiting southern France: "The south of France is perfectly unknown to all of us so that your material is all new. What a bully time you must have had seeing it all. It must have been even more exciting than I found Rouen when I stopped there first on my way to Paris in 1877." KC to AC, 5 November 1916, KC Papers, AAFAL.

3. See KC to HFC, 28 October, 4 November, and 26 December 1877, which has the quotation, and KC to parents, 11 November 1877, in KC, *Letters,* 38–42, 50–51.

4. Dorothy Weir Young, ed., *The Life and Letters of J. Alden Weir* (New Haven: Yale University Press), 86–88.

5. Richard Whiteing, "Henry Bacon," *Art Amateur* 7 (November 1882): 115; and Phebe D. Natt, "Paris Art-Schools," *Lippincott's Magazine* 27 (March 1881): 269.

6. KC to HFC, 4 November 1877, KC, *Letters,* 39–40. KC later wrote home critically of Healy: "I find him very polite, but it seems to me exaggeratedly and rather hollowly so. I never feel that he is quite frank in anything. His painting I do not like at all, neither do I think father would. Of course I try to be always respectfully and deferentially polite with him."; KC to HFC, 22 July 1878, ibid., 104. See also KC's critical view of Healy in reviewing the painter's memoirs, "Memoirs of Three Painters," *Nation* 59 (29 November 1894): 411.

7. KC to parents, 11 November 1877, KC, *Letters,* 41–42.

8. KC to HFC, 4 November 1877, ibid., 39–40.

9. The KC quotation is from KC to HFC, 18 December 1877, ibid., 49–50. The story from Low is in his "The Primrose Way," 59–60, typescript, Low Papers, AIHA; see also Low's *A Chronicle of Friendships* (New York: Scribner's, 1908), 16–18. There is no biography of Carolus-Duran, but there is some valuable information in an essay by a former student, J. Carroll Beckwith, "Carolus Duran," in *Modern French Masters,* ed. John C. Van Dyke (New York: Century, 1896), 73–82. There is a good deal of contemporary comment in Marie

Bashkirtseff, *The Journal of a Young Artist* (New York: E. P. Dutton, 1919), esp. 320–21, entry for 25 May 1882. For the studio and home, see Evan Charteris, *John Sargent* (New York: Scribner's, 1927), 25–26; Charles Merrill Mount, *John Singer Sargent* (New York: Norton, 1955), 26–47; Stanley Olson, *John Singer Sargent, His Portrait* (New York: St. Martin's, 1986), 33–42; and John Milner, *The Studios of Paris* (New Haven: Yale University Press, 1988), 45–46.

10. The Bouguereau question is in Low, *A Chronicle of Friendships*, 15, and the answer in Low, "The Primrose Way," 55. The quotations from Carolus-Duran, and other information like them, are in Carolus-Duran, "A French Painter and His Pupils," *Century Magazine* 31 (January 1886): 373–76. Albert Wolff, *La capitale de l'art* (Paris: Victor-Havard, 1886), 285–96 has some shrewd observations on the changes in style and the marketplace that Carolus-Duran represented. C. H. Stranahan, *A History of French Painting from Its Earliest to Its Latest Practice* (New York: Scribner's, 1907), 354–57 has some information. Philip G. Hamerton, "The Poet with the Mandolin," *Scribner's Magazine* 16 (August 1894): 134, 232–35 notes that Carolus-Duran worked outdoors in landscape without figures and was not exclusively a studio painter.

11. Bashkirtseff, *Journal* (9 February 1881): 255; Eliot Gregory, *The Ways of Men* (New York: Scribner's, 1900), 108.

12. KC to HFC, 26 November and 18 December 1877, KC, *Letters*, 43, 49–50.

13. KC to HFC, 13 January 1878, ibid., 55–56.

14. KC to HFC, 27 January 1878, ibid., 60–61. Gregory, *The Ways of Men*, 110–11, recounts works on the ceiling, which is now in the Louvre. Other pupils who worked on it and were later KC's friends included J. Carroll Beckwith and John S. Sargent. The work is illustrated in Carter Ratcliff, *John Singer Sargent* (New York: Abbeville, 1982), 40.

15. KC to JDC, 20 February 1878, KC, *Letters*, 64–65.

16. KC to HFC, 20 May 1878, ibid., 80. For KC's later comments on Carolus-Duran, see his books: *The Classic Point of View* (New York: Scribner's, 1911), 198–99; *Artist and Public* (New York: Scribner's, 1914), 153; and *Concerning Painting* (New York: Scribner's, 1917), 188–89.

17. For the Ecole in general, see: S. G. W. Benjamin, "Practice and Patronage of French Art," *Atlantic Monthly* 36 (September 1875): 259–60; Will H. Low, *A Painter's Progress* (New York: Scribner's, 1910), 167–68; Young, *Life and Letters of J. Alden Weir*, 70–71; Natt, "Paris Art Schools," 269–76; Richard Whiteing, "The American Student at the Beaux-Arts," *Century Magazine* 23 (December 1881): 259–72; and Henry O. Avery, "The Paris School of Fine Arts," *Scribner's Magazine* 2 (October 1887): 387–403. For scholarly analyses, see especially, H. Barbara Weinberg, "Nineteenth Century American Painters at the Ecole des Beaux-Arts," *American Art Journal* 14 (Autumn 1981): 66–84; and her "The Lure of Paris: Late Nineteenth-Century American Painters and Their French Training," in *A New World: Masterpieces of American Painting, 1760–1919*, ed. Theodore E. Stebbins (Boston: Museum of Fine Arts, 1983), 16–32; and her *The Lure of Paris: Nineteenth-Century American Painters and their French Teachers* (New York: Abbeville, 1991); and Albert Boime, *The Academy and French Painting in the Nineteenth Century* (New York: Phaidon, 1971).

18. KC to JDC, 24 March 1878, KC, *Letters*, 69–70.

19. KC to HFC, 8 April 1878, ibid., 72–73; and Richard Murray, "Kenyon Cox and the Art of Drawing," *Drawing* 3 (May–June 1981): 1–6.

20. The first quotation is from Whiteing, "The American Student at the Beaux-Arts," 263; the second is from KC to HFC, 3 June 1879, KC, *Letters*, 161. There is no biography of Cabanel, but see: Georges Lafenestre, "Alexandre Cabanel," *Gazette des Beaux-Arts*, ser. 3, vol. 1 (April 1889): 265–80; C. Stuart Johnson, "Famous Artists and Their Work. III. Alexandre Cabanel," *Munsey's Magazine* 6 (March 1892): 635–41; and Stranahan, *A History of French Painting*, 398–401.

21. KC to HFC, 14 April [1878], KC, *Letters*, 74 mentions the two drawings. The first of these works was a first-century B.C. Greek statue attributed to Apollonius; the second was a torso fragment from the Parthenon. KC to HFC, 20 May 1878, ibid., 80, has the quotation on training. KC to HFC, 16, 21 June 1878, ibid., 88–90, deal with going upstairs.

22. KC to JDC, 31 May 1878, KC, *Letters*, 83–84.

23. The journal of this trip is in ibid., 90–103. The quotation on churches in Rouen is from 91; that on St. Eloi is on 92; the description of his painting is on 94–95. KC marked the painting "From Grosse Horloge, Rouen, 30 June 1878," which should read "Gros-Horloge."

24. KC first mentioned the trip in a letter to HFC, 22 April 1878, KC, Letters, 78. The quotation is from KC to HFC, 20 May 1878, ibid., 80–81. He mentioned the trip in KC to JDC, 8 June 1878, ibid., 85. He reported the concours results in KC to HFC, 13 August and 24 September 1878, ibid., 109, 119. He noted giving up Switzerland in KC to Will C. Cochran, 30 July 1878, AC Papers, AAA.

25. KC to HFC, 1, 2 September 1878, KC, Letters, 113.

26. KC to HFC, 4 September 1878, ibid., 114.

27. KC to HFC, 8 September 1878, ibid., 114–15.

28. KC to HFC, 21 September and 13 October 1878, ibid., 118, 124.

29. Box 1197, Folder 1, "Figures," KC collection, CHM contains sketches from this Italian trip. The quotation is from Theodore Robinson to KC, 1 August 1880, KC Papers, AAFAL.

30. KC to JDC, 11 September 1878, KC, Letters, 116–17.

31. KC to HFC, 13, 15 October 1878, ibid., 124–25.

32. KC to HFC, 23 October 1878, ibid., 130–31. KC devoted a good deal of attention to Michelangelo in his mature years, when he had become a classicist. Perhaps recollecting this visit, he wrote in 1905: "No person, at all impressionable by art, who has ever stood in that chapel is likely to forget his emotion. Nothing in the whole range of art is so overwhelming, so 'intolerable.' Its enormous melancholy catches one by the throat and chokes one with the poignancy of sensation. One gazes with a hushed intensity, one cannot tear oneself away, and yet one breathes a long sigh of relief when one gets out at last into the sunlit air of Florence." See KC, "Michelangelo," International Quarterly 11 (April 1905): 66.

33. KC to HFC, [?] April 1879, KC, Letters, 155.

34. KC to HFC, 31 October 1878, ibid., 133–34.

35. KC to HFC, 28 December 1878, ibid., 145–46.

36. KC to HFC, 9, 19 November 1878, ibid., 134–36, describes these events.

37. For contemporary comment and recollections of Julian's, see: Whiteing, "The American Student at the Beaux-Arts," 266; Alice Fessenden Peterson, "The American Art Student in Paris," New England Magazine 2 (August 1890): 669–70; Corwin K. Linson, "With the Paris Art-Student," Frank Leslie's Popular Monthly 34 (September 1892): 289–302; J. Sutherland, "An Art Student's Year in Paris," Art Amateur 32 (January 1905): 52; Edward Simmons, From Seven to Seventy: Memoirs of an Artist and Yankee (New York: Harper, 1922), 118–20. See also Catherine Fehrer, "New Light on the Académie Julian and Its Founder (Rodolphe Julian)," Gazette des Beaux-Arts, ser. 6, vol. 103 (May–June 1984): 208–16; The Julian Academy (New York: Shepherd Art Gallery, 1989); and Milner, Studios of Paris, 11–12; Montreal Museum of Fine Arts, William Bouguereau 1825–1905 (Montreal: The Museum, 1984), 55–58.

38. KC to HFC, 9, 19 November [3], 15 December 1878, KC, Letters, 135–41.

39. KC to HFC, [?] April 1879, ibid., 154–55; Murray, "Kenyon Cox and the Art of Drawing," 3; and Whiteing, "The American Student at the Beaux-Arts," 262, which mentions Cabanel's growing reputation for slackness in instruction.

40. KC to HFC, 12 October 1877, 13 January 1878, KC, Letters, 31, 55.

41. For contemporary comment see, Eugene Benson, "Jean-Léon Gérôme," Galaxy 1 (August 1866): 582; "Jean-Léon Gérôme," Appleton's Journal 1 (20 November 1869): 438–40; Lucy H. Hooper, "Léon Gérôme," Appleton's Art Journal 3 (1877): 26–28; "Gérôme," ibid. 4 (September 1878): 279–82; Stranahan, A History of French Painting, 308–20; Fanny Field Hering, Gérôme, The Life and Works of Jean-Léon Gérôme (New York: Cassell, 1892); Will H. Low, "Jean-Léon Gérôme," in John C. Van Dyke, ed., Modern French Masters, 31–46. For recent studies, see Gerald M. Ackerman, Jean-Léon Gérôme (1824–1904), exh. cat (Dayton: Dayton Art Institute, 1972); Gerald M. Ackerman and Gilles Cugnier, Gérôme (Vesoul, France: Musée de Vesoul, 1981); H. Barbara Weinberg, The American Pupils of Jean-Léon

Gérôme (Fort Worth: Amon Carter Museum, 1985); and Gerald M. Ackerman, *The Life and Work of Jean-Léon Gérôme* (New York: Sotheby Publishers, 1986).

42. "Open Letters," *Century Magazine* 37 (February 1889): 635. This is a selection of letters about Gérôme from his former students, such as Brush and Cox.

43. Earl Shinn, "Frederic Bridgman," *Harper's Weekly* 63 (October 1881): 198–99; and Low, *A Painter's Progress*, 165–66; and KC's own letter on Gérôme in "Open Letters," 635.

44. The quotation is from Stephen Wilson Van Schaick in "Open Letters," 636. KC's friend J. Alden Weir commented many times on Gérôme's methods and demands; see Weir to John F. Weir, 11 January 1874 in Doreen Bolger Burke, *J. Alden Weir* (Newark: University of Delaware Press, 1983), 53, and Weir to John F. Weir, [May 1874], in Young, *Life and Letters of J. Alden Weir*, 37. Gérôme's atelier is described in Low, *A Painter's Progress*, 164–65; John Shirley-Fox, *An Art Student's Reminiscences of Paris in the Eighties* (London: Mills and Boon, 1909), 73–75, 88–100; and Ackerman, *The Life and Work of Jean-Léon Gérôme*, 168–77. Gérôme's studio is described in Whiteing, "The American Student at the Beaux-Arts," 261–62; William C. Morrow, *Bohemian Paris of Today* (Philadelphia: Lippincott, 1900), 38–41; "The Home of Gérôme," *Art Amateur* 13 (August 1885): 47–49; and Milner, *The Studios of Paris*, 140–41.

45. KC to HFC, 2, [?] April 1879, and KC to JDC, 14 May 1879, KC, *Letters*, 152, 155, 158.

46. KC to HFC, 3 June 1879, ibid., 161.

47. KC to HFC, 7 May 1879, ibid., 157.

48. KC to HFC, 28 May 1878, ibid., 83. See also S. G. W. Benjamin, *Contemporary Art in Europe* (New York: Harper's, 1877), 96–98.

49. KC, "The Paris Salon," *Cincinnati Daily Gazette*, 5 July 1879, p. 4, from the second of three reports on the Salon of 1879 that KC did for his hometown paper; and KC to JDC, 30 September 1879, on Bouguereau, in KC, *Letters*, 176–77. KC retained his dislike of Bouguereau, referring in 1911 to "the sweet insipidity of Bouguereau. The drawing of Bouguereau, with its superficial correctness and its entire lack of functional expression; with its hands which never grasp anything and its feet which never support any weight; with its apparent idealization which amounts to no more than prettifying studio models—this is the drawing most trying to the soul of anyone capable of understanding what real draughtmanship is." KC, *The Classic Point of View*, 146.

50. KC to JDC, 16 January, 31 May 1878, KC, *Letters*, 58, 84.

51. KC to HFC, 2 April 1879, ibid., 152–53; KC to Blum, 3 September 1879, cited in Weber, "Robert Frederic Blum," 78–79; KC to JDC, 30 September and to HFC, 23 December 1879, KC, *Letters*, 177–78, 185. KC did later call on Madame Fortuny to see some of her husband's sketches; see KC to HFC, 29 January 1880, ibid., 190. See also KC's much later remarks on Fortuny and Boldini in his "Naturalism in the Nineteenth Century," *Art World* 1 (February 1917): 318.

52. Good contemporary reactions to this realism when KC was in Paris include Benjamin, *Contemporary Art in Europe*, 76–78; Natt, "Paris Art Schools"; and a three-part series, "Glimpses of Parisian Art," *Scribner's Monthly* 21 (December 1880): 169–81, (January 1881): 423–31, and (March 1881): 734–43. For recent studies see Gabriel P. Weisberg, *The Realist Tradition: French Painting and Drawing, 1830–1900* (Bloomington: Indiana University Press, 1980); William S. Feldman, "The Life and Work of Jules Bastien-Lepage (1848–1884)" (Ph.D. diss., New York University, 1973). See also Lois Marie Fink, "The Role of France in American Art, 1850–1870" (Ph.D. diss., University of Chicago, 1970), and her "American Artists in France, 1850–1897," *American Art Journal* 5 (November 1973): 32–49. Current studies emphasize Courbet as the greatest realist, but the contemporary comment on the Bastien-Lepage school was enormous.

53. Albert Wolff, *La Capitale de l'art*, 253–67, gives a good sense of Bastien-Lepage's appeals. See also David Sellin, *Americans in Brittany and Normandy, 1860–1910*, exh. cat. (Phoenix: Phoenix Art Museum, 1982), 45–46.

54. KC to JDC, 10 June 1878, KC, *Letters*, 87–88.

55. KC, "The Paris Salon," *Cincinnati Daily Gazette*, 11 June 1879, p. 4. KC began to doubt Bastien-Lepage in KC to JDC, [?] July 1879, KC, *Letters*, 167–68. In a letter to HFC,

29 January 1880, ibid., 189–90, he reported visiting Bastien-Lepage's studio with friends to see the just completed *Joan of Arc,* which was to be the sensation of the Salon of 1880. It was a realistic scene of a bewildered but entranced Joan in peasant garb listening to the voices of floating allegorical beings clad in armor, an effort to combine traditionalism and modernism. KC thought it an astounding piece of verisimilitude and praised it again in a report to the *Cincinnati Daily Gazette,* 12 March 1881. He changed his mind and wrote a perceptive piece on the limitations of this realism and of Bastien-Lepage later in "Bastien-Lepage," *Nation* 54 (May 5, 1892): 343–44. See also KC, *The Classic Point of View,* 15.

56. KC to JDC, 5 September 1879, KC, *Letters,* 172.

57. KC, "The Paris Salon," *Cincinnati Daily Gazette,* 9 July 1879, p. 4. Gérôme became a deadly enemy of impressionism, seeing it as a passing fad; see Kirk Varnedoe, *Northern Light: Nordic Art at the Turn of the Century* (New Haven: Yale University Press, 1988), 59–60. He counseled Dennis Miller Bunker, a student just a little later than KC, to avoid harsh sunlight: "Jamais de la violence." See Bunker to Anne Page, 1 September 1886, cited in Sellin, *Americans,* 133; and R. H. Ives Gammell, *Dennis Miller Bunker* (New York: Coward, McCann, 1953), 70–73. Gérôme was referring to the manner of execution, not necessarily to subject matter.

58. KC to JDC, 16 January 1878, KC, *Letters,* 57–58.

59. KC to HFC, [8 April] 1878, ibid., 74 deals with the pen drawing; KC mentioned showing the painting from Venice at Julian's in KC to HFC, 9 November 1878, ibid., 135; the quotation about Mrs. Noyes is from KC to JDC, 23 May 1879, ibid., 159; KC's comments on himself are in KC to HFC, 3 June 1879, ibid., 160–61.

60. Grez figured largely in the lives of this generation of painters. On Stevenson, see Sidney Colvin, ed., *The Letters of Robert Louis Stevenson,* 2 vols. (New York: Scribner's, 1899), 1:118, 133; and Robert Louis Stevenson, "Fountainebleau, Village Communities of Painters," in *Across the Plains, With Other Memories and Essays* (New York: Scribner's, 1922), 134–37. See also Low, *A Chronicle of Friendships,* 33, 136–37, 172–73; Simmons, *From Seven to Seventy,* 196–98; May Alcott Neireker, *Studying Art Abroad* (Boston: Roberts Bros., 1879), 59–60; TBL [*sic*], "Grez par Nemours," *Studio* 2 (July 1883): 15–18; R. A. M. Stevenson, an art student at the time and later a well-known art historian, wrote a survey in "Grez," *Magazine of Art* 17 (January 1894): 27–32. See also Michael Jacobs, *The Good and Simple Life* (Oxford: Phaidon, 1985), 29–41; Varnedoe, *Northern Light,* 162–63, 182; Sellin, *Americans,* 9–10; May Brawley Hill, *Grez Days: Robert Vonnoh in France,* exh. cat. (New York: Berry-Hill Galleries, 1987); and Elizabeth de Veer and Richard J. Boyle, *Sunlight and Shadow: The Life and Art of Willard L. Metcalf* (New York: Abbeville, 1987), 36–38.

61. The wordless letter is reproduced as plate 8 in KC, *Letters.* The fête and gypsics arc noted in KC to JDC, 26 June 1879, ibid., 162–63. The soldiers are mentioned in KC to JDC, 5 September 1879, ibid., 173.

62. KC to HFC, 26 August 1879, KC, *Letters,* 171–72.

63. KC to HFC, 7 September 1879, ibid., 174.

64. KC to JDC, 1 July 1879, ibid., 164–65.

65. KC to HFC, 7 September 1879, ibid., 174.

66. KC to JDC, 29 October 1879, ibid., 180.

67. KC described Miss Brown in KC to HFC, 12 November 1879, ibid., 181–82; and noted her posing in KC to HFC, 23 November 1879, ibid., 183; and recounted the Gérôme story in KC to JDC, 8 December 1879, ibid., 184.

68. KC reported Dyer's role in KC to HFC, 23 December 1879, KC, *Letters,* 185; Miss Brown's posing for him in KC to HFC, 30 December 1879, ibid., 186; and on falling in love in KC to HFC, 29 January 1880, ibid., 189.

69. KC's disappointment is in KC to JDC, 10 January 1880, KC, *Letters,* 187–88. The noted critic Mariana Griswold van Rensselaer said of the work in 1880: "Another new name, I think, is that of Mr. Kenyon Cox, who shows two small canvases. The most important, 'A Lady in Black,' is charmingly original and 'taking.' The frame is black, the background too, and also the dress, fan, and gloves. There is only the head, with its reddish-brown hair and the thin white scarf to relieve the uniformity. The way in which the blacks are differentiated and the forms brought out by their sole use is very clever, and so natural that there is no note

of strangeness or affectation in the effect. In spite of all this, the principal charm of the canvas lies in the face, which is admirably rendered and peculiarly interesting in itself." See "The Philadelphia Exhibition," *American Architect and Building News* 8 (11 December 1880): 280. The second work, not discussed, was *Dans les herbes*. Van Rensselaer recalled the picture a year later in reviewing another show; see "The New York Art Season," *Atlantic* 48 (August 1881): 193–202. AC to Frank H. Goodyear, 6 January 1980, and AC to Jennifer Martin Bienenstock, 22 April 1981, both in AC Papers, AAA, mention the painting's subsequent role in the family, and the fact that it became one of AC's favorite works.

70. The town of Robinson, named after Robinson Crusoe, is described in Low, *A Chronicle of Friendships*, 305, and in KC to HFC, 14 April 1878, KC, *Letters*, 74–75. Posing for Sargent's picture is mentioned in David McKibben to AC, 15 July 1958, and AC to McKibben, 22 July 1958, AC Papers, AAA. KC's later views of Sargent, as a facile but unreflective painter, are in KC and W. A. Coffin, "Society of American Artists," *Nation* 50 (8 May 1890): 380–82, which says that "Sargent is the Paganini of painting;" and KC, "John Sargent, Painter," ibid. 77 (26 November 1903): 426–28. KC did an impressive sketch portrait of Robinson in Italy in 1878, which was the cover for John I. H. Baur, *Theodore Robinson, 1852–1896*, exh. cat. (Brooklyn: Brooklyn Museum, 1946). Robinson's return is in KC to HFC, 12 November 1879, KC, *Letters*, 182. After Robinson's death, KC referred to him as "the regretted Theodore Robinson" in reviewing John C. Van Dyke's *Modern French Masters* (New York: Century, 1896), in which Robinson had written an essay on Corot; see KC, "Van Dyke's French Masters," *Nation* 63 (19 November 1896): 389. KC mentioned Dyer many times, but especially in KC to HFC, 23 December 1879, KC, *Letters*, 185. Dyer left few clues for his later life, but he did show occasionally, as in "The National Academy of Design: Fifth Autumn Exhibition," *Studio*, n.s., 2 (December 1886): 92. KC tried to get him illustration commissions later, as in KC to Robert Underwood Johnson, 12 July 1894, Century Collection, NYPL. Jacobs, *The Good and Simple Life* has a passing reference to Dyer as a member of the St. Ives art colony in England. The quotation about Stott is from KC to HFC, 12 November 1879, KC, *Letters*, 182. Robinson referred to Stott's "Bacchanalian countenance" in a letter to KC, 8 December 1880, KC Papers, AAFAL. Shirley-Fox, *An Art Student's Reminiscences*, 112–13 notes his work. Kenneth McConkey, *British Impressionism* (Oxford: Phaidon, 1989), 34 also mentions Stott. Shirley-Fox, *An Art Student's Reminiscences*, 115–16, reports on KC the caricaturist. Herbert F. Sherwood, ed., *H. Siddons Mowbray, Mural Painter, 1858–1928* (Privately printed, 1928), 23, has the quotation on KC and friends. KC later noted how art students matured or became dull in KC, *Artist and Public* (New York: Scribner's, 1914), 46. KC reassured his mother about student morals in a letter of 29 January 1880, KC, *Letters*, 189.

71. KC to HFC, 19 November 1878, KC, *Letters*, 136–37. Material on KC's social life in the preceding paragraph is drawn from numerous references in ibid.

72. KC to HFC, 24 [25?] November 1878, KC, *Letters*, 137.

73. KC to JDC, [26 December 1878?], which has the quotations, and 27 December 1878, ibid., 143–45.

74. KC to Will Cochran, 4 August 1879; and KC to JDC, 21 September 1879, ibid., 169–70, 175–76.

75. KC to JDC, 10 January 1880, ibid., 188; JDC to James Monroe, 6 February 1880, James Monroe Papers, OCA; Monroe was married to Helen F. Cox's sister, Julia. The comment from Robinson is in KC to JDC, 19 March 1880, KC, *Letters*, 192. The panorama story is in KC to JDC, 27 March, 2 April 1880, ibid., 193–95.

76. There is an untitled notebook with sketches dated for the summer of 1880 in KC Papers, AAFAL. Robinson to KC, 1 August 1880, ibid., has his remark. KC mentioned wanting to visit London in KC to JDC, 19 March 1880, KC, *Letters*, 192. Earlier after commenting on the work of Bouguereau, he had said: "I think the same fault in another way characterizes most of the English painters. Their boasted 'sentiment' is in most cases false sentiment—sweet, sickly, and untrue. In technical matters they are usually beneath contempt. Puerile to the last degree." KC to JDC, 30 September 1879, ibid., 177.

77. KC to JDC, 14 October 1880, KC, *Letters*, 195–97.

78. The illustration is from Whiteing, "The American Student at the Beaux-Arts," 267, and is reproduced in KC, *Letters*, pl. 9. KC described the work in a letter to HFC,

13 December 1881, ibid., 205–6, and tried to soothe her complaints that he was not mentioned by name in the accompanying text.

79. KC to JDC, 3 November 1880, KC, *Letters,* 197–98, has the quotation from KC. H. E. Johnston to KC, 26 May 1881, KC Papers, AAFAL, has the directions and "carteblanche." KC to HFC, 13 December 1881, KC, *Letters,* 206, suggests that Johnston is to be in Paris. KC to HFC, 22 June 1884, KC Papers, AAFAL, written after KC left, says that he has not done the Johnston child portrait. KC to JDC, 9 May [1882], KC, *Letters,* 210, says that he is going to start a picture for Johnston in the country, which may have been *Hay time.*

80. The quotation is from KC to HFC, 7 March 1880 [1881], KC, *Letters,* 200–201. One George E. Hopkins of Cincinnati, who had just returned from Europe, criticized the work in a story in the Cincinnati *Gazette,* 15 June 1881, noted in KC to JDC, 8 July 1881, KC, *Letters,* 201. The work was also criticized and compared to *Dame en noir* in a review of the Pennsylvania Academy exhibition, in *New York Tribune,* 25 November 1881.

81. KC described his work with Becker in letters to his parents, KC, *Letters,* 201–7, with the quotation on this last page.

82. KC reports beginning the head in KC to HFC, 7 August 1881, ibid., 203. Pennsylvania Academy of Fine Arts, *Fifty-third Annual Exhibition, October 24–December 9, 1882* (Philadelphia: PAFA, 1882), has the ownership of the three KC works showed: *Afternoon* (Brown), *Autumn Sunshine* (Groesbeck), and *Hay time* (Johnston). [C. H. Moore], "The Sixth Annual Exhibition of the Society of American Artists," *Nation* 36 (12 April 1883): 328, says: "'Afternoon,' by Kenyon Cox, is an unaffected bit of quiet (apparently French) landscape in the sketchy French style." Jennifer Martin Bienenstock to AC, 25 March 1981, AC Papers, AAA, offers the description of *Afternoon,* from an unidentified review clipping. The whereabouts of all these pictures is unknown.

83. Gregory's payment is in KC to JDC, 7 April 1882, KC, *Letters,* 208. Theodore Robinson to KC, [February 1882], KC Papers, AAFAL, says: "I am sorry the portrait of Gregory doesn't please Gregory more." The Ullmann portrait is mentioned and the quotation is in KC, *Letters,* 209–12. The Fine Arts show is reviewed in *Portfolio* 13 (August 1882): 147–48.

84. KC notes beginning the work in KC to HFC, 13 September 1882, KC, *Letters,* 212. The work is well described in "Americans in Paris," *Studio* 1 (6 January 1883): 3, which KC probably gave the editor as he went through New York City. The price is in KC to George Corliss, 26 October 1883, KC file, PAFA. The quotation is in KC to JDC, 7 November 1883, KC Papers, AAFAL. The picture was praised, and its debt to Bastien-Lepage noted, in Roger Riordan, "The Exhibition of the Pennsylvania Academy," *Art Amateur* 10 (December 1883): 7. The work is mentioned but not reviewed in "Pennsylvania Academy," *Studio* 2 (10 November 1883): 213.

85. The quotation is from KC to HFC, 13 September 1882, KC, *Letters,* 212. William Stott to KC, [May 1883], KC Papers, AAFAL, suggested that KC was upset because of Ullmann's death. JDC to LEO, 20 June 1882, KC Papers, AAFAL, suggests that he try to visit KC in Grez, "both to see Ken and to see a little place which is quite a favorite among the artists in France." For their meeting, see KC to LEO, 24 August 1882, KC, *Letters,* 211, and KC to HFC, 13 September 1882, ibid., 212. The exact date of KC's departure is unclear. A letter from a friend in London suggests that he was leaving at the end of November or beginning of December; see Percy [illegible] to KC, 30 November 1882, KC Papers, AAA. Robinson to KC, 19 December 1882, KC Papers, AAFAL, notes their near miss. "Studio Notes," *Studio* 1 (6 January 1883): 6, says: "Kenyon Cox has arrived in New York from Paris, but has not settled down yet."

III. AN ARTIST IN NEW YORK

1. For the elder Coxes, see Schmiel, "Jacob Dolson Cox," 382–442. Will Cochran to KC, 24 June 1911, KC Papers, AAFAL, recalls his early interest in being an artist. Cochran's obituary in the *Cincinnati Times-Star,* 19 September 1936, has the basic information on his life. JDC to T. H. Robinson, 5 June 1879, JDC Papers, OCA, details John Black's career to that date. His story is in "John G. Black, 1847–1936," *Wooster Alumni Bulletin* 50 (February

1936): 85–86, and in his obituary in the *Wooster Daily Record,* 13 January 1936. Dolson's story is in his *Building an American Industry,* esp. 27, 85–86, 146–47. Information on Charles is scant, but Box 4 of the JDC Papers, OCA, has correspondence between him and his parents. The quotation is from Hope Cox to KC, 12 May 1908, KC Papers, AAFAL.

2. The Cleveland story is in Carl Lorenz, "Art Life in Cleveland," *Ohio Architect and Builder* 11 (June 1908); "Studio Notes," *Studio* 1 (10 February 1883): 45; William Ganson Rose, *Cleveland: The Making of a City* (Cleveland: World, 1950), 411; and clippings from W. R. Rose's "All in a Day's Work" column for 19 March 1919, which has the quotation on KC, and 21 March 1919, in KC alumni file, OCA. The quotation on the *Sketchbook* is from the issue of May 1883, 55–56. There is a copy of the journal in the Cleveland Public Library.

3. Becker to KC, 15 May 1883; and Stott to KC, [May 1883], both in KC Papers, AAFAL.

4. See Robinson to KC, 19 December 1882, 26 February 1883; 15 April 1883, which has the quotation about the West; 1 May 1883, with the comment on *Afternoon;* and 20 June 1883 on decorating work; all in KC Papers, AAFAL.

5. JDC to James Monroe, 27 March 1883, James Monroe Papers, OCA with the quotations; HFC to KC, 20 May 1883, and Robinson to KC, 22 May 1883, both in KC Papers, AAFAL.

6. The Duveneck portrait of Fry is in Quick, *An American Painter Abroad,* 33. There is more information and a reproduction of KC's work in Cincinnati Art Museum, *The Golden Age,* 41, 124. *Landscape,* 1883, oil on canvas, 16″ × 30″, is in MMA, gift of LEO.

7. Mary Rudd Cochran to author, 2 July 1971, and her interview with W. E. Bigglestone, 10 October 1975, OCA, recount the family pressure and help. The quotation to Low is in KC to WHL, 30 September 1883, Low Papers, AIHA. There is interesting information on Low in Laura L. Meixner, "Will Hicok Low (1853–1932): His Early Career and Barbizon Experience," *American Art Journal* 17 (Autumn 1985): 51–70, and Douglas S. Dreishpoon, "Will H. Low: American Muralist (1853–1932)" (Master's thesis, Tufts University, 1979). Typical of KC's memory of this year is his incorrect remark, "I returned to New York in 1883 and opened a studio," in KC to Mrs. Lew F. Porter, 22 March 1914, typescript copy in Jersey City Museum. The quotation from the Cleveland group is in *The Sketchbook* 1 (September 1883): 111, probably a late issue, because KC was in New York only by October. The last quotation is from "Studio Notes," *Studio* 2 (13 October 1883): 164.

8. Barye is mentioned in KC to JDC, 15 October 1883, KC Papers, AAFAL. The article did not appear for some time, which was not unusual, and was Henry Eckford, "Antoine-Louis Barye," *Century Magazine* 31 (February 1886): 483–500. KC to HFC, 22 November 1883, KC Papers, AAFAL, notes his move. The story of the Holbein is told in Lula Merrick, "Holbein Studios, First in City, Are to Go, But Memories Will Be Bright," *The Sun and the New York Herald,* 7 March 1920, sec. 7, p. 9. KC to HFC, 5 October 1885, mentions his boardinghouse; and KC to LEO, 10 August 1887, suggests where he might rent rooms in proximity to the art scene; both in KC Papers, AAFAL.

9. See Arthur John, *The Best Years of the Century: Richard Watson Gilder, Scribner's Monthly, and the Century Magazine, 1870–1909* (Urbana: University of Illinois Press, 1981), 76–91.

10. The first quotation is from KC to JDC, 15 October 1883; the second from KC to JDC, 19 October 1883; the comments about gloom are from KC to JDC, 7 November 1883; all in KC Papers, AAFAL.

11. See G. W. Prothero, "A Greek Play at Cambridge," *Century Magazine* 28 (July 1884): 411–17; Henry Burden McDowell, "The Chinese Theater," ibid. 29 (November 1884): 27–44; Ernest Whitney, "The Glory of the Year," ibid. 30 (August 1885): 550–52. The quotation about Franklin is from KC to HFC, 12 January 1886, KC Papers, AAFAL, and the article was John Bigelow, "Unpublished Letters of Benjamin Franklin" *Century Magazine* 32 (June 1886): 260–72, with KC's drawing of the bust as a frontispiece on p. 174, with the date marked. One review of the magazine commented: "The very weird and alert expression which Mr. Cox has contrived to give to the philosopher's white countenance is in lively contrast with the placid and cow-like aspect under which he is usually represented."; see "Art Notes and

News," *Art Interchange* 16 (19 June 1886): 193. KC's illustrations are scattered throughout *Century* and *Scribner's* magazines, and show a considerable variety of approaches. There is a large number of proofs of the works in Box 43, in the KC collection, CHM.

12. The comment on bad engravers is in KC to HFC, 22 November 1883; their slowness of the work is noted in KC to HFC, 30 May and 22 June 1884; all in KC Papers, AAFAL. Critical reviews are in "The Library," *Art Interchange* 16 (2 January 1886): 2; and "'Lalla Rookh,'" *Art Amateur* 14 (January 1886): 48.

13. The first quotation is from KC to HFC, 9 August 1885, KC Papers, AAFAL; the second quotation is from a letter to the editor, answering recent criticisms of reproduced art works, KC, "Traduttore Traditore," *Nation* 45 (24 November 1887): 415.

14. The quotation is from KC to R. U. Johnson, 21 February 1917, KC file, AAIAL; and KC, "The Fool's May-Day," *Century Magazine* 28 (June 1884): 176.

15. The first quotation is from KC to LEO, 3 January 1885; the second from KC to LEO, 3 June 1886; both KC Papers, AAFAL; and KC to WHL, 9 September 1886, Low Papers, AIHA.

16. See KC to JDC, 23 May, 26 June, and to HFC, 9 July 1879, which has the quotation, in KC, *Letters*, 158, 163, 165–66.

17. KC to HFC, postmarked 8 November 1885, admonishes the family to secrecy about the criticisms and has the quotation; KC to LEO, 30 November 1885, does the same; KC to LEO, 30 June 1885, comments on the need for simplicity in popular writing; all in KC Papers, AAFAL.

18. The first quotation is in *New York Evening Post*, 9 November 1885. The comment on Millais is from ibid., 16 November 1885, reviewing a show at the Union League Club. The Academy review is in ibid., 21, 30 November 1885, which has the quotation. Silva's letter and the reply, which KC may have written, are in ibid., 4 December 1885. These reviews are unsigned but clearly are KC's. The newspaper is unpaginated.

19. JDC to KC, 21 December 1885, has the quotation. KC to HFC, 12 January 1886, comments on specific antagonisms and has the quotation about himself. KC to LEO, 23 January 1886, has the last quotation; all in KC Papers, AAFAL.

20. His review of the oriental material is in *New York Evening Post*, 23 December 1885; of etchings, ibid., 3 February 1886. The Morgan review is in ibid., 18 February 1886; reprinted in KC, "The Morgan Collection," *Nation* 42 (25 February 1886): 176. The comment to his mother is in KC to HFC, 20 February 1886, KC Papers, AAFAL.

21. The first quotation is from KC to JDC, 21 March 1886, KC Papers, AAFAL. He notes dislike among critics in KC to WHL, 10 May 1886; the quotation is in KC to WHL, 9 September 1886; both Low Papers, AIHA.

22. Unidentified newspaper clipping, KC Papers, AAFAL.

23. *New York Evening Post*, 14 December 1885, reviewing watercolors from the Bahamas and Santiago de Cuba.

24. Robinson to KC, 20 June 1883, KC Papers, AAFAL.

25. "New York Art Schools," *Art Amateur* 12 (December 1884): 13; John C. Van Dyke, "The Art Students League of New York," *Harper's Monthly* 83 (October 1891): 688–700; "In the Art Schools," *American Art News*, 4 (21 October 1905): [2], for a later date; Marechal E. Landgren, *Years of Art: The Story of the Art Students League of New York* (New York: McBride, 1940); and Lois Marie Fink, "American Renaissance, 1870–1917," in National Collection of Fine Arts, *Academy: The Academic Tradition in American Art* (Washington, D.C.: Smithsonian Institution Press, 1975), 54–56.

26. KC to HFC, 27 May 1884, mentions being considered; KC to HFC, 22 June 1884, reports getting hired and the salary; KC to HFC, 20 May 1885, has the quotation; KC to LEO, 27 October 1885 mentions that he can just live on the salary; KC to HFC, 11 August 1889, notes his pay raise; all in KC Papers, AAFAL.

27. "New York Art Schools," *Art Amateur* 12 (December 1884): 13; *New York Evening Post*, 28 November 1885; "Art Notes and News," *Art Interchange* 15 (17 December 1885): 168; KC to HFC, 5 October 1885, KC Papers, AAFAL.

28. LKC memoir, KC Papers, AAA. Dan Beard, *Hardly a Man is Now Alive* (New York: Doubleday, 1939), 277, is by a student at the League in the 1880s and notes KC's appearance.

"Among the Artists," *American Art News* 4 (18 November 1905) has a good photo of KC and a small biography for a later date. *New York Times*, 2 February 1908, sec. 1, p. 8, has a photo of KC with women students. F. O. Matthiessen, *Russell Cheney, 1881–1945* (New York: Oxford, 1947) shows KC instructing a class about 1905 with an unusual view of the left side of his face.

29. Landgren, *Years of Art*, 42, briefly notes KC's later teaching. Lawrence Campbell, of the League, to author, 6 March 1985, outlines KC's career there. "Art Notes," *Art Interchange* 23 (14 September 1889): 81 notes the new seal's appearance on League circulars. KC's preliminary drawing of the seal is reproduced in Fink, "American Renaissance, 1870–1917," 56, and it is still in use.

30. KC and the specially posed model is in Russell Cowles interview, April 16, 1869, pp. 27–28, Russell Cowles Collection, AAA; KC, *The Classic Point of View* (New York: Scribner's, 1911), 187–88; KC, "The Museum and the Teaching of Art in the Public Schools," *Scribner's Magazine* 52 (July 1912): 127, with the quotation; [Clarence Cook?], "American Notes," *Studio*, n.s., 5 (31 May 1890): 260, notes improvements at the League. "In the Art Schools," *American Art News* 6 (9 November 1907): 2, reports he is demoting students to cast drawing.

31. KC, "Van Dyke on Painting," *Nation* 56 (20 April 1893): 295–97, reviewing John C. Van Dyke, *Art for Art's Sake: Seven University Lectures on the Technical Beauties of Painting* (New York: Scribner's, 1893) is a bravura performance on the technical steps and skills necessary to do a good picture in KC's view. KC to LKC, 15 May 1906, KC Papers, AAFAL, notes his tutelage of a woman painter. Nude life classes were apparently segregated at the League until 1929, according to Fink, "American Renaissance, 1870–1917," 63. KC's anatomy lectures are noted in "In the Art Schools," *American Art News* 5 (16 February 1907): 2, which says: "These lectures are well attended, and no one is better able to impart knowledge concerning the anatomy of the human figure than Mr. Cox." Exhibition of KC's pictures at the League is noted in "In the Art Schools," ibid. 4 (31 March 1906): 2. A fund drive for the League is announced in *Hyde's Weekly Art News* 11 (7 February 1903): 1. Burke, *J. Alden Weir*, 94, notes receptions at the League.

32. The commission is reported in KC to HFC, 12 February 1886; the quotation about success is in KC to HFC, 20 February 1886; the book is described in KC to LEO, 26 September 1886; HFC to KC, 15 February 1886, has her answer; KC to JDC, 21 March 1886, has the last quotation; all in KC Papers, AAFAL.

33. The dates of beginning and completing the work are in a ribbon drawing at the end of the book. There are a few ink studies in Box 38, KC collection, CHM. The original paintings are in the Brooklyn Museum. KC to WHL, 9 September 1886, Low Papers, AIHA has the quotation.

34. KC to LEO, 3 June 1886, KC Papers, AAFAL; and "'The Blessed Damozel,'" *Art Amateur* 16 (January 1887): 47. The display is also noted in "Holiday Books. III," *Nation* 43 (9 December 1886): 480–82.

35. Gérôme's copy was apparently sold as part of his estate and ultimately found its way into a Rossetti collection in the rare books department, PUL. Gérôme is mentioned in KC to HFC, 15 December 1886, KC Papers, AAFAL, and in KC to WHL, 4 February 1887, Low Papers, AIHA. Cochran to KC, 22 November 1886, and WHL to KC, 15 January 1887, both in KC Papers, AAFAL, have those remarks.

36. KC to HFC, 15 December 1886, KC Papers, AAFAL.

37. "Holiday Books. III," *Nation* 43 (9 December 1886): 480–82, and KC to HFC, 15 December 1886, KC Papers, AAFAL. Mariana Griswold Van Rensselaer, an important critic who had liked some of Cox's Paris work, wrote a thoughtful afterward to the book that tried to anticipate criticism of the nude. She thought that KC's were palpable but appropriate to the text, because they imparted substance and energy as well as idealization. There is a mass of unidentified clippings of reviews in KC Papers, AAFAL. See also reviews in: *Boston Post*, 29 November 1886; "The Blessed Damozel," *Literary World* 17 (27 November 1886): 427–28; "Christmas-tide Customs," *Art Interchange* 17 (18 December 1886): 205; "The 'Blessed Damozel,'" *Art Amateur* 16 (January 1887): 47; "Illustrated Books," *Atlantic Monthly* 59 (February 1887): 263–65. The quotation about training is from KC to WHL, 9 September

1886, Low Papers, AIHA; that about his decorative bent is from KC to Mrs. Lew F. Porter, 22 March 1914, typed copy, Jersey City Museum.

38. KC to HFC, [December 1886], KC Papers, AAFAL; and KC to WHL, 4 February 1887, Low Papers, AIHA.

39. KC to WHL, 9 September 1886, Low Papers, AIHA.

40. Frank Jewett Mather, Jr., "Kenyon Cox," *Scribner's Magazine* 65 (June 1919): 765, an obituary in which Mather tried to explain why KC's nudes were not acceptable to his generation. See also William H. Gerdts, *The Great American Nude* (New York: Praeger, 1974), 103–52, for the issue in this period.

41. The first quotation is from KC to JDC, 16 January 1878, KC, *Letters*, 57–58; the second is from KC to Dear Madame, 15 March 1893, Miscellaneous Manuscripts, AAA.

42. For varied discussions of this issue, see: James Harding, *Artistes Pompiers: French Academic Art in the 19th Century* (New York: Rizzoli, 1979), 44–51; Elizabeth Ewing Tebow, "Arcadia Reclaimed: Mythology and American Painting, 1860–1920" (Ph.D. diss., University of Maryland, 1987), 42–44, 73; Leila Bailey Van Hook, "The Ideal Woman in American Art, 1875–1910" (Ph.D. diss., City University of New York, 1988); Martha Banta, *Imaging American Women: Idea and Ideals in Cultural History* (New York: Columbia University Press, 1987).

43. HFC to KC, 31 March 1885; KC to HFC, 4 April and 14 June 1885; all in KC Papers, AAFAL.

44. KC to HFC, [December 1886?], KC Papers, AAFAL. This letter may be in response to her tempered congratulations on *The Blessed Damozel*. On models, see also Charlotte Adams, "Artists' Models in New York," *Century Magazine* 25 (February 1883): 569–77, and Landgren, *Years of Art,* 49–55.

45. Coffin, "Kenyon Cox," 335; KC and WHL, "The Nude in Art," *Scribner's Magazine* 12 (December 1892): 747–49; KC, "The Making of a Mural Painting," pt. 2, p. 3, manuscript, KC Papers, AAFAL, which has his quotation. See also KC, *The Classic Point of View,* 43; KC, "What is Painting?" *Art World* 1 (October 1916): 32.

46. The reviews of KC's nudes seem generally hostile; see [W. J. Stillman], "Fine Arts: Exhibition of the Society of American Artists," *Nation* 38 (29 May 1884): 473–74, and "Seventh Exhibition of the Society of American Artists," *Art Interchange* 12 (5 June 1884), both referring to *A Rose* (whereabouts unknown); "Saunterings," *Town Topics* 15 (8 May 1886): 6, and "Book of American Figure Painters," *Art Amateur* 16 (January 1887), both referring to *Evening* (1886, NAD), and reviewing *Book of American Figure Painters* (Philadelphia: Lippincott, 1886); W. A. Coffin, "The Academy Exhibition. II," *Nation* 44 (28 April 1887): 373, referring to *Flower de luce* (whereabouts unknown); "Society of American Artists," ibid. 46 (26 April 1888), referring to *Indian Summer* (whereabouts unknown); "The Monthly Exhibition of the Union League Club," *Studio* 5 (22 February 1890): 116, referring to *Birth of Venus* (1889), oil on canvas, 29⅛″ × 17″, Dixon Gallery of Art, Memphis, now known as *Nude on Beach with Seagulls;* "The Society of American Artists Exhibition," *Art Interchange* 32 (May 1894): 135, referring to *A Study of Sunshine* (whereabouts unknown). *The Approach of Love* (1890), oil on canvas, 18⅛″ × 30¼″, is in the Cincinnati Art Museum. KC's general view of the modern nude is in his "The Nude in Art," *Scribner's Magazine* 12 (December 1892): 747–49. The Pennsylvania Academy show is noted in *New York Evening Post,* 7 March 1891, p. 11, with KC's response on p. 15. KC's works there with nudes were *Evening* (1886), *Painting and Poetry* (1887), *A Nymph* (1889), and *An Eclogue* (1890). His private response is in KC to Louise King, 12 March 1891, KC Papers, AAFAL. The Century story is in KC to Mr. Fraser, 2 April 1895, Century Collection, NYPL, apparently referring to KC, "Puvis de Chavannes," *Century Magazine* 51 (February 1896): 558–69. The note on eroticism is from KC to Blashfield, 18 January 1900, Blashfield Papers, NYHS. Comstock is in Landgren, *Years of Art,* 87–89. The destroyed work is in "Cox Picture Slashed," *American Art News* 8 (15 January 1910): 1. Dolson's comments are in DC to KC, 26 January 1907, KC Papers, AAFAL. The Buffalo story is in KC to Cornelia Sage, 27 April 1909, AKG. The Moser affair is in Moser to KC, 27 March [sent 2 April] 1911, and KC to Moser, 10 April 1911, James Henry Moser Papers, AAA. The Cornish models are noted in KC to W. H. Troy, apparently of the *Boston Sunday Post,* 17 September 1913, HL.

47. For an example of KC's late critical writing style on nudes, see "Some American Figure Painters," *Cosmopolitan* 32 (April 1902): 585–600. The quotation is in KC to AC, 7 January 1918, KC Papers, AAFAL.

48. KC Diary, 12 March 1876; Robinson to KC, 31 May 1883; and KC to HFC, 27 May 1884; all in KC Papers, AAFAL.

49. The first quotation is from KC to HFC, postmarked March 27, 1885; a letter of that same date has the illustration and the second quotation; the comment about the photo is from KC to HFC, 20 May 1885; the letter to his father is dated 3 June 1885; he noted finishing the picture, with the quotation, in KC to HFC, 14 June 1885; the last quotation is from KC to HFC, 5 October 1885; the retouching is mentioned in KC to LEO, 30 November 1885; all in KC Papers, AAFAL. The picture is also described in "Art Notes and News," *Art Interchange* 15 (3 December 1885): 152.

50. There is a review in "The Eighth Exhibition of the Society of American Artists," *Art Interchange* 16 (8 May 1886): 145, and one in an unidentified clipping in the KC Papers, AAFAL. Coffin, "Kenyon Cox," 335, notes the work with approval. KC mentions reworking the picture for the NAD in KC to August Jaccaci, 16 September 1911, Jaccaci Papers, AAA. The quotation is from KC to LEO, 30 June 1885, KC Papers, AAFAL.

51. The reviewer's comments on the original illustration are in "Christmas-tide Customs," *Art Interchange* 17 (18 December 1886): 205. KC's report on starting the work is in KC to WHL, 4 February 1887, Low Papers, AIHA. KC is shown standing in front of this and other of his works in *Heroes in the Fight For Beauty: The Muralists of the Hudson County Courthouse* (Jersey City: Jersey City Museum, 1986), 50. The work is described in "The Society of American Artists," *Art Amateur* 17 (June 1887): 5. See also [W. A. Coffin], "Society of American Artists. I," *Nation* 44 (12 May 1887): 415.

52. KC to JDC, 3 June 1885, KC Papers, AAFAL.

53. "Art Notes," *Art Interchange* 24 (29 March 1890): 97. Coffin's comments are in "The Society of American Artists," *Nation* 50 (8 May 1890): 381. This review is unsigned, but the magazine's index attributes it to KC and Coffin jointly. Coffin presumably wrote about KC's work, and the style seems to be his.

54. See "Art Notes," *Art Interchange* 21 (1 December 1888): 178. The quotation is from KC to William Rothenstein, 24 March 1912, HL. KC to H. W. Kent, 27 March 1912, and Kent to KC, 28 March 1912, KC file, MMA, refer to the picture.

55. KC to HFC, postmarked 10 August 1885, KC Papers, AAFAL; and "Art Notes and News," *Art Interchange* 15 (8 October 1885): 92; "Saunterings," *Town Topics* 15 (8 May 1886): 6. Whereabouts of both pictures unknown.

56. Opdycke's biography is in *The National Cyclopedia of American Biography* (New York: James T. White, 1937), 16:218–19. In 1960, after reviewing his father's correspondence, Allyn Cox wrote his sister Caroline Cox Lansing, on 4 June 1960, AC Papers, AAA: "I have discovered, by the way, that Mr. O was a saint, something I never suspected." KC to LEO, 23 January 1886, KC Papers, AAFAL, declines a loan but says: "Your offer was like yourself, and was only another proof of what I have long known, that you are a friend to be counted on." KC's designs for the books are in Box 1197, Folder 7, KC collection, CHM. The titles were: Baldassare Castiglione, *The Book of the Courtier* (New York: Scribner's, 1901); and Demetrios Bikelas, *Tales from the Aegean* (Chicago: A. C. McClurg, 1894). The quotation is from KC to LEO, 16 November 1888, KC Papers, AAFAL. The 1888 portrait was noted in "Art Notes," *Art Interchange* 21 (1 December 1888), and Coffin, "Kenyon Cox," 335. The *Portrait of Mrs. Emerson Opdycke* (1888), 16½" × 13", and one of her husband, *Portrait of Emerson Opdycke* (1902), from photograph, 16½" × 13", are both in possession of Henry Peltz of New York City. *Portrait of Mrs. O* (1897), oil on canvas, 16½" × 14", is in possession of Leonard E. Opdycke, Poughkeepsie, New York. The progress of the last work, LEO's wife, is reported in KC to LEO, 1, 20, 24, 26 February 1897, all in KC Papers, AAFAL; and LEO to JDC, 12 February, 3 May 1897, both in JDC Papers, OCA.

57. The whereabouts of this work are unknown, but an engraving of it is reproduced in Coffin, "Kenyon Cox," 336.

58. KC notes writing the first article in a letter to LEO, 11 May 1884, KC Papers, AAFAL. He often mentioned Saint Gaudens in voluminous publications, but his principal

direct writings on him are "Sculptors of the Early Italian Renaissance," *Century Magazine* 29 (November 1884): 62–66; "Augustus Saint-Gaudens," ibid. 34 (November 1887): 28–37; "Rodin," *Architectural Record* 18 (November 1905): 327–46, which contrasts Rodin and the moderns with Saint Gaudens; "Saint-Gaudens's 'Sherman,'" in KC, *Old Masters and New* (New York: Scribner's, 1905), 278–85; "In Memory of Saint-Gaudens," *Architectural Record* 22 (October 1907): 249–51; and "Augustus Saint-Gaudens," *Atlantic Monthly* 101 (March 1908): 298–310. Secondary works include: Louise Hall Tharp, *Saint-Gaudens and the Gilded Era* (Boston: Little, Brown, 1969); Burke Wilkinson, *Uncommon Clay: The Life and Works of Augustus Saint Gaudens* (New York: Harcourt, Brace, Jovanovich, 1985); National Portrait Gallery, *Augustus Saint-Gaudens: The Portrait Reliefs* (Washington, D.C.: Smithsonian Institution Press, 1969); John Dryfhout, *The Work of Augustus Saint-Gaudens* (Hanover, N.H.: University Press of New England, 1982); and Kathryn Greenthal, *Augustus Saint-Gaudens: Master Sculptor* (New York: Metropolitan Museum of Art, 1985).

59. Typical reviews of the portrait are in "Art Notes: Society of American Artists," *Art Interchange* 20 (21 April 1888): 130; "Society of American Artists," *Nation* 46 (26 April 1888): 352; "The Society of American Artists," *Studio* 2 (May 1888): 96–97; "The American Artists' Exhibition," *Art Amateur* 18 (May 1888): 130. See also Coffin, "Kenyon Cox," 335. The medallion is illustrated in Dryfhout, *The Work of Augustus Saint-Gaudens*, 181. The replica is virtually exact except for the formal lettering in the original's upper left-hand corner: AVGVSTVS SAINT GAVDENS SCULPTOR. IN HIS FORTIETH YEAR, PAINTED BY KENYON COX. 1887. The original is illustrated in an engraving in Homer Saint-Gaudens, ed., *The Reminiscences of Augustus Saint-Gaudens,* 2 vols. (New York: Century, 1913), 2:frontispiece.

60. W. B. Spear to HFC, 1 January 1891, KC Papers, AAFAL. This was in response to the thoughtful profile by William A. Coffin, "Kenyon Cox," *Century Magazine* 41 (January 1891): 333–37.

IV. ART LIFE AND NEW RELATIONSHIPS

1. KC, "The Fool's May-Day," *Century Magazine* 28 (June 1884): 176.

2. The description of the work is from KC to HFC, 19 January 1878, in KC, *Letters,* 59–60. The remark about a cult is in AC to William Gerdts, director of the Newark Museum, 22 October 1962, AC Papers, AAA. The sketch is in the Newark Museum. The bust is now attributed to Francesco Laurana, and is ca. 1487–88. William C. Morrow, *Bohemian Paris of Today* (Philadelphia: Lippincott, 1900), 21, notes the bust casts; see also David C. Huntington, *The Quest for Unity: American Art Between World's Fair, 1876–1893,* exh. cat. (Detroit: Detroit Institute of Art, 1983), 34–35. The draft of the poem is dated 25 July 1883, Bellaire, Ohio, in poetry notebook, KC Papers, AAFAL. The poem appeared at the conclusion of the article by KC, "Sculptors of the Early Italian Renaissance," 66. KC noted careful changes in proofs of illustrations of the bust in Box 1197, Folder 1, and in Box 43, Proofs Folder, both in KC collection, CHM.

3. KC, "The Gospel of Art," *Century Magazine* 49 (February 1895): 533.

4. His daily schedule is in KC to HFC, 16 October 1885; the quotation on socializing is in KC to HFC, 12 February 1886; both in KC Papers, AAFAL. The boarding house is described in Howard Russell Butler, typescript memoir, p. 133, Butler Papers, AAA; JDC to James Monroe, 9 June 1886, James Monroe Papers, OCA, notes the quinsy. The quotation about reading is from KC to WHL, 9 September 1886, Low Papers, AIHA.

5. See Coffin, "Kenyon Cox," 337. KC to Richard Watson Gilder, 11 October 1890, Century Collection, NYPL, concerns his liking for Coffin, who did not like Cox's classical works. There is a brief biography in "William Anderson Coffin," *Art Amateur* 17 (September 1887): 75. The Chase story is in Mrs. Daniel Chester French, *Memories of a Sculptor's Wife* (New York: Houghton Mifflin, 1923), 158.

6. See French, *Memories,* 154–73; Young, *Life and Letters of J. Alden Weir,* xxi–xxii; KC to JDC, 23 December 1884; and KC to HFC, 29 May 1888, both in KC Papers, AAFAL.

7. KC to HFC, 5 December 1883, and KC to JDC, 16 December 1884, both in KC Papers, AAFAL.

8. Baker, *Stanny*, 87–88 has the history of the concerts. Homer Saint-Gaudens, *The American Artist and His Times* (New York: Dodd, Mead, 1941) notes his father's opinion of KC's writing. Homer Saint-Gaudens, ed., *The Reminiscences of Augustus Saint-Gaudens*, 1:288–89 has a Saint Gaudens letter from 1886 on KC's work. This same source has a photograph of one of the concert audiences, facing p. 308, with KC showing his right profile, at the rear, in the middle. The studio quotation is in KC, "Augustus Saint-Gaudens," 300. The Gosse incident is in KC to JDC, 16 December 1884, KC Papers, AAFAL.

9. The area is described in Helen M. Knowlton, *Art-Life of William Morris Hunt* (Boston: Little, Brown, 1899), 116–18, and in Jacobs, *The Good and Simple Life,* 168–70. The first two quotations are in KC to LEO, 24 June, 6 July 1884, KC Papers, AAFAL. The last quotation is from KC to WHL, 31 July 1884, Low Papers, AIHA.

10. The quotation on landscape fever is from KC to HFC, 20 May; the send-off is in KC to HFC, 19 June; the quotation on haying is from KC to HFC, 8 July; the picture description and the quotation on color are from KC to HFC, 8 August; the comments on autumn landscape are from KC to HFC, 20 September; the importance of the summer is noted in KC to LEO, 27 October; all 1885, in KC Papers, AAFAL. KC noted Ballast Island in KC to WHL, 28 July 1887, Low Papers, AIHA.

11. KC to HFC, 22 November 1883, and KC to HFC, 20 February 1886, both KC Papers, AAFAL.

12. See Jennifer A. Martin Bienenstock, "The Formation and Early Years of the Society of American Artists" (Ph.D. diss., City University of New York, 1983), 30–31, 409. The quotations are in KC to HFC, 27 May 1884, and KC to LEO, 27 May 1884, both in KC Papers, AAFAL. KC noted his regard for the SAA in KC and W. A. Coffin, "Society of American Artists," *Nation* 50 (8 May 1890): 380–82. See also "My Note Book," *Art Amateur* 14 (January 1886): 28; "Art Society Elections," ibid. 17 (June 1887): 25; "American Notes," *Studio* 6 (2 May 1891): 217; [no title], *American Art News* 3 (22 April 1905): [1].

13. On his first rejection, see KC to JDC, 19 October 1883, KC Papers, AAFAL. Three Hallgarten Prizes were established in 1883, to be given for the best oils in the annual spring exhibition that were the work of American artists in the United States under age thirty-five. See "Notes and News," *Art Interchange* 11 (6 December 1883): 145; "The Academy Prizes," *Studio* 2 (15 December 1883): 277; "Art Notes," *Art Interchange* 22 (27 April 1889): 129. The whereabouts of *Autumn* are unknown. On KC's election as an associate in 1900, WHL wrote what must have been a common feeling: "In the Academy I am as dangerous a young man from the S.A.A. as I am an old fogy Academician in the Society, and have little influence (in either place) . . ."; see Low to KC, 9 January 1901, KC Papers, AAFAL. See also Eliot Clark, *History of the National Academy of Design* (New York: Columbia, 1954), 251; Fink and Taylor, *Academy,* 89; Paul D. Schweizer, "Genteel taste at the National Academy of Design's Annual Exhibitions, 1891–1910," *American Art Review* 2 (July–August 1975): 77–90.

14. See Gilder to T. Wayland Vaughan, 26 December 1906, in Rosamund Gilder, ed., *Letters of Richard Watson Gilder* (Boston: Houghton Mifflin, 1884), 372. Gérôme's letter was dated 18 November 1884, reprinted in *New York Times,* 18 December 1884, p. 4. The basic story of the league is in *Report of the Work of the National; Free Art League* (n.p., [1895]), copy in BUL; and in "Art Notes," *Art Interchange* 23 (31 August 1889): 65.

15. His testimony is in U.S. Congress, 51st Cong., 1st sess., Misc. Doc. 176, *Revision of the Tariff: Hearings Before the Committee on Ways and Means* (Washington, D.C.: Government Printing Office, 1890), 616–18; and "Art Notes," *Art Interchange* 24 (18 January 1890): 18. The quotation on leaving art alone is from KC to [James B. Carrington], 31 March 1889, Carrington Papers, BL. KC's basic articles are "'Protection' for Artists," *Nation* 49 (11 July 1889): 24–25; "Art no Luxury," ibid. 49 (18 July 1889): 46, which has the quotation on civilization; and "Why Not Pictures?" ibid. 49 (19 December 1889): 488. KC to John Sherman, 3 September 1890, Sherman Papers, LC, has that quotation. KC alluded to enhancing the art market with repeal in KC, "The Edinburgh Art Congress," *Nation* 51 (18 September 1890): 230–31. KC notes the House action in KC to LEO, 30 March 1890, KC Papers, AAFAL.

16. The first quotation is from KC to F. W. Barrett, 9 March 1892, in Grenville H. Norcross Autograph Collection, Massachusetts Historical Society, Boston; the Gilder quotation is in KC to Gilder, 13 February 1893, Gilder Papers, NYPL; the letter is KC to Cleveland, 6

November 1893, Grover Cleveland Papers, LC; the league disbandment is in *Report of the Work of the National Free Art League;* the Gardner visit is in KC to Gardner, 24 November 1904, Isabella Stewart Gardner Museum, Boston; the Wilson encounter is in KC to Wilson, and Wilson to KC, both 13 September 1913, Woodrow Wilson Papers, LC.

17. The first quotation is in KC to HFC, 9 August 1885; his desire to go is in KC to HFC, 20 February 1886; the last quotation is in KC to JDC, 21 March 1886; all in KC Papers, AAFAL.

18. Annette Blaugrund, *Paris 1889: American Artists at the Universal Exposition*, exh. cat. (New York: Abrams, 1989), 14–17, details the jury; KC to Hawkins, 24 November 1889, Hawkins Papers, BUL, is his acceptance, which is noted in "Our Artists and the Paris Exposition of 1889," *Studio* 3 (November 1888): 188–89; *New York Herald*, 8 March 1889, notes the shipping date; "The Fine Arts at the Paris Exposition. X. The United States," *Nation* 49 (17 October 1889): 310, has good coverage; Cox's entries are noted in Exposition Universelle Internationale de 1889 à Paris, *Catalogue Général Officiel* (Lille: Danel, 1889), 1:176, 188; the drawings were *Bust of J. Alden Weir, Portrait bust, Disciple of Saint Joseph, Lecture in a Chapter house, At the forge,* and *At work,* the last two probably from the Pennsylvania vacation in the summer of 1885, whereabouts of all unknown. The whereabouts of *Jacob Wrestling with the Angel* are unknown, but a version is illustrated in John Hay, "Israel," *Century Magazine* 34 (May 1887): 126. KC's medals are noted in *Journal officiel de la Republique Française*, no. 263 (29 September 1889): p. 4707 for oil works, p. 4709 for drawings; Coffin, "Kenyon Cox," 335, notes that the awards were for categories, not individual works; see also Blaugrund, *Paris 1889*, 27.

19. KC to LEO, 16 July; KC to HFC, 24–27 July, 11 August 1889, which has the quotation; all in KC Papers, AAFAL.

20. KC to HFC, 11 August 1889, KC Papers, AAFAL. The quotation about *Painting and Poetry* is from E. Durand-Grevitle, "Notes on the Pictures of American Artists at the Paris Exposition," *Studio* 5 (18 January 1890): 68–69. The work is mentioned in "The Paris Exposition," *Art Interchange* 23 (6 July 1889): 209. It is shown in place in a contemporary photograph in Blaugrund, *Paris 1889*, 55. Harold Frederic, "American Art in Paris," *New York Times*, 16 June 1889, p. 11, has his remark. Theodore Child, "American Artists at the Paris Exhibition," *Harper's Monthly* 79 (September 1889): 520–21, mentions Cox's work. William A. Coffin, "The Fine Arts at the Paris Exposition. X. The United States," *Nation* 49 (17 October 1889): 310–11, notes the portrait.

21. KC to HFC, 11 August; and to unaddressed, 23 August 1889; which has the quotation; both in KC Papers, AAFAL.

22. KC to HFC, 6, 8 September 1889, KC Papers, AAFAL. For KC's later views, see his "Michel's Rubens," *Nation* 69 (14 December 1899): 448–51, reviewing Emile Michel, *Rubens: His Life, His Work, His Time* (New York: Scribner's, 1899).

23. The king quotation is in KC to HFC, 12 September; the remarks on Rembrandt and Vermeer are in KC to HFC, 10 September; the Hals quotation is in KC to HFC, 12 September; the quotation on realism is in KC to HFC, 15 September; all 1889, in KC Papers, AAFAL. KC's later views on Hals are in "The Master Painter of Haarlem," *Nation* 75 (9 October 1902): 287–88, which says: "His range is too limited, his sense of beauty too restricted, his intellectual value too slight to allow us to place him among the great ones of the earth."

24. KC to Family, 20 September 1889, KC Papers, AAFAL.

25. KC to HFC, 5 October 1889, ibid.

26. Her basic biography is in *Cyclopedia of American Biography* (New York: James T. White, 1909), 11:301–2. The quotations are from her loosely typed memoir in KC Papers, AAA. The basic secondary source is Patricia C. Ronan, "Louise King Cox—Her Life and Work" (Master's thesis, City University of New York, 1988).

27. His comment on falling in love with her is in Lucia Fuller to LKC, 18 March [1919]; her visit is in Louise King to KC, 15 June 1886; the recommendation is KC to Whom It May Concern, 22 October 1887; all in KC Papers, AAFAL.

28. KC to Louise King, 6 September and 24 November 1888, KC Papers, AAFAL. Louise alluded to this time in Toledo years later in encouraging her own son Allyn, then studying in Rome: "I know only too well that terrible, nervous tension of surroundings that pull and tease

and try. I have had some pretty bad ones myself, when there seemed no hope for any life or art, but one dreary grind. And the surroundings weren't a palace in Rome, but a horrid room in a country town where I did all the cooking and I gave lessons in copy for a living." The letter is dated 26 March 1917, AC Papers, AAA.

29. KC to HFC, 1 January 1880, KC, *Letters*, 189, is on falling in love; KC to HFC, 8 August 1885, has the quotation about marriage; and KC to HFC, [December 1886], is about ladyhood; both in KC Papers, AAFAL. There are several versions of the story of their confrontation in class; see French, *Memories of a Sculptor's Wife*, 158–59; and Saint Gaudens, *The American Artist and His Times*, 156. The last quotation about awe is from Mary Rudd Cochran to author, 2 July 1971.

30. KC to Louise King, 6, 17, 23 July, 17, 21 August 1891, which has the quotation, are about Magnolia; KC to Louise King, 9 October 1891, concerns the fellowship; Hope Cox to KC, 1 May 1892, recalls her visit; KC to Louise King, postmarked 23 January 1892, is his response to her wish to be "honest with me," though it does not mention the exact circumstances; all in KC Papers, AAFAL.

31. HFC to KC, 31 March; and JDC to KC, 7 April 1892; both in KC Papers, AAFAL.

32. The quotations in order are KC to HFC, 3 April; HFC to KC, 5 April; KC to HFC, 14 April 1892; all in KC Papers, AAFAL.

33. HFC to Louise King, 24 April; JDC to KC, 28 April; HFC to Louise King, 5 May; DC to KC, 9 April; all 1892, in KC Papers, AAFAL.

34. Samuel Isham to Stanford White, 16 May 1892, White Papers, NYHS, is an invitation to the dinner, which cost five dollars. The organizing committee consisted of J. Carroll Beckwith, Herbert Denman, and Robert Reid. KC's report on the meal is in KC to HFC, 25 May 1892, KC Papers, AAFAL.

35. KC to HFC, 25 May 1892, KC Papers, AAFAL, notes his work on the portrait. See also the comments of Kathleen A. Pyne in Detroit Institute of Arts, *Quest for Unity*, 99–100.

36. KC to HFC, 21 June 1892, KC Papers, AAFAL, has his presence in Belmont and calming influence on Louise. The marriage license is in KC Papers, AAA. HFC's description of the wedding is in a long letter to her daughter Helen Black, 2 July 1892; and KC's comments on Louise's looks are in KC to HFC, 7 July 1892; both in KC Papers, AAFAL.

V. MURAL PAINTER

1. KC to LEO, 16 September 1893, KC Papers, AAFAL.

2. KC to HFC, 14 April 1892, KC Papers, AAFAL, has their desire for a calm summer. AC to Dick West, 23 November 1970, AC Papers, AAA, notes the commission. The effort is covered in Frank Millet, "The Decoration of the Exposition," *Scribner's Magazine* 12 (December 1892): 692–709; Will H. Low, "The Art of the White City," ibid. 14 (October 1893): 504–12; W. Lewis Fraser, "Decorative Painting at the World's Fair," *Century Magazine* 24 (May 1893): 14–21. Blashfield's comment is in Edwin H. Blashfield, "A Painter's Reminiscences of a World's Fair," *New York Times Magazine*, 18 March 1923, pp. 13–14. French, *Memories of a Sculptor's Wife*, 176, is good on the excitement. The quotation from Saint Gaudens is in many places, but see Helen Lefkowitz Horowitz, *Culture and the City: Cultural Philanthropy in Chicago from the 1880s to 1917* (Lexington: University Press of Kentucky, 1976), 87. See also Elizabeth Broun, "American Paintings and Sculpture in the Fine Arts Building of the World's Columbian Exposition" (Ph.D. diss., University of Kansas, 1976).

3. The working conditions are described in Blashfield, "A Painter's Reminiscences of a World's Fair," and in J. Alden Weir to Ella Weir, 11 August and 9 September 1892, in *Life and Letters of J. Alden Weir*, 181–83. Louise's report is in a letter to HFC, 1 September 1892, and the poem is undated; both in KC Papers, AAFAL.

4. The quotation is in KC, "The Relation of Mural Painting to Architecture," *House and Garden* 2 (February 1902): 100. KC's plan is drawn in an undated fragment, KC Papers, AAFAL. He did not describe the final work methods, but they surely resembled Weir's, summarized in Burke, *J. Alden Weir*, 200–202. See also David F. Burg, *Chicago's White City of 1893* (Lexington: University Press of Kentucky, 1976), 160–61.

5. This description is drawn from the studies KC did for each of the figures in watercolor, 13½" × 10", in Box 1197, Folder 3, KC collection, CHM. The works, of course, did not survive.

6. The works are noted in Broun, "American Paintings and Sculpture," 256. The Blashfield quotation is in his "A Painter's Reminiscences of a World's Fair," 14.

7. Theodore Robinson heard of the stillbirth at an SAA jury meeting and noted it in his diary, 2 April 1893, Frick Art Reference Library. There is a deed of trust dated 19 December 1931, AC Papers, AAA, for the maintenance of a grave site in Fairhaven, Massachusetts, which apparently included the infant and Louise's mother, Anna T. King. The quotations are in KC to LEO, 19 January 1895, and LKC to HFC, 11 May 1893, both in KC Papers, AAFAL.

8. KC to McKim, 6 April 1893, copy in Walker Papers, Bowdoin College Museum of Art, Brunswick, Maine; and LKC to HFC, 9 June 1893, KC Papers, AAFAL.

9. LKC to HFC, 9 June, on the departure; LKC to Hope Cox, 14 June, on the trip; KC to HFC, 16 June, on his activities; all 1893, in KC Papers, AAFAL. The Kodak story is in Hutchins Hapgood, *A Victorian in the Modern World* (New York: Harcourt Brace, 1939), 84–85. KC to HFC, 13 July, is on Veronese; LKC to HFC, 23 September, is on the return; both 1893, KC Papers, AAFAL; and AC to Richard West, 23 November 1970, AC Papers, AAA.

10. The contract is in KC Papers, AAFAL. The basic story of the building and decorations is in Richard V. West, *The Walker Art Building Murals* (Brunswick, Me.: Bowdoin College Museum of Art, 1972), esp. 4–14 for KC.

11. The entry of 1 March 1894, Robinson Diary, FARL, notes his visit. The quotation is from KC to Opdycke, 14 May 1894, KC Papers, AAFAL. LKC to KC, [May 1894], ibid., encourages him to set the color as he wishes. The thanks are noted in KC to Mary Sophia Walker, 5 June 1894, Walker Papers, Bowdoin College Museum of Art. The other artists had their views. Thayer at first disliked Cox's work but changed his mind. Vedder thought Thayer's was "poor trash, [and that] Cox is far better but so weak." See Nelson C. White, *Abbott H. Thayer* (Peterborough, N.H.: Bauhan, 1951), 66–67; and Regina Soria, *Elihu Vedder* (Teaneck, N.J.: Fairleigh Dickinson University Press, 1970), 214–16.

12. For some contemporary comment, see: "Mural Decoration in This Country," *American Architect and Building News* 59 (5 March 1898): 73; Russell Sturgis, "Mural Painting in American Cities," *Scribner's Magazine* 25 (January 1899): 125–27; William Walton, "Mural Painting in this Country since 1898," ibid. 40 (November 1906); Pauline King, *American Mural Painting* (Boston: Noyes and Platt, 1901); Samuel Isham, *The History of American Painting* (New York: Macmillan, 1905), 538–60; Charles H. Caffin, *The Story of American Painting* (New York: Stokes, 1907), 313–14; and Edwin Howland Blashfield, *Mural Painting in America* (New York: Scribner's, 1913). Important later works include: Richard Murray, *Art for Architecture: Washington 1895–1925* (Washington, D.C.: Smithsonian Institution Press, 1975); the same author's "The Art of Decoration," in National Collection of Fine Arts, *Perceptions and Evocations: The Art of Elihu Vedder* (Washington, D.C.: Smithsonian Institution Press, 1979), 167–239; H. Barbara Weinberg, "John La Farge: Pioneer of the American Mural Movement," in Carnegie Museum of Art, *John La Farge* (New York: Abbeville Press, 1987), 161–94; and her "The Decorative Work of John La Farge" (Ph.D., diss., Columbia University, 1972).

13. See H. Wayne Morgan, *New Muses: Art in American Culture, 1865–1920* (Norman: University of Oklahoma Press, 1978), 50–56; Michele H. Bogart, *Public Sculpture and the Civic Ideal in New York City, 1890–1930* (Chicago: University of Chicago Press, 1989), 58; and William H. Wilson, *The City Beautiful Movement* (Baltimore: Johns Hopkins University Press, 1989), esp. 75–95.

14. WHL, "The Mural Painter and His Public," *Scribner's Magazine* 41 (February 1907): 254. For similar views, see Irene Sargent, "Comments Upon Mr. Sheean's 'Mural Painting From the American Point of View,'" *Craftsman* 7 (October 1904): 28–34; Edwin H. Blashfield, "A Definition of Decorative Art," *Brochure of The Mural Painters* (New York: The Mural Painters, 1916), 7–10; and the comment of KC's friend in Herbert F. Sherwood, ed., *H. Siddons Mowbray, Mural Painter* (Stamford, Conn.: p.p., 1928), 56: "I was tired of the photographic realism of the school in which I had been educated and its blighting

dependence on the model for everything. I wanted above all things to do mural work." See also Bogart, *Public Sculpture*, 54–55.

15. See Aimée Brown Price, "The Decorative Aesthetic in the Work of Pierre Puvis de Chavannes," in *Puvis de Chavannes,* ed. Louise d'Argencourt, exh. cat. (Ottawa: National Gallery of Canada, 1977), 21–25. There is some thoughtful criticism of Puvis in Michael Andrew Marlais, "Anti-naturalism, Idealism and Symbolism in French Art Criticism, 1880–1895" (Ph.D. diss., University of Michigan, 1985), 239–49; and in Van Hook, "The Ideal Woman in American Art," 108–10.

16. KC to HFC, 4 July 1893, KC Papers, AAFAL; and KC, "Puvis de Chavannes," *Century Magazine* 51 (February 1896), 569. This essay was reprinted in John C. Van Dyke, ed., *Modern French Masters* (New York: Century, 1896), 19–30. See also KC, "Some Phases of Nineteenth Century Painting. Part III. Mural Painting in France and America," *Art World* 2 (April 1917): 13.

17. KC to John Ferguson Weir, 24 October 1904, Weir Papers, YUL; KC, "Veronese," *Scribner's Magazine* 36 (December 1904): 668–80.

18. The quotations are from KC, "The Subject in Art," *Scribner's Magazine* 50 (July 1911): 12–14, reprinted as chapter 2 of KC, *The Classic Point of View*, 36–76; and KC, "The Sherman Statue," *Nation* 76 (18 June 1903): 491–92, reprinted in KC, *Old Masters and New*, 278–85.

19. KC, "Washington Allston," *Nation* 56 (12 January 1893): 32–33 with the quotation on place; KC, "Indifference to Art," ibid. 75 (25 September 1902): 240–41; and KC to Frank Jewett Mather, Jr., 12 November 1915, Mather Papers, PUL; see also KC, "The Relation of Mural Painting to Architecture," 100–101.

20. The first quotation is from KC, "Mural Decoration," *The Scrip* 50 (January 1906): 116. The second on figure drawing is from KC, "The Making of a Mural Painting," pt. 2, pp. 1–2, and the third on drapery is from ibid., pt. 2, pp. 3–4, and the finishing process is from ibid., pt. 3, pp. 1–8, manuscript in KC Papers, AAFAL. KC stated these views many times, but see KC, "School Decoration by Art Students," *Nation* 92 (1 June 1911): 563–64. See also Murray, "Kenyon Cox and the Art of Drawing," 4–6.

21. KC, "Puvis de Chavannes," 569.

22. The basic contemporary work on the subject is Herbert Small, *The Library of Congress: Its Architecture and Decoration,* rev. ed. (New York: Norton, 1982). See also John Y. Cole, "A National Monument for a National Library: Ainsworth Rand Spofford and the New Library of Congress, 1871–1897," *Records of the Columbia Historical Society; Washington, D.C.* (Washington, D.C.: The Society, 1973), 468–507; Genevieve Rose Sheridan, "The Art and Architecture of the Library of Congress" (Ph.D. diss., George Washington University, 1977); Beverly Elson, "The Library of Congress: A Merger of American Functionalism and Cosmopolitan Eclecticism" (Ph.D. diss., University of Maryland, 1981).

23. KC to Bernard Green, 2 December 1894; and KC to General Thomas L. Casey, 1 January 1895, both in Central Services Division files, LC; JDC to KC, 19 January, with the quotation, and 30 March and 27 September all 1895, in JDC Papers, OCA, deal with the loan; KC to LEO, 19 January, 24 March, with the quotation, both 1895, in KC Papers, AAFAL.

24. KC to LEO, 24 March 1895, notes the first sketches; JDC to KC, 19 February 1896, is on Cochran and Puvis; JDC to KC, 23 March 1896, mentions the photo; all in KC Papers, AAFAL. The review is Royal Cortissoz, "Painting and Sculpture in the New Congressional Library. III. The Decorations of Mr. Kenyon Cox," *Harper's Weekly* 40 (21 March 1896): 276–78.

25. KC to Green, 18 April, 16 May 1896, Central Services Division files, LC. The first quotation is in William A. Coffin, "The Decorations in the New Congressional Library," *Century Magazine* 53 (March 1897): 695; the second about the hat is in notes of Edwin H. Blashfield, cited in Leonard N. Amico, *The Mural Decorations of Edwin H. Blashfield (1848–1936),* exh. cat. (Williamstown, Mass.: The Sterling and Francine Clark Art Institute, 1978), 15.

26. The first two quotations are from KC to LKC, [26 May 1896]; the next two from KC to LKC, [27 May 1896]; the last is from LKC to KC, 28 May 1896; all in KC Papers, AAFAL.

27. KC to LKC, [27 May 1896], KC Papers, AAFAL. KC was more fulsome later: "And in such a figure as that of the 'Adams Memorial' in Washington, his imaginative power reaches to a degree of impressiveness almost unequalled in modern art. One knows of nothing since the tombs of the Medici that fills one with the same hushed awe as this shrouded, hooded, deeply brooding figure, rigid with contemplation, still with an eternal stillness, her soul rapt from her body on some distant quest. Is she Nirvana? Is she The Peace of God? She has been given many names—her maker would give her none. Her meaning is mystery; she is the everlasting enigma." KC, "Augustus Saint Gaudens," *Atlantic Monthly* 101 (March 1908): 308.

28. KC to LKC [27 May 1896], KC Papers, AAFAL; and KC, *The Classic Point of View*, 186.

29. For contemporary comment, see: "Sculpture and Decoration for the New York Appellate Court House," *American Architect and Building News* 59 (5 March 1898): 73; James Brown Lord, "The Appellate Division Court House, New York," *Architects' and Builders' Magazine* 2 (January 1901): 127–36; Charles De Kay, "The Appellate Division Court in New York City," *Independent* 53 (August 1901): 1795–1802; and Art Commission of the City of New York, *Catalogue of the Works of Art Belonging to the City of New York* (New York: The Commission, 1909), 97. The basic history is in Gary A. Reynolds, "The Mural Decoration of the Appellate Division Courthouse," in Architectural League of New York, and the Association of the Bar of the City of New York, *Temple of Justice: The Appellate Division Courthouse*, exh. cat. (New York: The Associations, 1977), 29–30.

30. KC described the work at some length in a letter to the family, dated 1 January 1899, KC Papers, AAFAL. There is a summary description in *Temple of Justice* 51, no. 9. See also KC to Opdycke, 5 April 1898, KC Papers, AAFAL. KC's pencil drawing for the figure "The State," 15⅝" × 9", item 1923-6-2, shows his attention to the color scheme; and his pencil study of "Equity," 13⅛" × 19⅜", item 1923-6-5, shows his notes on light and shade; both in KC collection, CHM.

31. There is a color photograph of the court seated before the work in *Appellate Division of the Supreme Court of the State of New York, First Judicial Department* (New York: The Court, n.d.), 3. Overdecoration is mentioned in KC, "Mural Painting in France and America," *Art World* 2 (April 1917): 11–16. The quotation is from KC to Blashfield, 18 January 1900, Blashfield Papers, NYHS.

32. Leonard's arrival is noted in KC to LEO, 6 July 1894; the household disorder is mentioned in KC to LEO, 19 November 1894; the name "Leo Minor" is in KC to LEO, 29 December 1895; Allyn's arrival is reported in KC to LEO, 5 June 1896; Caroline's is in KC to Family, 1 January 1899; the quotation from Louise is in LKC to KC, [1903]; and that of KC on jobs is from KC to LKC, 21 October 1900; all in KC Papers, AAFAL.

33. KC to LKC, 1 June 1901, KC Papers, AAFAL; and "The Evolution of a Kenyon Cox Mural," *Pencil Points* 4 (February 1924): 30–32.

34. KC to LKC, [1903], and untitled brochure of the Citizens Savings and Trust Company, both in KC Papers, AAFAL. KC's drawing, *The Sources of Wealth*, pencil on paper, 5⅞" × 14⅛", no. 1923-6-32, is in KC collection, CHM. Gertrude Underhill, "Mural Decorations in Cleveland," *Art and Archaeology* 16 (October–November 1923): 203, illustrates the work. The sale to Gilbert, with his notes, is in a KC memo dated 29 December 1903, Gilbert Papers, LC.

35. KC to LKC, 13 November 1903, KC Papers, AAFAL.

36. Channing Seabury to Cass Gilbert, 21 June 1904, reports Gilbert's desire for KC to do the work; KC to Gilbert, telegram, 27 June 1904, accepts; both in Gilbert Papers, NYHS; Gilbert to Board of State Capitol Commissioners, 5 July 1904, Commission Papers, MiHS, notes the price and arrangements.

37. The drawings are in Box 38, a folder marked "Minnesota," KC collection, CHM; the changing design is noted in KC to Gilbert, 2 August, with the quotation on Eastern ideas; 8 August, with the quotation on restlessness; and 19 August 1904; all in Gilbert Papers, NYHS.

38. KC to Gilbert, 24 October 1904, Gilbert Papers, NYHS, notes that the cartoon is done; KC to Gilbert, 4 November 1904, Gilbert Papers, LC, reports that he is painting; KC

to August Jaccaci, 4 November 1904, Jaccaci Papers, AAA, has the elephant quotation; KC to Gilbert, 28 September, and 18 November 1904, deal with the wings; KC to Gilbert, 5 December 1904, reports the reception; and Gilbert to KC, 31 December 1904, reports the placement; all in Gilbert Papers, NYHS; KC to Gilbert, 25 January 1905, Gilbert Papers, LC, thanks him for the praise; KC to Channing Seabury, 26 November, undated December, and 8 December, all 1904, in Channing Seabury and Family Papers, MiHS, deal with finishing the canvas; and Elmer Garnsey to Frank Hanson, 14 March 1905, Board of State Capitol Commission Papers, MiHS, has the final payment for the work.

39. [No title], *American Art News* 3 (17 December 1904): [1]; Rena Neumann Coen, *Painting and Sculpture in Minnesota, 1820–1914* (Minneapolis: University of Minnesota Press, 1976), 98–99; KC to Gilbert, 6 May 1905, Gilbert Papers, LC; KC, "The New State Capitol of Minnesota," *Architectural Record* 18 (August 1905): 95–113; Neil B. Thompson, *Minnesota's State Capitol* (St. Paul: Minnesota Historical Society, 1974), 65–72.

40. KC to LKC, 21 April 1906, KC Papers, AAFAL.

41. See Peter A. Day, "Recollections of the Old Capitol and the New," *Annals of Iowa* 7 (July 1905): 81–101. The quotation is from an untitled memorandum, with the contract, in Capitol Commission Records, Iowa State Historical Department.

42. *Sioux City Journal,* 2 June 1907; State of Iowa, *The Capitol of Iowa* (Des Moines: State Printer, 1954), 18.

43. "Among the Artists," *American Art News* 4 (4 November 1905): [3]; and KC to HFC, 1 March 1906, KC Papers, AAFAL.

44. KC to LKC, 16 April 1906, ibid.

45. KC to F. D. Harsh, 7 June 1906, Capitol Commission Records, ISHD; and KC to Saint Gaudens, 10 September 1906, Saint Gaudens Papers, DCL. See also Minna C. Smith, "The Work of Kenyon Cox," *International Studio* 32 (July 1907): iii–xiii; and Gladys E. Hamlin, "Mural Painting in Iowa," *Iowa Journal of History and Politics* 37 (July 1939): 244–50.

46. KC to Gilbert, 2 April, accepts the commission; the contract is dated 28 April; KC to Gilbert, 20 September, reports on the legend; all 1906, in Gilbert Papers, NYHS. The Barrymore quotation is in her *Memories* (New York: Harper Bros., 1955), 154. Progress on the work is noted in KC to Gilbert, 15 September, 20, 31 October 1906, all in Gilbert Papers, NYHS, and in "Among the Artists," *American Art News* 5 (3 November 1906): [3]. The Barrymore controversy begins in Leslie D. Ward to Gilbert, 5 November enclosing the clipping of the same date; KC's response, including the story of the interview and the remark on sitters, is in KC to Gilbert, 9 November; alterations are noted in KC to Gilbert, 9, 11, 13 November, 2 December, with the quotation about newspaper chatter, and 10 December, with Gilbert's note of his visit; all 1906, in Gilbert Papers, NYHS. The newspaper quotation is in *Newark Evening News,* 20 November 1906, p. 4, col. 2.

47. KC to Gilbert, 27 December 1906, Gilbert Papers, NYHS, notes the exhibit and has the final quotation about rubbish; the exchange between them is in Gilbert to KC, 29, 31 December 1906, KC Papers, AAFAL; and KC to Gilbert, 3 January 1907, Gilbert Papers, LC; the installation is mentioned in KC to Gilbert, 31 December 1906, Gilbert Papers, NYHS.

48. Wyoming Historical and Geological Society, *Luzerne County Court House* (Wilkes-Barre, Pa.: The Society, 1986), 9; KC to August Jaccaci, 31 July 1908, Jaccaci Papers, AAA; "The Luzerne County Court House," *American Architect* 96 (15 September 1909): 97–104.

49. KC, "The Making of a Mural Painting," 1:3–4.

50. KC reports the final design in KC to August Jaccaci, 24 November 1908, Jaccaci Papers, AAA. The progress of the work is in "With the Artists," *American Art News* 7 (14 November 1908): 3; "In the Art Schools," ibid. 7 (20 February 1909): 2; "Among the Artists," ibid. 7 (10 April 1909): 3; "Among the Artists," ibid. 7 (24 April 1909): 3; "Drawings by Kenyon Cox," ibid. 8 (4 December 1909): 3; "Architects' League Dinner," ibid. 8 (5 February 1910): 3. His liking for the work is in KC to Mrs. Lew F. Porter, 22 March 1914, typed copy, Jersey City Museum.

51. Cox insured the work for thirty-five hundred dollars, which was probably the fee, as noted in KC to W. S. Budworth and Sons, 9 January 1910; the quotation is from his description of the work in KC to Cornelia B. Sage, 27 January 1910; he noted its installation

date in KC to Sage, 6 February 1910; all in KC file, AKG; the "bully" quotation is from KC to LKC, 5 June 1911, KC Papers, AAFAL; the building's history is in Helen B. Lybarger, *Old Federal Building* (Cleveland: Ben Franklin Press, 1985), [11–12].

52. DC to KC, 6 November 1908, KC Papers, AAFAL; progress on the work is noted in "Among the Artists," *American Art News* 8 (20 November 1909): 3; reports of the dedication are in *Winona Daily Republican-Herald,* 29 April 1910, which has the quotation on p. 7; KC mentioned his satisfaction with the work in KC to Mrs. Lew F. Porter, 22 March 1914, typed copy, Jersey City Museum.

53. Millet to KC, 1 February 1910 outlines the work, and Millet to KC, 9 February [1910], settles it, with the quotation; the cameo notation is in KC to HFC, 14 June 1910; all in KC Papers, AAFAL. The basic story is in *Heroes in the Fight for Beauty: The Muralists of the Hudson County Courthouse* (Jersey City: Jersey City Museum, 1986), esp. 16–18, 85.

54. KC to Jaccaci, 16 September 1911, Jaccaci Papers, AAA. The contract is dated 23 January 1912, in the Capitol Commission Papers, SHSW.

55. The descriptions of the setting and the quotations from KC about the figures, are from Stan Cravens, *Wisconsin State Capitol Guide and History,* 31st ed. (Madison: Wisconsin Department of Administration, n.d.), 15–17; this is taken from KC's handwritten description of the works in KC to Porter, 12 February 1914, Capitol Commission Papers, SHSW; the quotation about drawing and mosaics is from KC to Mrs. Lew F. Porter, 22 March 1914, typed copy, Jersey City Museum.

56. KC to Porter, 14 July 1912, Capitol Commission Papers, SHSW; and KC to Opdycke, 25 December 1912, KC Papers, AAFAL.

57. KC to Porter, 21 November 1913, and KC to George B. Post and Sons, 5 August 1914, note choosing the company; George B. Post and Sons to Porter, 3 August 1914, has the quotation about Barnes and artists; KC to Porter, 12 August 1914, is on the bid; KC to Porter, 8 December 1914, has KC's quotation on Barnes; all in Capitol Commission Papers, SHSW. There is some background information in Henry A. La Farge, "Painting With Colored Light: The Stained Glass of John La Farge," in Carnegie Museum of Art, *John La Farge,* 210.

58. KC to Porter, 24 May, 19 July, with the quotation; and 20 October 1913; Capitol Commission Papers, SHSW.

59. KC to LKC, 19 May 1914, KC Papers, AAFAL, describes the work on site; the quotation about placement is from KC to Porter, 8 May 1914; George B. Post and Sons to Porter, 3 August 1914, KC to George B. Post and Sons, 5 August 1914, and Porter to KC, 24 October 1914, all deal with cost overruns and changes; the quotation about subcontractors is from KC to Porter, 20 October 1914; KC's satisfaction with the work is from KC to Porter, 26 October 1914; Post's views are reported in KC to George B. Post and Sons, typed copy, 5 August 1914; Porter's quotation is from Porter to KC, 24 October 1914; all in Capitol Commission Papers, SHSW.

60. KC to Porter, 30 October 1913, has his suggestion; Porter to KC, 11 November 1913, has the response; KC to Porter, 5 December 1911, is a reminder; Porter to KC, 9 December 1913, has the quotation on Alexander's possible withdrawal; KC to Porter, 11 December 1913, has the report of talking to Alexander; all in Capitol Commission Papers, SHSW; KC to Blashfield, 19 December 1913, Blashfield Papers, NYHS, the day of the meeting, shows his anxiety.

61. KC to Edward Burlingame, 14 May 1914, Scribner Papers, PUL, notes his trip to Madison; KC to LKC, 19 May 1914, KC Papers, AAFAL, reports he has checked the chamber; the room is illustrated in Cravens, *The Wisconsin State Capitol,* 27–28; KC to LKC, 21 May 1914, KC Papers, AAFAL, reports on the commission's acceptance of the subject; the contract is enclosed with Porter to KC, 14 August 1914, and is in Capitol Building Contracts, Series 837; all in Capital Commission Papers, SHSW.

62. KC to Porter, 2 June 1914, notes Croton-on-Hudson; KC to Porter, 2 August 1914, has the quote on Europe; KC to Porter, 3, 13 December 1914, reports his progress; KC to Porter, 17 February 1915, has the quotation about Blashfield; KC to Porter, 24 May 1915, has his remarks on the hard work, and the needed time extension; KC to Porter, 22 July 1915, mentions photographs; all in Capitol Commission Papers, SHSW. KC to Robert Underwood

Johnson, 24 May 1915, KC file, AAIAL, mentions his frantic workpace. There are studies for the project in Box 1197, a folder mislabeled "Wisconsin State Capitol, Supreme Court Room," Cox collection, CHM.

63. KC to Porter, 4 October 1915, Capitol Commission Papers, SHSW; and KC to LKC, 5 October 1915, KC Papers, AAFAL. KC to Porter, 17 October 1915, notes the exhibition and the shipment to Madison; Porter to KC, 29 October 1915, has his praise, and KC to Porter, 1 November 1915, his response; all in Capitol Commission Papers, SHSW.

64. Oberlin College, *Annual Reports . . . for 1914–1915* (Oberlin, Ohio: The College, 1915), 13–16.

65. DC to KC, 24 December 1913, and 7 January 1914, with the quotation; 28 January 1914, on the design; all in KC Papers, AAFAL. The design is on Roll 3060, frames 89–90, KC Papers, AAA. See also Henry C. King, "The Administration Building," *Oberlin Alumni Magazine* 11 (March 1915): 219; and Paul B. Arnold to W. E. Biggelstone, memorandum dated 12 April 1976, KC alumni file, OCA.

66. DC to KC, 28 January 1914; KC to LKC, 19 May 1914; both in KC Papers, AAFAL.

67. KC described the works in "Remarks of Mr. Kenyon Cox at the Dedication of the Administration Building of Oberlin College," 2–3, with the quotation, KC Papers, AAFAL; and in KC to W. F. Bohn, presidential assistant, 12 February 1915, Presidential Assistants file, OCA; drawings of the works are in Box 38, a folder marked "Oberlin," KC collection, CHM; the review is in *New York Times*, 8 November 1914, sec. vii, p. 3.

68. DC to KC, 29 December 1914, KC Papers, AAFAL. KC on the painters is from KC to George M. Jones, 22 January 1915, Henry Churchill King Papers, OCA; King to KC, 28 January 1915, ibid., invites him to the ceremonies. KC to LKC, 9 February 1915, recounts the museum tour; and Hope Cox to KC, 3 June 1915, expresses her satisfaction with a photograph of the work dedicated to her mother; both in KC Papers, AAFAL.

69. KC to Hale, 28 July 1914, Hale Papers, AAA.

VI. AN ESTABLISHED ARTIST

1. JDC to KC, 7 April 1892; and DC to LKC, 27 January 1916; both in KC Papers, AAFAL.

2. JDC to KC, 20 July 1897, KC Papers, AAFAL; Cox, *Building an American Industry*, 162–66; Schmiel, "The Career of Jacob Dolson Cox," 466–67.

3. HFC to KC, 27 October 1908, KC Papers, AAFAL; questionnaire in HFC alumni file, OCA.

4. Cox, *Building an American Industry*, 146–47, 166–67; DC to KC, 20 November 1907, and 24 December 1913, with the quotation; both in KC Papers, AAFAL.

5. See Hope Cox Pope to KC, Munich, 10 April 1911; and DC to KC, 24 December 1913, with the quotation; both in KC Papers, AAFAL.

6. DC to KC, 20 November 1907, KC Papers, AAFAL; and KC to Wilson, 18 May 1909, Wilson Papers, LC.

7. LKC to KC, 14, 27 June 1910, KC Papers, AAFAL.

8. Caroline Cox Lansing to author, 8 October 1983, and 12 March 1984; Ronan, "Louise King Cox," 98 n. 89; Katharine Smith, KC's great-niece, to author, 8 October 1988.

9. KC to LKC, 1 June 1901, has the quotation, and KC to LKC, 26 May 1904, mentions illustration work; both in KC Papers, AAFAL. See also KC to August Jaccaci, 12 April 1904, Jaccaci Papers, AAA; and KC to Edward Burlingame, 11 June, 28 August 1914, Scribner Archive, PUL.

10. DC to KC, 16 October 1906, with canceled receipt, also enclosed in DC to KC, 22 November 1907; DC to KC, 2 February 1907, with the quotation; and 6 February 1907, enclosing the $6,500 down payment; all in KC Papers, AAFAL. See also Ronan, "Louise King Cox," 31.

11. KC to LEO, 8 November 1907, KC Papers, AAFAL; AC interview with author, 11 March 1982; KC to August Jaccaci, 12 April 1908, Jaccaci Papers, AAA; KC to President, National Society of Fine Arts, 12 April 1909, Miscellaneous Manuscripts, Roll 3134, AAA;

NOTES TO PAGES 184–91

and John Tauranac and Christopher Little, *Elegant New York* (New York: Abbeville Press, 1985), 170–71, for a picture of the building.

12. AC told Richard Murray of the National Museum of American Art that his father had suffered a mild stroke, and had painted for a time with his left hand. The first quotation is from HFC to KC, 1 April 1908; Hope's advice is in Hope Cox to KC, 12 May 1908; both in KC Papers, AAFAL; KC reported on his progress to August Jaccaci in letters of 12 April, 24 June, and 24 November 1908, in Jaccaci Papers, AAA; he noted declining speaking engagements in KC to Henry C. King, 27 April 1908, King Papers, OCA; and slowness in answering correspondence in KC to Robert Underwood Johnson, 24 October and 14 November 1908, KC file, AAIAL; the last quotation is from KC to LEO, 22 December 1908, KC Papers, AAFAL.

13. KC to Senator John Sherman, 3 September 1890, Sherman Papers, LC; KC to LEO, 5 August 1894, KC Papers, AAFAL.

14. French, *Memories of a Sculptor's Wife*, 181–83, is a good contemporary description of the area. The basic coverage is Shirley Good Ramsay, *A Circle of Friends: Art Colonies of Cornish and Dublin* (Durham: University of New Hampshire Art Galleries, 1985), and Deborah Elizabeth Van Buren, "The Cornish Colony: Expressions of Attachment to Place, 1885–1915" (Ph.D. diss., George Washington University, 1987). The quotation is from *New York Tribune*, 11 August 1907.

15. LKC to Stephen Tracy, 20 January 1896, Virginia Colby collection, Cornish; KC to Tracy, 29 January 1896, cited in Van Buren, "Cornish Colony," 57 n. 7; Ramsay, *A Circle of Friends*, 81; AC to Virginia Colby, 4 September 1982, Colby collection; JDC to KC, 11 August 1897 and 17 September [1897?], KC Papers, AAFAL. See also William H. Child, *History of the Town of Cornish, New Hampshire, with Genealogical Record, 1763–1910*, 2 vols. (Concord, N.H.: Rumford Press, 1910), 1:225–26; and Henry Mason Wade, *A Brief History of Cornish, 1763–1974* (Hanover, N.H.: University Press of New England, 1976), 56–57.

16. Tharp, *Saint Gaudens and the Gilded Era*, 312; Ramsay, *A Circle of Friends*, 70–72; St. Gaudens, *The American Artist and His Times*, 156, with the quotation.

17. LKC to KC, [1906], KC Papers, AAFAL; Ronan, "Louise King Cox," 29; entry of 9 September 1903, Lucia Fairchild Fuller Diary, Colby collection; St. Gaudens, *The American Artist and His Times*, 156; KC to Churchill, 26 August 1900, Churchill Papers, DCL.

18. KC to Saint Gaudens, 2 August 1903, and 3 February 1904, with the quotation, Saint Gaudens Papers, DCL; and Saint-Gaudens, *Reminiscences*, 2:93–94.

19. See KC, "An Out-Door Masque in New England," *Nation* 80 (29 June 1905): 519–20. There is a good description in Tharp, *Saint Gaudens and the Gilded Era*, 335–50. For comments on the meanings in such efforts, see Van Buren, "Cornish Colony," 45; and Trudy Baltz, "Pageantry and Mural Painting: Community Rituals in Allegorical Form," *Winterthur Portfolio* 15 (Autumn 1980): 211–28.

20. The preface for *Artist and Public* (New York: Scribner's, 1914) is signed in Croton-on-Hudson. He worked there on the Wisconsin capitol sketches, as reported in KC to Lew F. Porter, 2 June 1914, Capitol Commission Papers, SHSW. The place is described in Alexander Calder, *Calder: An Autobiography with Pictures* (New York: Pantheon, 1969), 28–30. KC to AC, 19 August 1917 notes his drivers; and the quotation is from KC to AC, 22 July 1918; both KC Papers, AAFAL.

21. KC to Opdycke, 10 March 1902, KC Papers, AAFAL. "With the artists," *American Art News* 7 (14 November 1908): 3, mentions a portrait of one Mrs. Sales, whose husband had donated a library to Pawtucket, R.I.

22. "Annual Society Display," *American Art News* 3 (8 April 1905): [1], for Carlsen; [No title], ibid. 4 (15 September 1906): [1], for McKim; "In and Out the Studios," ibid. 9 (31 December 1910): 3, for La Farge.

23. Parrish to KC, 15 May with the quotation, and 16 November 1905; both in KC Papers, AAFAL.

24. KC to Gilbert, 14 November 1906, 17, 22 January, 27 February 1907; all in Gilbert Papers, LC.

25. Saint Gaudens, *Reminiscences*, 2:247–48 mentions the fire. KC to Robert Underwood Johnson, 26 January 1915, KC file, AAIAL, notes the photograph. Jaccaci to Reginald

Cleveland Coxe, 6 December 1907, refers to the conversation with KC; Jaccaci to Coxe, 9 December 1907, mentions the fee; KC to Jaccaci, 10 January 1908, has the quotations on his progress with the work and Orchardson; KC to Jaccaci, 12 April 1908, has the quotation on the finished painting; all in Jaccaci Papers, AAA.

26. KC's friend Will Low had some interesting observations on glass in "Old Glass in New Windows," *Scribner's Magazine* 4 (November 1888): 675–88. Candace Wheeler, "Decorative Art," *Architectural Record* 4 (April–June 1895): 409–13, is a good contemporary summary of the movement. A good survey is La Farge, "Painting with Colored Light," 195–223.

27. See KC, "The Work of Burne-Jones," *Nation* 55 (24 November 1891): 395–96, reviewing Malcolm Bell, *Edward Burne-Jones* (New York: Macmillan, 1892); S. W. W., "Stained-Glass Windows," *Nation* 55 (8 December 1892): 431, which takes issue with KC, and his reply, "Stained-Glass Again," ibid. 55 (15 December 1892): 448–49; and KC, "Holiday's Stained Glass," ibid. 64 (20 May 1897): 382–83, reviewing Henry Holiday, *Stained Glass as an Art* (New York: Macmillan, 1896), with the quotation.

28. The design and making of the window are noted in detail in "Memorial Window for General J. D. Cox," *Oberlin Review* 28 (11 April 1901): 442–43, from information which KC furnished. Some of his preparatory drawings and a color sketch are in Box 38, a folder marked "Stained Glass," KC collection, CHM.

29. The first quotation is from Ben Foster to KC, 14 March 1901; Wendell Garrison to KC, 18 March 1901; Weir to KC, 15 March 1901, with the quotation; and KC to LKC, 1 June 1901, with the report of dinner with Weir; all in KC Papers, AAFAL. Weir had done a stained-glass window in memory of his first wife and small son in 1897–98; see Young, *Life and Letters of J. Alden Weir,* 194–95.

30. KC to LKC, 6 April 1900 [1901], has his report on events; DC to LKC, 17 March 1919, recalls the reception story; both in KC Papers, AAFAL. KC, of course, received his higher education at the Ecole des Beaux-Arts.

31. KC to HFC, [1901], KC Papers, AAFAL. There is a sketch of a window dealing with the Annunciation, no. 1923-6-69, KC collection, CHM. The Pittsburgh window was titled *Hope and Memory.* On the chapel, see Geoffrey Blodgett, "The Completion of Finney Chapel," *Oberlin Alumni Magazine* 78 (Autumn 1982): 1–3.

32. The works are illustrated in place in Tauranac and Little, *Elegant New York,* 186–91. KC wrote a detailed and fascinating account of making the windows in "A Novelty in Design for Leaded Glass," *Architectural Record* 26 (December 1909): 453–54.

33. William Walton, "An Alliance of Architecture and Sculpture," *Outlook* 92 (26 June 1909): 463–75; "The Statues and Their Meaning," [Brooklyn] *Museum News* 6 (December 1910): unpaginated; Bogart, *Public Sculpture,* 171–76.

34. Bogart, *Public Sculpture,* 170–71; and Daniel Chester French to Edward C. Potter, 24 April 1907, French Family Papers, LC.

35. On Dubois, see KC to HFC, 28 May 1878, and 12 March 1879, and to JDC, 1 May 1879, in KC, *Letters,* 83, 150, 155–56; and also KC, "Michelangelo"; and KC, "Rodin," *Architectural Record* 18 (November 1905): 327–46.

36. KC to Jaccaci, 19 May 1907, for the first quotation, and KC to Jaccaci, 3 July 1907, for the second; both in Jaccaci Papers, AAA; and HFC to KC, 17 July 1907, KC Papers, AAFAL.

37. [No title], *American Art News* 5 (15 June 1907): 1, for the first quotation; and KC to Jaccaci, 4 September 1907, Jaccaci Papers, AAA.

38. "In the Art Schools," *American Art News* 6 (14 March 1908): 2; unsigned carbon memorandum to Michael J. Kennedy, 22 July 1909, which notes approval of KC's statue on 9 June 1908, Art Commission of the City of New York archives.

39. MacVeagh to KC, 10 October 1912, KC Papers, AAFAL.

40. KC described his original efforts and progress in KC to Will Cochran, 2 February 1913; Allyn's posing is noted in AC to Mr. Hassler, 26 July 1981, both in AC Papers, AAA.

41. The *New York Times,* 5 December 1912, p. 1, has a brief story on acceptance of the preliminary design. The quotations from MacVeagh are in MacVeagh to KC, 1 February 1913; KC to LEO, 25 December 1912, notes the hard work, both in KC Papers, AAFAL. KC to Cochran, 2 February 1913, AC Papers, AAA, has those quotations.

42. DC to KC, 7 February 1913, KC Papers, AAFAL.

43. Clark, *History of the National Academy of Design*, 108–9, 251; Coffin to KC, 28 August 1903, KC Papers, AAFAL; the book is at the academy library, New York City; Robert Underwood Johnson to LKC, 11 April 1919, KC file, AAIAL; the muralist and Fine Arts Society lists are in Roll 3976, frames 1004, 1089, AC Papers, AAA.

44. These honors are catalogued in KC to Mr. d'Hervilly, 14 June 1911, KC file, MMA; the quotation is from KC to Will Cochran, 2 February 1913, AC Papers, AAA.

45. KC to LEO, 24 December 1906, KC Papers, AAFAL; KC to Blashfield, 24 February 1909, Blashfield Papers, NYHS.

46. On Yale, see KC to HFC, 14 June 1910, KC Papers, AAFAL; and KC to Will Cochran, 2 February 1913, with the quotation, AC Papers, AAA; for Oberlin, see King to KC, 8 June 1908, KC to King, 10 June 1908, and King to KC, 31 May 1912, and KC to King, 4 June 1912; all in King Papers, OCA; for Dartmouth, see Ernest Fox Nichols to KC, 16 April, KC to Nichols, 4 May, Nichols to KC, 5, 25 May, 4 June, with citation text enclosed, all 1915, in Dartmouth College archives, DCL.

VII. CLASSICS AND MODERNS

1. I have discussed KC's formal thinking in much greater detail in *Keepers of Culture: The Art-Thought of Kenyon Cox, Royal Cortissoz, and Frank Jewett Mather, Jr.* (Kent, Ohio: Kent State University Press, 1989), esp. 1–10, 39–51. The quotation is in KC to James B. Carrington, 31 March 1889, Carrington Papers, BL.

2. KC, "Raymond's Theory of Art," *Nation* 58 (24 May 1894): 393–94, reviewing George Lansing Raymond, *Art In Theory: An Introduction to the Study of Comparative Aesthetics* (New York: Putnam's, 1894), with the quotation; and KC, "New Books on Art and Artists," ibid. 80 (9 March 1905): 194–95, for the comparisons of artists.

3. The quotations on modern life and on Millet are from KC, "The Art of Millet," *Scribner's Magazine* 43 (March 1908): 332; that on Corot is from KC, "More Books on Art," *Nation* 75 (18 December 1902): 483–84.

4. KC, "Realism and Idealism," *Nation* 42 (7 January 1886): 10–11; KC, "Symonds's Art Essays," ibid. 58 (1 February 1894): 87–88, reviewing John Addington Symonds, *Essays Speculative and Suggestive* (New York: Scribner's, 1893), with the quotation on realism and idealism; KC, "Stillman's Essays," ibid. 66 (13 January 1898): 31–32, reviewing W. J. Stillman, *The Old Rome and the New* (Boston: Houghton Mifflin, 1897), with the quotation on harmony.

5. KC, "Michel's Rubens," *Nation* 69 (14 December 1899): 448–49, reviewing Emile Michel, *Rubens: His Life, His Work, and His Time*, 2 vols. (New York: Scribner's, 1899).

6. KC to Johnson, 20 March 1897, Century Collection, NYPL, for both quotations; KC to Wendell Phillips, 1 June 1898, HL, for fuzziness; KC to Jaccaci, 18 July 1903, and Jaccaci to KC, 22 July 1903, Jaccaci Papers, AAA, referring to August Jaccaci and John La Farge, *Concerning Noteworthy Paintings in American Private Collections* (New York: Jaccaci, 1909); KC to LKC, 19 November 1913, KC Papers, AAFAL.

7. KC to Robert Underwood Johnson, 3 November 1910, Century Collection, NYPL.

8. National Collection of Fine Arts, *Academy*, 118–19; KC to Will Cochran, 2 February 1913, AC Papers, AAA, on Columbia; undated typescript titled "The Venetians," marked for slides; William A. Goodyear to KC, 5 June 1906; both in KC Papers, AAFAL. The academy apparently did pay a small stipend during the Columbia arrangement; Marion E. Jemmot, Secretary of Columbia University, to author, 22 March 1988.

9. KC to August Jaccaci, 1 September 1911, has the quotation on the godsend; William M. R. French to KC, undated, and 8 March 1911, Art Institute of Chicago archives, has the terms; and Harriet Monroe, "Fine Exhibit of Small Bronzes Attracts Art Lovers," *Chicago Tribune*, 2 April 1911, sec. 2, pt. 2, p. 7, has the times.

10. KC to WHL, 3 May 1911, Low Papers, AIHA; KC to Moser, 10 April 1911, Moser Papers, AAA; KC, *The Classic Point of View*, v–vi. The two most important sources for the book are probably KC, "Symonds's Art Essays," and KC, "Raymond's Theory of Art." AC to Caroline Cox, 3 August 1980, AC Papers, AAA, notes his work on the project; the published

articles were: "The Classic Spirit in Painting," *Scribner's Magazine* 49 (May 1911): 542–54; "The Subject in Art," ibid. 50 (July 1911): 1–13; and "Design," ibid. 50 (September 1911): 335–48; KC to Charles C. Curran, 13 May 1911, KC Papers, AAFAL, notes that the book was already printed.

11. Unsigned to KC, 16, 21 March 1911, on the club, Art Institute of Chicago archives; KC, "An Example from Chicago," *Nation* 92 (4 May 1911): 455.

12. KC to LHC, 22 April 1911, KC Papers, AAFAL, has the quotation on Hutchinson. KC, "Art: An Example from Chicago," *Nation* 92 (4 May 1911): 455–56, treats the art community, and KC, "Collections of the Art Institute of Chicago," ibid. 92 (15 June 1911): 610–12, covers that topic. KC to James B. Carrington, 20 March 1911, Carrington Papers, BL, and KC to WHL, 29 April 1911, Low Papers, AIAH, both deal with his favorable impressions of Chicago. There is additional information in Horowitz, *Culture and the City,* 86, 199–200.

13. KC, *The Classic Point of View,* 3–5, 34, 80–81, 123, 231–32.

14. KC to WHL, 29 April 1911, Low Papers, AIHA; KC to LKC, 15 April, and 3 May 1911, with the quotation, both in KC Papers, AAFAL.

15. The modernist poet Harriet Monroe noted KC's interest in American art in an interview with Joaquin Sorolla, a Spanish painter also visiting Chicago, who agreed with KC; see "Sorolla Admits America's Supremacy in Art," *Chicago Tribune,* 16 April 1911, sec. 9, p. 7. KC's hope for American art is in a letter to James B. Carrington, 31 March 1889, Carrington Papers, BL. Coffin's remark is in his "Kenyon Cox," 337. KC and Coffin, "Society of American Artists," *Nation* 50 (8 May 1890): 380, has the comparison with France. KC's view of European art about 1900 is in his "Picture-Books," ibid. 71 (29 November 1900): 428–29, reviewing Victor Champier, *Exposition Universelle, 1900. Les Chefs-d'oeuvre* (Philadelphia: Barrie, 1900), and *Royal Academy Pictures 1900* (London: Cassell, 1900), and KC, "Books on Painting," *Nation* 73 (7 November 1901): 363–64, reviewing Walton, Saglio, and Champier [*sic*], *Chefs d'oeuvres of the Exposition Universelle,* pts. 8–15 (Philadelphia: Barrie, 1901). KC, "American Art at Buffalo," *Nation* 73 (15 August 1901): 127–28, dissects American art at the Pan-American Exposition. KC, "Art: The Carnegie Institute Exhibition," ibid. 84 (18 April 1907): 370, notes decadence. KC, "The Winter Academy," ibid. 85 (26 December 1907): 595–96, has the quotation on attainment. KC, "The Pennsylvania Academy Exhibition," ibid. 86 (23 January 1908): 88–89, notes the level of quality. The Homer quotation is from KC, "The Winter Academy," ibid. 83 (17 December 1906): 565, and see also KC, *Winslow Homer* (New York: privately printed, 1914), and KC, "Some Phases of Nineteenth Century Painting," *Art World* 1 (February 1917): 315–20. On Henri, see KC, "The Winter Academy," *Nation* 83 (17 December 1906): 565. KC, "The American School of Painting," *Scribner's Magazine* 50 (December 1911): 767, has the quotation on old fashions. KC, "American Art and the Metropolitan Museum," *Century Magazine* 83 (December 1911): 204–13, is another survey, with a plea for more museum purchases of current American works. The last quotation is from KC to Cochran, 2 February 1913, AC Papers, AAA.

16. Edward Marshall, "Our Art Has a Terrible Attack of Ugliness," *New York Times,* 30 April 1911, sec. 5, p. 4; KC to LKC, 3 May, and KC to Curran, 13 May 1911; both in KC Papers, AAFAL.

17. The first quotation is from KC to LKC, 29 March 1911, KC Papers, AAFAL; the last two are from KC to WHL, 3 May 1911, Low Papers, AIHA.

18. Art Institute of Chicago, *Exhibition of Paintings and Drawings by Kenyon Cox* (Chicago: The Institute, 1911). There is a photograph of the exhibition in place, numbered 1959. 69.137, in Box 39, the folder marked "Non-mural Painted Works," KC collection, CHM.

19. LKC to KC, 12, 13 May 1911, KC Papers, AAFAL; Caroline Cox to AC, 3 August, 30 November 1980, AC Papers, AAA.

20. KC to LKC, 29 March, 31 May 1911, deal with the drawings purchase; KC to LKC, 16, 26 April 1911, mention lectures; KC to LKC, 15 April 1911, has his quotation on Sorolla; KC to LKC, 31 May 1911, has his quotation on pulling through; KC to LKC, 15 June 1911, mentions borrowing from DC; all in KC Papers, AAFAL. KC to Low, 3 May 1911, Low Papers, AIHA has the quotation on money. The Sorolla exhibition was from mid-February to mid-March and attracted about one hundred thousand visitors. It then moved to

St. Louis for a month. When Sorolla left for Europe in mid-May, he had earned some eighty thousand dollars in sales and commissions, many of them portraits. See San Diego Museum of Art, *The Painter: Joaquin Sorolla y Bastida*, exh. cat. (San Diego: The Museum, 1989), 247.

21. KC to LKC, 16, 26 April, 3, 22 May 1911, all in KC Papers, AAFAL.

22. Moser to KC, 27 March [sent 2 April] 1911, with clipping dated 18 March, and KC to Moser, 10 April 1911, Moser Papers, AAA. The notice is in *New York Times,* 15 March 1911, p. 13.

23. KC to LKC, 29 May 1911, KC Papers, AAFAL, notes his last duties. On the visit to HFC, see Hope Cox to KC, 10 April 1911; KC to LKC, 31 May, 5 June 1911; and KC to LEO, 18 June 1911; all in KC Papers, AAFAL.

24. KC to Blashfield, 16 June 1911, Blashfield Papers, NYHS; KC to August Jaccaci, 1 September 1911, Jaccaci Papers, AAA.

25. "Modern Art, Its Malady and Cure," *New York Times Book Review,* 1 October 1911, sec. 6, p. 588; Hamilton Wright Mabie, "Some Recent Books," *Outlook* 99 (25 November 1910): 783-84; Mather to KC, 15 January 1912; KC to LKC, 20 April 1912; both in KC Papers, AAFAL.

26. Will Cochran to KC, 24 June 1911, KC Papers, AAFAL; KC to Will Cochran, 2 February 1913, AC Papers, AAA.

27. KC, "The Illusion of Progress," *Century Magazine* 86 (May 1913): 39-43; KC to Johnson, 16 December 1912, Century Collection, NYPL.

28. The basic study, with a catalogue of the works, is Milton Brown, *The Story of the Armory Show* (New York: New York Graphic Society, 1963); and Royal Cortissoz, "Kenyon Cox," in his *American Artists* (New York: Scribner's, 1923), 87; and KC, "The Modern Spirit in Art," *Harper's Weekly* 57 (15 March 1913): 10.

29. "Cubists and Futurists Are Making Insanity Pay," *New York Times,* 16 March 1913, sec. 6, p. 1.

30. Gilbert to KC, 16 March 1913; Tarbell to KC, 19 March 1913; Cortissoz to KC, [22 March 1913?]; all in KC Papers, AAFAL.

31. KC to Blashfield, 19 December 1913, Blashfield Papers, NYHS.

32. KC, "Artist and Public," *Scribner's Magazine* 55 (April 1914): 512-20.

33. Burlingame to KC, 30 December 1913; KC to Burlingame, 1 January and 11 May 1914; all in Scribner Archives, PUL.

34. KC, "Indifference to Art," *Nation* 75 (25 September 1902): 241; KC, "Rembrandt," *Architectural Record* 20 (December 1906): 439; WHL, *A Painter's Progress* 58. WHL later reported a variant of the remark. "No, after five or six years of experience, I am convinced of what I had long suspected. Our people can be crammed with knowledge, can be educated to some appreciation of literature, but can, as I love to quote my dear departed Kenyon Cox, get along 'quite comfortably' without art." WHL to Royal Cortissoz, 5 August 1920, Cortissoz Papers, BL.

VIII. LAST YEARS

1. KC to LEO, 18 May 1914, KC Papers, AAFAL; KC to Hale, 7 March [1914], on the first drawings; KC to Hale, 28 July 1914, with the quotation on working; KC to Hale, 12, 25 August 1914, settling the details; all in Hale Papers, AAA. The review is in the *Boston Evening Transcript,* 18 December 1914, p. 4. See also *Exhibition at Saint Botolph's Club, Boston, Paintings, Decorations and Studies by Kenyon Cox. Monday, December 21, 1914 to Friday, January 1, 1915* (Boston: The Club, 1914).

2. There is a brochure for the war committee in a volume labeled "World War Correspondence," including KC's name, in Blashfield Papers, NYHS; and KC to Mather, 12 November 1915, Mather Papers, PUL.

3. The poster's antecedents are discussed in Marianna Doezema, "Kenyon Cox and American Figure Painting," *Georgia Museum of Art Bulletin* 10 (Spring 1985): 1-32. Item 1923-6-62, and a study titled "Columbia Appeals to the Sword," in Box 1197, Folder 5, are about the cover for *McClure's Magazine* 11 (July 1898); a copy of the finished poster is in Box 43,

item 1959-69-389; all in KC collection, CHM. The poster is reproduced in Peter Stanley, *What Did You Do in the War, Daddy? A Visual History of Propaganda Posters* (Melbourne: Oxford, 1983), 57, and in Walton Rawls, *Wake Up, America! World War I and the American Poster* (New York: Abbeville, 1988), 22, and 150, 153. The quotations are in KC to Ruckstuhl, 11 May 1917, KC file, AAIAL; KC to LKC, 30 May 1917; and KC to AC, 7 June 1918; both in KC Papers, AAFAL.

4. Information on Leonard Cox is scarce, but there is a basic obituary in the *New York Times,* 19 August 1963, p. 25, col. 5. The first quotation is from KC to AC, [?] October 1916, and the long quotations are from KC to AC, 16 April 1918, both in KC Papers, AAFAL.

5. Forbes Watson, "Art Notes," *New York Evening Post,* 16 October 1915, p. 7; KC to Mather, 12 November 1915, Mather Papers, PUL.

6. KC to Robert Underwood Johnson, 6 July 1916, KC file, AAIAL, reports beginning the picture; Box 38, the folder titled "Studies for *Tradition,*" KC collection, CHM, has the sketches; KC to Robinson, 17 September 1916, KC file, MMA, has those remarks; DC to KC, 12 December 1916, KC Papers, AAFAL, has his comments; Ruckstuhl is quoted in KC to AC, 5 January 1917, ibid; the *New York Times,* 16 December 1916, has the review; KC's remarks to WHL are in a letter of 12 December 1916, Low Papers, AIHA; the photograph is in "Kenyon Cox," *Literary Digest* 61 (5 April 1919): 30–31.

7. Forbes Watson, "The National Academy," *New York Evening Post,* 30 March 1917, p. 9.

8. KC to LKC, 31 May, 6 June, and to AC, 15 June, all 1917, in KC Papers, AAFAL. The work is *John J. Fitzgerald* (1917, oil on canvas, 25½" × 20¾"), in the House of Representatives Appropriations Committee room, U.S. Capitol, Washington, D.C.

9. The drawings are in Box 38, a folder marked "Prentiss Monument," KC collection, CHM; the quotation on old and new forms is in KC to Henry Churchill King, 18 February 1918, King Papers, OCA. Dolson's first responses are in a letter to KC, 3 January 1916; the work's progress is noted in KC to AC, 25 March, with the quotation, 8 April 1917, and Nellie Cox to KC, 1, 9 April 1917; Dolson's responses are in letters to KC, 10, 20 November 1917; his offer to buy the model is in a letter to KC, 11 February 1918; all in KC Papers, AAFAL. KC to Henry Churchill King, 18 February 1918, describes the work and offers the model to Oberlin; King to KC, 19 February 1918, accepts it; and King to KC, 5 August 1918 notes its appeal; all in King Papers, OCA.

10. The first works are *Plenty* (1910, oil on canvas, 25⅛" × 35⅜" and *A Book of Pictures* (1910, oil on canvas, 30" × 36", repainted in 1917), both in National Museum of American Art, Smithsonian Institution, Washington, D.C. KC to AC, 15 June 1917, has the drawing and description of *The Education of Cupid;* KC to AC, 19 August 1917, has the quotation on its merits; KC to AC, 24 February 1918, mentions the NAD show; KC to AC, 16 April 1918, has the words on laymen's taste; DC to KC, 26 December 1917 and 11 February 1918, show his enthusiasm for the work; all in KC Papers, AAFAL.

11. Proofs of some of these are in Box 43, and drawings for others, including those mentioned, are in Box 1197, KC collection, CHM.

12. KC to H. W. Kent, 17 February 1912, KC file, MMA; "Lectures to Teachers," *Bulletin of the Metropolitan Museum of Art* 7 (April 1912): 79–80; KC, "The Museum and the Teaching of Art in the Public Schools," *Scribner's Magazine* 52 (July 1912): 124–28; the larger series is noted in KC to H. W. Kent, 20, 27 June, 9 July, 17 August 1914; all KC file, MMA; and "Three Lectures by Kenyon Cox," *Bulletin of the Metropolitan Museum of Art* 9 (October 1914): 204.

13. KC to Weir, 3 December 1908, with the quotation, and KC to Weir, 27 January 1913, declining again, both in Weir Papers, YUL; KC to Cochran, 2 February 1913, AC Papers, AAA; memorandum, dated 25 May 1914, and KC to Edward Burlingame, 27 May 1914, Scribner Archive, PUL; KC to H. W. Kent, 20, 21 October 1914, and KC to Edward Robinson, 27 September 1916; "Lectures by Kenyon Cox," *Bulletin of the Metropolitan Museum of Art* 11 (December 1916): 264.

14. KC to LKC, postcards dated 26, 27 April 1917, KC Papers, AAFAL.

15. KC, "Painting as an Art of Imitation," *Art World* 1 (October 1916): 30.

16. KC, *Concerning Painting* (New York: Scribner's, 1917), vii.

17. KC to Kent, 30 January 1918, KC file, MMA.

18. DC to KC, 10 November 1917, mentions reproducing *The Education of Cupid,* as they had done with *Hope and Memory;* DC to KC, 10 July 1914, deals with the apartment; DC to KC, 12 December 1916, establishes the trust; all in KC Papers, AAFAL. LKC to AC, 26 March 1917, AC Papers, AAA, has that quotation. Caroline Cox Lansing to author, 12 March 1984, recalls the trust arrangement and the relationship with DC.

19. H. W. Kent to KC, 13 February, and KC to Kent, 27 February, 27 March; all 1912, KC file, MMA; KC to LKC, 28 November 1913, and to AC, 4 February 1917; both in KC Papers, AAFAL; KC to Arnold Brunner, 23 October 1917, KC file, AAIAL. The apparent contraction of tuberculosis is derived from comments of Caroline Cox to her son Cornelius Lansing, delivered in turn to Patricia Ronan, who incorporated the material in "Louise King Cox," 96 n. 69.

20. KC to WHL, 12 December 1916, Low Papers, AIHA; and KC to LKC, 6 June 1917, KC Papers, AAFAL.

21. H. W. Kent to KC, 29 January 1917, KC file, MMA, notes the special arrangements for a lecture. Maxfield Parrish to LKC, [?] March 1919, remembers KC's improvement in Cornish. KC to Johnson, 29 October 1918, KC file, AAIAL, has that quotation. AC to LKC, 23 June 1918, AC Papers, AAA, has that quotation. KC to AC, 19 December and DC to KC, 21 December, both 1918, in KC Papers, AAFAL, refer to his being bedridden.

22. KC to Johnson, 22 August 1918, KC file, AAIAL; KC, "German Painting," typescript, KC Papers, AAFAL.

23. LKC to AC, 2 January 1919, AC Papers, AAA; LKC to Johnson, 10 March 1919, KC file, AAIAL; DC to LKC, 12 March 1919, KC Papers, AAFAL; *New York Times,* 18 March 1919; "Kenyon Cox on German Art," *New York Evening Post,* 20 March 1919, the text of the essay Johnson read.

24. *New York Times* and *New York Tribune,* 18 March 1919; Blashfield to LKC, 23 March 1919, KC Papers, AAFAL; Frank Jewett Mather, "Kenyon Cox," *Scribner's Magazine* 65 (June 1919): 765–67. Mather to LKC, 17 March 1919, KC Papers, AAFAL, was his personal condolence and contained the line: "His was an extraordinarily vigorous, just, and honest mind." Years later, in a letter to LKC, 7 March 1945, AC Papers, AAA, Mather wrote: "I recollect with great pleasure my association with your husband whom I admired as an artist, critic, and superior human being."

25. Augusta Saint Gaudens to LKC, 23 March; Lucia Fuller to LKC, 18 March; DC to LKC, 17 March; all 1919, in KC Papers, AAFAL.

26. Unsigned memo of advance for $262.50 to KC, 8 October 1917; LKC to Charles Scribner's Sons, [1920]; unsigned to Dear Madame [LKC], 7 January 1920; all in Scribner Archives, PUL.

27. AC to Virginia Colby, 22 May 1982, Colby collection, has the first quotation; AC to Caroline Lansing, 7 July 1966, AC Papers, AAA, has the second.

28. Ronan, "Louise King Cox," 96 n. 69; Caroline Lansing to author, 12 March 1984, with the quotation.

29. DC to LKC, 7 October 1922, KC Papers, AAFAL, notes that she is thinking of leaving the apartment; Ronan, "Louise King Cox," 41–45, summarizes information on her late years; AC to Caroline Lansing, 7 July 1966, AC Papers, AAA, notes her unhappiness; Caroline Lansing to author, 12 March 1984, deals with LKC's death. DC to LKC, 31 March 1919, KC Papers, AAFAL, offers the family plot for KC's ashes, but they were stored at a New York crematorium. The cremation certificates for both KC, dated 20 March 1919, and for LKC, dated 13 December 1945, are in the AC Papers, AAA. A handwritten memo dated 16 August 1945, signed by Allyn's wife, Ethel H. Cox, ibid., certifies that the ashes of both are in Cornish, "according to their expressed wishes." Ethel Cox to AC, 26 April 1936, ibid., requests that she be cremated and the ashes scattered, though "I do not ask that my ashes be kept to scatter with yours someday, as did your dear mother and father."

BIBLIOGRAPHIC ESSAY

THE COLLECTION AND DISPOSITION OF Cox's papers and residual art works is an interesting story. Allyn Cox returned to the United States in 1920 after four years of study at the American Academy in Rome, and a year after his father's death. He cleared out both the New York City apartment, which his mother vacated shortly thereafter, and the Cornish summer home, which he sold. He placed a large quantity of uncatalogued art works in storage. They would be available for any retrospective exhibitions of his father's work, and he ultimately meant to give them to a public depository. In the meantime, his own career developed and the material simply languished. He performed the same service for his mother after her death in 1945.

Allyn was conscious of his father's roles in American art history and knew that his name never disappeared from the art debates. In the late 1950s he began to gather the family's papers. Kenyon did not save or copy much correspondence, but Louise kept a considerable number of letters from family and friends, including much of the correspondence between her and Kenyon. Cox's sister Hope, who died in 1937, also kept family papers, which passed to Louise and then to Allyn. This collection included Cox's correspondence with his parents from his youth to his mother's death in 1911. Other family members contributed their surviving documents. Leonard Opdycke, Kenyon's friend from boyhood until his death in 1915, seems to have kept all of Cox's letters, which his family gave to Allyn. This large collection went to the AAFAL, which is the basic primary source for Cox's life and work.

Allyn's own voluminous papers ultimately went to the AAA. On his death, a small amount of residual material relating to his father went to the same depository as the KC papers, AAA. As is the nature of historical sources, a good many of Cox's letters survived in the collections of friends and public bodies, which are noted in the footnotes here. The most important of these is probably the small number of significant letters in the WHL papers, AIHA. There is also some material relating to the Cox family, especially the early years, in the JDC papers, OCA. A fair amount of correspondence relating to Cox's writing and publishing is in the Scribner Archive, PUL, and the Century Collection, NYPL. The most detailed record of any single Cox commission is the file on his work at the Wisconsin state capitol, in the Capitol Commission papers, SHSW, Madison.

Cox was an excellent letter writer, whether dealing with friends or patrons. He was frank, pithy, and exact, as in his published writings. He naturally tended to report on his own views, his emotional and physical state, and his opinions of people and their work. He often wrote about the state of a given work in progress, but seldom explicated on exactly how he was working. I have edited a set of his letters that make a coherent whole, *An American Art Student in Paris: The Letters of Kenyon Cox, 1877–1882* (Kent, Ohio: Kent State University Press, 1986), and hope to do a second volume covering the years 1883–1919.

Cox produced an array of criticism and art history for genteel magazines such as *Century* and *Scribner's,* as well as for art periodicals. He collected what he considered the best of these pieces in five books: *Old Masters and New* (1905); *Painters and Sculptors* (1907); *The Classic Point of View* (1911), which is the Scammon Lectures of that year, and a clear and masterful statement of the classic ideal; *Artist and Public* (1914); and *Concerning Painting* (1917). These books did not include all of his lengthy essays and contain only a fraction of the criticism he wrote for the *Nation.* This last work was usually unsigned but can be identified in Daniel Haskell, comp., *The Nation. Vols. 1–105. New York, 1865–1917. Index of Titles and Contributors,* 2 vols. (New York: NYPL, 1957), 2:106–110. These short reviews and essays are important statements of Cox's thought and bear reading for their thoughtful tone and conciseness.

At about the same time, Allyn began to organize the large mass of residual art works. It was virtually impossible to trace works that had been sold, and many others simply disappeared. These apparently included several canvases of major significance to Kenyon, such as *Vision of Moonrise* and *Painting and Poetry.* Several important and representative works were already in major museums, such as the Metropolitan Museum of Art and the Cleveland Museum of Art. But Allyn understood that taste changed over time among curators as well as the art public. He insisted on dispersing the residual works among many museums, so that "we should not have to depend on one board of trustees, which if the thing were all under one roof, could order it all thrown out one day" (AC to Leonard Cox and Caroline Lansing, May 5, 1958, AC papers, AAA). He gave most of the drawings to the CHM in New York City. Most of the paintings, some drawings and sketchbooks went to the NAD, which in turn distributed them to numerous museums around the country while keeping a basic collection. Both Allyn and Caroline bequeathed examples of their father's works to the National Museum of American Art in Washington, D.C. These collections of documents and art works are necessarily incomplete, but they are a substantial and enlightening basis for Cox's complex career as an artist and critic. The materials also testify to his family's sense of responsibility to history and should be an example to others of like mind.

INDEX

Italicized page references indicate illustrations.

KENYON COX, 1856–1919
was composed in 11/13 Garamond Number 3
with Weiss display type
on a Xyvision system with Linotronic output
by BookMasters, Inc.;
printed by sheet-fed offset
on 60-pound acid-free Glatfelter White Smooth stock,
notch case bound into 88' binder's boards
in Holliston Kingston Natural cloth
with 80-pound Rainbow endpapers,
and wrapped with dustjackets printed
on 100-pound enamel stock
in two colors with film lamination
by Braun-Brumfield, Inc.;
designed by Will Underwood;
and published by
THE KENT STATE UNIVERSITY PRESS
KENT, OHIO 44242